INSIDE OUT

INSIDE OUT

A Memoir of Entering and Breaking Out of a Minneapolis Political Cult

Alexandra Stein

NORTH STAR PRESS OF ST. CLOUD, INC.

Some names and places have been changed to protect privacy.

Printed in the United States of America by Versa Press, Inc. East Peoria, Illinois.

Published by
North Star Press of St. Cloud, Inc.
P.O. Box 451
St. Cloud, Minnesota 56302

Dedication

To Rosa, Carlos and Sunna

ACKNOWLEDGEMENTS

First, I would like to thank those former members of the O. who got out with me as well as those who left during the following year. You know who you are. Also, I thank the others who left years before we did who generously, and sometimes bravely, shared their stories with me.

Grateful acknowledgement is due to the people who helped when I first emerged from the O.: Heather Svoboda, Doug Agustin, and Lynell Agustin from Free Minds, and Bruce Laughton from Answers, Inc. Their work is unsung but tremendously important.

Many writers, writing teachers, and friends helped as I wrote this book. Myrna Kostash saw the promise in this work early on and understood its political and historical focus. She has continued to provide both friendship and advice. Larry Sutin and David Pink may not know it, but they nurtured my first tentative steps back into writing after my unwelcome ten-year hiatus. Claudia Poser, Liz Weir, Cheryll Ostrom, Lynda McDonnell, and Erin Hart listened to and critiqued many passages in first draft.

Others read all or part of the manuscript at different stages and encouraged me along the way: Ellen Hawley, Richard Solly, Duke Klassen, Teresa Whitman, Martha Roth, Jon Odell, Anthony Porter, Abe, Scott McLemee, Tim Wohlforth, Dennis Tourish, Reva Rasmussen, Ron Engel, Hilary Krivchenia, Cilla Walford, Kasia Polanska, Mary Hourigan, Ida Susser, Mervyn Susser, and the late Bill Truesdale.

Lai Ying, Gunilla Bjorkman-Bobb, and Marc Ricciardi provided friendship under extraordinary circumstances.

A week-long residency at Norcroft introduced me to the beauties of the North Shore, which allowed me to write the most difficult scene in the book. Thank you to Joan Drury, Norcroft's founder, and to the wonderful caretaker there who quietly delivered apricot juice and other delicacies that I request-ed via the chalkboard.

Special thanks go to Tammy McKanan for her deep understanding, ap-preciation and multiple readings of this book. Janice Lee Porter put my expe-rience into more than one picture, helping me make beauty out of a difficult story. Janja Lalich, who lived and wrote about a similar slice of history, has been an invaluable advisor, colleague, and friend.

Robyn Slovo told me to just start writing the story, and Jenny Diski said, "Put words on paper." These phrases were more helpful than either of them might have imagined.

Finally, I would like to thank, again, Lyndall Stein. She continues to pro-vide unconditional support, encouragement, and the magical ability to laugh during even the darkest times.

I know there are many others to whom I owe thanks. Despite writing memoir, my memory is actually abysmal, so I hope that those whose names do not appear here will accept my apologies. And on the subject of memory—of course this is my version of events; these are my memories and my interpreta-tions of the stories that others told me. I have tried to represent the truth as best I could, but, as I learned during the life represented herein, absolute truth is a dangerous concept, and so I offer this story solely as my own perspective.

INSIDE OUT

If I Had a Hammer

Pete Seeger and Lee Hays

If I had a hammer,
I'd hammer in the morning,
I'd hammer in the evening—
All over this land.
I'd hammer out danger,
I'd hammer out a warning,
I'd hammer out love between my brothers and my sisters
All over this land.

CHAPTER 1

His arm rose up in the fight, perhaps to ward off a blow to the head—for the other man was pistol-whipping him, the other man said so, later, to Betty. Or perhaps his fear was raised, like an arm, to strike, for the gun went off then, so said the other man, and its bullet dug through the soft skin under the arm, his soft black skin, and—how fast did it go?—it found, on its way, a strong, hard muscle and ricocheted from that muscle, which nudged the hurrying bullet around and directed it away from its upwards course where it may have exited the young body with only an injury. Detoured by the body itself, the bullet traveled sideways, quicker than a cry, and it entered the heart, which it stopped, and it stopped his breathing too, and the other man reported later, to Betty, who was to become my friend, "I was pistol-whipping him, and the gun went off."

Oh, and the body, the shiny black body of the young man, I see it still in my imagination as his feet lift off the ground an inch or two, I see his whole body coming up, up off the ground, then falling, falling like the Little Prince of my childhood tales who falls like a tree but slowly, gently, in an arc that turns and falls until the body bloodies the floor. The same floor that later was overlaid with the green shag carpet on which my infant son would learn to walk.

Meanwhile, the man who was still alive sweated and shook in fear and ran to Chicago where Kristin and Sara hid him: an underground existence that has eluded me until now.

I sit, surrounded by the shadows of the dead man's life. It is to this that I have come as I sift through the dusty contents of a crumpled brown grocery bag that Betty has kept for ten years at least and at last been courageous enough first to open, and then to give me for she knows that I need to know, need to make an understandable story of the random events, the decades of not knowing. I must pry the hands off the monkey's eyes, ears, and mouth, those three cream-colored stone monkeys of my grandmother's, sitting next to grandpa's whiskey on the teak bookshelves. I used to look, look at them and now I understand altogether what they mean. First I must understand, and then I will look, listen and speak.

Out of the grocery bag that I can barely touch—I feel the old blood will spill upon me—I pull the paper remainders of a life: the parking tickets; a letter from his mother in LA; a smudged calendar noting the birthday of his daughter with whom he does not live; pay stubs; rolling papers; weather reports for his KMOJ radio show.

The stone monkeys must come to life and tell how I arrived here. They will look back and trace the path traveled; they will mark it "Danger."

I was fourteen in 1968. Martin Luther King, Jr., was killed that year. Malcolm X was already dead, and George Jackson was killed soon after. There were riots in the cities of America. Riots by white youth in the streets of Chicago, riots by blacks in LA and Detroit. There was war in Vietnam. There were demonstrations and riots in all the major cities of the Western world.

In London I argued with my mother to be allowed to go on a demonstration at the U.S. embassy against the killing in Vietnam. I too had seen the babies covered in napalm, the children running in flames from their own skin. At night I cried for the horror of it. During the day I traveled from the city out to school in the safety of the suburbs. Here we were a world apart—conjugating Latin verbs, calculating numbers of molecules or the relative cooling properties of a cup of tea—but at night I smelled burning babies and rebelled.

I argued and argued until my mother finally agreed I could go but on the condition that she go with me. My older sister Lyndall and brother Jeremy were going too, but with their own contingent. Lyndall, whose bedroom was decorated with posters of Che Guevara's bloody corpse and angelic portraits of him still alive, was my mentor—she had helped shape my pity into a political anger.

My mother and I arrived at Marble Arch and joined the small clusters of people heading to the embassy. As we approached, the groups grew thicker, banners started to unfurl. We could see black police vans and coaches—policemen began to appear, first the regular street cops with batons; then, as we got closer, the helmeted cops grouped in formation. We began to hear the sounds of protest: unintelligible megaphoned voices and sing-song chanting, "HEY, HEY, LBJ, HOW MANY KIDS HAVE YOU KILLED TODAY?" or simply, "U.S.—OUT OF VIETNAM; U.S.—OUT OF VIETNAM."

That surge of feeling came to me, deep in my ribcage, adrenalin becoming political power in the company of strangers who, like me, came to shake off the nightmare of slaughter that announced itself with unbearable regularity in the evening news.

Soon we were marching in the street, heading for the square that housed the U.S. embassy. By the time we arrived, Grosvenor Square was already filled with thousands of people. Hundreds of police flanked the embassy itself, and others had begun to cordon off the square to stop the flow of demonstrators. My mother and I were right at the point where the police were splitting the march. Ma grabbed me, "Oh, god!—they've got horses."

She held on to me tightly, and I felt her fear traveling through the hot clasp of her small hand. In front of us, a line of cops on horses were making their way into the crowd to cut us off from the square. People started to push. There were so many people behind us, we couldn't go backwards, but ahead were the horses, held in by their riders but straining and sweating and high-stepping, shaking their heads in the bridles. The cops seemed so high up, looking down on us through reflective plexiglass visors and bullying the horses on through the crowd.

We found ourselves pushed to one side, up by a building whose entrance was blocked by more policemen. Behind them press photographers and reporters stood on the stone steps of the entrance, safe from the crush and the mounted police. Ma pulled me over and tried to get to the steps. She ordered one of the cops to let us through to the press area, "For god's sake, let us in. My daughter, she's only fourteen!"

"Jesus Christ! what the hell did you bring her here for?" the cop said. But he let us in, and we stood with the press, behind the iron railings, and watched as the police finally forced back the marchers, away from the square. The thousands left in the square were still trying to break through the police lines to get to the embassy or to get close enough to smash windows. But the police line held, and, in an hour or so, people were dispersing and heading back to the tube station. Ma and I joined the retreat.

"We should have had marbles," she said. "That's what we used in the thirties—in the Great Depression demonstrations—we used to bring marbles and throw them under the horses' hooves. I didn't think they still used horses . . ." She paused. She was scared of police horses the way that South African or American blacks were scared of police dogs—she had seen the viciousness they were used for.

I forgave her then for the embarrassment I felt when she hauled me to the safety of the press area. She had a history. She had been fifteen years old during the time of the Depression demonstrations and the great sit-down strikes. On Saturday mornings she'd sold the *Daily Worker* at the local market. She too had felt the need to act, and she knew enough to try to protect me.

Later, people said it was a damn good thing no one had broken through the police lines. The embassy was filled with U.S. Marines—and, so it went, if we'd gotten in, then it was just like being on American soil, and the Marines would have let loose. In our minds hung grainy images of U.S. soldiers—soldiers with helmets and guns shooting civilians half a world away.

Politics, of the save-the-world and contribute-to-humanity variety, had always been my guiding light since as far back as I can remember. Born in South Africa to left-liberal parents, I had an early education in injustice and inequality and was exposed to many people fighting the system. The name of Nelson Mandela was spoken with affection and respect in my house from before he began his twenty-seven-year prison term. Our family photo album included a photograph of him boxing, and of other South African fighters against apartheid, as well as literary and artistic figures from South Africa and England and other countries: Doris Lessing, Miriam Makeba and Hugh Masekela, Ruth First and Joe Slovo, Alan Sillitoe, and others.

In the late 1050s in South Africa, friends of my parents were being arrested and jailed regularly. These were the years of the consolidation of apartheid. Decisions and commitments had to be made—there was no fence to straddle. My mother feared that friends would ask her to hide an illegal printing press in Rose Cottage, the thatch-roofed house in Johannesburg where I was born—or that my father would be asked to assist in some other illegal activity.

"How could we have refused? But with four children, how could we do it?" she told me, explaining their decision to voluntarily exile themselves from the place they loved. By 1958 we had joined the exodus from apartheid and left South Africa for London, my mother's birthplace.

The stakes were high for those who stayed. Most paid with arrest and some with death. The exiles suffered too: loneliness and loss, a cold that struck to the heart. Some became alcoholics, others depressives—all of us, children too, embraced forever a longing that could not be filled.

* * *

Our house in London became a social center for one part of the progressive cultural community. An international assortment of poets, writers, artists, actors, musicians, and political figures came to eat my mother's soup on Sunday nights. Every Christmas, by tradition and word of mouth, a hundred or so gathered to talk and drink and dance to Motown music until early on Boxing Day. In between times, to raise money for the African National Congress, we had parties, loud and fun with the old South African dances and the sound of penny whistles rolling in memories of the townships and the ghost of Sophiatown.

This was the mad color of my upbringing. The music of Ginger Johnson sliding out of the living room window in rainbowed bubbles wafting, the trebles dancing, hopping happily above the bass notes, which boomed up through my feet as I sat by the shutters hidden away, watching Ginger's green and gold robes flying as his hands magicked upon the steel drum creating in me, for a moment, glory. From my protected spot at the feet of the band, I looked over to my father on the dance floor. His hips twisted to the *kwela*, danced in drunken courtship to a young English woman who knew nothing of the *kwela*, our African dance, the dance of Sophiatown and Jo'burg. His arms were held high and outstretched, the glass in his hand slopping wine with the beat. For me the outstretched arms were never for the Jewish circle dances, that was another culture entirely, one which, but for knowing it had been my father's, never touched me in a conscious way. No, the outstretched arms were strictly the balance for the stomp-stomping of the *kwela*, where the weight was carried low in the body, close to the ground, and the arms were used to draw in the spirit, or the Other, or the girl for sex.

This was the country I came from. Dancing the *kwela* in London, the music raining out of the open window and people crowding into the house, paying money for the African National Congress at our front door and passing damp hats and coats up the stairs, past the breathless dancers and the embracing lovers, up the stairs to the bedroom to rest precariously on my bed at the top of the silent mound of dark wool coats, quiet and unnecessary as a grave.

Television

1970. The ten-year anniversary of Sharpeville. I am fifteen. We gather in Trafalgar Square to commemorate the event. Television cameras document our protests and record speaker after speaker standing in the gray London air on the old black stone parapets surrounding the famous fountain. We have displaced the pigeons, the tramps, and the tourists who usually occupy this space. Not far from the demonstration is South Africa House, the target of our wrath, a place of evil, that we can imagine as nothing else.

The speakers come one after another denouncing in similar language the familiar terrors of the South African government. I stand with my hands deep in my pockets, watching the TV reporters roaming the perimeter of the crowd, reminding myself to check the evening news that night.

Something is happening on the speaker's parapet—I can't quite make it out—there are men in uniforms pushing speakers out of the way. They are young men, white, wearing khaki uniforms and peaked caps; leather belts—or are they ammunition belts?—strung obliquely across their chests. I am confused. They are not policeman—besides British cops don't carry guns. *Wait. Guns? That's right, Jesus! They've got guns! No, something's wrong here. What's going on?* Several of them stand up on the parapet with their legs apart, owning the stage from which they have pushed the speakers. Their chests are pushed out arrogantly. One of them, thin and aggressive, raises a bullhorn to his mouth.

"This is an order to disperse!" he shouts. His South African accent echoes through the bullhorn. I look around, frowning, meeting the stare of a woman I do not know standing next to me, also looking around, craning her neck, trying to see what is going on. Maybe they came from the embassy?

"You must disperse immediately! This is an unauthorized demonstration. Disperse!"

Before I can decide what to do, there is a terrific explosion. I jump back. I hear shooting. The khaki uniforms have raised their guns. In front of the parapets, I see a crowd of black people running towards me, their arms lifted to the gray sky. The sound of the guns firing is immense. I cover my ears but keep my eyes open. It dawns on me that this is an agit-prop performance. As I realize this, I see the bodies of the black people falling. There are children, and women, and men. They are falling, falling onto the cold paving stones of Trafalgar Square. The shooting stops. There is quiet. A carpet of bodies lies in front of us. I begin to cry. This is Sharpeville.

That night the scene is replayed on the evening news.

For eleven years England had been a kind of home. Our four-story Victorian house overlooked the leafy chestnut trees of Primrose Hill and the steel-mesh aviary and artificial goat mountain of London Zoo. At election time, the huge window of our living room sported a poster exhorting the neighbors to "Vote Communist." We were middle class, comfortable, crazy and, indeed, communist.

Then, at the age of fifteen, I ran away. In the public bathroom of Charing Cross train station, I shed my brown and mustard-yellow school uniform like a used cocoon. In its place I wore a floor-length black victorian skirt, a white silk shirt and a black velvet jacket that fitted close to my young, barely blossomed body. I ran to Paris where I lived an itinerant life among a group of Sorbonne graduates who had blazed their way into adulthood through the great year of 1968 when they had almost, but not quite, brought down the government of Charles De Gaulle.

I had run from the delicate etiquette of my upper class school that had no bearing on any other part of my life. I ran from the crazy scenes in the family kitchen where my mother held my sister Hatty's head back and tried to force barbiturates down her manic-depressive's throat, while Hatty fought back and spit the pills anywhere—into the sink, on the floor, at my mother. I ran from the sight of my father shrugging off my mother's embraces. I ran from my best friend, another South African child of exile, who had left me for a world of quaaludes, speed and, finally, junk, used in furniture-less apartments. Here her working-class Irish boyfriend frightened me in his stupor as he unzipped his boot beneath his ass-hugging velvet bell-bottoms and pulled out plastic packets of multi-colored pills to share.

I ran from an intense isolation where I could speak to nobody about what it felt like to be me. I ran from my role as the good child, a role that had stuffed me into a space in which I could no longer live.

In Paris I was accepted as I tagged along from one drawn-out, smoke-hazed, three-hour dinner to the next where the food (biftek frites, steak au poivre, oysters with lemon, succulent rabbit stew, tripes cooked buttery soft in tomato stock) was as important as the discussion dissecting the failures of 1968, the philosophies of the nascent women's movement, the meaning of existence, of self, of other, the complex analyses and shifting of the sexual relationships that flowed in and out, cracking among us like glacial ice.

After a couple of years I learned, finally, that I could not make Paris my home, and that I needed to become an adult. By eighteen I had arrived in San Francisco, independent and looking, still, for a place to belong. In San Francisco I found a wonderfully mixed culture that could include me and my complicated past.

By 1974 I was living with three other women in a rented, four-bedroom house in the mostly Latino Mission district. Our landlord was a Nicaraguan. On one side of us lived a rotund young Chicano garbage man who rehearsed his salsa band on the other side of the adjoining wall to our house. Our neighbors on the opposite side were a church-going Mexican family with three daughters whose picture I still have—they are dressed up in pastel taffeta (pink, yellow, and blue, with matching bows in their hair), perhaps for a wedding, or a confirmation. They giggle coyly into the camera, hiding behind young hands. Across the street from us was a corner store run by a Palestinian family. My bedroom window faced the west, and in the evenings I sat and watched the red sunset as it embraced the city. When the sky grew dark, the corner store became the light on the block, its red sign flashing "Miller High Life" in a soundless heartbeat.

The Mission district was close to the Castro area, the center of the gay men's scene in San Francisco. To its north was downtown, to its east was Potrero Hill, a mostly white working-class neighborhood, and to its south was Bernal Hill, a slowly gentrifying spot with a magnificent view of the city and of the industrial part of the Bay where the World War II shipyards still provided jobs for welders and machinists who labored like ants in the great gray hulks of the docked ships.

I loved the Mission; it was sunny, set in a natural valley that protected it from the fog that dominated the rest of the city. Flowers bloomed year round. Music drifted out onto the sidewalks. Languages and accents played like music also, moving in and out of harmony, but always calling to me, making my heart swell in some old memory of a multi-lingual life in South Africa, or even London. Here life became bright and warm for me as I became part of the Left community that added its mark to the character of the neighborhood.

I had begun by working in the Berkeley Free Clinic and continued into the world of the Women's Union, the Peace and Freedom party, the food co-ops, and the many grassroots collective organizations that sprang up during the 1970s. For five years or so, life was filled with meetings and social activity of a fertile and vibrant nature. We had women's consciousness-raising groups, political study groups covering everything from Marx's *Capital* to the new women's poetry that was coming out, groups to discuss our work in the various collectives. We had sing-alongs with old Woody Guthrie songs and the songs of the 1930s, Civil Rights era songs, and the new songs: reggae and Holly Near and Sweet Honey in the Rock. Weekly house meetings kept things under control in our collective houses. The personal was political and vice versa.

There were health clinics, graphics collectives, art exhibitions in the food co-ops and, of course, constant and ubiquitous, the many anti-imperialist and third world support groups. One meeting flowed into the next; the personnel changed, rotating from one house or collective storefront as we switched groups and formations.

I met my closest group of friends in a study group I led that had formed out of the Peace and Freedom Party Food Conspiracy—a volunteer-run buying club. I taught a kind of Beginner's Guide to Marxism. We read Marx and Engels: *The Communist Manifesto*; *Wages, Price and Profit*; and the new feminist economist theory: Mickey Ellinger's *We Can't Go Home Again*. At every class, I gave my small group of students study questions: "Describe an example of when surplus value was extracted from you?" or "Show the class movement of your own family over the last three generations."

The focus of the group was on encouraging everyone to speak out and on applying the history, politics, and economics we were learning to our own lives and our work in our various collectives.

Leah worked at the collectively run Honey Sandwich Childcare Center. Barney, disabled with a club foot, was one of the main organizers of the People's Health Collective. Cathy worked as a mechanic at the Perpetual Motors Garage. Jannie volunteered for the Food Conspiracy. Leonard worked two shifts a week at the Noe Valley Food Co-op.

At the second meeting of our Peace and Freedom study group (recruitment accomplished by placing flyers in the grocery bags of food), I fell in love with Leonard suddenly and without restraint. He was a handsome Italian-American, a black frizz of hair hung over sweet and deep-set eyes that made my heart squeak when I looked at them. He had a big nose that beaked over his red lips which I traced with my thumb while I cupped his broad, bearded face in my two small hands. I could smell him when he entered a room—but I never identified what the smell was. I sniffed at his chest, at his flannel shirts, his hair, his thick beard. His smell was sweet like candy or flowers or hot chocolate. When he came home from his job as a union carpenter the smell was overlaid with pine dust and the mixed odor of wood preservatives and resin and the rusty smell of framing nails, but under all that, still, was Leonard and that sweet tang that went straight to my head.

Leonard was quiet and shy, like me, but when he spoke he was thoughtful and intelligent and always looking for the practical applications of our theories. Our study groups were not the debating societies that made up much of the Left—we attracted, deliberately, women who were intimidated by the mostly white male middle-class Left, and working-class men like Leonard.

Leonard continued to live with two other women who worked with him at the Noe Valley Community Store while he and I spent half the nights of the week at each other's houses. Leah was lovers with Barney—later she moved into my house in the Mission. Cathy found Paul, a physics teacher who played guitar in La Frente, the community song group.

Meanwhile, I continued my education informally. I took classes at the Liberation School—on economics, on feminism and on the Israeli/Arab war. At San Francisco City College I studied occupational safety and health and its place in labor organizing. Through the community education service, I learned about holistic health.

Within the larger Left community, my friends and I formed a kind of loose-knit family, centered around our women's house on Twenty-third Street. We saw this arrangement duplicated by others and reflected also in our political work in our community organizations. We began to feel that we were building an alternative community: a comprehensive set of institutions on which we could rely, and which could grow beyond us, reaching out to other people who needed a human structure in which to live. The established structures of the United States had so clearly failed us, time and again, leaving people adrift in the crushing loneliness that had become the human face of Marx's alienation. We saw alienation and were driven by our own needs to build an alternative.

From the anti-war movement, and the newer anti-imperialist support committees, people had ties with liberation struggles overseas, and, in a tortuous route, via Vietnam, the lessons of China were coming to us in the form of books like *Away with All Pests* (a glorious description of the power of the collective in solving public health issues). The collected works of Mao began to appear on people's bookshelves, and we studied Mao's elegant essays, finding therein simplicity and light. He brought to us the compelling concept of the New Man, embodied for us in our vision of Che Guevara and his poetic pronouncement that "a true revolutionary is guided by great love." Through Mao we learned that our path to revolution involved our conscious self-transformation—that by examining our attitudes and our actions we could transform our ingrained bourgeois habits into the selfless purity needed for successful collective action. "The personal is political" took on a new meaning. With China's criticism/self-criticism, we challenged not only the enemy of U.S. imperialism, but also, the enemy within.

I stopped and touched a rose one night, on my way home from a meeting, feeling euphoric, as I did so often those days. The rose was black in the nighttime, and it confused me because I wanted it to be red, but the streetlights could only illuminate blackness. I breathed in its odor anyway, and reached my hand out to touch its soft petals, smooth and silky, a rose petal between my fingers that I touched ever so gently, wishing only to share it, not to keep it for myself.

We were working together! I felt it. In my chest, under the soft skin and the bone, I felt it with a joy that ached with intensity. We were working together. Each of us bringing something from our past that was good or wise or capable. Once in the house, I shed my yellow cotton jacket, kicked off my sandals and put a record on the stereo. I picked out an album by Quilapayun; on the cover a group of black-caped, mustachioed Chilean men. They were in exile, singers of the New Song, cultural brothers to Victor Jara—they sang liberation songs and resurrected the folk songs and instruments of the indigenous Chileans. "Together," they sang, "United by blood—let us walk, side by side . . ." and in the background the soft whistle of pan pipes and the beating resonance of a hide drum.

"Libertad, Libertad, Libertad . . ." they sang in sad tones—in their country there was no liberty, only the echo of the machine guns that had slaughtered the prisoners of the stadium and the armed shadows of the Junta that continued to disappear those who spoke out.

I lay on the living-room carpet, listening to the music, my arms stretched out, trying to calm my breathing, knowing that to get too excited would mean I'd get sick. But sometimes, after a good meeting, when we left each other with hugs and a feeling of closeness and a vision beginning to come true of what we were trying to build, then the adrenalin just took off on its own, and I had learned, finally, that I must relax, allow the energy to flow on and through me.

This was happiness then. I opened my eyes and looked up at the ceiling and the dusty light fixture etched with a design of California grasses. I drew in another deep breath to calm me. This was happiness . . . these natural compounds in my body that twitched my muscles and made me want to dance or make love or drive to the beach down by Daly City and slide down the scrubby cliffs and pound my feet along the sand in a kind of joyful rage.

Everything fit. We were not a cadre organization, but we were cadres in training. Working to a plan in our organizations, review-

ing our work weekly in the study group, helping each other with criticism and self-criticism, trying to gently guide our mass organizations in a common direction.

Sometimes I felt as if we were a team of horses, driving together, turning together, galloping along a road with power and beauty. This is what it meant to not be alone, to work with others, to have organization.

These were heady days. We felt that the beauty of nature was ours. That time was on our side.

CHAPTER 2

I went to visit Leonard one day at his cottage on Noe Street. He was cooking at the stove when I came in, and he turned to me: his great black beard was gone, and in its place was a thick Zapata-like bristle of a moustache, and the stunning lines of his wide jaw. The smooth plains of his cheeks caused me to blush. I was shy with him that whole day.

"It's still me," he said, as I looked up at him, catching my breath at his new face.

But it was already clear that Leonard was slowly shutting down to me. A distance came between us. Perhaps my emotional volatility was scaring him off: my life generally proceeded in sweeping peaks and valleys that echoed the genetic manic depression in my family. My household on Twenty-third Street was beginning to break up, and Leonard had to deal with the bitter emotions in which I was caught up.

These ruptures reflected the slow disintegration of our political efforts. Somehow, despite our deep desire, something was evaporating. The North Vietnamese had taken Saigon in April of 1975 and "Our War" finally ended leaving a political vacuum in its wake. It appeared that the FBI's ruthless counter-intelligence program, known as COINTELPRO, had worked: the leaders of the Black Power movement had been killed or jailed. I listened to the somber music of Bernice Reagon as she sang in an aching tenor: "they are falling all around me, the strongest leaves of my tree. . . ." Her words echoed my deepening sadness.

Early on, the young Black Panthers, Mark Clark and Fred Hampton, had been murdered bloodily in their beds, and COINTELPRO continued its work, infiltrating and manipulating progressive groups. The path on which I wished to walk was crumbling beneath my feet. The childcare center Leah and I had built fell apart; the various collectives were running aground in the absence of a mass movement, and people began to float away, most into an individual soul-searching, while others, like myself, tried even harder to find, or create, revolutionary organizations.

Wars of liberation were underway around the world, and we followed them closely. But in the United States our struggle stuttered, and then fell quiet, leaving thousands of us hanging, ready to give our all to the Movement, only there was no Movement left to give to.

The people with whom I had worked and lived moved off in different directions. One of my old friends became a radical feminist and then a witch, finally ending up as a massage therapist in the country. Leah became pregnant and beat a partial retreat to the safe suburban lifestyle of a Jewish housewife. Leonard, although still distant, was talking about starting a family which sent me into a state of panic. Cathy was in school studying ecology and the environment. Barney had moved to New York in a surprising and sudden conversion and had joined a Yeshivah—he was becoming a Hasidic Jew. At our goodbye dinner for him, he provided his own food and plates and he turned his back to us to wash his hands the required three times before eating. We tried to tackle him with a feminist perspective: "But, Barney, don't you have to pray every morning that thank God you weren't born a woman?"

He nodded mutely, his head hanging as he pulled on the strings of his prayer shawl that poked out, to us, offensively from beneath his sweater.

"Barney—you were always such a believer in feminism—how can you accept that?"

We had no effect. He left us. Leah married Ron soon after. Cathy started seeing a therapist three times a week. Jannie lived quietly on her own with her cats and simply stopped coming to any of the study groups.

I felt my one-time comrades had abandoned me, and while I was angry for a while I didn't exactly blame them; these were choices they could make. But they were choices unavailable to me; my past had branded me with this path. For each emaciated child for whom I had cried when I was still a child, for each black South African who endured apartheid, for each of the figures in my life who had fought or spoken out against these or other abuses, for my own emptiness inside: for these reasons I hung on. I saw no other future for myself than to be an organizer—and then to write of my experience. This was going to be my life, and I stayed active.

* * *

It was through the Black Panther Party newspaper that I first learned about the Inter-Communal Survival Committee (ISC). They were a part of the Panthers but were a white group organizing white working-class people in the Uptown area of Chicago. They, too, had practical community programs: food give-aways, health-screening programs, block clubs, and a lively magazine titled *Keep Strong*. The newspaper mentioned they were opening a new office in San Francisco.

I set out to find them. When I tried to contact them, they were suspicious and unwelcoming; clearly this was a tightly knit group not seeking to recruit or gain publicity. They were working from their own plan and had little interest in proving themselves to the local Left—in fact, they wanted to keep well away from the Left, and for a while it seemed that included me.

But I persisted and finally convinced the local leader, Marc Zirulnik, that I was sincere and willing to work. A couple of weeks later, I was already in a kind of routine. Two or three days a week I met Laurie, one of the ISC cadres, at their Church Street office, a basement filled with bundles of *Keep Strong* and the week's BPP newspaper. There was a typewriter, a coffee maker—not much else.

One morning I arrived at 7.00 A.M. Marc was already there. As I headed down the stairs to the basement office, I saw him and Christine, another local recruit—they were hugging, their mouths together in a kiss. I retreated for a few minutes. Then started my descent again—they were separate now. I kept my eyes low, looking at the ground, picking a pile of papers from which I would count my daily quota of one hundred.

"Hi," said Marc casually as he drifted past me up the stairs, leaving for his own work that day—perhaps he would be organizing the Thanksgiving food giveaway we were planning or the big new program in Stockton, or the fundraiser at a local bar owned by a Greek sympathetic to the Panthers.

"Hi," I replied. I kept my thoughts to myself. But I was surprised. I had thought he was with Jerry—a tall, blonde, rather hard-edged woman who, Laurie had told me, had once been a model. I knew that Jerry took care of him, bringing him coffee at the "crib" (the house that four of them shared—sparse and barely furnished—they had no time to make it a home), touching him with love in her eyes, while for the rest of us she reserved only a hard look.

And, what was hard to acknowledge, was that I was attracted to Marc too. I didn't quite understand it—I was still with Leonard and loved him. Leonard couldn't figure out why I liked Marc (he knew I did). Marc was burned out, pale and skinny from years of overwork. And I began to have this feeling that Marc, whether consciously or not, used the effect he had on women to recruit them or at least bond them to ISC. I could see that. And watching Christine, her body pressed up to his that morning, yes, I could see it. He was someone with whom a woman, me perhaps, wanted intimacy. He had this intensity about him—driven, dedicated, his blue eyes small openings into what must be the great love of which Che had spoken. There was a feeling that if the eyes would turn your way, then the great love would meet your own, and this imagining of passion was what drew us to him.

Laurie arrived in the office just as I had finished counting out my papers. Short, squat, her long brown hair pulled back into a pony tail, her face squashed up a little like her body, Laurie was part American Indian. She was a streetperson—this was how she described herself to me. And she had given herself to ISC because here was an organization that respected her, that valued her streetwise abilities, that gave her a roof, food, a stipend (barely), and a purpose. Laurie's center of gravity rode low—she had been struck down many times, but like one of those spherical toy clowns weighted on the bottom with magnets or lead, she just rocked back into place each time. She was probably in love with Marc, too, only being small and plain and plump the way she was, she must have known there was never a chance for her. I am sure she loved him nonetheless and felt fed by that.

I came to be fond of Laurie. She taught me how to sell papers, showed me how to work the street, steered me away from trouble more than a few times, and was honest and direct.

Laurie and I rode the bus to Haight Street. She knew hundreds of people in and around the Haight. We sold papers to the storeowners, to aging hippies, to black men who high-fived Laurie and hugged her with affection. We wandered into the Free Clinic and peddled papers in there or talked young people into trying their first copy as they entered the Haight Street Co-op to buy their week's vegetarian groceries. In the morning, we'd each move fifty or so copies this way and then take the trolley downtown to Powell Street where the cable cars turned and the Moonies recruited students and young travelers.

Selling 100 papers took around twelve hours. By nightfall my fingers were black with newspaper ink. I was tired but satisfied, having pushed myself out of my shy shell far enough to convince 100 people to part with twenty-five cents each to buy the Black Panther Party newspaper. To young mothers I spoke of the party grade school—there were often articles about it in the paper. To others, I pitched the international news. To the elderly, I opened the paper to the sections covering health-care news or talked to them about the clinics that the Panthers had set up. I rarely stopped people, except for the regular buyers who came looking for the paper, but I would turn and walk with my potential customer, matching my stride to theirs, firing off several topics until I met a response. If they responded, then I knew there was a good chance of a sale. I believed in the Panthers program, and this belief came into my sales pitch with energy and enthusiasm.

I gave my money to Laurie at the end of the day and climbed, exhausted, onto the bus back home to the Mission.

ISC's plan was to open a permanent office in rural Stockton—a town in the heart of the San Joaquin Valley, the birthplace of agribusiness, of the giant factory farms. Marc explained to me that Stockton was populated with Appalachian hillbillies and Okies who had fled generations of poverty out east only to find equally grinding conditions in the valley. When Marc talked to me about the Panthers, or about ISC's plans, he spoke with such dedication and seriousness, with such insight. These few times we spoke together I felt I could touch a heroism in him that I was searching for also in myself.

After a couple of months Marc took me to meet Slim Coleman, the Chicago-based leader of ISC. He was staying for a few days in Huey Newton's Oakland apartment. I was doubly awed: to be in Huey Newton's place and to be meeting Slim, a veteran, so I understood, of the Freedom Rides and the Civil Rights Movement in the South.

Marc and I entered the building. It was secure, with both a doorman and intercom system. The lobby was pristine, white, high-ceilinged. Marc announced us through the intercom, and then we were buzzed in. We climbed into the white-and-gold elevator and rode it up twenty-five floors to the penthouse.

Huey, facing murder charges, was keeping a low profile—he had vacated the apartment for a while and was living in a house in the Oakland hills. I believed he had been framed and would be exonerated of the prostitute's murder and wished only that the government's harassment of him would stop.

I entered the living room, trailing Marc, and saw Slim sitting on the white leather couch, slouched back, his long, large legs crossed. I sat across from him, embarrassed, not knowing what to say or do, just waiting quietly while Marc and Slim conversed. The view through the ceiling-high penthouse windows was impressive—into the night the city lights glittered across the blackness of Lake Merritt.

I was there to be checked out by Slim before I applied for membership to ISC. I imagine that he relied simply on his intuition for this review, since he barely acknowledged me during our visit. I was not ISC material—they recruited working-class whites generally. They were already working hard to recruit Leonard, who was cynical and resistant—but he came with iron-clad class credentials and, better still, he was a man. I tried not to mind that they were far more attentive to him than to me, even though I was more eager than he and had already volunteered weeks of my time. But here I was, finally getting to some point of acceptance—although I realized that, as a Jewish intellectual, with my roots deep in the radicalism of the struggle in South Africa, this would be a stretch for both ISC and me. The cultural differences, as ever in my life, were vast. but they took me in after all, and I passed their tests of selling papers and working on the food giveaways, and I had sat in the kitchens of poor Okies in Stockton and found a way to talk—my strange accent and vocabulary notwithstanding.

As I watched the two men I remembered my one visit to Stockton.

I sit in the shabby kitchen of a large-breasted white woman. Laurie and I are in Stockton for the Thanksgiving food giveaway —one of ISC's organizing drives. We are going door to door explaining ISC's purpose and trying to sign up likely community recruits who will spearhead ISC's block organizations.

We are working on only a couple of hours sleep. Last night we worked until 3.00 A.M. setting up a school gymnasium for the food giveaway where we are to hand out paper grocery bags filled with donated food, including one small turkey per bag. At four, we fell asleep in sleeping bags on the floor of the Stockton "crib" and woke at 6.00 A.M. to finish the setup. There was no food in the kitchen and so, for breakfast, Laurie and I picked up paper cups of coffee and a sugary doughnut each at Dunkin' Donuts.

Now we are in this stranger's kitchen. Laurie pulls out copies of the ISC magazine and opens it on the plastic, checkered tablecloth. She leans toward the woman's pockmarked and pink-lipped face and describes with enthusiasm ISC's Chicago programs.

The red-and-white squares of the tablecloth and the greasy smell in the air remind me of the kitchens of my school friends when I was small. We were new in the gentrifying London neighborhood and in the back streets my fellow school children lived in Victorian-era slums (two-up, two-downs they were called), where the cold blew in through broken windows.

*My friend Sheila lived in one of these run-down brick buildings;
her mother worked in the local workmen's cafe, and they survived
on a diet of soft white bread and strong tea. I was sad and shy
when I visited them after school, and I shared the white bread
spread with yellow margarine, and then later, Sheila was ashamed
when she walked into my house and she looked up at the domed
glass ceiling of the entranceway, which the ivy grew towards in
symmetry from two plaster plinths (and I knew what the word,
plinth, meant, because we had them in my house). The hallway of
my house was bigger than her whole flat, and I felt her subservient
shame and carried it as part of my own.*

*This is the memory that comes to me as feisty little Laurie and I
are welcomed by the woman who is probably not much older than
I am, but looks it. She is white and pallid and obese in the way that
poor people in the U.S. become obese: from a diet rich in fats and
sugar and salt and empty of education.*

*The woman lets herself down slowly in the kitchen chair;
behind her a curtain is strung up to separate what is supposed to
be a dining room but is by necessity made into a bedroom for three
of her children. Laurie leans forward and extracts the woman's
promise that she will come with her children to the food giveaway
later that day. Laurie is lively and caring and tough as nails, while
I watch quietly in the background and remember Sheila.*

I sat in Huey's penthouse with the cold glass windows and the white
leather furniture heavy as a threat and glossy with the fame of the absent
occupant. I thought to myself, *Here I am, in Huey Newton's place. I am serious now, I am organizing white people, and we are here, really, allied with
blacks, doing real work, organizing.*

Slim lounged comfortably on the couch, stroking his square chin, looking
at me from the corners of his eyes, and I imagined that I was working on the
front lines and that, sometime, ISC would acknowledge my dedication, effort
and intelligence, and for that I would work tirelessly.

This quiet determination of mine, however, did not last long. I began to
have political arguments with Marc, pointing out how little actual political
education ISC offered either their cadres or the people they were organizing.

The end of my involvement finally came after they asked me to raise two
hundred dollars from my friends. They were quite specific: I was to ask ten
friends for twenty dollars each. The problem was, my friends didn't have

twenty dollars each to spare; they were mostly on food stamps and living the marginal existence possible in the seventies for young single people. But more than that, it would have been a strange threat to those friendships. Nearly all my friends were involved in some kind of political activity, from working in a shelter for battered women, to running La Casa, a support group for Nicaragua. All their projects were in need of money. The act of going to them for money somehow implied that my work in ISC was more important than theirs. It would also imply that I was out of touch, that I didn't understand their financial and political situations. In any case, it would cast a shadow on the friendships, and I didn't feel comfortable with that. I offered instead to develop a fundraising program, saying that it would be more beneficial. This was ignored, and I resigned soon after when it became clear that I would be violating organizational discipline by refusing the assignment.

I understand now that the request was designed to test me and alienate me from those friendships. Not consciously perhaps, but that would have been the effect. At that point I had seen enough of ISC that I knew to stay away. Even though they were doing things that I respected (in particular the work in Stockton), there were too many things that didn't add up.

In Stockton I had worked on a free blood pressure screening program as part of ISC's organizing there. And indeed there were many poor people who came who had seriously high blood pressure. But all we did was to tell them their BP was high and suggest they see a doctor. There was no follow-up. They weren't told how to see a doctor. There were no lists of medical clinics, or discussion on how to get Medicaid coverage. It dawned on me that ISC was simply using the screening as a tactic—they didn't really care about the fact that these people were sick. Yes, ISC was working on concrete programs with poor whites, but no, they didn't give a damn about them as people. And they didn't give a damn, either, about us, the "cadre." We dedicated ourselves to the group, sleeping only a few hours a night, spending twelve hours on the street hawking papers, and getting little in return—no study, no culture, no friendships. I resigned, sadly, and returned to my journal.

July 15, 1978

Write a short story. Write about cadre parties and "Moonie-ism." Why do they become top-heavy and squash the life out of people?

Marc has a bad back. You can watch him holding it when he's in a kitchen, papers on the table and coffee boiling on the stove, and there he feels comfortable enough to feel uncomfortable. He is not a tall man, and the pain in his back causes him to stoop forward slightly making him look even shorter. Even when bent, he keeps his shoulders square and thrown forward aggressively, taking attention away from a belly beginning to round out and sag.

His eyes are very blue and hard for me to look at. There is kindness behind them, but he cannot look back there—the pain, too, is buried beneath layers of priorities, barely noticed in his numbness from himself. He is caught in something and his arm is twisted, and as he struggles he is twisted tighter and tighter by a history of forces that he cannot look at.

Marc is an organizer.

The woman sits in her room, alone. The thoughts and feelings inside of her take up so much space that she hardly knows her physical borders anymore. Sometimes she sees herself from outside: a woman a little curled over in a corner of the room, or sitting at a big, worn desk. She looks much smaller than she is because of how she curls in on herself. She is actually of average height, slender, but not thin. She feels big—inside of her the thoughts and feelings are very big. They fill the room. It's why she likes to keep her room empty, sparse—to have a place to fill up, a place where she can breathe easy.

She is a strong woman with weak edges.

CHAPTER 3

Television

1979. Truncated hourglass shapes are stuck on the land—over-sized, concrete Gullivers rising from the dirt of Harrisburg, Pennsylvania. The pictures on television are still—these structures are without roots, yet they cannot move. Helicopters fly around the gray stillness, cameramen filming the fat-waisted nuclear reactors, the whir of the engines and the blades giving us a background noise.

A hundred and fifty thousand people are evacuated: mostly pregnant women and children. Fear is broadcast over the airwaves. There has been too much heat in Three Mile Island's Unit II, but despite mistakes and malfunctions there is no meltdown, no release of radioactive cesium. At least, not this time.

Leonard and I broke up. Even though I had left ISC, the fact that I had wanted such an organization—one to which I could commit myself fully—stood between Leonard and me like a wall. While I wanted the life of a full-time revolutionary, he wanted to be settled, to have children to care for and to worry about the details of domestic life. I would not get married. I would not live with him. This was not to be my future.

The irony, of course, was that what separated us was, equally, what most drew us to each other. Leonard was my core and my grounding. When I got sick with tension-filled days and responsibilities that scared me, he sat by my bedside and held my forearms with his square, strong hands, and, through my fever, I felt his coolness blow into me, bringing me down, earthing me in him. I imagined him a tree, with his roots sunk deep in the ground and his body being able to bend but not break.

22

And he loved in me my courage and adventurousness, my dedication and my strength of purpose. For him I opened up a world of ideas and possibility. But in the end my world was too open-ended for him and his too predictable and closed for me. What we wanted did not match. For a while we pulled on each other and thrashed about in anticipation of loss. The break-up devastated me. I tried to negotiate with him, to find a compromise that would work for us, but by then he had met another woman from the co-ops who shared his desire for a settled family life. In a deep and lonely depression, I mourned the loss of him.

Leah and I still got together, just the two of us, to try to figure out what we were doing and to plan out our organizing work, but we no longer had the support of a larger community.

Leah talked about Andy, a gay typesetter who worked with her at a downtown print shop. He was helping her to organize the other workers, and she spoke highly of his abilities. Together Andy and Leah developed a clear strategy for their organizing, systematically evaluating each worker in the shop with an assessment of their motives, allegiances, and potential to help or hinder the unionization effort. I was impressed: here was someone else who thought along the same lines as we did—who believed in an organized yet personal approach to working with people. I wanted to meet Andy, but for weeks Leah put me off.

"I like what he's teaching you about organizing. I just want to know where he learned that," I persisted.

"He was out in Minnesota for a while—he's mentioned a group out there that he worked with, but I know he doesn't like to talk about it."

This intrigued me. I was back in that familiar, agitated state, looking for an organization. How could I have a political life without others? And it was precisely in order to be able to have a political life, and to have (perhaps contradictorily) my independence, that I had let go of Leonard, the person I had loved more than anyone. Andy's efficient but mysterious organization became a beacon for me: maybe *this* was the group that would allow me to use my skills and commitment. And if not all that I expected, at least some kind of political work might lift the veil of pain under which I lived since Leonard's departure.

Finally, Leah invited Andy to meet me. I answered the door to a compact man, thin and neatly dressed, wearing brown-framed glasses and with short brown hair and a closely-trimmed moustache. We shook hands, and he smiled and didn't look quite directly at me. He seemed shy or restrained, or self-contained, perhaps.

We sat in my sunlit living-room, drank tea and juice and began to talk. After some time and small talk he began to loosen up.

"So," I asked, "where did you learn your organizing techniques?"

He raised his eyes up, hesitating, then looked back at the notebook he had with him. "I was involved in something in Minnesota. It wasn't a very public group."

"Can you tell me anything about it? I'm interested in learning about any grassroots work that's going on."

I told him about my experience with ISC and laid out some of my political views. While I admired the liberation struggles in Nicaragua, or Zimbabwe or Mozambique, I had always believed that the real struggle—for me, at least—lay in organizing working- and middle-class whites in the United States. As white people, that was where we could best contribute: to combat the alienation and isolation of U.S. whites before the Right wing could exploit those weaknesses.

Andy continued, "We have strong alliances across racial lines. But it's mostly a white group. Right now we're involved in community work. We grew out of the food co-op movement, and it's expanded since then. There are certain open programs: a childcare center, bookstore, health workers' group—that kind of thing. I'm afraid that's about all I can tell you."

However, over the next weeks we talked more. I had a vision of the work I wanted to be doing, and as we talked, Andy described it to me, as he had lived it. This organization was working in the food co-ops in the Twin Cities of Minneapolis and St. Paul. Their position was that the co-ops must serve poor and working people, not just the hippies who could afford not to work. The group was against the hippie and private-property philosophies of the co-op owners and refused to enter into the polemics of the Left (of which I had experienced more than enough and was thoroughly tired).

Andy and I became friends. He came from a Calvinist farm family in South Dakota that was deeply religious, forbidding dancing or contemporary music. But he had extricated himself and found his way to San Francisco. I was interested in his history, and I liked his gentleness and dedication. His personality when I met him was a strange combination. On the one hand he was serious and reserved and spoke in an emotionless yet lucid way about the practical details of organizing. But I began to see another side of him; he would stop in the street to stroke a passing cat, picking it up to nuzzle it, or coo baby-talk at the lucky feline. Or after a discussion he would relax all of a sudden and a sly sarcasm would steal out of him, escaping from behind his formal mask. These odd contrasts endeared me to him. Soon he joined Leah and me, and we became a threesome working together in our union work.

Andy was my introduction to the O. The O.—standing simply for the Organization. *The* Organization: the one and only, as if there were no other. It built community programs at the same time as developing its cadres, and this cadre development, Andy stressed, was given high priority, unlike in ISC. The belief of the O. was that nothing could be done if cadre weren't educated and transformed through criticism and self-criticism into strong, capable, independent yet disciplined revolutionaries.

"So why did you leave?" I asked him. Because he spoke with a kind of nostalgia and clearly a great deal of respect for the O.

"I was ready to come out of the closet. It didn't seem appropriate there. I didn't see how I could. The O. didn't exactly encourage that kind of thing."

He lived in the Castro area now, sharing a pretty, wooden Victorian house with two other gay men and was taking on the life and identity of a gay man, with encouragement from me and Leah. I didn't, then, stop to question further why he could not have stayed in Minnesota and in the O. and come out as a gay man. I didn't grasp the significance of a gay man feeling himself pushed out of an organization that claimed itself a leader against sexism and for the liberation of women.

Andy and I worked closely together over the next two years and I grew to love him for his kindness, his humor, his affection.

Over and over again I talk about the people I love. It's like I've lost something that I'm trying to get back, or reaching for, like hands pulled apart in a crowd, and there they are receding into the past. All I can think of is how I loved them and they are gone now. I never go back to those I care for and they are just lost out there with no past or future, just that little spot of time I knew them in, light of that time shining down on the memories. There is no home there to go back to.

Andy introduced Leah and me to the Assessment Process. He brought out a dog-eared, faded and much-copied paper that he had kept from his days with the O. It was a single sheet titled, "First Stage of the Assessment Process." I never did find out what the second stage was. The purpose of the process was to analyze a person in order to support their political practice and to help transform them into a more effective revolutionary.

In the setting of a small group of would-be cadres, we used the list of detailed questions presented on Andy's faded paper to extract a life history from the person being assessed. The questions included the educational background, work history, religion, ethnicity, neighborhood, and so on of each side of one's family, and also had broad questions such as: "What is your conception of yourself as a man/woman?" or "What are you to yourself, and what is your purpose in life?"

The assessors took detailed notes and then analyzed the information and wrote up a formal "assessment." This was a class-based analysis of that person's personal and political outlook, a summary of their strengths and weaknesses and, finally, a set of recommendations of steps to take that would enhance their developing, rising, proletarian side and negate their bourgeois side.

Having experience, as many of us did, with, not only the counter-culture version of Maoism (as practiced by, for instance, having ten minutes of criticism-self-criticism at the end of every food co-op meeting, or women's group, or childcare collective meeting), but also having been politically weaned on women's consciousness-raising groups and other products of the women's movement, the assessment process fit well in the natural progression we were going through of trying to link the political with the personal. In the early years of the seventies, we had already started unearthing our hidden histories. The immigration patterns of the century became something alive; we could see our own families as part of a demographic and economic movement: whether it was Leonard, who could now understand why his mother refused to have Italian spoken in the household (striving for assimilation as a response to anti-Italian prejudice), or Leah, who found a cultural comfort and pride in learning about the Russian *shtetls* and the persecution her great-grandparents had fled. My family's history, which included Communist trade unionists and Lithuanian Jewish peddlers, became part of a whole; no longer something that set me apart from others. We discovered a deep and rich radical history that was our own.

We were now the downwardly mobile—at least temporarily—and this dislocation was the source of our discontent. Yet, when we looked at our histories, a surprising number of us discovered that the upward mobility of our families had lasted less than a generation. We were not all as middle class as we thought. The assessments were another tool to trace our histories and to understand the influences on us of our class and cultural backgrounds.

In our first use of the assessment, Leah, Andy, and I gave each other assessments that were generous and sympathetic. We treated each other delicately and with respect.

Leah had straight brown hair cut in a pageboy style that fell neatly around her face: a pretty round face with a bumpy, freckled nose—she looked like a young Russian peasant. I could imagine her grandmother in her strong, firm-breasted body. Her assessment indicated she was too "subjective," too focused on personal issues and needing to study more in order to understand the social forces that motivated people. But, at the same time, we recognized her strengths: she was a good organizer precisely because she listened to people attentively and made a human connection with them.

As for me, I was a good theoretician and strategist, but my weakness was in implementing the ideas I had, in following through with things and, of course, in being shy. So I was encouraged to be more active in the groups in which I was working, to work more in mass practice. Andy? . . . I no longer remember his assessment. Strange, because these became a kind of blueprint for dealing with each other, the first thing we looked at in analyzing each other's work.

Our weekly "unit" meetings used the assessments as the basis for discussing our political work and reporting the week's developments in our union organizing. By this time I was a landscape gardener, traveling the glass-walled banks and offices of San Francisco and the grassy lawns of Silicon Valley with a watering can and a pair of pruning shears tucked into a leather holster that I wore at my waist.

Through this job, I'd been thrown into a rank-and file union struggle. My unionized co-workers and I had discovered that our employer, American Building Maintenance, was flagrantly shunting our work over to a newly formed non-union shop that openly operated out of our building and used our equipment. The day we received lay-off notices referring to a "lack of work," we began to organize, despite the fact that none of us had any labor union experience. The new "scab" employees were earning less than half of our union scale wages.

We found out early on that ABM and our local of the Laborer's Union had a sweetheart deal set up where the union had sacrificed our unionized jobs. A woman at the National Labor Relations Board, who we consulted to get an idea of our rights, told us to be careful: both the Laborer's Union and ABM were believed to have ties to the Mafia, and it was likely that the sweetheart deal was engineered through this connection. We figured this was true, as George Evancovich, the head of the local, looked like a caricature of a mobster, smoking cigars and sporting the scar of a bullet hole in the center of his forehead.

We were a motley group of gardeners: among us several working-class dykes, a displaced valley girl, a couple of middle-class drop-outs trying to be artists, a young and feisty black woman from Oakland, and two older white men who'd moved to the job after years working as janitors for the same company. At least half were alcoholics and the other half smoked too much pot. But with our jobs at risk, we closed ranks and decided to organize to force the union and ABM to negotiate with us. We filed grievances with the Laborer's Union and Unfair Labor Practice charges with the NLRB.

Over a jug of red wine, Dale, a former janitor and current alcoholic, helped me rewrite the words to some old labor songs. Our ad hoc group began a flurry of activity: we leafleted ABM's stockholders' meeting; Dale and his guitar led twenty of us in a musical picket of the downtown Hyatt Regency hotel; and we started discussions with the janitors who made up the bulk of ABM's workforce. The union and company had ignored us for months, but our enthusiastic singing on the picket line got immediate attention. The Hyatt Regency management was on the phone to the unsavory allies in a matter of hours, demanding that they get us the hell off their front entrance. That same evening we scheduled a negotiating session.

Chris, a prematurely graying woman gardener, and I, young and well read in labor history, represented our group. We met with the men from the Union and ABM in a smoke-filled conference room at the Holiday Inn. Chris and I were the only women present. With our co-workers we had worked out a clear strategy: we would go to the wire for our jobs, but the pension fund, which we had discovered was missing completely, we'd leave that be. We figured we could get twenty jobs back without too much trouble, but the hundreds of thousands of dollars of pension money might draw on us more fire than we were willing to take on.

I leaned back in the plush chair at the conference table, a toothpick dangling from the corner of my mouth, in my element at last: *this* was something I was good at. I had taken the lead in organizing so far and our tactics had forced them to deal with us. As Chris and I argued our position, I chewed thoughtfully on my toothpick or waved it around aggressively to punctuate a point. The middle-aged men across the table peered through the cigar smoke, jaws slack. I imagine we were helped by the element of surprise as I'm sure they had never negotiated with such women before, if any women at all.

Our co-workers, both union and non-union, crowded the hallway outside waiting for us. With this show of support, we won back our jobs and the
non-union company was folded into the union shop, doubling their workers'
wages. We were ecstatic, high on that bond that comes from working together with people on something we knew was right. I was proud of myself. I'd
led this group, found a way to unite both the union workers and non-union
workers to our mutual benefit, and together we'd forced the union and company to, at least temporarily, break up their sweetheart alliance. We'd done
our homework and understood the forces at work; we'd been brave, but in
letting go the pension fund we'd also been realistic. And we'd *won*. We celebrated with a drunken picnic and sang our songs one last time.

The woman at the NLRB had asked me during my talk with her if perhaps I should consider becoming a union organizer. I'd felt proud then, too.
Here was something I could do.

But of course, when the struggle was over, things dissipated, as they do.
Several of my co-workers left soon after; having been loyal workers for years,
they were now disgusted at the company and had no stomach for the job any
longer. As for me, I felt my future still lay ahead. Union organizing was fine,
but it had to be at a rank-and-file level—I'd seen such corruption first hand
after all, and without an organization to support me what good would my isolated efforts do?

At one of our weekly meetings, Andy announced that he had received a memo
from his leadership in the O.—until then I had not known that he was still in
touch with them. It was an unsettling, though not entirely unwelcomed, surprise.
The memo invited one of us to visit the O. in Minneapolis as the contact for our
unit. Andy and Leah nominated me to go. I was glad to represent them. Here I
was going to the source, to the creators of the assessment process, to people who
understood the need to relate the personal to the political in a human and practical way. And, according to Andy, the leaders were experienced organizers from
the Civil Rights Movement. In my prolific studying over the past years, I had
already read the history of that movement and of SNCC, the Student Non-violent Coordinating Committee. James Forman, one of the SNCC leaders, was
one of my personal heroes, and I had read with great interest and empathy his
book, *The Making of a Black Revolutionary*. What particularly appealed to me
was the description of his own breakdown and his ability to accept that as part
of the human struggle rather than as a fatal weakness.

When Andy showed me pamphlets of Forman's that had been reprinted by the O. and sold at their Working Woman and Man Bookstore, I read them eagerly. Forman, elder statesman of SNCC, had a clear and human grasp of how to organize people. He insisted on discipline without losing sight of the need to motivate people, to listen to people and to respect their experience. Without ever saying so directly, Andy implied that Forman had some connection to the O., and, indeed, from what I knew of the O., this seemed reasonable. I had followed Forman's career and had read of his work in Detroit with the black workers' movement there and Black Star Press. He had been with the Black Panthers for a while and then seemed to disappear.

Now here I was, nominated by my unit to travel to the Midwest as their representative to an organization that was the secret offspring of the militant black organizations of the fifties, sixties, and seventies.

CHAPTER 4

I flew to Minneapolis in early spring of 1980. My instructions were to take a cab from the airport to the Working Woman and Man Bookstore on Lyndale Avenue. I imagined myself a soldier, moving quickly, being flexible and willing to trust that the Organization, from which Andy had learnt so much, would make the necessary connections for me. Now I was grasping the real Movement. These were people schooled in the Civil Rights Movement of the '60s, the SNCC sit-ins and the voter registration drives. The roots of the O. were the Freedom Singers, the people who first sang We Shall Overcome, the song that was a nursery tune for me, sung as a child on the Ban the Bomb marches in England. The roots of the O. were the people who had battled police dogs and fire hoses in the South; the little girls killed by racists in their church had paved this way for me. I was finding a home and home was the Movement.

That first day in Minneapolis, an April snow was falling. Not a gentle and pretty snowfall but a wet dumping of coldness that piled up a foot or more. No one at the bookstore was expecting me. Al, the stocky, dark-haired man at the counter seemed thrown by my sudden appearance. He ran out into the snowstorm to make a call from a payphone to his 'contact' to find out what he was supposed to do with me. Payphones were always used in those years. It was assumed that home or program phones were bugged. The O., I was to learn, ran on high security. On his return from the payphone, Al nervously took me down to the basement of the bookstore to wait. And there I sat, on a folding metal chair, surrounded by boxes of Mao's Collected Works; back issues of China Periodicals; second-hand volumes of Malcolm X's autobiography; and Chinese children's books, full of colorful scenes of peasant life.

Hours later I was taken, through the blizzard, to a duplex on Garfield Avenue where I was to live for the six weeks of my visit. Richard and Ted lived there along with another man who moved out that evening so that I could have his room. It was a railroad style apartment where you had to walk through each bedroom to get to the kitchen or bathroom. There were no doors to the rooms—only accordion-like screens that were never pulled shut. There was no privacy.

I put my stuff in the bedroom and sat in the kitchen with Richard. The first thing he did, before even greeting me, was to put the telephone in the refrigerator and turn the radio on. Satisfied that the FBI wasn't listening in, he pulled up a chair and began to explain the house rules. These included a severely restricted use of the phone, a detailed schedule of chores, and a procedure to follow in the case where a criticism or self-criticism might be required. He then offered me a brief description of his background ("my mother was the kind of person who would burst into tears at the mention of FDR's name") and a summary of his ideological weaknesses. His suggestion was that I use this information as the basis to struggle with him to develop his proletarian side. Later I found out that Richard, Al and Ted all thought I was some political hot shot from San Francisco; they had no warning of my arrival or any idea why I was there, and they were as intimidated by me as I was by them.

The next day Richard came and, with the phone cooling nicely in the fridge, told me I was to get a job through a temporary agency, and that after work and on weekends I would be working with him and Al at the bookstore. The following week I would have my ideological assessment, which would be a great step forward for me and allow me to concentrate on fighting my weaknesses.

Meanwhile I entered into the life of the O.: a disconcerting mix of intense isolation combined with no personal privacy, and rigidly structured yet strangely intimate relationships with other cadres.

April 4

Well, here I am—in the Midwest. It was hard last night. People so formal and closed, so no connections are made. So little feeling. I wonder where the humanness comes in?

Above all I must be objective about what I see: what is leading us to our goal and what is holding us back. I mustn't let my ego and my insecurities get in the way. It's hard not to though.

I tell you, last night in bed when people were still typing at 1.00 a.m. and going to get up at 6.00, and I was too hot and couldn't sleep—oh—I wanted to cry. But I didn't. And now, this morning, I'm alone for a bit while someone went to get keys for me. And I'm tired—my eyes are fuzzy.

This evening I go to the Bookstore, and today I will explore and tomorrow is the Bookstore Club.

I don't know, it's very confusing so far.

Admitting that I don't know the reasons for it, this closed form of living together seems very alienating. And no pictures on the wall . . .

April 5

I was trying to summarize the Bookstore Club meeting, but my concentration is shot. Hell.

I should read more on the African struggles of cadre life. It might help.

I feel tired though. Perhaps tomorrow I could write up my feelings on the contradictions and begin to clarify them.

April 6

I've been depressed today—lonely. Lonely. All these weird trips flashed through my mind; going to church (!—something I've only ever done as a tourist), or a psychiatrist, emergency counseling—hell—anywhere where someone would talk to me. Christ. So I walked a lot instead, went to some lakes and sat.

And I decided: to treat all this as if I were in school doing an intensive 6 week training—and not to expect warmth or friendliness out of it—but just to expect to learn things.

Then just now, I went on another walk to the railroad tracks. The sun was setting red down the tracks and I stood on the bridge watching and I put my hands on the sun-warmed stone ledge and let the heat and the peacefulness seep into me. I cried a little. I decided I should buy myself some flowers —but where would I put them?

The lack of privacy is driving me crazy.

April 7

Today I found a job in a packaging factory. I'll meet some other "girls" which will be wonderful (I haven't met any O. women yet) and quite a relief.

In any case, this guy Ted, he's nice enough, not really "cute," but I like him. At least he talks to me—unlike anyone else here. It makes me smile to think of the sexual glances—the messages that pass between us. I wonder how that gets decided here? There's obviously not much room for this kind of thing. And if we went ahead we'd undoubtedly have to do a self-criticism of our "idealism" afterwards. It's so stupid.

But we live in such close quarters—it's always the chest that pulls me. Funny.

I don't much like the other guy, Richard. He's pompous and self-righteous.

I wanted privacy this afternoon, to rest and think, but Ted came home. And now someone else has arrived. No time to myself, no time to exercise. No door to shut.

Later that week I waited in my room for the assessment to begin. Richard was waiting too, in the room he shared with Ted. He was using the time to type a summary of his practice. Every moment of the day was used productively. I felt guilty sitting on my bed reading (there was no chair in my room) while he typed. Because I only had my bookstore shifts as my assigned task I had little to do in my first week in Minneapolis, so I borrowed a stack of books on the labor movement and spent my spare time reading. But as I never saw the others reading, this seemed not to fall under the heading of 'productive activity'. And as I could only read for so many hours at a stretch without needing a break, I would spend painful hours trying to keep my eyes open so that I wouldn't be caught sleeping, or I'd drag myself out of the apartment for a walk downtown, or around the lakes. Nights were the worst because I didn't want to roam around the dark city by myself, but I couldn't watch TV, I didn't have anyone to talk to, and I felt guilty if I went to bed too early.

There was a stereo in the living room, but no-one ever played it. Sometimes when Richard and Ted were both out and I was not expecting them back, I would put on a record and do some exercises. That would feel refreshing and revitalizing, but still, not a condoned activity and so always done with one ear to the door in tense alertness. This was where I first discovered Phil Ochs' music: plaintive songs of protest that I would stretch and feel to as I passed the long hours in that dark little apartment.

Now, as I waited for the meeting to begin, my stomach was already knotted up with anger and tension. This meeting had been postponed twice before and I was prepared for Richard to come in and cancel it again. "There are other priorities," was all he said when he'd canceled before. There were always other priorities, some life that was being led outside the house that I was not privy to. Richard and Ted would come in to eat and sleep, never for very long, and leave after a shower and a change of clothes. No-one else ever came to the house. And the only other O. members I saw were the two men at the bookstore.

But this time, George was coming to the house. He was in the tier of the hierarchy above Richard. This wasn't explicit, but I gathered it from the gestures between them, the way Richard would refer to his 'contact', Pedro (George's code name).

Finally the doorbell rang and Richard ran down the stairs to answer it. I'd met George briefly the day I'd arrived. He was friendly, more so than the others, and had asked me quite a lot about myself that first day. He was an attractive man, dark curly hair, intelligent dark eyes, a little overweight but not too much so.

We shook hands, and then Richard asked me to close the blinds in the living room while he and George went to talk in the bedroom. They closed the accordion partition and talked softly in there for a few minutes. When they came out, Richard completed the security arrangements by unplugging the phone and taking it to the next room, and turning the radio on by the couch. It seemed that security was always tightest during any discussion of an ideological nature. In the O. 'ideology' referred, not to a set of ideas, but rather to the values, thoughts and behaviors described in one's assessment. During these discussions people unplugged the phone, started using code names and lowered their voices several decibels.

I sat in the middle of the couch, a cheap old thing, probably bought on credit from Sears; it was a nondescript tweed, designed not to show the dirt. I wasn't sure what the proper posture was for an assessment. Usually I sat with my shoes off and my feet curled under me, or, when I was particularly animated, I would sort of crouch and hold my arms around my knees, which were drawn up to my chin. The more animated I became the tighter I crouched myself—trying to contain and channel the strong physical response I had to intellectual stimulation. My body was wiry, not through exercise or diet, but simply because of the amount of adrenaline that I could generate out of political excitement. Finally I decided to sit straight, with my feet flat on the floor. This seemed to be the appropriately serious and authoritative posture.

George sat across from me in a straight-backed kitchen chair, alert but relaxed, his notebook resting on his crossed legs, while Richard slumped nervously next to him in the ragged recliner.

"Shall we start?" George said. Richard and I glanced at him, and at each other, and nodded. Richard started the questioning, while both he and George took notes.

"Where were your father's parents from, where did he grow up, how many children were there in the family?"

We all had copies of the assessment questions, and I knew them by heart by now.

I began: "My grandparents on my father's side were both Lithuanian Jews." (I had a good guess, from the looks of him, that George was also a Lithuanian Jew.)

"When they were young their families were driven out of Lithuania by Tsarist anti-semitism and they joined the mass emigration of Jews—they went to South Africa at the turn of the century. My great-grandfather became a peddler and traveled the countryside trading ostrich feathers. Later he had a dairy. My grandfather became a well-respected mathematician and had something to do with one of the first computers, ENIAC, or UNIAC. My grandmother's family owned an inn. My grandma always wanted to teach, but wasn't allowed to because teachers training college meant traveling on Friday night, the Sabbath.

"They had three children—my dad was the eldest. He's close with his sister who's a successful epidemiologist here in the US, and he has a brother in Israel who's a microbiologist. My father was a bit of a rebel—his college friends in South Africa were mostly Jewish radicals, and they were radical-ized more by the second world war. Many of them joined the Communist Party afterwards—I'm not sure if my father did or not, but I know he was involved in a certain amount of activism. He rebelled against his parents by refusing to follow a scientific career. He tried to be an actor early on, and told stories of appearing as a walk-on at the Old Vic with Laurence Olivier as the leading man. But he finally settled on becoming a journalist and writer. At one point he edited an African magazine, *Drum*, which was a gathering place for a generation of black writers, intellectuals and photographers. And he wrote several novels. He resigned his job at *Drum* because of a political fight with the white publishers. A lot of his friends were in the African National Congress as well as the Communist Party, and I know at least some of them were involved in risky political work—sabotage attempts, that sort of thing. A good friend of his is in jail now, for life. He was arrested just for distributing pamphlets. Many other friends were exiled. I think my parents' activity was limit-ed, mostly to do with raising funds for the ANC.

"Anyway, he met my mother in England during the war while he was in the navy and she came back to South Africa to marry him. It was his second marriage; he'd been married briefly to someone else in South Africa. This was one of the many family secrets.

"Now he runs a publishing company, he publishes newsletters, things like 'Business Ideas' for would-be entrepreneurs, and investment newsletters. He makes a lot of money now.

"He split up from my mother last year—he's had a long-standing affair with a much younger woman. Not the first, from what I understand. They live together now.

"He was basically an absent father—classic, I suppose. I don't remember that much about him. He'd come home from work with a migraine and sleep on the couch. Get mad at my mother a lot—pretty sexist really; you know, he didn't know how to boil an egg, and expected her to do everything in the house, then criticized her for over-cooking the chicken."

George interrupted me, "What kind of ideas did he impart to you? Can you give us any quotes or sayings that he used that would be typical of his outlook on life?"

I thought about that for a while, and couldn't get any impression of my father at all. Apart from a visual image of him, curly hair that had been grey-white as long as I could remember, blue eyes behind heavy glasses, a good-looking face, but one which usually had a little frown as he rubbed his face with his hand, I couldn't think of any words he used, or lessons he may have tried to teach me. It was a blankness that reflected his absence in the family. Stark and surprising to find so little there.

"No," I replied, "I really can't think of anything. I don't have much of a relationship with him now. There's a distance there that neither of us seem able to bridge."

Richard looked up from his notes: "Will you give us your mother's history now? Answer the same questions about her."

I took a deep breath and sighed. "This one is always a long story," I said, "but I'll try to keep it short.

"My sister and I like to joke that we're fourth generation atheists—we come from a long line of them on my mother's side. Her father grew up with the Russian Revolution—he was a student at Cambridge University during the early years of the Revolution, and this was the shining light of his life. From his college days he was a committed communist, an early member of the British Communist Party. The 1920s were the days of the victory of communism,

free love, culture and bohemianism. Allen was a renowned typographer, journalist and a witty, fast-talking, crude kind of character—he could swear in six
or seven languages. He wrote history books on British trade unionism, communism and the working class as well as books on printing and typography.

"He married Norma Garwood, my grandmother. She was brought up
without a father, by her mother, Marion, who worked in munitions factories
all over England to support herself and her daughter. Norma worked as a secretary—at one point to a Soviet trade delegation that became implicated in a
spy scandal. Norma and Allen separated when my mother, Jenny, was quite
young. Jenny grew up in a house that was divided in two: on one side lived
Allen with a succession of his various lovers, and on the other lived Norma,
with hers. My mother says she had more "uncles" and "aunts" in those days
than I've had hot dinners. When she was just four years old, my mother was
sent to Summerhill, a progressive boarding school in the country. She always
felt abandoned, that she was sent there so her parents could just get on with
their lives and loves and politics.

"In 1944, Norma killed herself. She put her head in the gas oven, while
her new baby was in the next room and Jenny was at the cinema. Jenny
came home and found her. Norma's lover Joe, the father of the baby, had left
her—he was a Left-wing folk-singer, that's all I know about that. Anyway,
Jenny, whose grandmother had just died, had also just had an abortion. She
met my dad right after all this—she became a war bride, fleeing crisis, I suppose—then moved to South Africa to marry him.

"She never went to college, but worked for a couple of years as a film
editor. She later regretted her limited education. I think she always wanted to
be an artist, but she told me that her art teacher at school had also killed herself and she could never bring herself to paint after that. I suppose she had too
many tragedies in her life. Anyway she always had artists around her, and
worked for years in and around art galleries. She discovered and promoted
several now well-known artists. But I still think of her as someone whose
potential was lost. Now she's bitter and hard for me to deal with.

"Because of her family history she always wanted a big and stable family—she invested a lot in trying to create that, but when my dad started running around it tore things apart for her. Things were pretty bad between them
for a long time before they broke up. I've often resented the fact that they did-
n't separate sooner because ours was an unhappy household. I mean, we had
wonderful high times, they knew how to throw a party, or have marvelous
adventures on holiday, but daily life was a shambles. I was unhappy as a kid.
I couldn't wait to grow up and get out of it all."

"And what about your mother," said George. "What lessons, what sayings did she have that would illustrate her outlook on life?"

"'It takes two to tango', 'It takes all sorts to make a world', or 'Don't cut off your nose to spite your face.' The funny thing is that's what she always does. She is constantly doing things that hurt her to get back at other people. Like, when she's angry at anyone, family or friends, she'll just cut them off for months, sometimes years at a time. Actually, I've only just come back into her 'good books'—she cut me off for a year, right after my niece was born. And she still hasn't seen my sister since the birth. Then she'll just show up one day, probably bringing presents, and act as if nothing happened. I'm used to it now, it's happened so often to me.

"In terms of values: she never let us litter—she'd always tell us a street sweeper would have to pick it up, and she said it in such a way that I grew up respecting the work of street sweepers and my responsibility not to make more work for them. She had that about her a lot, a kind of gut-level class consciousness. Even though she lived in an artistic and intellectual elite, her mother and grandma were working class and that comes through in her, her respect and affection for working people. She has not really been separate from working people in a funny way. Like, the artists she has worked with have often been from working-class backgrounds, I think that's something she is very comfortable with.

"But she's very dramatic and theatrical, eccentric I suppose. When I was young she used to sweep through London like a misplaced queen—wearing a floor-length olive-green cape with a matching green velours cowboy hat and leather boots. People either love or hate her, depending which side of her they see. Since Dad left I've been closer with her, but she's unpredictable so I don't know how long that will last.

"Jenny wasn't really political, except in this gut-level kind of way. She reacted pretty much against the organized politics of her parents. But she did get arrested once in South Africa—it was during a bus boycott and she was giving rides to Africans from the township to their jobs in the city. This was something the Left did to support the blacks in the boycott. Anyway a cop made the mistake of stopping her—oh Christ! She gave him hell, and Jenny's hell is no joke, she scares people when she's angry. She got fined for that. But it wasn't like our other friends who went underground, or went to jail, or fled the country. My mom and dad supported the struggle but were clear on their limits, they wanted to raise their family in safety, and this was why they finally left South Africa for London in 1958 when things were beginning to get much more repressive."

The assessment continued: I discussed, briefly, my siblings, in particular my closest sister, Hatty, and her illness; how her manic depression affected my growing up. We discussed the ideas, events and people that had influenced my life including my earliest hero, Albert Schweitzer; the still-imprisoned Nelson Mandela; the Vietnam War; the events of May 1968 in France; the Chinese Revolution and Mao Tse Tung; the Black Panther Party; the Bolshevik Alexandra Kollontai and my eldest sister, Lyndall, who had introduced me to so many of my heroes.

I described, in some detail, my long history of involvement in political organizations, from my teenage years in London as a shy observer of the Youth Campaign for Nuclear Disarmament, through a host of tight-knit Marxist study groups in California, to my most recent experience in the Laborer's Union.

And I laid out for Richard and George, both of whom were carefully transcribing my words into their notebooks, the schools I'd attended: my early school life, lonely in a working-class London school—a mix of English, Irish, West Indian, Greek-Cypriot and Indian kids, and my subsequent entry to an elite girls school in the suburbs—an all-white enclave that was far more foreign to me than my primary school. Richard and George heard my story of how I ran away at fifteen, searching for meaning and love in post-1968 Paris.

I ran down the main relationships I'd had, both women friends—the strong, creative connections I'd always had with one best friend or another: Robyn and Anne in school, Leah in San Francisco—and men: Pierre, my first love, in France, and Leonard, who I never stopped loving, but nonetheless, for whom I wouldn't compromise my yearning for a political life. I described how men came and went for me in two to three year stretches, broken by a driven searching and sampling of others, handfuls of men that I tried loving, slept with, and left. The latest was Barney—another two-year man—a Pittsburgh-born Irish-Catholic, reconstructed as a California healer. He paid attention to the aches and pains of my body and taught me to feel sympathy for myself. Barney had been a welder in the San Francisco shipyards but he was leaving that world behind and was searching instead for spirituality in the California hills. He could understand, but could not live, the life I was seeking.

Finally I described the miscellany of jobs I'd held: all occupations that, for me, were sidelines, fillers to earn a subsistence wage while in my 'real' life I put my time and effort into political work, the struggle, the real work of revolution.

We'd come to the end of the assessment questions. I was tired—I'd spread my life out in that room for examination. I uncurled my legs from where they had crept up onto the couch and stretched.

My part of the assessment being done, George and Richard moved into the bedroom and whispered together. They left me sitting on the Sears couch. My mind was filled with the images of my life, connections between one event and another making sparks in my brain as the patterns formed and reformed, seen clearer now, or perhaps even for the first time, in this retelling of my story. Like waking from a dream and trying to remember it, I tried to hold each spark, each new connection. "Remember that one," I'd say to myself. "So, that's why I did that—oh, I see now—see, I was so alone at school . . ." Or, "Yes, there's that pattern again, I'm always the quiet one, but the one with ideas."

I struggled to hold on to the new images and clarities and felt full and rich, listened to—they had taken time to listen to this complex and confusing story and now, there were George and Richard talking it over as I watched their silhouettes against the light coming through the bedroom window blinds, heads together, talking about me, my history.

I felt a kind of peacefulness. I felt they had listened to me.

George and Richard returned to the living room.

"We'll need to take a couple of days to produce the assessment analy-sis," said Richard. "It will be sent forward for review and then we'll get togeth-er to discuss it with you."

Then they both left and I, too, to get to the bookstore to put in my shift.

CHAPTER 5

April 11
This is crazy to be feeling this way. I should be having some kind of contact with people. Just friendliness, just straightforward niceness and concern like you should show your fellow workers.
Damn.
I should go out tomorrow night—get my work done in the day and then go to a movie, or the women's coffeehouse, or something. I want a friend.

April 13
I'll laugh to see how long they last this way. I've got to struggle too, but it's hard to be so isolated.
I have a lot of friends in California. I will remember them. I will remember.

* * *

Milieu Control
The most basic feature of the thought reform environment, the psychological current upon which all else depends, is the control of human communication. Through this milieu control, the totalist environment seeks to establish domain over not only the individual's communication with the outside (all that he sees and hears, reads and writes, experiences, and expresses), but also—in its penetration of his inner life—over what we may speak of as his communication with himself. . . .

Many things happen psychologically to one exposed to milieu control; the most basic is the disruption of balance between self and outside world. Pressured toward a merger of internal and external milieux, the individual encounters a profound threat to his personal autonomy. He is deprived of the combination of external information and inner reflection which anyone requires to test the realities of his environment and to maintain a measure of identity separate from it. . . .

He undergoes a personal closure which frees him from man's incessant struggle with the elusive subtleties of truth.

Robert Jay Lifton, Thought Reform and the Psychology of Totalism

A week later we were back in the living room, all three of us. I'd left work at the packaging factory early—I'd lied to my foreman half way through my shift, said I was ill and had come back to the apartment. This was the only time the others could meet, so, as my job was only temporary, it had been decided that I would miss work for the meeting. I was nervous again, not knowing what to anticipate. What had they discovered from my history, my life? Had they found some clue I had missed? Would they offer me small jewels of wisdom acknowledging my self and giving me a place in which to grow?

But by this time I also knew that "struggle" was the order of the day, and they would give nothing to me easily. I was distressed by the coldness of the people I met. Only Ted, and perhaps poor scared Al, had offered me any warmth or humanness. Richard was one whose humanity eluded me. He was a small man, with a round, pale face and lank colorless hair. Today he hadn't shaved and dirty-yellow bristles gave his face even less definition than usual. He sat hunched over in the armchair deferring to George. Obviously George had done many of these assessments, and Richard was in the role of apprentice, taking notes but leaving the major part of the discussion to George, who opened the meeting, looking at me with intense eyes and a kind expression. Richard passed out copies of my assessment.

We began to go over it line by line. My Principal Internal Contradiction (PIC) was stated as "Seeking enlightenment based on personal judgment." I didn't understand what this meant. I brought the paper closer to me and read it again, squinting a little as I did, and tried to understand what "seeking enlightenment based on personal judgment" could mean. I moved on. The next two lines described my father as my Dominant Influence. I tended to a rational, intellectual view of the world, like my father, and so I didn't have trouble accepting this part of the analysis.

The character of his influence on me was described as "Personal Independence." Again, I did not dispute this. It had been my father who had allowed me to stay in France when I ran away, and it had been he who had paid for my first trip to the United States. But, other than that, he had never given me money; he was a firm believer that one should pull oneself up by one's bootstraps, and I recognized in myself an almost desperate independence and self-sufficiency.

It was also noted that I was "Metaphysical" in my "Mode of Thought." This was a concept directly lifted from the library of Marxism-Leninism-Maoism. Metaphysicians were supposedly capable on a practical level, but lacked vision and a global view. Idealists, on the other hand, could see connections between things and were conceptual and visionary. I always wanted to be seen as Idealist—being visionary was preferable in my mind to a practical mechanistic way in the world—also, it seemed apparent that being dominant, as Metaphysicians were supposed to be, was a less preferred position. If I were dominant, then clearly, in the dialectical view of things, I was the side that needed to be overthrown.

The paper went on to describe how my independence had allowed me to "move to areas of attraction with relative ease." Well, again, this was true: I'd run away from home, and then moved to the United States when I was only eighteen. People always thought I was brave, but to me it was simply a part of myself, an adventurousness that came naturally. George also noted that I did not stick with things for long; I changed jobs and political groups and men, for that matter, rapidly. Consequently I'd had a lot of experience with different things but had never settled on anything for long. This was an accurate perception—I had been aware of this for a long time.

George picked up the paper and began to read: "Basically, the PIC stated means that you think you know best what is needed for your development. This subjective view has resulted in relative non-development. You have not developed an occupational skill. You have taken leadership in groups without sticking with them, and, because of this lack of commitment you have, in fact, upheld capitalist relations of production. In essence, you have a pattern of running from struggle."

I sat silent, waiting for George to finish. I felt sick inside and wrapped my arms around my middle, holding myself in.

"The recommendations are that you develop an occupational skill and work with a group to develop it in a process. Specifically, it is suggested that you become a machinist while continuing to work on your development within the O."

George then quoted the last line of the paper to me: "If factors of stability are not introduced, you will not be able to develop and contribute to the revolutionary struggle."

I remained quiet, my mouth down turned and my brow furrowed. This was not what I had expected at all. They were blaming me: they had told me that my prized independence was, in fact, "running from struggle." They had told me that I led people nowhere and in fact kept people oppressed within capitalism. There was no rising side described; how could I know what I was supposed to be, what part of me was right, what part should be encouraged to supersede the old?

George smoothed the papers on his knee and repeated, "It is your bourgeois intellectual arrogance that makes you think you can determine the best way to contribute to the revolutionary struggle."

This last silenced me. The whole reason I was in Minneapolis was because I was searching for an organization, for a common discipline—I knew that I needed something larger than myself, that I needed leadership. And here I was, and the structure, the organization I had found, was telling me that it was exactly my strength, the independence that had saved me from my family, that was impeding my ability to become a professional, selfless revolutionary.

I kept my anger to myself, bitterly holding my tongue. But I could not stop thinking about the odd internal logic in what George was saying. Surely if I was the best authority on my own development than why would I be here, precisely seeking the guidance of those more experienced than me?

George could see how angry I was, even though I remained silent in a quiet turmoil that I could find no logical way of expressing.

"It's a normal reaction for people to get angry when they get their assessment. In fact, it's predictable. After all, you have a lot of value tied up in your bourgeois side, and until you have an opportunity to develop your proletarian side it's very threatening to give up that value. But with struggle, you will be able to identify how your PIC operates and how it holds back development. Remember, the Left in the U.S. failed because it never addressed people's internal stake in the system, and their bourgeois values. Until we are able to struggle internally we will be unable to sustain a successful revolutionary process."

The meeting broke up with the understanding that I would "struggle with the assessment," talk to others about it and try to lower my defensiveness in order to give the process a chance.

Doctrine Over Person

This sterile language reflects another characteristic feature of ideological totalism: the subordination of human experience to the claims of doctrine. This primacy of doctrine over person is evident in the continual shift between experience itself and the highly abstract interpretation of such experience—between genuine feelings and spurious cataloguing of feeling. It has much to do with the peculiar aura of half-reality, which a totalist environment seems, at least to the outsider, to possess. . . .

. . . doctrinal primacy prevails in the totalist approach to changing people: the demand that character and identity be reshaped, not in accordance with one's special nature or potentialities, but rather to fit the rigid contours of the doctrinal mold. The human is thus subjugated to the a-human. And in this manner, the totalists, as Camus phrases it, "put an abstract idea above human life, even if they call it history, to which they themselves have submitted in advance and to which they will decide quite arbitrarily, to submit everyone else as well."

Robert Jay Lifton, Thought Reform and the Psychology of Totalism

* * *

April 19th

Depressed again. And exhausted. I feel so uncomfortable with Richard. Anything I say he responds with, "Well, that's your Mode of Thought," and then he gives me these abstract answers that I don't understand at all.

I talked to Ted a little about his new assessment—he is depressed by it. Not surprising. I asked him what he thought his rising side, or his positive side was, and he couldn't say. All they see here is the negative! There is no attention paid to people's strengths. No wonder they are so demoralized.

When I questioned Richard about this, he skirted the issue entirely and replied, "Well, further down the road the working-class and petty-bourgeois Left will be taking our leadership." I almost laughed in his face. I mean, apart from us poor souls, who else is taking their leadership? They are completely alienating.

I've been busy—crazy busy now. Working full time, every night a four-hour shift at the bookstore (where there are no customers—night after night—no customers!), writing summaries of my practice and preparing the bookstore's union newsletter when I get home.

Apart from Ted and Richard, I talk to no one. Except the women at work—who are wonderful. Strong working women—most of them single mothers. This is the work I want to be doing, organizing women like this. The conditions are such crap in this factory—one twenty-minute break in a whole day! And people are terrified of being fired because they are the sole supports of their families. And remember, that's why I'm here—that's my long-term goal, to be in an organization that is serious and disciplined enough it can develop real programs for people like this.

Perhaps the O. can do it, perhaps not. But I must remember that that is what I'm after.

April 20th

No touching. I think of San Francisco and all the people who touch me—Leah, Cathy, and even Ron and Andy give me hugs. I wish there was someone I could hug and cry with.

Tomorrow Ted is taking me to his company's annual party. He needed a partner—and I've been complaining about how people here never seem to do anything fun.

I am depressed. I should make an appointment with a counselor tomorrow. How would I do that?

April 21st

Today I feel much better. A good time last night with Ted. We relaxed and laughed and danced. I liked seeing him relax.

It was strange though—it seemed that Ted hardly knew his co-workers—he's been there three years or so. I suppose he has no time to get to know them.

I wore my yellow shirt. He asked me to slow dance. I laughed and told him the last time I'd slow danced was when I was twelve. I didn't tell him that was the first time I'd ever been kissed, and I still remembered the young man's (and he was a man—they were always too old for me, even then) smell from that night.

And now I have Ted's smell to remember. A little acrid, but like sweet soap as well, and it made me close my eyes as we danced. Oh, touching. . . . The scent of him stayed on my hands until I went to sleep last night.

Whoever invented slow dancing should get a prize. One is so close—bodies touch, breasts touch chest, legs one between the other, the rhythm of love-making in the music.

It was good to be touched. My period, which was two weeks late, came during the night. I must have relaxed inside.

I wonder what he feels? I will not initiate anything. I'm not at home here; I don't know the "etiquette," the rules in this group. Although I'm sure one has to analyze the whole thing up and down and get the Central Committee's approval!

Perhaps with Ted I could look at my assessment with less defensiveness than with Richard. Perhaps he can help me see if there is anything useful in it for me.

April 23rd

Ted came home early today, and we went running together. I feel he is trying to keep a connection—but everything is so held in.

We ate together after and sat for an hour and a half talking—of course Richard walked in and looked at us with such animosity—like we were doing something terrible. I'm sure he'll criticize us for wasting time.

But I asked Ted why he is in the struggle—he said it was to develop himself with meaning—not to sell himself on the marketplace. A strange answer. But I suppose I understand it—he wants his life to have some meaning, same as me.

I like talking to him.

April 25th

Richard is sick and cancelled our meeting. People get so little sleep, of course they get sick.

I had a dream. I met an O. woman; she was human and warm. She was going to live with Ted. She didn't think he was very politically developed, but she liked him anyway. She turned into me. I was embarrassed because Ted and Richard came home, and my papers were scattered all over my room, disorganized, and every time I picked them up, they fell down again. Ted and Richard went into the backyard to talk about me. My blouse was ripped, and I didn't have any nice clothes to wear. I was worried about my typewriter being stolen. My words were disappearing. A carnival appeared, and I marched out with everyone else to the insistent, unfriendly beat of drums.

* * *

The next week I met with Richard again. He had given me two more papers to study: "Ideological Forms of the Capitalist Relations of Production" and the "Ideological Handbook of Bourgeois Mannerisms." Both these documents were secret and to be kept locked up when not being studied. Richard and Ted each had their own locked file cabinet in which their various summaries and theoretical papers were stored. Richard indicated to me that these papers were "closed" and should not be shared with anyone unless so instructed. There was always a great deal of talk about "open" and "closed" forms relating to, respectively, mass work and organizational, or cadre, work.

These were terms with which I was familiar from my work in California. Several of our study groups there had been closed or semi-secret. When we pulled various people together from the different food co-ops and child-care or health-care collectives in order to study Marxist theory and to discuss our work in these programs, we had been clear that it was best not to advertise the links between us. In San Francisco this was to prevent suspicion developing that we were trying to take over anything and also because we believed in the Leninist model of organizing in the cell structure; we also believed that if our organizing were successful, our groups would eventually be targeted by the police. The massacres of the Black Panther Party leadership and the workings of the FBI's COINTELPRO were fresh and bloody in our memory. We had many connections to targeted organizations: the Panthers; the Central America support organizations that actively supported the struggles of the FSLN in El Salvador and the FMLN in Nicaragua; the Peace and Freedom Party. There were also underground connections to the Prairie Fire Organizing Committee (the follow-on group to the Weather Underground) and to black groups such as the African People's Socialist Party or the Seize the Time newspaper collective.

The need for security was a given in this climate. For those of us who wanted to pull the mass programs and collectives that had grown out of the 1970s under a common umbrella and use them as a political power base for the "People," it was clear that a core of committed cadre would have to be organized. Most of the study groups in which I had been involved in San Francisco had had this long-term goal.

I was not only aware of the need for closed cadre groups to be organized but I had also seen how people's individual personality issues obstructed the organizing process. So-and-so had such a big ego that he always took over the meetings and gave no one else room to speak. Or someone else, usually a woman or a working-class man, had good ideas when spoken to individually but was unable to stand up in a group to present them. For myself, I knew that

I could outline a strategy in broad strokes and make it compelling to people, but I was too disorganized to bring it down to the nuts and bolts of daily tasks—for this I had always relied on a friend for whom this was a strength.

So reading the papers on Ideological Forms began to fit in with my own experience. The theory behind the IFs, as they were known, went like this: any relationship between people in capitalism can be looked at strictly as a class relationship implying domination and subordination. Depending on the conditions of each individual's life, each person embodied part of this rela-tionship in his or her "Ideological Form."

The pamphlets that Richard had given me described the possible IFs and their respective attributes as: working class (financial insecurity), petty bour-geois (social power), bourgeois (financial security), sexism (obedience), male chauvinism (personalized supremacy), racism (cultural degradation) and white chauvinism (cultural supremacy). Each of these IFs was described in detail, even giving examples of "mannerisms" that typified an IF. For example, male chauvinists had a know-it-all attitude, were above the small tasks and were braggarts. People with the sexism form either "reacted" to it by having a poor personal appearance and habits, or "conformed" by being overly nice, serving others and being apologetic.

It was not hard to see elements of myself, or others, in these descriptions. And equally, I could see, from my own organizing experience, how these dif-ferent traits held people back from developing their own potential and from developing the group. In our San Francisco assessment group, and in women's groups before that, we had also tried to identify ways in which we had internalized our "place" in society and develop strategies for challenging these stereotypes, both politically and personally. The concept of IFs and PICs was, in a sense, the logical development of this. The difference was in how rigid the O.'s theory was, and in the level of secrecy that surrounded it.

But when Richard asked me what IF I thought I had, I could not recognize any one of them as being a complete picture of how I saw myself. I could see parts in each description: my shyness and social unease seemed to reflect sex-ism, whereas my geographical and occupational mobility reflected the petty bourgeois form. My intellectual ability and group leadership could fit into the male chauvinist form and the cultural elitism I had learned in my family was described by the white chauvinist form. I did not know how to answer him.

Finally he quoted one of the papers to me: "Whoever is the Dominant Influence [my father] automatically determines one's Ideological Form. How can this be? The Ideological Form of one's Internal Contradiction is a bourgeois birthmark inherited from one's Dominant Influence. Thus, the only way to erase the bourgeois birthmark from one's life is to transform one's bourgeois world outlook to the proletarian world outlook of dialectical materialism. The only way one can do this is by developing one's proletarian PIC with the objective material condition being a Marxist-Leninist organization."

"Now," said Richard, "Given that theoretical basis, what do you think is the IF of your DI, your father?" He leaned forward in his chair, pushing his glasses up further onto his pale nose, his equally pale eyes looking at me searchingly.

My face flushed a little. I rubbed the back of my neck and felt the sweat dripping down the sides of my ribcage. I was supposed to name my own IF. He was pinning me down here, and I couldn't bear it—I wanted to leave the room, to elbow him out of the way, to push back his pallid face—but I couldn't. I had been told already that I ran from struggle. I would not run from this struggle. I would hold my ground; I would damn well deal with it.

But I could not answer him. I sat silent and sweating, the smell of anxiety lifting from me and evaporating into the air.

Richard tapped his fingers on his notebook.

"Don't you think his IF could be Male Chauvinist?"

Well, yes, it could be, I thought. My father was an old-fashioned kind of sexist, and I had complained about this to him more than once. But I could see where Richard was leading—if I agreed with him, then I was naming myself a Male Chauvinist also, by virtue of the inherited qualities of Ideological Forms.

"But how can I be male chauvinist?" I said. "I've spent years working on how I've been oppressed as a woman, and organizing other women—how can I possibly have the objective material conditions, in particular, not being a *man*, to be a male chauvinist?"

I was genuinely confused. I could follow the logic that I would have things in common with my father, that I had inherited bourgeois traits from him, but how this could translate into my being a male chauvinist was beyond me.

"Oh, it's not to do with you being a man or a woman," Richard replied. "Look, it's about your position in the relations of production. From your DI you have gotten intellectual superiority, an ability to move from one thing to another at your whim, thinking you always know what's best even when you don't have the material basis for that, and your DI's position in capitalism gives you the same leverage that he has. It's not a personal thing—no one's saying you aren't also oppressed as a woman. It's just that, if you're serious about com-

mitting your life to the revolution, there is really no point unless you are equally serious about transforming your PIC and your IF.

"You can carry on flitting about from one thing to the next, you can go
back to San Francisco and try to organize working women, but if you don't
deal with your *own* male chauvinism, how you always act like you know
what you're doing without really knowing where you're taking people, well,
what kind of favors are you doing them?"

I was silent. I didn't accept at all that I was so-called male chauvinist. I
wasn't sure if I agreed that my Principal Internal Contradiction was "Seeking
Enlightenment Based on Personal Judgment"—it still seemed too abstract a
phrase for me to grasp. But I did accept the perceptions of my experience: that
I'd flitted from one project, job, man, to the next; that I was afraid of a certain
kind of long-term responsibility and commitment.

Richard and George left the discussion at that. They did not push me to
accept the analysis but said that I should think about the recommendations: to
develop an "occupational skill" and to struggle with a group in a long-term
process. At that point I had grave doubts that the group I would choose to
struggle with would be the O.

I stayed angry. But I decided to be principled and to channel that anger, so
I wrote up a formal criticism of the O. and gave it to Richard. I challenged the O.
on the problems that I saw: the isolation in which people lived, the coldness
between people, the disconnection from mass organizing, the way people didn't
seem to think for themselves but parroted certain phrases over and over again.

A day or so later, Ted came and talked to me. For a week I hadn't seen
him; he was working eighteen hours a day between his printing job and his
shifts at the O.'s bakery. I'd missed him—he was the only one I could talk to.

"You've seemed so withdrawn the last few days. I've been wondering
what's going on with you?" he asked.

I opened up to him, relieved to have someone who would listen to me.

"I've just been feeling so sad. So overwhelmed. So *alone*. It feels so
wrong here. Don't you feel it?"

"Sure, sometimes I feel that way. When contradictions get really heightened, when the struggle gets intense. Why don't you tell me how you're feeling?"

"It's like I'm crazy. I see these things that no one else does—the way people act here . . . But I've taken a step. I wrote up a paper and sent it to leadership. I'll just put out my disagreements clearly."

Ted nodded. "If that's how you feel you should best be spending your time . . ."

April 27th

Ted said I'd seemed withdrawn the last day or two. I haven't seen anyone for days, so I don't know how he could even have noticed. I told him I felt totally isolated. He said I should look at why those conditions had been set for me—that they were conditions set for my development so I could reflect on my practice.

So, I am trying to look at it. What is it I'm supposed to get out of this process? I feel like they are trying to break down my identity. Ted offers some kindness—not much, but some small reaching out to me.

I've been thinking about Leonard and how that's over. How I just about feel resolved about it—seeing how it could not have continued, how it would have held me back to stay with him.

Normally I would have left here like a bat out of hell. But changing the external conditions is what I always do. This time I suppose I must look at myself, my internal response. That's what must change this time, even if I don't understand it.

But my response is to scream inside of me—"Leave me alone, leave me alone!"—when what I want is to come closer to people.

My back hurts. I want to go to sleep, but Richard is here. I am isolated, yet never alone.

Later Ted let slip that he'd been assigned to talk to me. I felt winded, like I'd been punched in the stomach. I thought he had felt my sadness and cared. But no, he was just acting on the plan to set conditions for my development. What was real here? My head began to feel heavy and then heavier, I felt a blurriness setting in, that I couldn't trust what was happening around me.

Mystical Manipulation

The inevitable next step after milieu control is extensive personal manipulation. . . . Initiated from above, it seeks to provoke specific patterns of behavior and emotion in such a way that these will appear to have arisen spontaneously from within the environment. This element of planned spontaneity, directed as it is by an ostensibly omniscient group, must assume, for the manipulated, a near-mystical quality.

Ideological totalists do not pursue this approach solely for the purpose of maintaining a sense of power over others. Rather they are impelled by a special kind of mystique, which not only justifies such manipulations, but makes them mandatory. Included in this mystique is a sense of "higher purpose," of having "directly perceived some imminent law of social development," and of being themselves the vanguard of this development. By thus becoming the instruments of their own mystique, they create a mystical aura around the manipulating institutions—the Party, the Government, the Organization. . . .

Whatever [the group member's] response—whether he is cheerful in the face of being manipulated, deeply resentful, or feels a combination of both—he has been deprived of the opportunity to exercise his capacities for self-expression and independent action.

Robert Jay Lifton, *Thought Reform and the Psychology of Totalism*

* * *

April 28th

I dreamt this man came into bed with me. We started hugging; it felt so good. Our legs were entwined. I felt him resist even though I knew he liked the hugging too. I tried to touch him more, but he got up and turned to me and said, "No." I asked him why he didn't want to make love, and he told me he knew it would hurt me, and it was bad for us. He was like a monk, as if he had nearly broken a religious vow.

Oh, god. The three of us are in the house, and no one ever talks to each other. I can't stand it.

Later that week, a unit meeting was held at the bookstore. Like most unit meetings this one started at 11:00 P.M., squeezed in after the store had been closed up for the day and after everyone had completed their daily summaries or attended any other meetings they had scheduled.

By eleven o'clock we were all exhausted already. We sat in the basement, an overheated, airless room, with the radio turned on for security purposes. The meeting was mind-numbing—the heat made me long for sleep, and the crackling music from the radio meant I had to strain to hear what people were saying (people always talked softly in these meetings; again, the FBI . . .).

Al and I had criticized Richard at the last meeting—he had a habit of dumping work on us at the last minute, which left us scurrying all week to complete our assignments. The criticism of Richard had opened the meeting up a bit, and Al joined me in questioning the problems we saw at the bookstore: the lack of mass participation, the lack of customers, the almost complete absence of initiative on any of our parts, and the general decay and stagnation that was evident in the place. We had a lively discussion addressing these issues and had agreed to continue this at the meeting today.

But in the stuffy heat, Richard opened the meeting saying, "It is seen that it is more important to discuss Claire's [my codename] practice rather than allowing ourselves to become distracted by her criticisms of the program. She does not have the basis or the history of practice here to be able to contribute significantly until she has examined her own practice."

Al looked at me, open-mouthed. He had shared equally in the discussion the week before. But he said nothing. He bowed his head. Richard turned to me and asked, "What have you summarized about your practice this week?"

Tears pricked my eyes. The radio babbled in the corner. I could think of nothing to say. I wanted to close my eyes and sleep.

Later I discovered that criticism of the O. was always diverted. This was true with an awesome consistency. The only criticisms that were allowed (in fact, encouraged) were those against other individual members. Apparently I was never to gain enough seniority to make criticisms of the organization itself. Soon I learned the important lesson that the more I criticized the O., the more I was criticized myself. I took this lesson to heart, not in a conscious way, but deeply nonetheless.

Chapter 6

Ted and I continued to skitter around each other like water beetles, the surface tension of our feelings keeping us afloat, and the frenetic activity level of the O. holding us apart. For a couple of weeks all I saw of him were the brief hours when he returned to the duplex to eat or sleep between work shifts. He would move about the apartment in a purposeful manner, eyes down for the most part, unless he had time to talk. Sometimes he would say nothing at all; he was too exhausted. Or he would come in depressed, having been criticized for some intransigence.

Other times all he had to offer were criticisms of me: "Why haven't you done the dishes?" or "What is the internal basis for not completing your tasks?" These criticisms were done for form's sake; he was too tired, or disinterested, to listen to my answers. I felt pretty clearly that he was criticizing me because he was supposed to. This was another condition for my development.

Ted worked nights at the print shop, came home to change into his bakery whites and to eat, and then went to put in a full shift at the bakery. In the late afternoon he returned to sleep. I would be home from my job at the packaging factory and on my way to, or just back from, a shift at the bookstore. I waited for him to come home, desperate to talk to someone. But by the time he arrived, there was nothing left for me; he was reserving his resources for his own survival.

He slept in the room that he and Richard shared, just off the living room. He never thought to close the accordion partition. This meant I could not comfortably use the living room when he was there and could only wander through it to go between my bedroom and the kitchen. But as I wandered through, I watched him sleeping—he usually lay on his back with his arm resting on his chest and his knees bent. I knew that I shouldn't watch him sleeping; it was an invasion of his privacy. But that concept of personal space, of the right to anything private, was already being broken down in me.

I would drift into his room when he and Richard were out. It was grim, spartan. Two beds. Two desks at which to study and summarize. An assorted collection of Marxist and Maoist literature. And the one human element: a picture of Ted's brother Sam pinned on a bulletin board. It was a big photograph, a portrait of Sam as a teenager, dressed up in a military uniform (perhaps ROTC, or his military school). He looked handsome and dashing. I used to study that photo of Sam intently because it reminded me so much of Ted: the same jaw, the same clear and trusting gaze. Ted's "nom de guerre" was Sam.

Outside the apartment, our lives were totally separate. The security rules meant that Ted could not talk to me about any of his O. work. I only guessed he worked in the bakery. I couldn't discuss the bookstore with him or the people with whom I worked. This was supposedly based on the "need to know" principle of the communist cell organizing structure. And so our paths crossed only in this fitful and unsatisfying way, while I imagined, or hoped, at least, that his life outside held meaning and purpose.

Meanwhile, I was in a state of rage and loneliness. I could not fathom the methods of this organization. It went counter to all I had learned and appreciated about my political life in San Francisco: about the need for a deeply human and sympathetic connection between people, the need for programs that helped them in their daily lives in order to organize and unite them against the great profit motive driving the machine of the United States. I still thought perhaps I could teach the O. something of this.

But I could not find a way in. The one skill in which people were well-trained was the ability to turn a question or a criticism back onto the questioner. "What is your interest in pushing this issue?" "What have you done that gives you the basis to say you understand how to organize?" "Where are the people *you* led?" It was a relentless denial that I was unable to overcome. I called my friends in San Francisco for support. I called my mother and my sister, Lyndall. Of course, as I couldn't break security to tell them what I was doing, the conversations were limited, but they understood, at least, that I was unhappy.

After one of my phone calls, my mother sent me an article about Alexandra Kollontai who had been my heroine for many years. She worked with Lenin in the years of the Russian Revolution and wrote of women's issues, of the need for socialized child care to enable women to participate in the life of the external world. And she wrote of women's struggle for love, for the need for equal relationships based on work and respect. Her clear and passionate eyes gazed out from the photograph that accompanied the text. A fur hat and high-collared coat protected her from the wintry Russian cold. Elegant Kollontai led the movement for Worker's Democracy—against Lenin, finally. She was a woman who was able to be strong, who'd stood up for what she believed and, despite her non-conformity, had escaped Stalin's purges.

The article rekindled my yearning to give myself totally to the movement—the movement in the world to create equality. To me equality meant the world's children would not go hungry; that nature, the food source, would not be destroyed; that people would not be tortured for trying to feed the children; and that we could again live in communities where the common good prevailed. That feeling in me, that drive to contribute, to live with meaning, was enormous. It was a kind of grandiose ambition turned inside out. Only in the movement did I feel I could become completely myself, where my potential would be fully realized. So into my rage against the O. crept something a little sacrificial: a romantic determination, a giving up of myself in order to more fully exist. This tender spot of ego weakness took up residence in me, nothing more than a little bruise at first.

After weeks of seeing Ted only asleep, or for too-brief moments in the house, he finally invited me to go out with him one evening. We left late, after 9.00, and went to a bar, the CC Club. People were dancing there, but we sat on the red vinyl seats, drank a modest amount of beer and talked. The yellow lights shone and reflected in diagonals off the crimson plastic that I smoothed with my hand as I talked to him, feeling the intimacy of just the two of us out drinking and talking among the other couples in this bar.

It was a great relief to me to finally talk. It had been a few days since I'd forwarded my criticism of the O., and there had been no response yet. I was tense, but now I could talk to Ted about it.

"You know, there are things I respect about the organization—you get things done, you're well organized, if nothing else. But the *process* is so alienating. And it seems to me that it's really male dominated. No one ever takes the time to talk to anyone else. There's no discussion about why people have become cadre in the first place. People have to be connected to their own rea-

sons for struggling—we can't act simply out of altruism—that creates guilt politics. I've seen it happen over and over again. You have to struggle, on some
level, for *yourself.* Otherwise there's no way to keep up this level of sacrifice."

Ted listened attentively and nodded his head to encourage me.

"If you're doing it for your own feelings somehow, then you can hon-
estly join up with others. Otherwise, you become academic, or oppressive—
trying to take over other people's struggles, like I saw in San Francisco. That's
something the women's movement taught me. But that all seems to be lost
here. I don't understand it. You talk about women being in leadership, but I
don't see any women here at all."

Ted looked up, "Oh, there are women in leadership. Just because you
don't have personal knowledge of them doesn't mean they're not there. My
contact is a woman."

I shrugged. "I still don't see people dealing with what their own oppression is, except for this one-sided criticizing that goes on."

I felt a kind of trust in Ted. I could say things to him that I couldn't to
Richard—and he didn't attack me for it. I felt Ted would listen, that he would
be on my side.

It was getting late. Couples held each other on the small square of the
dance floor and moved together to old Beatles' songs, the music slowing down
as the night progressed. Ted's fingers were curled loosely around his glass. His
shirt was open at the neck and I imagined the smell of his chest and remembered
his arms around me as he had led me slow dancing (me so awkward, never having learned to slow dance during my teenage years as a barefoot hippie). I
sipped on my beer, tasting the bitter coolness beneath the warm white froth.

Ted turned his head from the dancers and moved his weight forward on
the bench to lean towards me.

"So. What do you think your particular oppression is?" he asked. "I
mean, you get into these positions of leadership—in your study groups and
that union struggle—and you seem to be trying to do that here somehow.
Talking to people about all your complaints about the O. Trying to organize
them. But then you don't know where to take people. You leave. So what do
you think it is in you, what is your oppression that makes you do that?"

He opened his hands, laid them face up on the table between us. I
wanted to touch them.

"You see, you think you are so crucial to things. But that's not objective.
You just manage to make people dependent on you—but how does that further the struggle? What is it that makes you do that?"

I wanted to think about what he was saying. I respected him for his commitment. For ten years I had searched for a way to tackle the problems I'd seen and I'd run into every variety of obstacle: Trotskyists, Maoists, Existentialists, Hippies, Radical Feminists, Witches, Bourgeois Democrats, and Social Democrats. Among them were nice people and not so nice people, but they were all pretty damn useless at organizing as far as I could see.

But here was Ted. Living and breathing and drinking beer across from me—someone who was dedicating his life to the Cause. I thought of Alexandra Kollontai—perhaps here was the resolution to my personal and political crisis. Perhaps with someone like Ted I would never again have to be pulled in opposing directions between my desire to be active and a complete person in my own right on the one hand, and my love for a man on the other. Ted wanted to understand me, to help me become a committed political person. He would not resent my activity or try to draw me away from it into a conventional life. He would support it as an equal because his primary commitment was to the movement. Here it was, wrapped together: an organization of committed revolutionaries (though possibly misguided—but that could change with struggle) and a man who would not chain me down, but would help me realize my potential.

And in that moment, as Ted reached out to me, asking me about myself and my commitment, something shifted in me. Not permanently, or in a final way, but enough to plant a seed that would settle and remain rooted in me for a decade. Ted's words made me question my anger at the O. and its methods. A glimpse of the O.'s logic came to me then as I opened myself to Ted; I began to see it as he talked. I was here because I had failed in my attempts at organizing.

The candle on our table flickered, sputtering inside the red faceted holder that dimmed its light. Ted slouched in his chair, but his shoulders were straight still. I was in love with him already.

I could not organize people because I carried in myself that portion of lived history handed down to me by the time and place of my birth and that of my parents. What I had seen as the burden of limited choices and opportunity that were mine as a woman—this was not so different as the limits I was under because of my middle-class background, my intellectualism, my lack of discipline. No, these were not personal faults—the O. was not saying I was a bad person—these were internalized bourgeois traits, and they felt as bad to me as the limits put upon me as a woman. It would be freeing to rid myself of them. It would help me become stronger and more effective.

In spite of the fact that I hated the intensity of the O.'s criticisms and their one-sidedness, I could see that they had devoted time and energy to me. They understood the internalization of oppression and made that a priority. Alone I was nothing. Joining an organization might mean compromise and struggle—but perhaps that was what I needed now. I turned to Ted, "Perhaps you're right. Things fell apart in San Francisco. I couldn't keep them together. I've never known how to keep things going."

I wanted to give him something, to please him so that he would give of himself to me. And he looked pleased. His eyes met mine, and his lips pressed themselves out into a small smile. I felt him breathe a sigh of relief; watched his chest rise and fall like a wave. Yes, this felt right. We were comfortable together. For a while we talked some more: about why I needed to commit myself to an organization, about the changes I needed to make to become a more effective organizer, about the work Ted had done to develop himself as a cadre and what he needed to be working on next.

Then, as if he were to become my lover, I asked him, "What about relationships? Are people in the O. in relationships? How does that fit in?"

"Of course. Many people are married. Some aren't. It depends what they need."

"What about you?"

"No, I'm not with anyone right now. I've needed to focus on my own development. It would have been distracting to be involved with anyone. Besides, I wasn't in a place where I could have contributed much to another person. Before the O., I was kind of a playboy. I had a few girlfriends, but I could never settle down and give any kind of commitment. So, that's what I need to work on—to be serious and respectful enough of the other person to commit to their development."

"Me, too. I've got to stop flitting around. That's been a problem for me . . ."

I told him about Leonard and the other relationships I'd had. And he recounted for me the women with whom he'd been involved. It struck me as odd that he hadn't been with anyone for a couple of years. We sat until 11.00 talking about our histories but keeping the topic of our obvious and mutual attraction well in the background.

Before we left the CC Club, Ted asked me if I had reached a decision yet about Richard and George's recommendation that I become a machinist. I had balked at the idea. My own plan, following the union organizing I'd done, was to get a job as a clerical worker in San Francisco and become active in one of the white-collar organizing drives that were going on. I wanted to connect women's needs on the job with their personal issues; I imagined running lunch hour support groups for working women, discussing children, relationships, families, and work. If women had a place to articulate their needs and problems, they might see the commonness of those needs and the social ties between them. Perhaps we could trace their economic ties and constraints to their family situations and the corporations for which they worked. I wanted to put the women's movement to work in union organizing and build, again, this alliance I dreamt of between the isolated and disadvantaged. I knew that I had a personal empathy that, when pulled out from behind my shyness, could be a dynamic and cohesive force in this kind of organizing.

So I hesitated to give this up. But at the same time I was weary of working alone, afraid of the position of responsibility where my ideas ended up leading me. To be a machinist? It was strange. I hardly knew what a machinist did. But Richard had explained it to me: a machinist ran machine tools to produce metal parts. I had always loved working with my hands and with mechanical things. At three years old, I hammered nails into bits of wood, and at sixteen I welded iron sculptures, wishing I could be making something useful, instead of an art I could not justify. Had I been born a boy I would, perhaps, have become an engineer, but as a girl the option of working with tools and shapes, volume and metal and the mechanically pleasing fitting of one working part into another only opened itself up to me in peripheral ways. The thought of cutting and shaping metal into moveable parts was alluring to me, my hands could feel the competence and toughness that would grow out of that.

And so I told Ted that, yes, I had thought about the recommendation, and that, yes, I supposed that I would do it.

Shortly after this, it was time to leave for California. Richard took me to the airport. He opened the trunk, pulled out my suitcase and slammed the trunk lid shut. An intense antagonism still existed between us—he was the tough cop to Ted's soft touch. But he stretched out his hand to shake mine, and a moment's warmth came from him. "Good-bye," he said, "I hope you keep struggling."

"Thank you for struggling with me," I said, wanting to respond a little to his warmth, and acknowledging to him that I had noticed the time and energy he had put into his role as my contact. I turned and walked through the automatic doors to find my gate.

I flew through the blue air, three hours across country, the thin air a bubble to my own world.

* * *

Barney, my friend and lover, met me at San Francisco airport. He kissed me and carried my bag to his rusty Toyota and touched me often in the car as we drove back to the city across the San Mateo bridge that snaked its precarious way over the flat, blue Bay. That first day home, he and I ate chocolate cake; walked around the Mission, my neighborhood; drove out to the beach to watch the sunset descend on the Pacific and ate and drank well in Little Italy. Later, in bed, he rubbed my shoulders until the tears came, and, when they did, I was almost hysterical, the tears falling like a brief thunderstorm until I was quiet.

But I couldn't relax. I knew now that our friendship was changing, that we wouldn't be the casual lovers we'd been before. In Minneapolis I had decided that. I was moving on again. My mind was on Ted already and a different world. And the specter of Leonard still haunted me as he and his new lover began to consolidate their life together.

Back home in San Francisco I walked on Twenty-Fourth Street in the Mission, the street filled with noise and music and smells. I passed the wide window of the *curandera*'s store that housed a mix of Santería religion and herbal first aid. Intense perfumes of myrrh and frankincense burning before plaster virgins wafted out onto the street.

Across the way was my local butcher shop where I bought hamburger and chicken from a cheerful Chicano teenager who chatted to me in Spanish. If he had been older, I would have flirted with him more. I passed by La Raza, a community art gallery, which showed an incredible assortment of works by local Latinos, celebrations of Frida Kahlo, and housed a color copying machine with an invitation to people of the neighborhood to come in and create copy art. The Cuban cafe down the street was run by an aging black boxer, an émigré (maybe an anti-Castro *gusano*, I never knew) and his pretty wavy-haired Cubana wife. She made squid and black rice, or Cuban sandwiches: crusty bread filled with ham and cheese and squashed in a hot iron to a melted deliciousness. I felt comfortable in their café and went there often to enjoy my solitude in reading or writing.

On each block, grocery stores spilled out fruits and vegetables onto the sidewalk. There were fruits from Mexico whose names I didn't know and dried salt codfish hanging from awnings, Mexican hot chocolate and hand-packed *horchata*, a powdered drink mix made of rice and sugar. There was cornmeal for tortillas, or sweetened, for porridge, and spiky *nopales* leaves from a cactus plant. Apart from my favorite restaurants on the street, where I would order tripe menudo and tortillas, spicy and greasy and good, or pork and rice with fried bananas, the next best thing, and especially good on Sunday mornings, were the *panaderías*, the self-serve bakeries selling turtle-shaped crumbly sweet buns, or foot-long *churros*, a straight and sugar-soaked doughnut eaten hot, or, just for looking at, beautiful breads shaped like crocodiles: green icing eyes and sharp white icing teeth hiding maraschino cherry tongues.

It was violence, though, that finally drove me out of the Mission. Not necessarily violence towards me, or even my friends, but the nightly violence that played out beneath my window. Knife fights that woke me up half-way through the night, gunshots that woke me too, or women screaming and running from men that were called their lovers. And the dog, Malo, that barked and barked every night next door. After my housemates and I complained a couple of times, its owner, Tino, drunkenly lurched out into his adjoining yard one night and started yelling, "You bitches, you bunch of fucking lesbians, I'm gonna kill you!"

The next day we seriously discussed getting a gun. The decision not to was made when we realized that a .22 might not be enough to protect ourselves, but a .45, which might blow a man's head off, was something none of us could imagine using.

But after years of the raw stuff that fills the lives of American big-city dwellers, my nerves were shot, I wanted it quieter and more peaceful.

Coming home to San Francisco, after six weeks in white, malled Minnesota, was a confusing paradox. The vibrancy that I loved came wrapped with a violence arising from poverty. And now there was no longer much structure to my life: my remaining friends made decisions based only on what they wanted as individuals, with no sense of connection to a whole, to how they could shape their lives in helping change what we all agreed needed to change. Suddenly I was in an atmosphere where I could "do my own thing" and no one would criticize. It was a relief to be free of the feeling of eyes watching and evaluating my every move, and it was a relief to be able to talk openly to my friends, but there was something deep that I missed. The unity of purpose. The seriousness of it. The fact that I could work with someone I barely knew, but who, because of our common commitment to a cause, and an organization, would be someone who shared a whole set of assumptions, and with whom a peculiar kind of intimacy existed. Despite the *verboten* status of feelings, there was an intimacy in knowing that, within the context of "ideological struggle" all sorts of personal things could be shared immediately.

But when I came home, I could not talk to anyone about the last six weeks. The security rules meant I had to lie to everyone except Andy and Leah with a vague and general story about volunteering at a bookstore. My friends must have wondered at me. The code of secrecy, the absolute underground nature of the group made "security" the number-one rule of acceptance. I came back to an intense culture shock and could talk to no one of it. Even with Andy and Leah, I was not to share the details of my trip. It was incredibly confusing and disorienting. I became more and more detached from my friends. And then I began to have nightmares.

CHAPTER 7

A man is coming, the woman is running, running, falling. She falls down the stairs, tumbling over and over. She doesn't feel the pain, the dream cushions her fall in vagueness—only her limbs are reeling around her in a gray fall. The man is running, running, and she gets to her feet, pushes the ground back with a giant step. Her other foot moves forward, grabs the ground and pushes back again. She is trying to run, but her legs encounter too great a resistance in the dream air; she cannot go forward faster than the heavy air will let her.

She turns around. The man has a gun. He is running towards her. Back come the stairs; she must hide. She tries to breathe, to grab a lungful of that gray, heavy air. She needs to cry louder, to scream, to get help, to get help . . . the cry won't come, the gray air sticks in her throat. Her heartbeats hurtle her through panic to a sweat-drenched terror. The man shoots the gun. The bullet smashes into her. She's like a marionette with the strings suddenly cut, her limbs collapse backwards around her spine into oblivion. Her throat is catching, trying to get air. The noise of the gun's explosion rushes along sound waves, reaches her ears in the delayed manner of thunder after lightning. The sound of the gun cracking jolts her awake.

I could hear my heart on overdrive, beating so hard I felt my body rocking with each pulse, the waves of blood pouring through me, creating pools of sweat in each small indentation of my skin.

The porch was dark. I looked up from my bed on the floor through the windows to the night sky of San Francisco. Through the city lights, and the reddish black of a polluted sky I could see some stars. It was a clear night, the fog hadn't come in yet, but the stars didn't calm me. I curled up on my futon clutching the covers around me and tucked my head between my arms. Tears wouldn't come to release the panic in my chest. I held tightly to myself while the rocking subsided, not yet feeling safe or able to relax my limbs back into sleep. *It's okay,* I told myself. *It's okay, you're all right now . . .*

The porch was built off the back of the house, on stilts in the California style. It was just big enough to fit my small desk and futon. Every night I unrolled the futon to sleep and rolled it up the next morning in the Japanese way so I would have room to dress and to pull the chair out from under the desk.

I had moved in with Penny—she'd lived with me for a while in the Twenty-Third Street house, which had finally fallen apart. Penny was from New England, looked New England in her L.L. Bean outfits and with her healthy coastal air, her fair and Waspish looks. She was a furniture maker, apprenticing in a chair shop, more or less a sweatshop. Her lover Lynette, a second generation French Catholic, was a cabinet maker. Lynette was skilled, competent, beautiful and tempestuous. They were constantly breaking up then loving each other and breaking up again, much like Leonard and I had done. Penny and I leaned on each other through our Leonard and Lynette heartaches.

I stayed on the back porch, every night hearing the creaking of the wooden stilts under my bed as delivery trucks drove by the front of the house.

For six months I stayed while I went to machine shop classes at the vocational technical school. At school I learnt the trade of a machinist. Every day I would come home and drink tea with Penny and Lynette full of excitement from my classes. I shared with them the sensuous details of lathe-work, or the fine control of thread cutting: the beauty of a diameter perfectly cut and measured to the exact tolerance required by the blueprint. Penny and Lynette, though accustomed to the softer and warmer world of wood, could perfectly appreciate the satisfaction I felt as a rough chunk of metal spinning in the chuck edged itself up to the cutter and steel chips peeled off with the heat of friction like blue-black butter from the knife.

As my teacher said, I took to machining "like a duck to water." Even on the 1900 vintage lathes and using only a caliper and steel rule, I could bring a diameter to one ten-thousandth of an inch precision. Blueprint reading came naturally to me; it was a language I understood without trying. The blocks of perspective were instantly apparent to me as a three-dimensional shorthand and soon I was tutoring the men and boys in my class in how to see the finished object, how to feel it in their hands, through the thin blue lines of squares and triangles and arcs given to us as maps. The fact of my femaleness presented an obstacle but never an insurmountable one. In the classic manner of women breaking into men's work, I earned respect through the quality of my work, always having to exceed that of the men. In that way, women in the trades become stars; they have to in order to survive.

After dinner, Lynette brought out the marijuana, and we would all smoke, talk and listen to music. I couldn't talk to them about politics, or about my experience in the Midwest with the O., so I drifted with them in a neutral world of a reserved but comfortable friendship. After we smoked they went off to bed leaving me to roll out the futon on the back porch. I was lonely then. I had broken off with Barney, and I still had this mysterious six-week chunk of my life that was unreal, as if I hadn't lived it at all, because there was no reflection in the rest of my life of that having happened. I couldn't mull it over with my friends. So I wrote in my journal and kept it inside.

September 20th, 1980

I have spent so many years trying to build something. And look at it now —it is all gone. The house, the last study group has broken up. All the people I've worked with over the years—they've gone. Have they given up? I think so—they've decided to live their own lives—children, houses, regular jobs— no time anymore for building the community. They have retreated to their own worlds and their own comforts.

I have lost Leonard to his need to provide—I've never wanted anyone to provide for me. I've lost Leah to her babies and suburbs. She said to me, "I've decided to try the life my mother had, perhaps it wasn't so bad, perhaps there is something I can learn from her after all." And all I can see is this large, purple-haired Jewish woman fussing and fretting, and Leah hating her for her meddling. And in our household we were all fighting because, for her mother's visit, Leah said the posters had to come down.

I raged when they took down my Vietnamese poster, the one on the landing, a glorious celebration of war and heroism; a young woman soldier in the foreground hurling out a grenade, her rosy cheeks and her fist in mid-air coming closer and closer to me as I walked down the stairs each morning. Every morning that woman fighter hurled her grenade against the gold and red of a sunrise heralding the new Vietnam. I loved that poster; it expressed what I felt, the terrible anger inside, released in the fury of a thrown grenade, and the love of the beauty that lay on the other side.

Have they all given up that dream? And how have I failed if all of that work has come to nothing? What do I do next?

On my own I am nothing. What is my life worth if I cannot stand up, join hands with my brothers and sisters and change the oppression that I see? I cannot sit and watch the pain pass by.

So what else is there but to fight? That is where I will feel whole and giving of myself and useful. That is when the blackness in me will be covered up, filled in, and turned to the outside in beautiful activity. Otherwise the emptiness will suck me in like quicksand and choke me in its grip.

I will struggle. This is what gives me an existence of which I can be proud.

Nicaragua is liberated. Zimbabwe is free. South Africa will be free. Because people dedicated themselves to freedom. I too, can dedicate myself to something greater than a personal victory.

I felt myself slipping. If I didn't find a way to hold on, I'd fall—and I'd seen the fall already, too many times.

Here are the nervous breakdowns (hospitalization required—this is to distinguish them from simple nervous tiredness, or the "normal" wear and tear of life and its crises) of my immediate family:

1966—Hatty's first breakdown. I am twelve years old; she is fourteen. I am made to put on her socks while my mother forcibly holds her down. I put one sock on and am unable to do the other. I run from our pink floral bedroom crying.

1968—Hatty's second.

1970—Hatty's third. I have run away from home and am living in Paris.

1972—Hatty's fourth. Every time I hear she is breaking down again, I burst into tears, am incredibly sad. I love her very much. Now I am living in the United States.

1978—Hatty's nth—I've lost count. I am still living in San Francisco.

1979—Hatty gives birth to her daughter, Joy. I come to London to be at her bedside, holding her hand, helping her. I see Joy arrive in the world, struggle for life in her first few hours. She is a "blue" baby—the doctors have given Hatty too many drugs too close to the birth, and baby Joy lacks oxygen. She spends her first four days in intensive care. Joy is a survivor, a beautiful, brave baby. After the birth, a nurse brings me a cup of tea, and I cry over it.

Hatty stays "sane" for the next seven years. We all assume that she hangs on for the sake of the baby. Perhaps her "sanity" is at too high a price; she is in a cycle of abusive relationships and has huge black-and-yellow bruises on her face—"Mad Mike," a violent clarinet-player, is obviously capable of murder. Everyone in the family tries to help her escape, but she mostly goes back.

1980—My mother, Jenny, goes mad. My father and she separated the year before, his long-standing affair with a woman my sister's age having been exposed.

1980—Jeremy, my oldest brother, also goes mad this year. I am surprised it has taken him this long. He has been under-functioning for years.

And what does the madness look like? The human thermostat goes haywire. Actually it simply turns off completely. All of a sudden the room gets too hot, but there is no mechanism in place to turn off the heat. The heat keeps cranking out, full speed ahead—hey! I thought someone said it was cold in here? I'm just trying to warm the place up—you can do exercises, too, you know, to warm up—oh, god, it's hot and beautiful. Let me just take off these clothes. God, what beautiful breasts—hey everybody, look, look, I'm running, I'm naked, don't you SEE MY BEAUTIFUL BREASTS. Yes, I know you want to sleep with me, but I really can't. I have a lover, you see. He is beautiful, too. YOU are a tart! You just open your legs for anybody. I haven't slept in three days. No I don't have time to sleep; I keep thinking things about when Ma told me, "Why don't you do something constructive—like slit your wrists." Poor Ma, she would never kill herself, you know, because her mother did—think about what that would be like—coming home from the cinema and finding your mother dead. Ma and I are both like that, we would never do that to our children.

Other times it is quiet, deeply buried, obsessive. She walks around the bedroom, hunched over, hunted; she looks like a sad tiger in a cage at the zoo. She's slowed down by drugs, Largactil, Thorazine, but she paces about in a rhythm, looks up sadly with confused eyes at each end of the room, then turns and paces again. Sometimes looking for things, or touching the wall in a certain pattern. Then she's gone to her cupboard, looking under the underwear for something that she can't find. She's looking up pained and confused again. Into the bathroom to wash her long spidery hands. Weeks later she is still washing her hands, all day long she washes her hands. Then her whole body. Her days are spent in the bath, washing, washing her whole body, her hair. We try to treat it normally, "Oh, Hatty, will you get out of the bath, please. I need to use it." An hour later she is still in. "Hatty, please, I really need to use the bath, what are you doing?"

"I'm rinsing my hair." An hour later, she's still rinsing her hair. She comes out of the bathroom at night to sleep. She doesn't eat, her body is shrinking, becoming long and stick-like. She rarely sleeps. Finally, when she refuses to come out of the bathroom altogether, someone—my father or brother—has to break the door down each time she goes in. The bathroom in our house has no lock. It is like living in a mental institution. I get to share a room with her madness. In the center of the room is a large porcelain bowl sitting on the floor. This was a concession to her when she was ousted from her occupancy of the bathroom. Now she brushes her teeth from morning to night, spitting into the porcelain bowl until the pale, flowered bottom of it is covered in a layer of her sputum, bloody because her gums bleed from hours on hours of brushing. Every few days my mother sneaks in and swaps her toothbrush for a new one, she wears them down to bristleless plastic in days. This is what my mother can do for her—she has called the dentist, and the dentist says that her teeth will be all right if she always has a nice new brush. So, into the jail cell (we are keeping her out of hospital for as long as possible; this seems to be the humane thing to do) of the bedroom that I still share with her, come a stream of nice new toothbrushes and out go the old ones gnashed to pieces by Hatty's emotion.

I have the kind of dream from which science fiction films are made. As I watch, my face begins to crumble and melt; the flesh beneath my eyes falls downwards, drooping like dough into my cheeks, down to my jaw. My forehead falls into my blue eyes, changing the round shape I'm so familiar with and attached to. The crumbling continues . . . a face is reforming. My face has destroyed itself. I am becoming Hatty. Her long, dirty-blond hair and her green eyes emerge from the doughy mess. I wake up screaming.

It's hard to imagine anything more frightening than to dissolve into Hatty's madness, but it is always there like Jiminy Cricket, sitting on my shoulder: my conscience, my limit, my navigator.

I will remain sane. Sanity is reason. Reason exists. Everything is knowable, at some point, at some time, everything can be understood. I will grab onto reason, and I will never let go. Reason will allow us to perform surgery on a world that is very ill. Hatty's madness cannot tolerate wars, the personal injury of war on a child, unerasable image of a single napalmed baby, only one of thousands, each a single child, suffering and mourned for by sister, brother, mother, father and aunt—if they are still alive, and not burnt up, each of them, also. The image of a generation, of my generation, who did not witness the other fires of the Holocaust, but read *The Diary of Anne Frank* and as teenagers bonded with her and could not believe her desperate courage and the unbelievable evil of the sick, sick world.

"No!" says Hatty and runs to the airport. She runs onto the tarmac, waving her arms. Her young American friend is on the plane, going home because he's been drafted. Hatty is desperate to save him. She is picked up by police, at the airport, and taken back to the psychiatric ward of the hospital because she is mad, because she is protesting the war in her own way, because one person she knows might die in Vietnam, might have to kill in Vietnam, and the only way she knows to protest is to keep him in England, safe from the draft. She mustn't let the plane take off. But it does, and she is hauled back to hospital, Hatty, the Mad Hatter.

Meanwhile, I study Marx and read about the Theory and Practice of Revolutions in progressive courses taught by Leftist academics. Hunger and napalm move me, too, but I have joined the camp that says it can all be thought out, and with the correct analysis a plan can be conceived to right things. Mao's theories are particularly beautiful and enlightening to me. They allow for mistakes—in fact insist on them. Mistakes are the raw material of "practice," and practice the raw material of theory. From practice arises theory, the mistakes and the successes are analyzed and produce a new plan, or theory. This new plan is then put into practice, from which further successes and failures arise as more matter for analysis. Without practice, theory is dross. Practice is the fabled pear, which must be eaten in order to be understood. Mao is such a poet, I can feel the texture of the pear and taste the sweet and grainy juice, sucked up before it reaches the chin; the morsel of pear is chewed, enters the digestive tract and is transformed (not only into muscle and blood, but the leavings are shit—even that honored as fertilizing nightsoil in the post-feudal Chinese culture that became our own during the China worship of the 1970s).

This science, this rational approach to life was succor to me. It was a personal salvation that involved no leap of blind faith, simply the application of scientific laws and the testing of the results in practice. It was absolute and self-correcting. It was simple and perfectly elegant. I found a deep satisfaction in grasping the cycles of knowledge and the dialectical patterns that made up the theory of dialectical historical materialism. It allowed me to feel control and to feel that I could contribute to truly changing the external world without lapsing into the internal state of chaos of my family.

As I went to bed, stoned, on my unrolled futon, the night terrors took hold of me again. In my panicked state, the creaking of the wooden stilts became alternately the imagined foreshocks of an earthquake or the spooky weakening of wood after the secret unleashing of a neutron bomb that would kill living things but leave buildings standing. The neutron bomb was in the news daily in those days and had entered into my imagination as a new phobia that only awakened itself in those long nights I spent on the porch. It was 1980 and Reagan had stirred up the Cold War again with his nomination of the Soviet Union as the Evil Empire.

That night I lay rigid in my bed, certain that the neutron bomb had been dropped on San Francisco. I could feel my limbs become poisoned and paralyzed. Waves of radiation crept through the house, seeping into me, and around the city into the blood cells of all the sleeping people. I heard a whimpering noise rising up and did not know it was from me. I curled into a ball, the defense position taught to children in the fifties, curl up under your desk, hands clasped over the head. I curled up like that knowing that against the neutron bomb, any physical barrier was useless, you would never know it had exploded, there would be no crash, no breaking down of walls or ceilings, no dust, no timbers crashing down, no use hiding under a desk or in a basement or, as for an earthquake, beneath the door frame to keep the strength of the building's structure around me for protection. No, with the neutron bomb came no warning, noise, or vibration, but just a silent, tasteless, invisible poison to burn and paralyze.

I was sweating again, my heart thrown about by fear. Finally I dragged myself out of bed and, unable to stand myself up straight—the back porch was so small it created in me a feeling, a need to be constantly curled up, so even in leaving the room I didn't feel I could stretch myself to my full height—holding on to the fridge, and then the stove and table, I made my way through the kitchen. Then leaning against the hallway wall, I got to Penny's room where she and Lynette were sleeping.

"Penny, Penny . . ."

"Hmmm. Alex, are you okay?"

"No, Penny. Can I come in. I'm scared. Can I sleep with you?"

I didn't usually cry easily in front of other people, but my chest hurt so badly, the tears just squeezed out of my eyes until my breath caught and I sat on the side of the bed sobbing and sobbing.

Penny sat up and held me. Lynette went off to get me a drink of water, and, after my crying subsided, they made room for me in the bed, and I slept close to Penny that night, not understanding the terror inside, but feeling safer and glad I'd been able to come to them.

During the day, I excelled at my classes, slicing up metal into cold and measured forms. But at night, I crumbled into loss, chased into panic by one nightmare after another.

CHAPTER 8

September 18th

It has felt like madness. I have been sinking into a world where I do not want to go. I know too well what lies there.

Yesterday I met Julie, a friend of Andy's. She left the O. because things were getting too heavy there—she talked about some kind of boxing matches being set up between people . . . It was supposed to "heighten struggle" but she couldn't take it anymore. It sounds strange. She moved here with Beth, her five-year old. Julie is forthright and warm, unlike the guys in Minneapolis; I like her. And she's someone I can talk to about the O.

September 28th

Julie invited me to the Women's Music Festival. So, here I am, with her and Beth up in the gray-green hills near the Russian River, camping among the sweet-smelling eucalyptus trees and eating desiccated three-bean meals served up to hundreds of us by loose-breasted, tank-topped dykes.

Leah and I broke, finally. She has gone, she said, to live an ordinary life. I feel she blames me for something, and I don't know what. I want to blame her right back. Julie, meanwhile, is ready to try again with the O. after her hiatus, and so she will join Andy and me in the unit.

I'm still having nightmares—since I got back from Minneapolis, night after night of this. In sleep, someone is trying to kill me, my friends are dying. I wake up with a dead emptiness inside as if I've lost everything, even my ability to know. My family feels so far, my friends too . . .

October 7th
    I must take myself in hand. I must struggle and face my fears. This chaos in my head has got to stop, or I'll drown. The noise is unbearable.
    Commitment and discipline will hold me up. This I can control: I will work harder for the struggle. It's the one thing I know I can do.

October 21st
    No more nightmares. I am moving on. I feel as if I've found solid ground. Although I still have my issues with the O., I've decided to join. I have to work in a group or go crazy, and I might as well struggle with them as anyone. And in joining, I'll have more credibility; they will have to listen to my criticisms and take them more seriously.
    I sent my formal request for membership to the center, via Andy. It's a big decision. But things are going well with Julie and Andy. I'm scared, but I feel relieved, positive and stronger, perhaps.

Soon after I formally joined the O., Julie and I got permission to move in together. Permission came in the form of a memo from P.S. (Program Secretary) agreeing to our proposal that we should live together in an organizational household. The memo came typed on a small beige piece of paper. This was mailed to Andy's post office box in an outer envelope addressed to him, the memo itself being enclosed in its own envelope addressed to Jo and Claire, (Julie and my respective code names), and then sealed and stapled for extra security.
    This formed part of the internal mail system, and reflected the cell structure of the O. An O. member always had a "contact," who sent and received internal mail to their contact at a higher level. Once it reached the "center," mail was then routed to the addressee. Most memos were to and from P.S., but there was other communication that flowed across the ranks. Apart from the work done in a specific program, or the communication between members of a household, nearly all communication within the O. took the form of these memos.
    So, in January 1981, with P.S.'s permission, Julie, Beth, and I moved into a little house in a mixed neighborhood of Oakland. I'd been wanting to get out of the rarified Leftist and gay and lesbian atmosphere of San Francisco for a couple of years, and I had still been sleeping in Penny's rickety back porch, so I was elated when we finally moved into the house on Penniman

Avenue. I had a real bedroom, where the sun shone in to wake me in the morning. I had a proper place in this house and I had Julie with whom I shared a political life and a developing friendship.

I was working at my first machining job, and Julie was commuting to San Francisco to work as a computer programmer for Bank of America. We soon established a routine. Julie woke early to get to her job, and then little Beth and I got up around eight. I'd feed her breakfast and get her ready for school. Beth was five, very friendly and self-confident, close to her mom, but glad to have another adult around to share her care and dilute the intensity of that single-mother/daughter bond. She worked herself into my heart with her natural affection; she didn't notice I was shy and climbed onto my lap for a hug the first day we met.

After breakfast in our little green cottage, I would try to fix her hair. She had a big brown afro that circled her small face. Julie and I knew we needed to tame that hair so that she could look neat at school like her classmates, but while Julie gained a semblance of finesse, studying African-American haircare from friends and magazines, I never managed more than a wobbly part down the center and two uneven top knots held by inelegant rubber bands.

Beth's father, Jefferson, was a black musician from Mississippi who Julie had met in Chicago where she'd been sent in the early days of the O. Her relationship with Jefferson came to an end soon after she got pregnant; Jefferson was strictly a biological father, he didn't participate in Beth's life in any other way. But before Julie lost contact with him, he gave her the name of his home town in Mississippi and told her to get in touch with his kinfolk there if she ever needed anything.

After the hair-fixing was done for the day, I'd drop Beth off at the Oakland Community School. This was the school run by the Black Panthers since the early 1970s, founded during the heyday of their community programs. Now Elaine Brown had left the party, Huey had returned from Cuba and was already isolated by rumors of his drug involvement and tyrannical rule. But the school was still solid, run by Ericka Huggins, continuing to win education awards and a symbol of black pride in Oakland. Julie and I ignored the rumors about Huey, both of us having a nostalgic attachment for him and the party.

Julie was a white woman from Minnesota of religious, though liberal parents. She had always been a rebel, had identified from a young age with the small black community in Minneapolis and now traveled to her straight-arrow job sporting a spiky punk haircut, a pin-striped jacket and skirt and bobby socks worn over her hose. She had inculcated in Beth a great sense of pride and identification with Beth's black American heritage. The South African Steven Biko became one of Beth's heroes, and at five years old she would cry at night over his picture—she understood he was dead, had died for freedom but only knew that death was sad, not final.

Julie, Beth, and I became very close in that little green house with the lemon trees in the backyard. I became Beth's second mother and learned to deal with the looks that a white woman and a brown child receive when they are together.

After dropping Beth at school, I'd go back home and spend the morning doing political work. I was still involved with the Rank and File Coalition; I helped to edit their newsletter, organized meetings and gathered support for the current hotel worker's strike going on in San Francisco. Or I would engage myself in our unit's work. Following another memo, on beige paper, from P.S., we were researching the various women's organizations in the Bay Area. We assumed this was as a preliminary step to organizing around women's issues—which was still, in my heart, what I wanted to be doing.

At this time I was "leadership" of our three-person unit, and it fell on me to organize our weekly meetings, to drag work and summaries out of Andy and Julie (they were both reluctant unit members—whereas I was full of energy and ideas about our strategic goals). On a weekly basis, I looked at the contradictions in my own practice, and at the unit's: Had we achieved our objectives? Where were our personal problems getting in the way of productivity? And how could we best offer leadership to each of the various Left and mass groups we were in?

Julie had been active for several months in the Organizing Committee for an Ideological Center (OCIC), a "pre-cadre formation." This was the type of group I'd learned to stay away from in my previous years of political work. I knew exactly how these things operated. They were part of an epidemic of party-building groups that the independent Left threw up in the 1970s. Even the groups that opposed party-building were the same. Overweighted with Jewish intellectuals (male) they theorized and polemicized on the nature of the Primary Contradiction at this point in history and the resulting strategy.

There were four positions activists in the Left could choose from: building a new communist party by arguing about Principles of Unity; building a Mass Socialist movement by arguing about who were the "leading workers" (we called this faction the Mealy-Mouthed Mass Socialists); organizing anti-imperialist support groups for third world liberation struggles or, last but not

least, organizing in the United States against the "internal colonization" of people of color and the racism of white people.

OCIC was in the last category—it was a multi-racial organization (in
itself a tricky formation to uphold this ideology) whose members were
involved largely in white-collar union organizing. The logical conclusion of
their line was to focus on the white members' "white-skin privilege" and to
demand they give this up, although how they were to do this was never made
clear.

I appreciated that Julie had had little of this type of political experience,
and we agreed that it would be educational for her to "struggle through the
process" with OCIC, but I wanted none of it and looked on with a told-you-
so attitude. I had already developed a firmly held set of beliefs that rested on
a rejection of guilt as the basis for organizing anyone. I believed that the way
to resolve the intense racial conflicts that divided the working class in the
United States was to organize people of all colors around issues central to
their own interests. I believed in *self-interest* as the only way to mobilize people, and I also believed that, if the Marxist class analysis was correct, then the
self-interests of these groups would overlap. There were global issues that
would unite people out of necessity. For instance, environmental issues, as
they related to working people; the neighborhood effects of pollution; the on-
the-job issues of occupational safety and health; even the lack of women's
rights—maternity leave, childcare provisions and so on. It seemed to me that
these issues crossed racial lines and, if properly addressed, were the basis to
organize people within their communities, and then to cross over to support
other communities with the same interests.

This was the goal for which I'd worked the last five years, and I hoped
that, by joining the O., I'd found a disciplined structure of dedicated cadre
who had a similar, non-polemical, non-guilt-ridden and community-based
vision of organizing.

To this end, I spent my mornings in an energetic flurry of paperwork and
phone calls. After a late lunch, I changed into my work clothes: jeans, baggy
gray or blue-cotton shirt with breast pockets (this served to protect my bra-less
state from the eyes of my fellow machinists) and Redwing work boots. I headed across town in my beat-up old Datsun to the industrial section of Oakland,
down by the docks.

CHAPTER 9

"Hey Alex! What's happenin', beautiful lady?" Ron greeted me as I entered the cavernous factory. I thought *he* was beautiful—a tall, lanky black man with a well-trimmed beard and a warm, polite manner. He was a jazz musician, but, with a wife and two young kids to support, he spent his evenings, along with the rest of us on second shift, churning out greasy truck axle parts at FABCO, a manufacturer in Oakland. I smiled at him and walked through to the women's washroom to put away my coat and lunch bucket.

Back by the old picnic table that served as our break area, two wide metal doors reached to the high ceiling. On this warm evening they were pushed open to let fresh air dilute the acrid smells of the shop. The sunset poured in over the flat black roofs of the adjacent warehouses, and bands of coral-pink and turquoise filtered through, making the grimy windows that skirted the top of the factory's concrete walls shine with color.

I brought back my thermos of tea to the production floor and waited for Steve, the young Chicano foreman, to give me my job sheet for the night.

"Hi, Alex, you're on machine 22. Just run off as many as you can. You've got them parts you were drilling yesterday, only turn 'em down to the outside diameter tonight. Say, Sam, you motherfucker! Where you been?"

Steve turned to Sam while I walked off to my toolbox to get ready for number 22. Steve and Sam joked in the background as I unfolded my blue machinist's apron, put on my safety glasses and selected my tools: the silver dial calipers I'd need to measure the diameter, a rough file to deburr the parts as they came off the machine, and a handful of small allen wrenches for adjusting the setup.

Sam was the most skilled of the swing-shift crew. He had been at FABCO at least five years and was sharp. He also had an "attitude" which meant he never got promoted. Steve, at twenty-three, was a good ten years younger, but he worked like a dog and, as Sam put it, "would eat shit no matter where it came from." And so Steve was foreman and supposed to tell Sam what to do, but in actual fact, Sam ran the shift, always in a good-natured way, running his own quota of parts on the hardest machines while helping anyone who needed it. He and Steve had an understanding: Steve wouldn't bug him, would let the shift proceed in a relaxed way (an advantage to swing shift was that none of the factory's white collar management were around), and Sam would ensure that production goals were met. They also had a personal understanding, of sorts. A mutual respect despite the difference in attitudes. Besides, they did drugs together, which gave them a common interest.

Sam had been a Black Panther back in the days when hundreds of young black men in Oakland were Panthers. But now he was a machinist, also our shop steward for the machinists' union. He had a "lady" at home, whom none of us had ever met, and was what he considered to be a "sensible" user of cocaine. He never did it on the job, unlike Tracy and Gary, two white urban cowboys from Oklahoma who had found themselves stuck in the FABCO factory while searching for the green pastures and golden hills of California. Tracy was also an alcoholic and had abandoned his wife and kids back in Tulsa. We feared for Tracy's life. He would duck behind the lid of his toolbox, thinking no-one would notice, and snort lines of coke, or tipple a bottle of Jack Daniels. While the majority of machinists with whom I'd worked were alcoholics of one sort or another, few were foolish enough to be less than totally sober running those machines.

Number 22 had been set up already by the day shift. Now I had to run the first couple of parts and take them in to quality control to get inspected. But first I needed to move a palletful of parts from the big drill at the back of the shop to the numerical control lathe that was number 22. I climbed up on the forklift, kicking off the sharp steel chips that had already collected on the bottom of my boots. This had been a major fight with Steve a few months earlier. He had refused to let me drive the forklift, and, whenever I needed parts, I'd have to call him to bring them over to my machine. I had fought and fought over this and finally, with Sam's support, had just started getting on the forklift whenever I needed it. Sam helped me learn how to drive it while Steve tried in vain to get me off.

I could see why it had been protected as I climbed up onto it. I sat up there, high up, a good view of the shop and felt like a cowboy. Straddling the black seat, high up and zooming in through the tight corners between machines, aiming for pallets and, with a pull on the black-knobbed levers, lifting hundreds of pounds of steel around easy as anything. It was powerful and macho, and I enjoyed it as much as any of them. Plus, it was a break from running the machines—always something to be nurtured in a machine shop.

Having delivered the parts to number 22, I organized my tools on the workbench and studied the blueprint, already black and fingerprinted from doing duty at previous operations. I found the outside diameter: three and five-eights of an inch, plus or minus five ten-thousandths. I slid open the metal and plastic door to the lathe and stepped on the foot pedal to release the three jaws of the chuck— opened up like that, I could see the smooth receptacle at the back end that held the machined end of the part, and the tooth-like serrations of each jaw. I grabbed the air hose and blew chips out of the chuck with a sharp hiss of compressed air.

. . . Then, pick up a part, one end smooth and machined already by day shift, the rest of it black and rough from the foundry cast. A short blast of air round the smooth end, and then lean into number 22 and seat the part in the jaws. If any steel chips find their way in there, you've lost the part for sure. The cutter will cut crooked, and then it's scrap. We're supposed to write down how many we scrap on the job sheet—it's part of the quality and cost-control program—but of course, no one does. We don't want to look bad, or even, in what passes for unionism, make anyone else look bad.

So turn that part in there, twisting it into the chuck, feeling for the scrape that means you've got to blow it out again. If it's good and clean, there's a satisfying smooth feel to it as you turn it back and forth. Push the foot pedal, watch your hands—always watch your hands—those jaws don't understand the language of pain, and flesh and bone isn't steel; the jaws will crush a hand or a finger that gets between them and that cold steel. Still, if you blew it out right, seated that part well, then the jaws will come together in a slow hydraulic motion and tie that part down solid.

You have to concentrate—that first part of the night is always the worst—is the setup right, will it hold? A machinist has to have a brain and hands that do what it tells them. You've got to be able to concentrate, to block out the noises: other air hoses blasting; drills cracking their way through steel or zipping through aluminum; men swearing in the background, constantly swearing; and country music or heavy metal from competing radios floating in between the industrial noises.

Turn on the spray of coolant, a dribble of milky fluid whose smell sticks to your clothes, hair, and the inside of your nostrils; let coolant run over the cutter and then push the green button. The servo motor wakes up, computer-controlled; it's been set up to run the cutter rapidly up to the part, which has been set off spinning now in the chuck. Then, right as it approaches the part, the motor slows, allows the cutter to edge on up, and then you hear the sound change: a grinding buzz as cutter meets metal, then a satisfactory whine while the coolant sprays out against the plastic of the door, and a long blackened thread of steel peels off like solid smoke, dropping into the lathe bin at the end of the run in a sharp, twisted heap. . . .

It was a short run. Just about thirty seconds or so for the whole cut. That meant I wouldn't be talking much with whoever was on 21. That was okay. I'd settle in, churn out some parts, let the evening ride by. I felt pretty happy that night, and my first part was beautiful—I'd blown off the spray and chips with the air hose, nestled the skinny stainless steel jaws of my calipers up on that diameter, and it was perfect. The needle on the dial swung to zero—spot on. Congratulations to day shift. Someone did a good job.

I kicked back, got my rhythm and started feeding those parts. One by one the black castings came out of my lathe cleaned up and shiny bright and started to fill up the empty wooden pallet on the other side of the machine.

Sam came by, "Baby! You're *cooking* tonight! I've never seen anyone get through those parts so quick. You better hold up sweetheart, you're gonna put these boys to shame."

He touched me on the shoulder, friendly, and said, "You coming by the Tip Top tonight? Some of the boys are going over. We'll see you there?"

It was one o'clock in the morning when I pulled my little red Datsun up behind Tracy's pick-up, which in turn was parked behind Sam's old Chevrolet sedan. They were both sitting in the Tip Top already drinking beer and whiskey. I ordered a margarita which came in a shallow, slender-stemmed glass, complete with plastic sword and a floating hazelnut. It looked like the shining neon sign outside that flashed TIP TOP, TIP TOP into the Oakland night while the neon cocktail glass poured endlessly pink toward the open bar door.

Drinking was a necessary release after a shift of dirt and noise and danger. A celebration that no cutters had flown out from drill or mill heads, no grinding wheels had exploded. No one had slipped on an oil patch or dropped a fifty-pound part on a steel-toed boot. Less attention was paid to the invisible dangers: toxic benzene used to degrease parts—workers using their bare hands to dip the parts in; or the acrid coolant, smelling of burnt hair; or the tiny particles that rushed from the grinder, glass-like, seeping into lungs for a shortened lifetime's residency. But I thought about these things, and so did Sam. We were the only ones to wear the rubber face mask at the grinder, or to complain about the open bucket of benzene.

But at the Tip Top, alcohol loosened the night's nerves, and we could sit back and breathe in our own uninterrupted time, only having to listen for a joke, or a gripe to add to, but not alert with all senses waiting for the machine's rhythm to unfold. Often we talked about the work: Sam would lecture whoever was around on how "they" were making money off leaving that benzene in a bucket on the floor. And I would chime in, supporting him, "Yeah, it's been banned in Europe, you know. So how come they still make us use it here?"

Sam knew his labor history and would talk about forced overtime, too. "You know," he would say, looking close up into whoever's face was nearby at the time, "You know, people *died* for the eight-hour day. Motherfuckers!"

He would open his eyes wide, enjoying his theatrical effect on his audience: "They blew people away fighting for that eight hours. And now you poor suckers think, 'Oh man, more money for my cocaine, or my truck,' or, goddamn it, pay your motherfucking mortgage with it. But the thing you got to remember is, some poor son of a bitch died so that you didn't have to work twelve hours every day and Saturday too. And now this goddamned union is giving it up to them. What about the guys who need the work? You've got to look at benefits, training, man! The company don't want to do all of that! No way!

"Pretty soon won't be any time for you to drive that brand-new pickup. You just be working your poor ass to death. Sitting in that place breathing up chemicals all night. 'Course they try to set up white on black, but Tracy, my man, you ain't the one doin' it to me. I'm no fool. I can see where my work is going, and the union? Just gives it up. Damn!"

Sam took a drink, scratched at his black afro and gave us a wide smile. He didn't take it all too seriously, but he liked to tell it like it was.

Sometimes Tracy would get homesick over his beer and whiskey at the Tip Top, and he would tell us about his kids and wife back in Tulsa. If he got really drunk then the guilt about leaving them would take over, and he would swear that, come the next paycheck, he'd be sure to send his child support. Sam seemed to have some feeling for him and would tell him how he didn't even know how many kids he'd left in his wake.

"I play it a little more careful now," he said. "I reckon that those poor motherfuckers are one day gonna wake up and wonder where the hell they daddy bin' all their life. It's too late now, but at least I don't have to do it no more. I got started young—before I knew that you can't just leave a trail of babies behind you."

Tracy nodded morosely. We ordered another round of drinks. One night, after we'd been going out together for several months, Tracy, oiled up on alcohol, looked up at Sam.

"Sam," he said, his blue eyes handsome, but watering a little from the drink, "Sam, my man, back in Tulsa I never knew any black people. I thought y'all were just some lower kind of life. But Sam, you have taught me this— you are one decent motherfucker. I am proud to know you Sam. You are black and beautiful!"

Sam burst into laughter, gave Tracy a bear hug and ruffled his hair.

"Hey baby, I love you too, brother. Oooh, man."

He was still laughing, wiping his eyes. I sat by in a warm and class-conscious glow fueled by my evening's two margaritas. I loved them both.

Some nights I would bring Sam and Tracy, or Sam and Steve, back home with me, and Julie would wake up and make us tea while I rolled a joint. We would stay up late listening to Peter Gabriel on the stereo, talking over life in Oakland and become blurry and comfortable and relaxed. Sam stayed several times with Julie. Steve and I had an odd attraction going on between us, totally unsuitable—he was quite a bit younger than me, and much more naive. But I was taken with his dark good looks, his rather gentle manner with me and a romantic image of his working-class background. While I knew that it could not possibly work between us, I was in the grip of one of my hopeless crushes. In our long discussions, when he would come up to my machine during the shift, and lean on the workbench, helping me to deburr my parts or pretending to be checking my work, we would talk about his family, or mine, about unionism and women's rights, or about his being Mexican-American and what that meant to him.

He boasted of having never read a book, but he had thought about things, and was sensitive to the suffering he had witnessed in his mother's life, as well as his own. I truly thought that there would be a way we could be lovers. One of those nights back at the house, after a stop at the Tip Top, we did finally make it into bed together. For the first time I saw Steve without his blue baseball hat. His straight black hair made him look very young, and his brown eyes were shy and scared. His chest was light brown and smooth, almost hairless. After we made love, he got up and put his clothes back on. He settled his baseball hat back on his head.

"Why are you going already?" I asked. I knew Sam was still there, with Julie.

"I never stay the night. It stops things getting complicated. I'll only stay the night with the girl I'll marry."

He backed out of the door, tugging on his cap. Before he left he turned to me again.

"Thanks," he said, embarrassed, and closed the door behind him.

I realized then that the cultural divide was vast, and I was finally able to give up my obsession with him.

The next morning, Julie and Sam and I woke up and had toast and coffee on the grass in our backyard, under the lemon trees. I was happy to relax there laying in the California sun, listening to Sam's low, barrel-chested laugh and watching Julie flirt so casually with him. Where I had intense, unbearable crushes that I had to work out to the end, Julie treated sex like a date at the movies: something to enjoy, and maybe repeat, but she never fell in love or allowed sex to interfere with a good friendship. Likewise, a good friendship always invited the possibility of sex, in her mind, as simply another activity to enjoy together.

After Sam left, I asked Julie how it had been with him.

"Oh, perfectly lovely," she said, "But I must tell you something—he's got a curly dick. I've never seen one before. It is Sam's secret. It must be why he's so nice."

I laughed, "Yeah, that must be what stops him from being macho. I mean, he's handsome, and strong and smart and all, but I suppose a curly dick must have made him suffer—that must be his internal contradiction! Oh, dear curly Sam!"

We lay together in the sunshine—Beth was off in San Francisco spending the night at Andy's, something she did every couple of weeks—and we drank tea and talked, and drank tea and cleaned house, and drank tea again. We were like sisters, comfortable together somewhere inside ourselves.

CHAPTER 10

Television

1981. The television broadcasts a photograph of Bobby Sands, a long-haired Irish youth who is an imprisoned member of the IRA. The television does not show his emaciated body or those of the other H-block men—the men "on the blanket." They are fighting for political status, and, in their refusal to follow the rules for criminal prisoners, they defecate in their cells, wrap their naked bodies in blankets, and now, as their final protest, they have ceased to eat. The British government does not yield.

One by one, like nine-pins, they fall into death, following the course of old-age with an unnatural rapidity: they lose their hair, then sight and hearing to finally drop into an endless coma. Bobby Sands is the first to die.

Every night we turn the television on and watch the self-willed death of young Irish men.

In London my sister Lyndall lives in the top floor apartment of my mother, Jenny's, house. Jenny lies on her bed. She is dressed in white and holds a bunch of Calla lilies in her hands. She looks like an angel, or the bride of Christ, or a corpse.

"I'm waiting to marry Peter," she announces to the empty room, or to the visitors who come by once in a while to check on her. Peter is a gay friend of hers who she can be sure will never marry her.

While she lies there, my sister is upstairs with her friends. Her living-room floor is covered with black cloth and wooden sticks. My sister and her friends are cutting and gluing and sewing. They are making black flags to take to a shopping center in Kilburn for a vigil commemorating the death of Bobby Sands.

In San Francisco, meanwhile, Julie gets dressed for work: pin-striped jacket and skirt, black pumps, a white shirt with a silk bow at her neck. Lastly she fashions a black armband from fabric in her sewing box. She pins the armband over her jacket sleeve. She wears the armband to her job at Bank of America, and after work she stops at the British Embassy and takes a post there at the vigil held for Bobby Sands' death.

Sometime later, mail came from P.S. Julie gave me the stapled envelope, with my code name, Claire, typed on it. I took it into my room and read it immediately, before changing my work clothes.

To: Claire
From: P.S.
Date: 12/01/81

You should look into taking classes in computer programming with the aim of becoming a programmer. This is an organizational step. Becoming a machinist indicated your commitment and willingness to struggle to transform your Bourgeois World Outlook and your PIC. It has also taught you the value of a production skill. This can never be underestimated as a stage in development.

Outside of a Marxist-Leninist Organization you were unable to reach this stage. However, now you have developed to the stage of organizational practice. Becoming a computer programmer will bring you in line with other organizational practice that is taking place.

I reread the memo. I had just finished a year's schooling in machine tool technology and had only been a machinist for a few months. Now this sudden change—Why? I felt knocked off center. I had assumed that I would be a machinist for some extended period of time. Now the meaning seemed to drop out of it—the relationships I'd been developing, the work I was doing in the Rank and File Coalition, the skill I'd been developing through my apprenticeship. Yet change was something I took on easily. I knew that soon I would be bored of machining, tired of the dirt and chemicals and the monotony of running jobs. I loved the setup work—this was where the skill came in—and I also liked working with the computer-controlled machines, figuring out how to adjust the programs, how to make them most efficient. But to go back to school *again*, while I was working and to immediately start a new career right on the heels of this one; this was change at a faster pace than even I was used to.

It appeared that, indeed, being a machinist had been a test; as P.S. said, a test of my commitment and willingness to struggle. Well, a year of my life devoted to it—I imagined that I had passed the test with flying colors. Inside, I felt confused still, cheated a little. For me being a machinist had been a real thing, I had taken it seriously, taken my co-workers seriously, and now, to learn it was just a test. . . . But, it was also to develop a production skill. I could understand this; I had certainly learned how to work, and I could see that this could transfer to other areas.

I could not grasp how computer programming fit into organizational plans for revolutionary struggle, but I was beginning to get used to the O.'s way of doing things. I was always given directions first, and then, in the process of struggling to implement the directions, I would either think it through on my own and come up with the political connections or discuss it with other unit members (where security allowed) or P.S. would occasionally clarify things in a memo. I was also concerned that I would not have time to continue much of the organizing work in which I was involved. I knew that working full-time, taking classes, helping to care for Beth and continuing with our unit meetings and summaries were going to take up all my time.

But by the end of the week, I was convinced this was a good move and sent off for brochures in computer training from the Oakland Community College and Golden Gate University. As with my machinist training, I put everything I had into the task at hand.

The new direction created a subtle shift in my identity and in my relationships. Now I was no longer a machinist, learning to be part of the Bay Area working class; no longer a woman who had fought her way into a male trade with persistence and determination. No, now I was a machinist who was to become a computer programmer: a skilled, white-collar job, well-paid, clean, well-dressed. Like Julie, my future now held a suit, blouse, and pumps, and commuting to work with lunch in a briefcase instead of a metal lunch bucket. I wasn't really a machinist anymore; I was a machinist waiting to become something else, something "better," something privileged.

At work, and in my other friendships, I began to drop hints. I showed a great interest in the computer-controlled equipment and acted as if computers had always fascinated me. It was important to make this sudden move into a new career seem natural, an obvious choice to make after all my work to become a machinist. I couldn't tell anyone, other than Julie and Andy, that I was following the direction of a revolutionary organization.

Before I finally left the Rank and File Coalition due to my new time constraints, I met Hector Morales, an Argentinean political refugee, at a Coalition meeting. He sat opposite me in the meeting, and I was immediately attracted to him. He was a small man with an intense, serious face. Wispy brown hair fell untidily around his sharp cheekbones which stood out thinly from his Indian features.

A mutual friend introduced us, and the following week Hector called to invite me out for a walk in the Oakland hills. He was even tinier when I stood next to him—smaller than me, and I am only five foot five. I was not sure how to behave; the first and last date I had been on was when I was fourteen, oddly enough with a fifteen-year-old Venezuelan. It had not been a success: Emilio had tried to kiss me wetly all the way through *Guess Who's Coming to Dinner* while I craned my neck around him to see Sidney Poitier on the big screen. Dating had not been a part of my social or sexual life since then.

But Hector had a polite and easy charm that I fell into. It was like being led in a dance. Letting the man take the lead in the courting ritual was something I hadn't often done, but Hector seemed sure of his role. It was a beautiful day in the hills, dry and scorched and kicking up the smell of burnt dirt and grass that I loved. We hiked for a little while until we came to a steep climb. Very casually, Hector reached back for my hand. I took it, and he held it firmly and didn't let go after he'd helped me up the rocks. I smiled when we reached a place to sit, and he pulled off his summer jacket for us to sit on. This was not how I was used to being treated, and it pleased me, not as a sign of respect, but because it was Hector and what he brought from his country and his upbringing. We sat and embraced and I felt his warm hand in mine.

I learned that Hector had been in jail for five years and had been tortured by the Argentinean Junta. The Trotskyist group to which he belonged had finally gotten him out of jail, and he had fled to the United States. Now he was working as a sewing machine repairman. Once he took me to the shop where he worked. In a small room was an entire machine shop in miniature—a doll-sized lathe, a mill that was less than a foot high, a drill with the tiniest drill bits I'd ever seen, and an assortment of diminutive machine shop accessories: files, clamps, vices, and other small and delicate hand-tools. It seemed to suit him so well, to fit his own thin delicacy. He traveled the textile factories on Market Street, fixing industrial sewing machines while the seamstresses gossiped with him about home and children, work and unions. This was how he had landed in jail in Argentina: organizing in textile shops, the mobility of his job being ideal for organizing.

When we slept together, I would feel his scars with my fingers, small ones on his stomach and gashes on his back, and wonder, "Is this a scar from his torture?" I didn't ask him much about it but listened hard the few times he talked of those years.

After a shift at the FABCO machine shop, I'd drive across the Bay Bridge at midnight and take a shower at his house, thinking of how Hector showered and how he would always brush the water off his body with his hands, force of habit from five years in jail with no towel. Then I'd come into bed with him. He was different from other men I'd been with, so small and thin to hold. I could wrap myself around him instead of being wrapped around.

Hector told me stories of his life in Tucuman in the mountains of Argentina. He was one of the few Argentineans left who had Indian blood— so many had been exterminated by European genocide. He lived in a mountainside barrio and when he was five went to work selling newspapers and shining shoes to earn money for his mother. At ten he'd been sent to live with his blind uncle. Hector cooked and cleaned for him—this he told me as he cooked me eggs fried with chopped onions. His uncle had taught him to cook, and he was glad of this—it wasn't normal for an Argentinean man to be proficient in the house. His uncle talked to him as an equal, about grown-up things, and spoke of history and class consciousness.

Hector never went to school, but in jail the political prisoners organized classes, and he learned to read and write there. He still wrote slowly when I met him, but he thought fast and wanted to study and write his "theories" until things changed so he could return home to Argentina, which he loved, and to his mother and family, and to the struggle there. Argentina was his home, and he was sick for the loss of it.

We were very kind with each other. He was quaint in ways, with a Victorian morality he consciously struggled with based on a somewhat abstract support for women's equality. Indeed, in jail he had learned great respect for the women prisoners, who, along with the men, suffered and sometimes survived the torture and the imminent disappearances of themselves or their loved ones. But he retained a patriarchal view and thought it strange that I would work in a man's job, dress like a man (I never wore dresses or makeup) and so often act like a man in my theoretical thinking and practical confidence.

We only fought once, yet this conflict led, eventually, to the end of our relationship. I refused to tell him about the O. He knew that I was dedicated to the struggle and that often I would not see him because I was busy. When it was with Rank and File work I could tell him this, but if it was a unit meeting, then I could not. He was trying to recruit me into his political group at the time and when he kept asking why I was not in a party, why I would not join his, or why I would not see him on such and such a day, I finally told him that I was already part of an organization but, beyond that, I couldn't tell him more.

He was infuriated: "Is it not enough that I spent five years in jail? Do you think I haven't proved myself an honest revolutionary? Five years of torture! A life like that!" He brought his hands up to his ears as if to block off the sounds he heard there.

"I'm sorry," I mumbled, hurting in my chest for him. "I'm sorry. But I can't talk about it. There is no reason for you to know. It's not that I don't trust you. Please believe that."

It was a deep rejection of him, at a time when he already felt politically isolated and helpless. The pain I caused him was a lesson to me never to tell anyone again the partial truth. This part of my life had to remain secret, people simply couldn't understand the need for the level of security required to build a serious organization that could withstand the violence of the FBI and other state forces. Even Hector, with his terrible experience, took the need for security as a personal affront. In the future, I would keep it to myself.

Perhaps if I had talked to him then the ending would have been different.

A little while later I let slip in my regular monthly summary to my O. contact that I was seeing Hector. P.S. sent back an angry criticism. I was accused of anti-organizational practice in entering into a relationship on my own initiative and without clearing it with the "center." I wrote back listing the good qualities that I thought Hector, and the relationship, had: his revolutionary background and experience, his respect for me, that I could learn about another struggle from him, that I was learning Spanish and so on. This justification was not accepted.

To: Claire
From: P.S.

Your relationship with H. is not developmental. It is opportunism to think that learning Spanish at this time is a relevant task. On the contrary, cadre will learn skills such as Spanish when organizational needs determine them to be a priority. Right now the priority is internal ideological development. Please forward a summary of steps you are taking for your ideological development.

There was no ultimatum in that memo, or absolute direction that I should break off with Hector, but I knew that to maintain our relationship would be a source of conflict with the O., and that I would have to continue to justify it. It was not an approved relationship and, as such, would be seen as my acting off my bourgeois side. Sooner or later I would have to make a choice; the O. would give me the time and space to make the right choice, the choice that was good for my development, but there was obviously only one right choice.

Hector and I finally parted in a friendly way, agreeing that it was time for each of us to move on. As I was committed to my organization, so he was committed to his homeland; as soon as the repression eased, he would go back there—and where would that leave us? We knew that it wouldn't work and said goodbye to each other in the Oakland hills again, green now with the winter rains.

Hector is one of the many people I wish I could find and see again. I would tell him how much he had meant to me—I laugh now when I remember him coming home one day very proud of just having his hair permed, tight little permed curls over that beautiful, lined Indian face of his. He would do that, try things out, just for the trying of them, to shake off the years of jail and limits and darkness. Perhaps if I went to Tucuman, I could find him one day. I am sure he is back there now, now that things are better in his homeland. I would go to Tucuman and ask for Hector Morales, the politico who fixes sewing machines.

CHAPTER 11

The computer classes I started taking in the daytime were tedious. I particularly hated the flow-chart exercises. I couldn't understand the need for such meticulous, mechanical detail to make such simple decisions. The diamond-shaped "decision boxes" irritated me the most. The only answers you could give were Yes or No. *How could everything be reduced to that?* I wondered. But, my teachers taught me, computers only understand two things: on or off, or in the binary world, one or zero. One is on, zero is off. Yes or no, there is no maybe. If you cannot flow-chart it, they explained, then it cannot be programmed.

Instead of my Rank and File work I now studied COBOL in the mornings. I resigned my co-editorship of the Rank and File newsletter and stepped down from the Steering Committee in order to make the time I needed.

At the kitchen table, I spread out my flow-charts, and Julie helped me walk through them while she stirred pancake batter or rolled out cookie dough. Writing the actual programs was relatively easy although it all seemed very long-winded. I made my way through the courses without making any friends with the other students. Julie and I had begun to discuss the issue of leaving California for Minnesota—we both felt that it was inevitable that we would be called there. After all, that was where the center was, and we knew that we were marginalized from the group by our geographical distance. So I did not feel in the mood to strike up any new relationships; I didn't need any more people that I would have to let down as my life changed.

We received another memo. This was a lengthy discussion about organizational development and the need for administrative skills to be developed in the O. P.S. pointed to the experience of the Congo, which had collapsed after Lumumba took power due to the white flight of the technical class who had supported the infrastructure and production facilities. Revolutionaries, wrote P.S., must be self-sufficient and know how to run things efficiently—we could not rely on the existing power structure. I agreed with this and believed that people had to control their own alternative institutions; that the co-ops of the 1970s were predecessors to the building of co-ops on a much larger scale, and that this work would eventually link up with the theory and practice of worker-controlled factories.

I could begin to see how computer programming fit in. Clearly this technology was the basis for efficient administration, as was the accounting the unit was beginning to learn through a textbook mailed to us by P.S. It made sense that, if we were going to build these community-wide alternative institutions, we had better educate ourselves. From my experience in San Francisco, I had seen the wasted time and energy that went into poorly run programs.

Julie and I took the administration and accounting seriously. P.S. praised us for our analysis of our household finances: the way we brought in our ideological strengths and weaknesses in how we each dealt with money, and the resulting budget that we employed. Complex budgeting forms were sent to us: the Household Budget Form and the Personal Expense Form. These we filled out weekly and forwarded to the center for a detailed accounting of our income and expenditures. The purpose was to develop organizational and financial accountability. Around this time we started paying dues. I centralized $100 per month while Julie paid $150. All our household expenses were also pro-rated by our income level.

During this period, we were sent some study materials. We were to read, and be tested on, *The Communist Manifesto* and Mao's *On Contradiction*. For long-term study, we were told to buy Ernest Mandel's *Marxist Economic Theory*. The first two assignments seemed extremely basic—I had studied these texts years before and taught them several times in the study groups I'd organized. But, as I always found something new on rereading them, I didn't resist.

There were some new texts assigned that I had not read before: Stalin's *Dialectical and Historical Materialism* and his *Strategy and Tactics*. I had always had a visceral, not an educated, distaste for Stalin—I equated him with the dogmatic groups I'd avoided in San Francisco, and of course with purges and repression. But Julie encouraged me to read him, saying there would be things for me to learn. Indeed, I found *Strategy and Tactics* interesting, particularly liking the concept of strategy as the Main Blow toward which all tactics must contribute and subordinate themselves. It was uncomplicated and fit with my desire to focus and organize things to achieve a plan.

Attached to the memo praising our financial analysis was a separate memo for me alone.

"Claire," it began, "It has been seen that you should engage in an organizational PR (Personal Relationship) with the strategic aim of having a child. This will be a critical step in your development. At present it is suggested you establish a PR with Stan. P.S. will entertain feedback on this suggestion."

I could feel my heart contract and pull my blood inward, making my skin cold. Stan, I knew, was Richard's codename, my pallid nemesis from the Bookstore and Garfield Avenue. Oh, God, I wanted to have a "PR," but please, not with Richard. I thought hard about the memo. Clearly P.S. understood that I wanted to be in a relationship and that non-O. relationships would just get disrupted again and again by the demands of cadre life. Obviously I should have a PR within the O.

The strategic aim of having a child startled me. But without actually having a PR yet I didn't take it too seriously. The idea of being a mother didn't come easily to me; motherhood had never been part of my self-image, but I had begun to think about it a little as I'd entered my late twenties. Living with Beth had taught me to love her, and shown me that I could be close and loving and responsible to a child. And politically I believed so strongly in the need to deal with the issues of women and children in order to empower both, that it also seemed intellectually appropriate for me to have a child.

There was nothing further said in the memo to explain it, but I discussed it with Julie. Together we concluded that being a mother would introduce stability and responsibility to my life. It would also, by throwing me into the condition of motherhood, give me the opportunity to break down the male chauvinist Ideological Form, which I was reluctantly beginning to accept as a part of my bourgeois character.

Life as a cadre was becoming more serious. Demands were being made. I'd changed careers twice, and was now entering a whole new realm where personal life was dedicated to a larger good. My life was a small thing, but part of something larger, where things were planned, where my development was taken seriously and where, eventually, the work I was doing would link up with the work of many other disciplined and dedicated cadre. I felt I was taking a deep breath and launching myself into the unknown.

In this state of mixed emotions, I sat down to write a reply to P.S. I knew I could not bring myself to have a relationship with Richard, let alone a child with him. However, I still thought about Ted from time to time—not obsessively as I'd done the first few months after my visit, but still, he was on my mind. Perhaps this was an opening to indicate my interest in Ted. Surely this was the appropriate time, going through the proper channels—in other words, a memo to P.S.—to "expose" my attraction to him. It took me a long time to formulate my memo. There was no grammar I'd learned in school, no form or template that indicated how to ask an unknown third party for permission to enter into a serious rela tionship with someone on whom I'd managed to maintain a crush for over a year. Eventually I decided to keep it simple:

To: P.S.
From: Claire
Date: 12/23/81

1. The unit has completed the assigned study. We will begin plan ning out a series of additional study sessions on Mandel's work.

2. I enclose dues for both Jo and myself. Our monthly summaries will be sent next week.

3. While I appreciated Stan's struggling with me when I was in Minneapolis, I found it very difficult to relate to him on a personal level. At this time, I do not wish to enter into a PR with him. However, I was attracted to his roommate, Ted, while I was there, and feel that we have much in common in our backgrounds and on a cultural level that would enhance a PR.

I was nervous as I mailed off my response. I didn't know if it was appropriate to refuse a recommendation, but I knew I couldn't do otherwise.

Meanwhile Andy had left our unit. He had been working as a typeset ter for Kaiser Hospital corporation for the past two years and was involved in the union organizing drive there. He had a close circle of gay friends, and was becoming more interested in art, calligraphy, and photography. Finally, he refused a directive from P.S. that he was to quit his job and become a com puter programmer. Within the unit we had struggled with him.

"Andy," I said, "Don't you see how important it is to develop these technical skills? We can't keep running our organizations like the hippies did."

Julie joined in, "The only way to make a contribution is by being in a disciplined organization. How can we change anything if we're not working together?"

But Andy held firm.

"Look, I don't have anything against the O. In fact I think it's a leading force in the struggle. I do believe the O. has the right conceptualization—people need to change internally. But I can't do it anymore. I left before because the level of struggle was too high for me. I'm not going to be a revolutionary. I realize I'm failing as a cadre—that I'm choosing individualism. But that's the only honest choice I can make right now."

I felt desolate.

"I'll miss you, Andy."

It was understood that we would have to stop seeing him. The same way that it was understood that by turning down the recommendation to be a computer programmer he was, in effect, resigning his position in the O. There were no half-measures in the O. If you weren't in, you were out, and the O. did not look kindly on consorting with ex-members.

Andy had introduced me to the O., and I had shared much of the last two years of my life with him. He and Julie and I had become almost like family, sharing Beth's care, and our double lives within the O. He was smart, caring, a hard worker and a creative person. I would miss his gifts. But I could see that he had been vacillating for a long time, resisting assignments and enjoying our social connection more than our unit meetings.

"What I really want," he said, "is to live with Tom. I want a house in the Midwest with a white picket fence . . . on a lake . . ."

He wanted to develop his art, to live life in a way he felt he had never been allowed. He had moved from his intensely religious South Dakota farm family into the parallel Puritanism of the O. Having come out as a gay man only recently, he wanted to live out the richness of life that he found in San Francisco and develop beyond the borders of his bespectacled Midwestern shyness.

A week or two after Andy's resignation, P.S. sent another memo:

To: Claire
From: P.S.

You will not have a PR with Stan unless your proletarian side continues to develop and you conceptualize the developmental
aspects of such a PR.

You and Jo should centralize a plan for moving to the Midwest in
May. Once you are in the Midwest, you will be able to be more
fully integrated into organizational life and political practice.
Without this daily practice and accountability, your development
and contribution to the revolutionary struggle will remain at a low
level.

Andy has indicated that he is not willing to struggle further with the
occupational recommendations made to him. His removal of himself from the discipline of a Marxist-Leninist organization is another case in point of political activists professing class struggle while
at the same time upholding Twenty Enemy Forces. Andy's political
practice shows that he favors personal freedom at all costs and
refuses to struggle for political and organizational correctness.

The O. is a cadre organization of Marxist-Leninist organizers, and
as such its members must and will internalize scientific principles of
ideological struggle.

Jo and Claire have yet to identify the basis of the relationship with
Andy. What might have seemed to be a political relationship
turned out not to have been one. The dialectical aspect of political disrespect is personal friendship that has an opportunistic basis.
How else can one explain Andy's behavior?

For several months Julie and I heard nothing more. We were sad to see
Andy leave the unit, but we proceeded to make plans for the impending move
to Minnesota. I had put the issue of the Personal Relationship out of my mind,
continuing with my studies and my job and writing monthly summaries about
my development. These I discussed with Julie and forwarded to P.S. I was
sincerely struggling to put my assessment to use—looking at my "practice" in

all areas of my life and attempting to analyze the primary contradiction within each. My overriding concern was to work through the old patterns that had prevented me taking responsibility and following through on the various things in which I was involved. To this end I noticed my fears and pushed myself to overcome them. I noticed the pattern of sloppiness in my work and my studies and determined to put my best into it—how could I be a good revolutionary if I was not prepared to struggle to present neat and complete flow-charts to my teachers?

This extended to the machine shop only in my commitment to master the skills of a machinist and to be conscientious in producing quality parts. It did not extend to subordinating myself to the company rules and manipulations. I continued to struggle for improved health and safety conditions and was constantly in trouble for refusing to work overtime. I became a vocal presence on second shift, noisily standing up for my rights and encouraging others to do likewise.

Late that winter my mother invited me to go on holiday for a couple of weeks to Florida. I was ready for a vacation and looked forward to seeing my mother again—it had been close to two years since our last visit together.

We met at Miami airport, hired a car and spent a week touring the coast from Sanibel up to Tampa. She was still recovering from the break-up with my father and her resulting breakdown. Together we collected seashells, swam in the sea, lay in bubbling motel jacuzzis and ate fresh fish every night. We drove up the coast through the Southern states. In Georgia we ate breakfasts of grits and eggs. In Mississippi we drove the country roads in winter greenery and warmth. On one of these roads we stopped outside a small house where a dozen handmade quilts hung on washing lines tied between trees. Like bees to honeysuckle, we were drawn to the multi-colored quilts, and my mother bought me the one I liked the best, on first sight, spotted from the road. Its pattern was called "grandmother's fan," but I always saw it as a hundred red suns setting on the white background and laying down patterned rays of red, white, and blue. In the corner was a tiny square embroidered with the words "Esther Smith, 1980." It had a fierce and ordered beauty that lay on my bed for the next ten years.

In New Orleans we ate freshly fried beignets, the crispy light doughnuts of the French Quarter, and leaned on a parapet in the sunshine listening to a jazz band play on the street. I kept looking at the young drummer: he was lean and black and serious and reminded me of Ron, my musician co-worker at FABCO. We connected, as strangers do sometimes, as I listened to him, among the tourists, feeling separate from them and yet not separate from the drummer and his band.

That night I had a vivid dream about Ted. He had faded from my mind over the past year, but suddenly he reappeared, very physical, holding me in my dream. I hadn't told my mother about him, but I began to talk to her the next day, as we drove along the freeway, about the fact I'd started thinking about having a child—that I hadn't decided, but was beginning to mull the idea over. After all, I was twenty-seven years old, my once-best-friend Leah had just had a baby, my sister had a two-year old, and it was time to start thinking about it. If this O. PR with Ted came about, I wanted her to feel that it was a "natural" development when I got pregnant.

Ten days into the vacation I decided to call home to Julie, to see how she was doing and let her know my flight home. My mother waited in the rental car while I squeezed myself into a telephone booth at a gas station.

Julie was curt with me: "I just spoke to my contact last night. You're supposed to come home."

"Sure," I said, taken aback by her tone. "I'm due home in four days. In fact, I wanted to give you my flight number."

"No. You're supposed to come home right *now*. You didn't forward anything about your vacation. You're acting out of personal independence, and without any organizational accountability. The method of correction is for you to cut it off now and get back to Oakland. Anyway . . . there's a memo waiting for you that you might be pleased about."

Julie was never that good at criticizing—she would start out tough, but soften it at the end, like she was doing now.

I stood in that phone box, with my mother waiting for me in the car outside, and I tried to think fast. It had not been apparent to me that I was breaking any kind of discipline when I arranged the vacation, but now that Julie said so, I could see that, indeed, I hadn't told P.S. about it, and that it was just something I was doing for relaxation and to be with my mother. It wasn't clear to me why that was wrong, but Julie was telling me I was engaging in anti-organizational activity. And there was a memo—maybe this was the reply to my memo about the PR. Somehow I thought it might be, from the way Julie spoke: she knew I'd had a crush on Ted all this time.

"Okay," I said, "I'll try to figure out a way—but it'll probably take me a couple of days. I can't just leave my mom stranded here. Damn. I didn't know I was supposed to report everything I do."

Julie replied over the long-distance line, "My contact said you should know that your relationship with your family is what upholds your bourgeois side. Any dealings with them have to be carefully looked at and developed as functional relationships—otherwise you just slide back into the family expectations and obligations without any consciousness of the dynamics. Family relationships have to be carefully conditioned, or they become a fetter on your development."

We said goodbye, and after she hung up I kept the phone to my ear for a few minutes as I tried to think of a plan. I had to come up with something right away that I could say to my mother—something that would justify why I had to leave immediately, and leave her in New Orleans for four days on her own, before her flight back to London. I thought up some lie about my job making me go back early, inserted myself into the lie like a method actor and walked out of the phone booth to join her in the car.

Whether she believed it or not, I don't know. But I left her there in Louisiana, found a flight to Oakland early the next morning and was gone. I felt terrible, I wasn't much given to lying, but something inside of me believed the argument, knew that I had to train to be a cadre, and knew only too well that my family had always been a suffocating blanket trying to hold me down with its own bizarre code of ethics and obligation. Even though I had begun to have a better relationship with my mother after my parents' break-up, I knew that I did not want to become embroiled with her and the rest of the family again. And if this was what it took to struggle to be in a serious organization, then so be it; I was willing to give it a try. I was sorry that my mother had to be inconvenienced; it didn't seem fair at all, but then, it was my fault for not having centralized my vacation plans. I was sure it would not be the last time that I would have to lie to my family or friends about my underground activities.

This was practice, practice for the cadre life about which I had read so much in the history of China, Mozambique, Angola, Nicaragua and all the other countries that had achieved their liberation through the subordination of individual needs to the collective struggle.

When I got back to the little green house in Oakland, Julie was at work and Beth was at school, but there was the letter, lying on the dresser by my bed. I opened it, very nervous, feeling that a future might await me inside that envelope. That was the feeling that always accompanied opening a memo in the O. A feeling that swung from intense fear to an exquisite anticipation and then settled around a general sense of nervousness. A memo could decide the next several years of one's life, exciting or fearful depending on the sentence. It could contain praise and a promotion to a new position or program, or, more often, a Criticism or Discussion Form from P.S. or another comrade. A criticism always included a Method of Correction: perhaps a demotion, or having to move to a different house or even city, or a new relationship, or a sacrifice or exclusion from some desired activity. Often the Method of Correction was for the cadres to write their own summary or self-criticism and propose their own Methods of Correction—this then involved coming up with what one thought was the correct answer—how had one's PIC or IF been the source of whatever error had been discovered?

If one knew how to work the system one could maneuver things so that a Method of Correction actually removed oneself from some undesired activity or responsibility, or, vice versa, the Correction could include, if properly justified, some preferred result: perhaps getting more exercise, or seeing family.

So, in a state of apprehension I tore open the envelope. Inside were three typewritten pages. The first was a memo from Ted.

To: Claire
From: Ted
Date: 02/03/82

It is my understanding that we are to have a Personal Relationship together with the strategic aim of having a child. I am enclosing a PR Summary. You should mail a summary of your PRs to Ted Brodsky, P.O. Box 10022, Mpls., MN 55440. When you arrive in the Twin Cities, arrangements will be made for you to move into the house where I am living.

That was all. The other two pages were his summary, describing his previous failings in his sparse history of relationships. I couldn't believe that the fantasy I'd held for almost two years was finally coming true. I had thought so often about Ted, played out in my head so many scenarios with him. It was hard to believe—to carry a crush for someone for a year and hold it in the dark corners of my mind another year and then, suddenly, there it was, put in my lap. I was breathless.

I'd felt such respect for his seriousness and his dedication, and felt such personal empathy in his warmth and his interest in me. And I thought I could still remember the feel of him—though we'd only touched once, dancing that night. Love and desire took hold of me. I laughed with Julie, celebrating my good fortune and let thoughts of Ted bubble up through the interstices of my brain, flooding me with feeling in every quiet moment.

I wrote poems to him, poems I never showed him, and decided once again to rededicate myself to the struggle, to work harder, to be more disciplined, to prove that happiness was a productive force, that I would share that energy and use it to move the struggle forward. The words I'd read of a Guatemalan guerilla organization came to me: "Those who wish to be couples may do so as long as they think about it carefully first, consider each side's feelings and don't put personal happiness before revolution."

This was a careful romance, a part of the revolutionary struggle, not an obstacle to it. Our partnership would be a creative, productive one; something to be proud of.

The next couple of months were filled with energy; I felt alive, not just because of Ted, but in anticipation of my new life in Minneapolis. But I also had nightmares that I didn't understand; the themes were always the same: war, death, and rape, men threatening me and my turning to my friends to get help.

My health had also deteriorated in the last year: I developed abscesses in my gums, and my chest was permanently constricted with a low-level bronchitis from the machine-shop fumes and dirt. My job had become something I hated, that was literally making me sick. I began to look forward to becoming a programmer in a clean, white-collar job.

Mostly, though, I was full of good feelings: for the friends to whom Julie and I were saying goodbye, for Julie and Beth as we prepared for our adventurous departure, for Ted who awaited me—and for the struggle. Leaving, after all, was something I'd always done well.

On May 1, 1982, International Worker's Day, Julie, Beth and I set off in Julie's battered two-door Fiat for Minneapolis. All our belongings had been sent off by train earlier in the week. I had packed up my ten years of life in California: my book boxes contained novels and books of poetry and works of political economy, demographics, oral history, labor history, medical books, political theory and philosophy, the complete works of Mao Tse Tung, feminist theory and feminist novels, African history and African novels, stacks of

Monthly Review and *Socialist Theory*, books on psychology and madness, books on Black America, notes and study guides from the Black Panther Party and the InterCommunal Survival Committee.

In other boxes were the letters I'd written and received since I'd left England fifteen years before, and a two-foot-high stack of journals I'd written since I was fourteen. There were pamphlets I'd worked on about childcare, Cuba, milk prices, rank and file unionism, the economics of women's liberation; my study notes on the books I'd both studied and taught; my notebooks full of ideas and notes for books I'd wanted to write but had never believed in enough to take the time. A short story of my teenage years in Paris and thirty pages of my poems lay side by side with the article on cadre organizing in the co-ops that I'd co-authored for the underground *Seize the Time* newspaper. Pictures I'd drawn and painted over the years and pictures painted for me by friends were rolled up into cardboard tubes.

My clothes: the bright yellow jacket I'd bought with my sister and mother in Camden Town; my baggy turquoise dungarees; the white silk shirt my roommate Penny had given me, off her back, when I had admired it; my black velvet jacket, also bought in Camden Town; and jeans, flannel shirts, and bright sweaters and Birkenstock sandals. Light, bright, California clothes, all went into boxes, sealed and addressed to a house I didn't know in Minnesota.

Into these boxes I packed away the threads of my life. Packed up and weighed at the train station: this is how much the boxes weigh, this is how much it will cost to send them. This is what a life looks like when you remove the people from it. I felt those boxes of papers, of my journals and letters, tied to me like a baby—this was my life's matter all boxed up, and it scared me to send it off like that, out of my grasp, on a train with no-one's protection.

Meanwhile, Julie, Beth, and I had spent our last night sleeping on the living room floor (all the furniture had been sold, or given away) of our little green house. The last person to say goodbye to us was Sam. He woke us late in the night, stopping by after his shift and shining his headlights into our empty living room, frightening us awake. We let him in, and Julie and I hugged him, one to each arm while his bushy beard and natural tickled our cheeks.

"We all are sure gonna miss you beautiful women—and that sweet Beth. You take care of yourselves now. Don't let the Midwest cover you in snow." He laughed at our ruffled sleepiness. "I'm off to the Tip Top—I just had to have one last hug. Goodbye, sweet ladies . . ."

Then he left, and Julie and I lay together, staring into the dark and taking a long time to get back to sleep.

May 8th 1982

*In four hours we arrive in the Twin Cities. We've had a good journey.
We saw beautiful desert, red rocks, mesas, canyons with cliffs going straight
up, hanging gardens dripping from them—this at Zion Canyon in Utah.
Awesome rocks of all shapes standing full and strong in the earth and giving
me force and solidity.*

*We saw small towns of Indians, the Mesa Verde with crazy kinds of cliff
dwellings and, all over the Southwest, dirt of yellow and orange and rich red.
And multicolored rocks exposing the layers of their development in one
expanse.*

*Then to Jemez in New Mexico—a hot spring perched upon a moun-
tain with a view of blue-green mountains further on and pine trees surrounding us. We camped in a deserted park there and had a fire and soup and in
the morning walked in the valley.*

*We missed Tulsa, and I thought, sadly, of Tracy mostly, and Gary and
Ron.*

*So, soon we'll arrive. To a new life, new home, work, friends, com-
rades, and lover. It has been a good journey. I feel well; beyond that I will
wait and see. This is a new period of my life. What will it bring me? It will
be a test—perhaps I've learned something about tests—to not be nervous, to
breathe, to do my best, to do what I can do.*

We drove into the Twin Cities on Interstate 94, past downtown Minneapolis
with its clean skyscrapers and wide blue sky, past the Cedar-Riverside buildings, scene of violent housing co-op struggles in the 1970s and into St. Paul,
the older, grayer and quieter sister of the Twin Cities. We found our way to
the address on Aurora Street sent to us in our last memo.

Julie was driving, Beth was asleep in the back seat. I was getting more
and more wound up and had curled myself into a snail-like spiral with my feet
squeezed up on the front seat, peering out at this city of freeways and buildings with no people on the street. Julie turned to me.

"I suppose we won't be seeing much of each other." She reached out
her hand and took mine. "You've been a good friend and comrade to me.

Don't give up the fight, even though it might be hard. You've got a lot to offer, you know."

I squeezed her hand. I couldn't quite believe what I had done. We had never spoken about it before, but there was always something implicit that we would be separated when we arrived. Our friendship was too close, it was too social—after all, we still smoked grass together, and we knew that would not continue. There would be no room for friendship, only comradeship, and somehow we knew that, for our development, we would be moved apart.

Beth was sucking her thumb, snuggled under blankets in the back seat. My eyes hurt, and I took off my glasses to rub them.

"I'll miss her, and you. You've been my family."

"You know," Julie replied, "There'll be a lot to replace what we had together. We'll both be in relationships, you'll be having a kid of your own. We'll be busy as hell. It'll be okay."

CHAPTER 12

We pulled up by a duplex in a run-down part of St. Paul. A man in his early thirties answered the door for us, took a look at Beth still sleeping in Julie's arms, at the Fiat filled with the debris of a cross-country trip, and nodded at us in mute understanding that he knew who we were and was expecting us. He led the way up a dark, narrow flight of stairs past neat stacks of papers, bathroom tiles, and two-by-fours piled along one side of the stairway. In the living-room he motioned to Julie to lay Beth on the couch and for me to put down the bags I carried.

"I'm Bill," he said quietly. "Welcome. I understand you'll be staying here for a while," he said to Julie.

I thought that perhaps Bill was who Julie was to have a relationship with, but I didn't know, and I wondered if she even knew yet. He seemed nice enough, good-looking, friendly, if a little serious and with his black hair cut a little too short for fashion, shaved, almost, at the back of his neck. He leaned forward in an earnest way when he talked to us, but his blue eyes sank back a little from contact. He showed us the kitchen and gestured with big hands to the cupboards, suggesting we help ourselves to whatever we needed, and then he showed Julie his bedroom where she and Beth would spend the night—he would sleep elsewhere until the living arrangements were sorted out.

As Bill spread out a sleeping bag for me on the couch, a tall, lanky woman with a permed frizz of hair came in and whispered to him. She looked at me and Julie curiously from the corners of her eyes. Finally, looking down at us from her considerable height, she introduced herself as Jerri.

"I'll be back in the morning," Bill said and, nodding to me, continued, "I understand someone will be coming by for you then, too."

He left with Jerri, and they closed the door with no further good-bye.

Julie and I sat together for a while on the bed where Beth slept. We looked at each other in a kind of tired and blank astonishment. What had we done? Julie's stocky body was slumped over as she sat, her gray eyes squinted up in the way they did when she was tired. The three of us had been so close the last couple of years and now this would be our last night together. We didn't know when we would see each other again. There was little left to be said, so we hugged and I felt Julie's large breasts soften up to my skinny torso. We said good night, and I crawled into my sleeping bag in the next room and remembered the nights I'd spent in Stockton with the InterCommunal Survival Committee, where I'd slept in strange places with strange people and did not know what to expect.

Early the next morning, I was awakened by two women coming through the living room: one was thin, dressed in a black coat, and the other was short and stocky with a scowl creasing her face. As they walked through, I sat up and greeted them. But neither of them turned, they just looked through me, said nothing and left the room. I felt I had made some faux pas, perhaps broken a security code by talking to people I didn't know; obviously they had some purpose being in the house, and it wasn't my business to know what it was or who they were.

Bill eventually returned in the late afternoon, but I had to wait until evening before Ted finally arrived to take me to my new living quarters.

He greeted me quietly, "Hi, how are you? Was your journey okay?" and, not really waiting for an answer went on, "Let's get your stuff. I've got my car downstairs. We'll get you over to the other place."

I could barely speak I was so nervous. He was how I'd remembered him: thin-faced, with a strong chin and soft green eyes behind his glasses. His shoulders were wide, but thin, and he stood very straight with an almost military bearing. He'd combed his sand-colored hair carefully back from his forehead and dense rust-red curls covered his forearms. What I hadn't remembered were his hands; they were small and delicate, with fine fingers that tapered at the ends. It was strange to be meeting him again like this, after all my dreaming.

We loaded up the car, I said a last good-bye to Julie and Beth, and then we drove through the spring night, back along the I-94 freeway and into Minneapolis. Ted was formal and restrained. We drove in silence.

Ted parked outside another duplex, and, as we entered the front hallway, he punched a code into an electronic security alarm. Then he flipped a numbered card hanging on the hallway wall. He explained that each person had a card with a number on it—they were Roman numerals—he was III, our roommate was IV, and I would be V. I and II lived in the upstairs apartment. Each card had a green side and a red side: green meant that the person was home; when one left the house, his or her card had to be flipped to red. If all the other cards were red, the last person leaving the house had to set the alarm. And, likewise, if one returned and saw that all the cards were red, that meant that person was the first one back, so the alarm was set and the siren would go off if it was not disarmed within sixty seconds. This seemed complicated to me, but fit with the pattern of security with which I was already familiar.

Ted opened the front door to our apartment, which was totally dark inside, and he went ahead to turn on the light switch. I stood at the entrance of the front room, waiting for him to find the light—it seemed to take a long time—and I tried making a joke: "I've been kept in the dark long enough . . ." I ventured, but he did not laugh, only brushed by me as he reached for the switch. As the light came on, I realized that, despite his calm and formal manner, he must have been absurdly nervous also—bringing me home to his house, to begin a relationship with someone he hardly knew.

I was put in the study at first. Ted had set up a bed for me in there. There were also two desks crammed in the room and a Hewlett-Packard personal computer, draped, icon-like, with a sheet for a dust cover.

The house was on a "good" block in North Minneapolis, in a largely black neighborhood. Further up, by Plymouth Avenue, near the McDonald's, were the crack houses and the corner hang-outs of the gang members who had drifted down from Chicago, looking for new territory, or, for some, a quieter life. The school kids hung out there, too, so it was a difficult mix, the cops as easily picking up the kids as the crack dealers. Our house, number 801, had damaged white stucco and green wood trim, a good-sized yard fenced off in the back with an incongruous five-foot mesh fence. The grass was kept short and neat, but there were few flowers, only a couple of peony bushes in the front and some low-maintenance day lilies. O. members, I discovered, did not have time for gardening, only for what was necessary to keep the house looking as unobtrusive as possible. On arriving, I had been told, by Jerri, my new roommate and my contact (she was the tall, imposing woman I'd met the day before), that there had been problems with the house a few years back. It had been known as an after-hours party house, and the O. had refurbished it and was trying to do its bit in saving the house to keep the neighborhood up. We were to keep a low profile in the neighborhood, not talk to the neighbors unless absolutely necessary and not get into social exchanges with them.

Ted, Jerri, and I occupied the bottom floor of the duplex. There were three bedrooms, all tiny. It had, indeed, been remodeled inside, and the paint was clean, and there was new woodwork in places. The third bedroom had been carved out of part of what was once a large living room, and was now the study. The living room was small and dark. Another woman cadre, Vida, (Roman Numeral I) lived on the top floor with a thirteen-year-old girl, Nancy (Roman Numeral II). Nancy's parents were both in the O., but, I was told, because of trouble in the family, Nancy had been sent to live with Vida. Vida seemed kind enough, and I envied Nancy the option of living away from her parents—I wished I'd been able to do that when I'd been a teenager, instead of having to run away from home at fifteen to escape my family troubles.

The first couple of days I spent settling in. Ted and I picked up my belongings from the train station where they'd been delivered, and I stored most of them in their boxes in the basement. I labeled all my boxes with the number V. Into the basement went my books, my boxes of letters and journals and writings, my cardboard tubes of pictures. I was worried someone might open the journal boxes, so these I wrapped tightly with silver duct tape and wrote "V's personal papers" on the labels. Then I hid them at the bottom of the stack. I would have to count on people's integrity not to open them.

The basement gave me a view into the life of the house. It was immaculate. Tools hung neatly from pegboards on one wall. Little plastic organizers contained nails and screws and staples in all sizes, all properly labeled and sorted. And by the lawn mower was a garden work schedule with the numbers I, II, III and IV represented, and the jobs divided into mowing, weeding, trimming and so on. A typewritten and numbered procedure for the safe and efficient use of the lawnmower and weedeater was taped next to it. Likewise, by the washing machine and dryer I saw a schedule posted of times each of the two apartments could do laundry. Apparently there had been problems in the past with a logjam on Sunday nights. There were assignments for cleaning the common areas of the house: the basement and the front entrance. Obviously the thirteen-year old, II, took an equal load of all these chores.

In the back end of the basement were two locked areas. These were filled with unidentified boxes that I could see as I peered through the slats of the wooden dividing walls. And then there were stacks of boxes labeled with various Roman numerals, belonging to the other members of the household.

One thing I had learned about the O. in my last visit was that they were deadly serious about things being organized. I respected this quality. Having lived in a chaotic collective household in San Francisco where house meetings were long and emotional as we tried to sort out the practical details of living together, I appreciated the cut-and-dried, no-nonsense methods I saw here. Clearly, the schedules and procedures that applied to almost every aspect of household life were the result of plenty of summarized experience. And it meant that these petty problems were cleared aside in order to make time for the serious work of organizing for the struggle. I was amazed by the detail to which this household organization had been taken.

But there was one thing I couldn't bear and against which I immediately rebelled. This was the food arrangements. The shopping list was printed off from the computer, all the items on it arranged by how the supermarket was laid out—this to maximize the efficiency of the shopping (which was generally done after midnight, the only time cadre had available after work and program shifts and meetings were done). There was a box of index cards of supposedly balanced menus from which the menu-planner and shopper for the week could choose. Most of these were mushroom-soup-based casseroles of one sort or another—quick and easy to make with canned, frozen or otherwise processed ingredients. Only the bread was of good quality, and that came from the O. bakery, brought in and frozen once a week by Ted. Ted and Jerri had instituted an efficient method (as recommended for all cadre, by P.S.) for making the packed lunches that they took to work every day. Once a month, one of them would set up a one-person assembly station in the kitchen and make up forty cheese or bologna sandwiches. These were put in individual sandwich bags and then frozen. In the morning all they had to do was grab a frozen sandwich and put it in a paper bag, along with an apple or banana. I was appalled at this, and slowly attempted to reeducate them both in enjoyable and healthy eating habits. It was hard because, as there was never enough time in the day for all the tasks one was assigned, naturally food preparation took a low priority.

On my week to shop though, I bought fresh vegetables and whole grains, and added good recipes using these ingredients to the set of index cards that sat on top of the fridge. Of course, we never ate together as we all ate irregularly in the brief free moments between work shifts, meetings and personal summary.

Apparently there had been a period shortly before I'd arrived when a lot of attention had been put into developing these household "systems." It was an organization-wide effort with the goal of streamlining and proceduralizing "household production" which was seen as a socially necessary form of labor, but one which, because of the Capitalist relations of production, had been left at a low level of development since it did not produce surplus value. As Marxists, and as upholders of women's liberation, the O. had placed a priority on resolving this contradiction of unpaid household work, at least within the organization. There was no sexual division of labor within the group. In fact, at a certain point in time, the childcare center had been run entirely by O. men as part of their learning to respect the realm of women's work. All the O. men I knew took equal responsibility for housework and child-rearing. Likewise, most of the O. women had had traditionally male jobs, either as machinists like myself, or auto mechanics, or printers. And O. women were expected to do heavy physical work, learn to use power tools and equipment, or learn to drive trucks in the various programs. This equality was a source of quiet pride to all of us; it wasn't advertised, or even talked about, but we were well aware that, as individuals, it set us apart.

"I'm an Idealist," said Jerri as we sat together at the kitchen table at our first formal meeting. "I'll be your contact, your, er . . . leadership," she announced, clearing her throat and sliding her eyes away from mine as she spoke. She was modest and didn't want to appear to be flaunting her rank, yet she was obliged to make the relationship clear. From that moment, I saw her in a different light; she was my contact, my leadership, and she must have earned this position through dedication and hard work.

Jerri was quiet, but the way she carried her height, and her internal steadiness indicated something else inside that thin and placid exterior: a powerful intelligence, a confidence in her abilities and an immense capacity for hard work. Her hair was light brown and permed every couple of months—this being the least time-consuming way to take care of it. She had just made the transition from machinist to computer programmer, the same path I was taking, and her job required her to have an appropriate appearance. To this end she had studied John Molloy's *Dress for Success* (recommended reading in the O. for people moving from blue- to white-collar jobs). She had purchased two navy-blue suits, an array of blouses and silk ribbons to tie at the neck. It pleased me that, despite the rigidity of the *Dress for Success* uniform, she had a taste and elegance that managed to show through.

Jerri was raised on a profitable soybean farm in Iowa, and she often recounted how she'd "walked the beans" in the summertime and assured me that this had taught her the meaning of hard work. She did indeed work incredibly hard. I remained awed by her for years by this. She would eat standing up in the kitchen so as not to waste time, and then, when at home, she would always be at her desk, studying, typing, making plans in triplicate to distribute to other cadres. She woke early each morning to finish her organizational work before going to her job. As soon as she got home in the evening she would change clothes, do her chores, and be off to the Bakery where she was now the manager. I think Jerri only ever slept four or five hours a night during those years. Her work was always of the highest quality—she had an instinctive ability to organize and administer things, though she lacked political savvy in dealing with people's quirks.

Even though Jerri would criticize me from time to time, she was not mean or vicious, and I had an affectionate admiration for her that lasted over the years. She had a warm and human side that perhaps only showed itself in our hurried conversations in the kitchen of 801, as she ate her stand-up meals. She was motivated by the same kind of desperate empathy I had for the streams of people whose suffering paraded the newspaper headlines. Her eyes would well up with tears talking about the poor young people she was organizing in the Youth Farm Program, how they'd never been in the countryside before, had never seen a cow or a horse. And her mind had an amazing reach and interest—when we had time, we would discuss world events; she would listen attentively as I told her the history of the struggle in South Africa, and she would, in return, explain to me, in a friendly and caring kind of way, the long-term importance of our work in the Bakery and the other programs and how this work would eventually develop into a nation-wide mass struggle against the U.S. state. Whenever I was in an "ideological crisis" (and there were many in my first year there) she would find the time to talk with me and give me a vision of what we were building.

"My Ideological Form is sexism," she continued, during this first meeting, "and my AI is with men."

This was something I hadn't heard of before. Introductions to other O. members commonly started with an exchange of one's ideological profile. In fact, O. members used to carry index cards around with them, listing these features; the theory was, they could just swap them with a new O. member, and each would immediately know each other's ideological framework. However, in practice, this didn't work, and the index cards were dropped.

"What's an AI?" I asked.

"It stands for Associative Identity. It's a new part of the Internal Transformation Process. You see, generally speaking, your AI is related to your DI. In my case, my Dominant Influence is my father, so I tend to have stronger relationships with men, rather than women. We call this one's Associative Identity. It's helpful to know what this is, then you can look at your relationships with people, who you're most likely to listen to, for instance, in the light of your AI."

"Oh." Apparently my AI was with men also, given my father was my DI. This was a new thing to think about—how had this affected my relationships with men? Obviously I'd always had strong male relationships, both lovers and friends. I hadn't thought of it as meaning I took them more seriously than women, or that I valued my women friends any the less.

"Anyway you'll need to get a job right away," she went on. "I understand you've been a machinist? You can try at Nortronics, where I used to work. They'll probably take you on. Then you should get a resumé together and start looking for a computer job. We'll have to get you into some practice as soon as possible—it will most likely be at the program where I work. I'm just waiting to check it out. Do you have enough study material?"

"Oh, I always have plenty to read, but if you've got anything in particular . . ."

"Well, there's *On Practice* and *On Contradiction* by Mao that I would recommend. It's really important to understand how contradictions are operating."

I groaned inside; *again*, did they not ever read anything else? I thought of my thick Gabriel Kolko book I was reading on the history of the United States in the twentieth century—this was the kind of thing that interested me. But, at her urging, I agreed to study Mao's pamphlets once more and to start pulling together my observations of O. life and its programs using the dialectical materialist method.

Three weeks later Ted and I sat in the kitchen, each with our notepads and pens ready, meeting, just the two of us, about our relationship. I'd only seen him two or three times since I'd arrived and had been looking forward to the meeting as, finally, a time to connect with him; to be able to have a personal conversation with somebody, and particularly him, was like food to a hungry child. We went over our schedules first, trying to find time in his overloaded week to get together. He was trying to respond to my complaints of feeling so distant and lonely. But as he worked full time and for eight additional hours a day at his programmatic work, it was hard for him to find any free time at all. We finally scheduled to go out for the afternoon two weekends from then, and, in the meantime, to run together on Saturday evening and to try to be in the house together for a meal on Sunday.

After sorting out the schedule, he suggested that perhaps now we should share the same bedroom. I agreed, and, knowing we would not find another time to do it, we decided to spend the rest of our meeting time moving my things from the study to his bedroom.

Without touching, but moving around each other carefully, we moved my bed and books and clothes from the study into the little bedroom off the kitchen. He hadn't lived with a woman before, while for me this was familiar territory—although I had never experienced this level of conscious planning and lack of spontaneity in a relationship. But I was willing to try it—after all, my previous relationships had fallen apart and had always held me back from my desire to do political work—so it seemed to be in the nature of an experiment to see how this way of doing things would work.

I claimed half of the dresser space, and set out my little baskets and carved wooden boxes of personal items, while he moved some of his clothes to the basement, stored in a box labeled III. The quilt my mother had bought me in Mississippi I laid on the bed. Ted wasn't sure he liked it, but I thought it brought brightness and beauty to the room, lighting it up with its repeating suns, and I asked that we keep it there.

From my tube of pictures I'd brought from California I found the one I liked the best, a silk-screen print of Victor Jara with a quote of his: *Happiness is putting one's heart, will and mind to work at the service of the people, helping to create that which is to be reborn. . . .*

Together we pinned this up on the bedroom wall.

That night he rearranged his schedule so that we could go to bed together. I lay in bed naked and nervous, waiting for him. We had never so much as kissed before, yet I still felt in love and wanted to feel his warmth close to me. I wanted to relax him with my touch, he was so guarded and brittle inside, although his outside was yielding with good manners, respectful and gentle as a revolutionary man should be. The inside and the outside were familiar territories to me; that people consisted of both was one of my fascinations, and I knew I had the ability to enter into the inside world of the people I'd known. Somehow I thanked my sister Hatty for that. She had gone inside when I was still young and curious enough to watch and accept and to understand the two worlds. My own also: I had prized my secret self, had kept it locked up and hidden in diaries and memories and letters that I never threw away. No one could take that part of me, the part that thought seriously about the world, that lived in feelings dark as violets, safe from the laughter of cynicism or greed.

He came to bed half-clothed, wearing his boxers, an undershirt and a soft purple sweatshirt. He began to stroke my hair, and we finally kissed, caressed each other, hugged and became warm. I reached under his sweat-shirt to feel his chest with my hands, and he pulled the two shirts over his head, giving me the wide hairiness of his chest to smell and bury my face in. Then, as I was used to doing, I started to extricate myself from his embrace and swung my legs over the side of the bed, reached over to the nightstand and found the blue drawstring bag that held my diaphragm. I took the diaphragm out of its plastic case and began to squeeze spermicidal jelly into it.

"Do you know how to do this?" I asked him, leaning closer to him so that he could see—for years I had taught my lovers how to prepare and insert my diaphragm so that it could become a shared and unembarrassed part of our love-making, and feeling close to Ted, I wanted him, too, to know about it. He frowned and leaned up on his elbow.

"Do you think you should be using that?" he said.

I looked at him, "Why not?—what do you mean? I've used a diaphragm for years."

I thought perhaps he wanted to use a condom instead, or was worried about the effectiveness of the diaphragm. It seemed odd to question it, my diaphragm was something with which I felt comfortable, and I couldn't see why he wouldn't.

"Well, I mean, we're supposed to have a child. That's the strategic aim of the relationship—that's my understanding anyway. Isn't it yours?"

The diaphragm sat in my hand, half-filled with jelly, still dusted with the cornstarch I used to keep it dry. My other hand held the open tube, a glob of jelly about to drip out onto the bed. It was like being punched so hard that I was see-ing stars, only the punch didn't hurt. I just felt my brain reeling, trying to clear away the pinpoints of light to regain my balance. When the stars had dissipated and dis-solved into furniture and floor, into bed and walls, the atmosphere in the room had changed. Suddenly I was dealing with something different—this wasn't just a memo from P.S. promising a new future that I could take up when I was ready. This was Ted, for whom I had waited two years. Words came to me.

"I hardly know you yet. I'm sorry, I'm not going to give up using my diaphragm the first time we sleep together. What do you think I am? You make me feel like a cow, just some animal to be poked and bred. It's disgusting."

"You're not a cow," he said gently. "You're a woman, who's going to have a child. We're going to have a child. And if you agree with the strategic aim, why wait? If that's the purpose of our relationship, then I don't see that we should have a sexual relationship if you're not in unity with the aim yet."

Now I saw: after these two years, and finally being with him, he was going to withhold sex from me, and love, I supposed, unless I put away my contraception. But I *had* agreed with the recommendation. I did want to have a child. But in a relationship that hadn't even begun yet? I sat on the edge of the bed, hunched up and naked, wanting only to rest myself in his arms. I couldn't agree, though, it was *crazy* to move on it so quickly.

Ted carried on talking. What did I think would be gained by waiting? Did I want to hold back my development? Did I think having a child would be good for my development? If I did, then couldn't I see that having a sexual relationship with him without implementing the strategic aim would be opportunist and would lead nowhere, like my previous relationships? I bristled at this, but I kept listening. I wanted to be with him. I wanted to settle down. I wanted to believe that I had found a relationship with him, and with the organization, that would last, that would allow me to grow, to realize my contribution to the world.

Inside myself again, curled up in defense, I put down the diaphragm and climbed back into bed. I didn't think about it—his words had begun to blur, I was suddenly exhausted, and all I wanted was to rest. I gave in, coming to him in resentful submission. Slowly Ted warmed me up again. I softened, and we made warm, wet love, both coming together, the first time.

"At least it looks like we won't have too many sexual contradictions," he said, holding me, my head on his chest as we rested, legs entwined, feeling, at last, love for each other.

CHAPTER 13

I got a job at Nortronics, as Jerri had suggested, and found myself doing precision machining in a small, clean shop—very different from the Oakland place. We made tiny parts: little bronze or aluminum pieces, a half inch long, serrated with narrow slots which divided up the sides of each part to look like the spindly legs of a metallic spider. The top was ground and burnished to a high polish and the finished product became a tape head to be used in the computer industry. I worked swing shift again, and grew to like most of my co-workers—though here racism ran rampant and went unchallenged because there were almost no black or brown workers in the entire company of 1,000 employees. Greg was one of my co-workers: a nice enough young guy, longish brown hair in a duck flip, shirtsleeves rolled up with a pack of cigarettes tucked in at his biceps, mostly interested in girls and guitars. When I told him that I lived in North Minneapolis, he said, "Jesus, I don't even drive there at night—all you see are the whites of their eyes flashing—you know—you can't see the rest of them in the dark," here he laughed, then continued, "And the whores and knives. . . . What do you want to be living there for? You're not a nigger-lover are you?"

I flinched and took a step back from him. I liked Greg. He'd helped me learn the ropes when I started, had given me extra drill bits when I kept breaking the thin ones they used—I had a heavy arm on the drill after my work on the big and greasy truck-axle parts at FABCO. The foreman harangued me every time I broke one of the needle-sized drill bits, and Greg was the one who had shown me where to get extras and how to stash them so I wouldn't have to face this humiliation. Later, Greg explained our foreman's problems to me: how he was a dry drunk who couldn't control his meanness.

Greg was decent enough to work with, but this was Minneapolis. Blacks made up only six percent of the population, and anyone living in the suburbs and working in a hi-tech company would stand a good chance of having no contact whatsoever with blacks. Despite Minnesota's progressive image, I discovered more virulent and undisguised racism there than I'd ever seen.

Now that I was in the O., however, I didn't get as close to my co-workers as before. I was friendly on the job, but I couldn't talk to them about the rest of my life, or go out to drink with them, or invite them home. All that part of my life was closed. The relationships were limited, and I kept mostly to myself. But I could not manage to stay out of trouble with the foreman and found myself constantly on "punishment detail" for talking pro-union, or against the shop's sexism, or for refusing to do overtime. The vertical mill was the most boring and tedious job in the shop, and I ended up there, week after endless week, pounding bronze bars into a vice, milling them down to size and pounding bars into the vice and milling them down and pounding and milling and pounding until my foreman felt me squirming adequately under his thumb and gave me a reprieve. Then he would allow me a few weeks on the skilled work of setting up to cut slots on the delicate saw-toothed arbor mills—until our next confrontation.

During the day I began my organizational work at the bakery: the People's Nutritional Bakery Co-op. Jerri took me in on my first day. The bakery was located in St. Paul, a fifteen-minute freeway ride through downtown Minneapolis, past the old grain mills and elevators of General Mills and Pillsbury that stood on the banks of the Mississippi, disused now and waiting for an urban planner to gentrify them in an attempt to bring life back into downtown from the white, malled suburbs where it had fled.

The building sat on the edge of St. Paul's black neighborhood, a block down from the two porn theaters owned by the Alexander brothers, St. Paul's resident vice merchants. Jerri unlocked the door and took me into the office. It was a narrow room partitioned off from the production floor by sheetrock, with room for two desks down one wall and a chair for each desk taking up the rest of the space. Both desks were occupied: Walt, a man I didn't know, sat at one, on the phone, making sales calls, and Vida sat at the other, one hand running numbers on a business calculator, the other flipping through a pile of invoices, matching them to checks and preparing them in a batch for computer entry. Neither of them looked up or greeted us as we came in—this would have been seen as "social exchange" and not productive behavior.

I learned quickly that the computer, housed in another tiny partition next to this office, was the center of operations. The bakery and its "systems" were the pride of the O. Years had been spent, after its takeover during the mid-seventies, (when it had been, first, Our Daily Bread and then later The People's Co-op Bakery) developing computerized procedures. The goal was that the procedures would be so precise and comprehensive that more or less anyone could come in and, by following them, become productive as a bakery worker. We were eliminating the need to rely on one or more skilled individuals; through effective administration and scientific methods, people would be empowered and anyone could make good, nutritious bread.

To this end the day's orders were typed into the computer, and recipes for the appropriate number of bread batches were printed out. The mixer started the process, clocking in at about 5.00 A.M. He or she dumped flour from the overhead hoppers into stainless steel mixing bowls and measured out blocks of moist, cheesy yeast, and then shortening, salt, water, and specialty ingredients for each type of bread. The mixing bowl was attached to a mechanical mixer, and the dough hook was set to churning the mixture around for several minutes until the gluten began to form, long elastic fibers of it keeping the dough wrapped cleanly around the hook. Then the dough sat for a period of time, and, by that time the bench worker had to be ready, cleaned up, hair net on and a white apron tied over white pants and shirt.

Bench was physically the fastest job—not as heavy or precise as mixing, and not as hot as the ovens, but one had to work to the dough's schedule. Once the yeast was mixed in, the dough had life, and if it wasn't cut and thrown into the rounder and then caught, one, two, three, four, five loaves at a time as they flew out, rounded and kneaded by the mechanical, grooved spiral of metal, then the dough died or became overheated and wet and unworkable. Bench was the most pressured job—but I'd liked it, the times I'd had to sub for a worker out sick. If I found the right rhythm with the mixer, then it went along smoothly like a dance, and I'd end the shift feeling happy and muscular, my arms tired to the shoulders with the weight of warm bread dough.

The bench worker loaded the bread pans and set them on the conveyor. From there the oven worker put the pans on a rack in the steam heat of the proof box to encourage the dough to keep rising. The oven room was, of course, hot, and even in winter we kept the back door open to cool it off. Oven workers had to be strong, preferably tall enough to reach the oven easily, able to work long shifts and stay alert enough to catch the staggered times of each batch of bread in the proof box or oven. The job was nearly always filled by a young man. Today Kelly was there—he was a twenty-year-old black man from the neighborhood—it was his first job. Kelly had rotten teeth which Jerri tried to help him with; she found him a dentist, set up an appointment, and gave him a lift there. She was roundly criticized for this act. As production manager, she was not supposed to "personalize" her relationships with the co-op workers—she was to have purely a functional relationship with them. It was believed that personal relationships with people would color one's judgment, leading to political or organizational errors based on a bias towards people's personal problems rather than the common good, in this case, the good of the organization. Without this overview, the O. and its cadres would cease to be objective and would be unable to perform their historic function.

Despite his problems with his teeth, Kelly was a good oven worker, generally arriving on time, unlike other workers who we often had to roust from bed at 6.00 A.M. Sweat would run down his face as he stretched his hands in industrial oven mitts up to the highest racks; he'd grab four pans at a time, smash them up against the oven to loosen the bread, and then upend the pans on the slicing racks and shake out the steaming hot loaves.

Once the loaves had cooled, they were wheeled into the slicing room next door, where Colleen, delicate and quick-muscled, fed the loaves, again, four at a time, down the feeder, through the oscillating blades and caught them at the other end, fast, before the loaf fell apart into slices, and then slid it into a plastic bag. Speed, and the accuracy of movement, not strength, was important in the slicing room. The slicer's shift ended at one in the morning, with the bagged bread left sorted for each customer, ready for the drivers to load when their shift began at 4.00 A.M.

Turnover was high at the bakery. No one could live for long on the minimum wages, or stand the crazy shifts that varied from three to sixteen hours a day depending on production levels. Then there was the bizarre management: the secretive O. cadres who floated in and out of the bakery before or after their other jobs as printers, lawyers, programmers, or machinists, and whose tight-lipped, sad features must have engendered interesting conversations among the workers who were told nothing, of course, about the O.

Colleen was a bright young woman with a child, recently moved to the Cities from up north where she'd been laid off from a factory job at Arctic Cat. She later got promoted to a data entry position in the office, supposedly a big step for her development. Kelly had just arrived from Mississippi—we often attracted young black immigrants from Mississippi; there were few other jobs they could get with their strong accents and thin work histories. High school students like Dave and Wally could earn school credits by working afternoons with us. It was either the bakery or McDonalds or another fast food joint. They liked not having to go to school, but I shook my head at the idea that this was considered education. Perhaps it qualified as a class in the School of Hard Knocks.

The truck drivers were the most colorful of the bunch. Perhaps it was something to do with having to get up at 3.00 A.M. to get to work on time (which few of them actually managed). Lisa sported a crimson mohawk which it fell to me to ask her to cover with a hat in the interests of maintaining good customer relations. She quit over the issue. Or there was the time I had to ask the plump and unkempt Angela to wear deodorant after the dietician at one of our largest accounts called to complain about her odor. Mike was skinny, cheerful and sweet-smelling; he just couldn't get out of bed in time to make the delivery deadlines. We were always short of drivers.

My work began after the slicing and sorting was done. I came directly from the machine shop, still in my work clothes which smelled of sour coolant and burnt metal. I'd arrive at one o'clock and let myself in to the computer room, greeting the slicer in the typically short and distant manner of O. cadre (remembering we were not supposed to have personal or social contact with the bakery workers). If slicing was done already, I'd have to open up the dark bakery myself, disarm the alarm system and make my way through the front office, past the desks dusted with the flour of the day's production, into the even smaller computer room. Here I flipped on the fluorescent lights, relaxed my breath for a moment and listened to make sure the night noises of the empty building were all familiar ones. Then I took the customer invoices, started up the computer and entered into it any shorts or overs from that day's orders and printed corrected invoices. Again, the process was highly proceduralized; I had to use a checklist for each step, check it off, double count all the totals, double check each entry. If any mistakes were made, I would be accountable, and all mistakes *were* tracked down, the offending party being made to make a self-criticism as to why they had made such an error.

I drove back to Minneapolis on the empty freeway early in the morning, finally getting home to bathe and get to bed just before dawn. I climbed into bed next to Ted, who was far into his own tense and dreamless sleep by then, and I'd sleep for four hours or so, until eight o'clock, and then get up, drive

back across the river, just missing the rush hour traffic, to get back to the bakery for a morning shift as the customer service clerk. Now I spent my time on
the phone: placating our customers who'd gotten late deliveries, or whose
orders were short, or who couldn't stand anymore to place their orders to the
answering machine and wanted to know that a real human being existed at
the bakery. At lunch time, after dropping by one of the customer sites, I'd get
home, eat lunch and prepare my dinner and thermos for work. If I had time I
napped for an hour and then set off again, out to the industrial suburbs, to
spend the next eight and a half hours in the machine shop.

Weekends were spent doing household chores, writing summaries, or
back at the bakery, fighting a losing battle to keep it clean and free of rats, mice
and cockroaches so that the city inspectors wouldn't close it down.

Most of the time I was angry. I was tired all of the time. I had no time to
think and no longer had time to read. I existed in a kind of suspension, marked
by freeway drives across the city at odd hours of the day and night, or by
stolen hours of sleep, at home or work, hoping my roommates, or my co-
workers would not find me. I tried to keep writing my journal, but after a couple of months I realized that I had to conserve all of my energy just to get
through the day, and the entries became more and more sparse, with just the
occasional line raging at Ted for never spending time with me and for the
unapproachable distance that he put between us. Other times, I would just
write a rushed and bewildered entry wondering what the hell I was doing,
and what was the sense of this work, the schedule, the inhuman quality to life
in the O. But soon the entries petered out as I became absorbed in surviving
the life, and as my ability to question it became dampened by mental and
physical fatigue.

When I raised questions, either talking to Jerri or Ted, or in written
memos to leadership, now known as P.O.O. (we all received a memo to this
effect: P.S. was now P.O.O., an acronym that was never translated), it was like
trying to punch a hole in a soft balloon, answers would come back to cover my
questions, all the same, from each source, suffocating and impenetrable. Mostly,
though, the questions I had were countered by questions back to me.

"Have you looked at your Ideological Form recently?" said Jerri when I
complained about the unrelenting work.

"How much summary have you done this week?" asked Ted when I
asked for an explanation of how the work at the Bakery was a political act.

"How do you think you'll understand things if you don't struggle with
them yourself?" I was told by Jerri and Ted and, in memos, by P.O.O.

Through struggle, I was assured, both with the practice of what we were doing, and within the conditions that had been specifically set for my development, and through struggle to understand the theory of dialectics in general, and of the Internal Transformation Process in particular, then both the level of my practice and my contribution as a cadre would grow, as well as my understanding of the organization's purpose and methods. Of course, it was always said, there is no mystery to the purpose of the organization: it was to develop cadre who were capable of leading the revolutionary struggle.

"Do you think you're ready to do that yet? Are you developed enough to take leadership of a revolutionary struggle?"

"Of course not," I admitted. I knew that I couldn't take on responsibility for leading the struggle. That was why I had sought out this group in the first place, because I wanted direction, guidance—leadership.

Ted and I were married the first weekend of July, by chance one of the most popular weekends of the year for marriages. P.O.O. suggested it in one his memos typewritten on beige paper. It seemed the right thing to do, that if we were to have a child (this miraculous, almost magical concept) then it would be practical to be married. I wanted to be married to Ted, to be in a revolutionary marriage. It was the only way I could imagine marriage for myself. It was just two months after I'd arrived in Minneapolis, but as it was to be a revolutionary marriage, and we had made the decision already, to have a kid, then why delay? After all, I could get pregnant any time now. And I loved Ted, and I felt that he loved me, even though he was distant so often, and I was lonely a lot, waiting for those infrequent moments with him.

He'd get angry sometimes—I didn't know why—and then he would withdraw from me, far away into a place he could not even find himself, just a place of coping with his tasks, with holding down the equivalent of two full-time jobs, plus the extra tasks of summary and criticism. He would fade away from me into his own survival, leaving me bereft. But I was slowly learning to grab him when he was there and shout into his comatose ears that I was a human being, that we were in a relationship, that there was a minimum of "connection" that needed to happen if we were going to be together at all.

Sometimes he heard this and reappeared. Then we would talk and find a layer of ideas and laughter to rest on, and feel comfortable together the way we had the first time we'd met.

Our marriage, anyway, was to be a practical thing. Ted made the appointments at the photographer's and at the courthouse. We told no one. Why advertise it?—that would just be angling for "exchange value"; our marriage was not to be a commodity exchange, but a practical acknowledgement of the future shared responsibility we would have for our children. We would use the mechanisms of the State as long as they were, indeed, useful to us.

Nonetheless, Ted insisted that I wear a dress to our wedding. This seemed absurdly traditional to me, but it was clearly important to Ted, and he spoke about it with a certain authority in his voice which I took as it was meant: if I disagreed, I might become the target of a formal criticism. I swallowed my objections—there was hardly a principle at stake here, after all. As I didn't own a dress I spent an agonizing day at the downtown Dayton's trying to buy myself a dress that seemed appropriate for a revolutionary tying of ourselves, the one to the other. Eventually I bought a beige smock with a bright blue-and-turquoise front, now immortalized forever in our wedding picture taken by a sordid photographer who resorted to telling dirty wedding jokes to try to squeeze smiles from our nervous faces. Ted looks even worse than I, a forced smile, a pair of glasses and an uncomfortable suit being all that the camera captured.

The week before we got married Ted finally told his parents—only because they were going to be in town and for some reason, we had decided it would be wrong for them to come to the "wedding" (it cannot really be called a wedding; a wedding connotes festivities, a celebration) and made them promise not to arrive until the day after. This was our private business, protected in the way we were now used to protecting the rest of our lives, and we did not want them interfering.

And so, on the Saturday of July 2, 1982, after I had fought with my foreman who wanted me to work overtime that weekend, and after he had finally been convinced by the other workers that, indeed, getting married was a valid excuse for needing the weekend off, Ted and I dressed up in our wedding clothes and drove to the county courthouse. Here a friendly judge invited in her receptionist and secretary as witnesses, married us in a brief but 1980s kind of ceremony (leaving out the "obey" clause of the marriage vows), and, after we'd said our "I do's," she prodded us gently to kiss each other, which we did rather shyly, feeling the seriousness of the event in our own way, our secret unity, the Cause of the People tying us in our own hearts, and the small heady feeling of actually, now, us, being married.

We drove home, sunny, arm in arm, married. Ted had to stop on the way to make a couple of phone calls from a phone box, and then we changed into jeans and took off for our honeymoon. This consisted of an afternoon at William O'Brien State Park, an hour's drive away from the city.

When we arrived, we walked for a while and then sat by a small lake. Ted had worked most of the night before, and, while I sat, full of an uncomfortable stirring inside me, he fell asleep on the grass. I looked at him there, sleeping, and suddenly felt so alone. I pulled my knees up to my chest and watched the lake, the reeds shadowing the water, and rocked myself while Ted slept away the hours that were to be ours together. Such few moments that we had, and he slept on for one hour and then two as I contemplated this terrible thing I had done.

But later that night I was happy again. After he woke up, we changed back into our wedding clothes in a picnic shelter at the park and drove back to downtown Minneapolis. Ted had booked a table at Murray's Home of the Silver Butterknife Steak, and here we had steak and wine, the steak, soft enough, indeed, to cut with a butterknife, as advertised, and it was red and womblike in there with Victoriana velvet, candlelight and a professionally romantic violinist who serenaded our adventure. Then it became warm and happy as marrying is supposed to be.

CHAPTER 14

I sat on the edge of the bed again, naked, after I'd taken my shower to clean off the oil and metal dust from the shop. Ted was already in bed, half asleep after I'd woken him—it was after 2.00 in the morning. I sank my head into my hands.

"Bastards. Bastards! Oh, God, those fucking South African bastards, they killed her!"

My body shook, cold inside with grief but hot on the outside, sweating in the night heat of a Minnesota August. Ted held me, tried to comfort me but did not know the words.

I'd read the news that evening at the shop. I'd been in the canteen, drinking my tea at break and reading the paper. A one-column-inch article had caught my eye, headlined, "South African woman killed by bomb." A sixth sense warned me, told me something so I was almost ready when I read the words:

Maputo, Mozambique. A prominent white South African Communist, Ruth First, was killed yesterday by a letter bomb which she opened in her office at Maputo University. A colleague was also injured.

I sat with the paper for a few minutes, silent, in shock. Then Greg came to sit by me. He took a look at me and asked, "What's the matter Alex?"

"I just found out a friend of mine got killed," I said numbly. "I'm sorry, I can't talk about it, I've got to . . ."

I didn't know what I had to do, but I left the canteen, with the paper open at the article, my thermos on the table. I got down the stairs and walked out of the front door and into the dark of the parking lot. Now I could feel the breeze, a hot August breeze blowing dust around the lot, and I started walking down the row of new industrial buildings. I needed desperately to cry, and I dared not do it by the buildings, so I walked on until I found a field behind one of them, not yet built on—there were remnants of farmland reverting to prairie all around the new suburbs. And here I stopped, surrounded by tall grasses and weeds and the blowing and stutter and rustle of warm wind. I sat among the growing things and wept. I thought of Ruth. And Joe Slovo, her husband. And her daughter Robyn, my best friend when I was growing up in England. And Ruth, again, who had written to me funny, child-like letters from Africa; who sat working endlessly in her book-filled study while Robyn and I played, or schemed in our teenage years. Ruth had been a model for me, a revolutionary who had dedicated her life, like Joe, to the struggle in South Africa. And they had been succeeding! I could see that, in tiny steps, things were changing in Southern Africa—in Mozambique and Angola and Zimbabwe. Their struggle wasn't isolated now, they had bases in friendly border countries. Even people in Minneapolis had become educated, finally, about South Africa, after the Soweto riots.

And they had killed her. Of course. I cried again, weeping into the grass, sitting cross-legged in my machinist's apron, knowing I was risking trouble because I would be late back from break. But I could not go back in until my tears had cleared.

I got up and walked for a while longer, and finally turned and went back to the factory. I was still disoriented and dazed and didn't know what to do, didn't know if I could face working. So I called Ted from the pay phone at the door. I told him what had happened, and he tried to reach for words of consolation.

"Will you stay at work?" he asked.

Somehow I already knew what the proper response should be. "I think it'll be hard. But I suppose it would be the best thing. It would be the most productive thing. I'll try to stay. I'll see you at home."

I put down the phone, blew my nose, breathed quietly in the corner there a few times and then shoved open the main door to the grinding noise of machine tools, and the tinny sound of country music played above it.

Either Greg had told the foreman, or I just wasn't noticed, but I didn't get caught coming in late, and I planted myself dully at my machine and started turning out parts. Greg tried talking to me, but I sat numbly, ignoring him as he talked until he finally looked at me quizzically and shut up.

I put in those brittle-edged, brass parts, ran them through the carbon-tipped cutter, hosed them down with the air hose and measured them, not really giving a damn if they were the right size, or how fast I was working. I would sit out the shift if it killed me. This was the most productive thing to do, this was in memory of Ruth, to stay at my post. I would remember her with work. Every tenth part I had to take into inspection for quality control. So in I went, to the scope that magnified the tiny rectangles for precision measurement, and checked my part. Jeff, the QA guy, saw me.

"Why so glum, Alex?" he asked kindly.

But I couldn't talk about it, or the tears would flood back. I kind of squeaked as I talked, not looking at him, trying to hide my eyes in the scope. "I just got some very bad news tonight."

He patted me gently on the back.

"Hang in there, girl—don't worry about the work too much—here, I'll check that for you."

He took the part, and sent me back out to the shop, and the rest of the evening he came by my station to pick up my parts for inspection, not asking me any questions but just trying to help.

These are the kinds of things I remember about people. The little things they don't need to do.

When the shift was done at midnight, I drove over to the bakery. I was glad it was night and the freeway was so empty because my eyes were still so blurry I could hardly see the road.

I was being trained in computer operations by Debbie, a cadre I'd recently met, and she was already waiting for me in the hot, cramped computer room. The work was all laid out and she was busy making notes about something, looking alert as if it were not after midnight, even though I knew she'd been up since six that morning. I hardly knew her, but she intimidated me. There was something about her that was hard edged, her lips pressed tightly together, her brown eyes only settling on me in expectation of an answer, always ready in judgment, somehow, that I would be found wanting. As I sat down I turned to her, "I might not be very productive tonight. I'm very upset, I just found out that a good friend of my family's was killed."

"What happened?" she asked.

"She was killed by the South Africans—I'm sure it was the Security Police or the Special Branch. They sent her a bomb—she opened a letter bomb."

Debbie was sympathetic.

"Well, we'll just do what we can. You must continue the struggle for her, for your friend, mustn't you?"

Later I wrote to Robyn and to Joe. A heartfelt expression of loss, one of thousands they received from around the world. And still later I got an envelope, addressed with my codename, Claire. Inside were two clippings. One was an reprint of a speech by Mozambique's president, Samora Machel, that eulogized Ruth and praised her contribution and sacrifice. The other was a copy of a poem by him mourning the death of his wife Josina. Debbie handed me the envelope at one of our late-night meetings. These clippings were precious to me, expression of a shared grief from my comrades, even though I didn't know which one had sent them.

I didn't know what had happened in that house, 801 Sullivan, the duplex where Ted, Jerri, and I lived. But something had. My first knowledge of it was when the doorbell rang. I'd already been there two or three months, and this was the first time the doorbell had ever rung. No one ever came to the house, no one knew our address; we all had post office boxes to receive our mail and I had been explicitly told never to give my address or phone number out, not to my old friends in California, and particularly not to my family. When I questioned this, I was told that it was, at this point, primarily for ideological reasons rather than security reasons. Of course, security was always important, but there was a need in my development to take a firm class stand in relation to my family and to connect to them only under conscious, planned and functional conditions. In a memo, P.O.O. told me that it was expected that I wouldn't understand this yet, but that I would in time.

Even other cadre didn't come to the house in those years. If we needed to contact each other, then we called from a pay phone (never from home—house-to-house or house-to-program calls were strictly forbidden). A special code was used. Each person in a house had a certain number of "rings" assigned to them—my code was two rings. If the phone rang twice, stopped, then rang again, it was a call for me, and only I was to answer it. The phone was never answered on the first set of rings, unless it rang more than five times, in which case it was assumed to be one of the rare outside calls, perhaps from a utility company or someone's workplace. This system prevented anyone in a house from knowing which cadre were in contact with the others and was part of the elaborate security procedures. It was a serious offence to pick up someone else's call and so, every time the phone rang, you stopped what you were doing and automatically counted rings.

I used to dread hearing my two rings. It usually meant that I had to come in for an extra shift at the bakery, to take up the few hours of free time I still had, or to cut into my sleep hours, already below what I needed to be able to effectively function. Or maybe I was being called in to help on some other program or was to receive a memo or criticism. Anyway, other cadre never came to the house, and if we needed to meet, then it was at one of various coffee shops, rotated so that we would not become noticeable as "regulars"—and we did tend to stand out because we usually went to all-night coffee shops, our meetings often having to take place after midnight due to our program responsibilities, and then we would huddle secretively in a booth, spending an hour over one cup of coffee, with papers spread out discussing ideological development, or the daily details of the bakery, or other programs.

So, when the doorbell rang that day, it was such an unusual occurrence that I was immediately on the alert. I opened the inside door and looked through the small glass pane. A young white man stood there, initially sympathetic in appearance: about thirty, with dark hair, just a little long, and a mustache. I opened the outside door a little—now I could see he was well dressed, in a black overcoat against the early cold of a Minnesota fall, with a scarf tucked neatly beneath his coat lapels.

"Hello?" I said.

He reached inside his coat without replying and pulled out a leather wallet, and in a kind of slow motion I saw him flip open an I.D. card. I had time to see the picture; the mustache stood out first of all, but then my eyes moved to the other side of the card and with a rush of blood to my face and an invisible gearing up of my heart I read the bold black letters: F.B.I.

"Is there a Kristin Olson living here?" he asked.

"No." I said.

"Do you know where she is?"

"No, I've never heard of her. Why do you want to know?"

He tried moving closer to the door, backing me up into the house. But I stood my ground and let him come into the no-man's land of space that surrounded me, usually kept free of other people, and I faced him, unyielding, in the doorway.

"We're trying to locate her for some inquiries. I'd like to come in, please. Just for a few questions."

"Uh . . . no!" I stepped back and grabbed the door handle, ready to close the door on him. Now that I knew who he was, I could recognize him without trouble. I knew that I didn't have to answer questions, and I certainly didn't have to let him in.

He hesitated. People were often misled by their first impression of me; I had a soft, babyish face that made them think I was a pushover. In fact, when my back was against the wall, I had reserves of persistence and force that surprised them. And so, he now was surprised as I shut the door and stood breathless in the hallway trying to think what to do next. Then I heard him shout through the door.

"You'd talk to me if you knew there'd been a murder in this house!"

I backed up further, through the inside door into the living room, and I waited there, with the door ajar until I heard him turn angrily and leave. My hands were shaking. Jesus, what were the F.B.I. after? I'd always hated the F.B.I.—they were the agents of COINTELPRO that had slaughtered so many Black Panthers, and hounded others active in the movement. The F.B.I. was my enemy, and here they were, trying to find someone I didn't know, but who I assumed was in the organization. They must be trying to infiltrate, break our security, I didn't really know what, but if someone was at risk from them, I needed to act quickly. Jerri was my contact. I needed to find her and report this. She would know how to notify the right people.

Grabbing my coat, wallet, and phone book, I flipped my number card in the hallway, set the alarm system (grateful for it now, and seeing its function clearly), double-locked the two doors and drove off to the pay phone at the Golden Valley shopping center. As I drove, I checked my rear-view mirror carefully and made sure no one was following me. My breathing was still out of control, but I felt strong, and this lifted me from my usual state of resistant resentment that characterized most of my work in the organization. My mission was a simple one: to notify P.O.O., through Jerri, of the threat. That others would deal with it, would know what the agent's visit represented, was a source of satisfaction to me; I was part of a cell structure, and it had proved effective. When our security was threatened, I could tell them nothing; the need-to-know principle meant that I could not jeopardize the organization, or even myself. We were part of the resistance, and I was going to do my bit efficiently and quietly. Without delay, the center would know and, with the information I passed on, would act.

So I called Jerri at work and, still catching my breath, gave her the details, then returned home and went to work at the machine shop as usual, feeling my separateness from my co-workers more necessary and acceptable now.

The next day Jerri woke me early to meet with her before she went to work. She unplugged the phone and turned on the radio.

"You should prioritize writing up a report about what happened yester-day," she said under her breath in a kind of stage whisper that I had to strain to hear. It aggravated me that with all the security precautions—the radio on, the whispering—it was always hard to hear what was being said. It made me so tired, like trying to decipher a conversation in a foreign language where one must lean forward and listen with every ounce of attention. It was exhaust-ing, but it was the normal manner of communication among most of the cadre. I, however refused to speak in a whisper; it seemed absurd to me.

"Okay." I said, out loud.

"Now, the tactic they use is to try to intimidate you. You mustn't ever open the door to them. I was told that another tactic is that they'll do something, and then sit back and watch how people act, like throwing a ball at a set of bowling pins and watching how they scatter. Then they can pick up on all the pieces. So, next time don't do anything out of the ordinary, like rushing out to call peo-ple. The important thing is not to make any unnecessary connections."

"I tried to make sure I wasn't followed," I said.

"No, that's fine. You did fine. It's just a good opportunity to learn how to respond in this kind of condition. And they'll say anything to try to get infor-mation."

Jerri was teaching me, not criticizing so much as guiding. Clearly she had reported the incident and was bringing back to me the learned lessons of leadership.

"Anyway, there was a problem here some years back—there was a drug house across the street, and there'd been a conflict with one of the drug deal-ers. That's why we've tried to clean the place up—one of the goals is to use our labor to help raise up the standard of the block.

"The other thing is, just in case they come around again, you should make an appointment to see a counselor at Group Health. We'll start build-ing a case that the State has been harassing you. Tell the counselor that you've been real upset by their coming round, scared that they'll come to your job—that kind of thing. Scared that you'll lose your job. It's a way for us to take the initiative, not just sitting back to let them have easy access."

She sat back in her chair and let her voice come up to its normal level. "Are you clear on that?"

"Yes. I'll make the appointment today, and I'll get that report done."

I felt I'd done okay. I would write a clear and detailed report, and I was almost looking forward to the bit of acting I would do at the doctor's office—portraying a nice suburban English girl, frightened to death by this unprecedented visit of the F.B.I., a question of mistaken identity, a sweet innocent being foolishly dragged into some dark world she couldn't even imagine existing. Yes, I would enjoy that. I was learning some of the skills of my chosen profession—I wanted to be a professional revolutionary, and I was learning to fight the State, turning its own tricks against it. And I was trustworthy. I would never breach the security of the organization. Despite my misgivings about some of the methods of the O., its seriousness and the tightness of its structure were attributes I respected deeply. I knew that the State could so easily smash us without that structure, and that the smashing would be a violent thing. The history of the progressive movement in the United States, which I had studied in such detail, was filled with murders and betrayals—from the Wobblies to the Panthers, people had paid with their lives for trying to change the country without adequate discipline, security, and structure. My heart ached when I thought of Ruth—security was a matter of life and death; this I knew. And so I carefully performed my piece of the task.

Later that day Jerri added some more work for the household as a whole, including Vida upstairs. We were to go through all our papers at once and remove anything of an organizational nature. That meant any memos about the organization's theory and ideology, any memos with our codenames on them, any memos of P.O.O.s and so forth. These would be stored in a special locked cabinet that had been bolted to the basement floor. We also reviewed the rest of our security procedures and were told to minimize any contact with other cadre for the next few weeks.

I padded down to the basement, not carrying the laundry basket this time, but instead a thin pile of manila folders holding the "closed" materials that were to be hidden from the prying eyes of the F.B.I. It occurred to me that, if the F.B.I. were to raid the house, perhaps they could just as well take a crowbar and jimmy up this cabinet and take it away with them. As a security precaution it didn't seem entirely rational, but I would do what I was told nonetheless.

I set my folders down on the concrete basement floor, took the little silver key that Jerri had given me and unlocked the cabinet. The others had already put their files away, stored neatly in green hanging file holders. I nudged them towards the back to make room for mine and as I did, one fell open and I saw the words: "Method of Correction: NB201 will be paddled by a member of the HH. He will terminate the PR." These words were highlighted in pink.

I knew what HH meant—that stood for Household. And NB201—that was Ted's code number at the bakery. I wondered what it meant to be paddled. I imagined an old wooden butter paddle, the kind of thing used on farms fifty years ago. Paddled? The only way someone could be paddled *by* someone (a member of the HH, in this instance), is if he or she was hit. Why had they hit him? Because of a relationship—a PR?

I shut the folder and stuffed my files in next to the others. My knees were sore from kneeling on the damp concrete. I stood up and brushed the dust off my jeans. I shook my head: an image of Vida dutifully beating Ted with a two-by-four played itself in my mind's eye. I pushed the image away. Away into the far corners. This was something about which I could not make sense, and I would not try. Better not to think about it at all.

I locked the box, climbed the stairs, shut the door to the basement and returned the key to Jerri's desk.

CHAPTER 15

I didn't know where Debbie lived, but I met her often, either in restaurants or at the bakery in the new basement office that a group of us cadre constructed over one weekend. We had expanded the upstairs production floor into our old office space following an announcement by leadership that our goal was to become the premier wholegrain bakery in the Twin Cities. By the next year, we were targeted to make two million dollars in sales—quite a leap from our current level of quarter of a million. Jerri and Debbie worked long hours devising and implementing a plan to meet these goals. First and foremost was the need to reorganize production in our small, crumbling facility so that our capacity could expand.

Debbie was now the production manager and my new contact. She and I were to transform the purchasing side of things. I started attending a vocational technical school out in the suburb of White Bear Lake in order to get my Purchaser's Certificate. I was now working full time, printing invoices late at night after my shift, taking morning classes and running back to the bakery before work to do the purchasing. I awaited our occasional days off with longing and anticipation as a time to sleep, or to be outside: out of the machine shop, out of school, out of the bakery's concrete basement. I soon learned that other cadre also looked forward to these holidays; to them a day off was precious—it was time to catch up on program work, to write long-delayed self-criticisms, or to do household chores. Having a holiday, to my comrades, was a chance to wade through the backlog that, if found out, would be a source of vitriolic criticism.

I was beginning to crack with the fatigue and pressure. One day I talked with Debbie about it during one of our late night rendezvous at Perkins. I waited until the uniformed waitress had brought our cups of coffee and left us alone again at the table.

"I can't keep up this pace—I have to get some space, to deal with what I feel about things. I don't have any time to think things through. That's what makes me so resistant to doing the work. I don't understand the point of so much of it."

"Do you think," she replied, "that is the principal problem, whether you understand it or not? Perhaps you need to look at why these conditions have been set for you?"

"Well, that's what I mean—I don't even have time to do that. It's all I can do to just keep my head above water. And now I'm just starting to get depressed and angry."

I leaned over the coffee shop table, hoping she would hear me.

"Nobody *talks* to each other here. It's all so *functional.*"

"Do you think you've learned anything so far, in the O?" Debbie responded, inching herself backwards in her chair, away from my dismay.

"Sure. Machining, programming, I'm learning the purchasing stuff now. And I guess, discipline. And looking at my internal contradictions and motivations."

"Do you think those are concrete, material things? Do you see those as necessary building blocks for the struggle? Were you doing anything material with people in California?"

"Yes, they are material things, and I can see it's been important for me to learn those skills. But what about *feelings*—isn't there a place for them too?"

I couldn't describe what I meant. I felt so childish, trying to grab at this *feeling* I'd had in San Francisco: the warmth of my friends, the open discussion, the support. Debbie looked stern, holding pen to paper, making notes about our discussion. She was obviously impatient—I was taking up so much of our meeting time with this wispy stuff. She was here to discuss purchasing arrangements for the new truck, and instead she had to deal with my internal ideological problems. But as a committed, high level cadre, she controlled herself and thought hard about how best to deal with me. As my contact, it was her job to bring me development and to struggle with me for clarity.

She looked up at me with her deep brown eyes and pursed lips and tapped her high-heeled foot under the table.

"You must struggle with the practice. We can sit here and discuss and discuss, but the only way to internalize it, to take your development seriously, is to work with it in practice. I will think about the issues you've raised, and I'll get back to you after I've done some further summary."

We left the coffee shop and arranged to meet the next night to continue the discussion.

* * *

The following evening I thought hard during my work shift, but I was unable to gather anything more concrete than this intangible concept of "feelings" that I knew would not satisfy Debbie. But I didn't have to worry because she came to the meeting fully prepared.

"I think the first thing is," she said, "to deal with the schedule problems. You've said that you don't have time to do all your tasks and that you don't feel you can keep your head above water. Well, other people are able to accomplish the same, or a heavier workload, so clearly it's not an objective problem. What you need to look at is where your time is going. This is the PSO3 form. You probably haven't seen it before, but it's very helpful in getting an objective assessment of your time usage."

She laid a piece of paper on the table. On it was a simple ruled grid with typed instructions on the bottom. There was a column for each day of the week and rows for each hour of the day—like a school child's class schedule. At the end of each day, she explained, I was to fill this out, using different colors for each kind of activity. Suggested categories were: work, programmatic work, study, summary, household chores, eating, sleep, and sex.

At the end of the week, the hours for each category were to be toted up and listed at the bottom of the sheet, and the form would be centralized, via Debbie, to P.O.O. She told me that P.O.O. would probably not respond to the form itself; it was primarily a tool for me to become conscious of how I used my time. It was for my own accountability. But, I thought, P.O.O. would now be in a position to know how many hours I slept, when I snatched a half-hour nap before work, or when I stole off to a lake to sit in the sun by the water—as I had done two or three times that year.

I took the forms with me and over the next weeks devised a pseudo schedule. Five to six hours a night were colored in blue for sleep. This was the maximum time deemed acceptable for such an unproductive activity. P.O.O., Jerri told me, rarely slept more than four hours a night. I colored in pink about an hour a day for study and summary and the rest was taken up by green and yellow for my two jobs at the machine shop and the bakery. I could not bring myself to pick up the sexual purple crayon. Let that be implied in the blue sleep hours.

And the lesson was learned. My schedule was no worse than anyone else's, even though my sleep was broken into two short slices every twenty-four hours. Obviously, if I concentrated on my work, and on that only, then I could get things done. It was only my selfish desire to have time to myself that was getting in the way. I would not complain about my schedule again.

* * *

In preparation for its projected eight hundred percent growth, the bakery was being transformed back into its original state: that of a co-operative. When the O. took over the People's Co-op Bakery, they had turned it into a corporation—supposedly to make it more attractive as a loan risk for the banks. Now there was a new initiative to return it to a co-op, which was to be a new, higher stage of development. Because there had been such an advance in the production and management procedures, we were told that now it was at a point where the workers could have a real relationship of ownership to it. The higher level cadres had developed a document of "Rights and Responsibilities" that the new co-op "worker-owners" would have to sign in order to keep their jobs. This transition had taken up much of leadership's focus for the last months, but I was at too low a level to be involved with it, other than attending a preparation meeting for the big announcement to the workers.

Everything was planned out to the minutest detail. The workers were assessed as to their possible responses; strategy and tactics were in place to isolate the dissidents and to support those who would stay. It was expected that some would react and they would either be encouraged to leave as soon as possible, or they would simply be fired.

A meeting was called for all workers and and the O. management staff. This itself caused ill-feeling because it meant that workers had to come in on Saturday, their one day off, as we refused to close down production for staff meetings.

The meeting was held in the basement. The basement flooded regularly when the rains were too hard for the St. Paul sewers to handle, and one time Debbie had been down there, broomstick in hand, trying to kill a pair of rats that had been flushed up along with raw sewage. After that incident I'd had a certain awe for Debbie, wading ankle deep in sewer water determined to kill rats for the common good. At the same time, I also became nervous of going down there whenever stocks of plastic bread bags and twist ties had to be replenished. I kept a sharp eye out for small, moving objects: rats scared me. (I was never able to re-read Orwell's 1984, much as I admired it, as I couldn't bear anticipating the rat scene. I could not shake the horror of it, fiction notwithstanding.)

An attempt had been made to brighten up the lunch area in the basement. A plastic, red-checkered tablecloth was laid over the wooden lunch table. Orange juice and whole wheat chocolate chip cookies were served. Large posters explaining the "Rights and Responsibilities" were hung around the dingy walls, along with charts showing the expected phenomenal growth of the bakery.

Cindy, who was an attorney and on the board of the bakery, had appeared for the meeting—this was the first time I'd ever met her. She'd come by the duplex at 801 once in a while to see Nancy, her daughter, but we had never been introduced. She was one of several O. lawyers. Most O. cadre had been instructed to become either computer programmers or lawyers. Other O. attorneys I knew included Kristin, a labor lawyer, and George, a successful corporate attorney. George drove a brand-new leather-seated Camry, and I'd been told, when I commented on it, that he needed it for his job; to gain legitimacy, it was important to keep up the external appearances.

Cindy was not an active member of the staff, and none of the workers had ever seen her before. I no longer remember how her presence was explained. But after Debbie opened the meeting and introduced her, she slowly and monotonously went over the long "Rights and Responsibilities" document. The Responsibilities had to do with the workers being accountable for production and quality, reducing absenteeism and tardiness and, most significant, as newly self-employed workers (because the structure of the co-op was that each worker owned a part of it and was, therefore, self-employed) they would be responsible for paying their own employment tax.

There was no corresponding pay increase to make up the extra seven percent tax that workers would now have to pay. Cindy assured them that the benefits would be long term for those who stuck with the bakery, and she then gave the floor to Debbie who painted a vision of the bright future we all had as the bakery moved towards its goal of dominance in the Twin Cities wholegrain bread market. There was no actual worker representation on the board of this newly-reformed worker-owned co-op. The board was hand-picked and consisted solely of O. cadres.

I was very distressed as I sat in that meeting in the basement. The bakery workers looked as cynical and suspicious as I felt as we heard the starry-eyed, deeply sincere presentations of Cindy and Debbie, each wearing their matronly interpretations of dress-for-success business wear: Cindy in her typically dull knee-length skirt and sweater and Debbie showing a little more life in a bright red dress that set off her dark cap of hair, dark eyes, and small, pale face.

I had asked Jerri and Debbie at the early preparation meeting for cadres, what the point of the whole thing was—didn't it seem like all the workers were getting was more responsibility and less money? It didn't seem like a real co-op to me at all.

"It's a new stage," replied Jerri.

"The benefits will be long term," added Debbie, "You can't just look at it in financial terms, but in structural terms. Each worker will get a dividend instead of a wage—this is a great step forward—we're changing the relations of production here. And as profits increase, their dividend will increase. They will finally have an actual interest in the productivity of the bakery. It has taken a lot of long-term planning to get here. We had to change the original form of the co-op because we couldn't make the leap to rationalized production in that old, ultra-Left form. We needed to pass through a stage of bourgeois management. But now we've achieved a great advance in the rationalization of production and we're offering the workers an opportunity to come in at the ground floor and benefit from all the labor that's gone into this."

"But isn't the effect that everyone's getting a wage cut?" I persisted. "I mean, they were already only earning minimum wage, and now it's gone below that."

"But they have *ownership* now. This is something none of them would ever have the opportunity to have before."

I couldn't shake my feeling of distress. This was not what I was fighting for: to bring the abysmally low wages of the bakery workers down still more and to set on their already overworked shoulders the additional burdens of their new "responsibilities." I was also disturbed by the combination of the planning behind their backs and the coldness of the relationships between them and us, the cadres. I had never wanted to be a manager, and here I was, filling in for Jerri as production manager, being discouraged from developing any friendship or closeness with the workers and feeling deeply alienated in the process.

Again I was told by Debbie: "What do you think will happen if you become socially connected with the bakery workers? How will you be able to have an objective relationship with them? We have to keep the overall goals in mind, and the bakery must raise production standards, raise sales, expand. Friendship networks invariably deteriorate into power cliques—just like in the old food co-ops. We learned that lesson through struggle. I know that you missed that stage, but you must have examples of that from your experience in San Francisco."

Well, I had. I remembered well the cliques of the Women's Union, of the Mass Intermediate Socialist Organization, of the Noe Valley Community Food Store, and of the People's Warehouse. I had so often been the victim of these cliques; excluded, made to feel inferior, not listened to. So I tried hard to accept the notion of political, ideological unity and of objective relationships designed to achieve a specific, material goal.

Nonetheless, I could not totally ignore what I felt about the new co-op structure. I thought it was a con, however sincerely Jerri and Cindy and Debbie believed in it.

After the meeting nothing much changed. There was some grumbling in the ranks, but no one left immediately. Only Helga and her husband threatened to cause problems. Helga was a large, tough woman who'd been born and brought up in a small German town in northern Minnesota. The town was so German that this had been Helga's first language, and she still carried a thick Minnesota-German accent. Her husband was also a large, tough German; a survivalist who kept a stock of rifles and canned goods in his basement and, if not a member, was certainly a good candidate for Posse Comitatus, the white supremacist vigilante group. He did not like paying taxes in the first place, even to Ronald Reagan's government, and he made a fuss when Helga's wages took that extra seven-percent hit. But, as she was our best worker, smart, and strong enough to haul 100-pound bags of flour, thus qualifying her for the senior position of mixer, Debbie paid a great deal of attention to mollifying her and offered up a rare raise to compensate. Helga's Jim calmed down for a while, but she left the bakery soon afterward for a job in a machine-screw shop. I admired Helga because she was tougher and smarter than her husband, this proven when she went hunting with him and his pals and the men came back empty-handed while she bagged two deer. One kill would have been a coincidence, a lucky break, but two showed a satisfying combination of female strength, intelligence, and ability. It was poetic justice that supremacist Jim found himself outmatched by his own wife.

As the transition to a co-op took place, I became more and more disaffected. I had done no political work in the year that I had been in Minneapolis, and I saw no indications of any being done in the organization. At the same time, Ted and I continued to be distant from each other. The days dragged on with their unrelenting schedule. Late at night, in bed, I would try to remember the sound of the crickets from the summer before, because that was the only thing that seemed alive to me. Life at the house was dead and stultified. Jerri would come in for a few minutes at a time and stand at the fridge picking at leftovers like an anorexic teenager. And when Ted was home, he'd sit at the table, his gaze far away, or his head bent to the sports pages. He ate and ate large quantities of calories to fuel his body for the twenty-hour days while his mind ached off in another direction so that he did not have to think about what he was doing.

At night we made love by the calendar, trying to get pregnant in a scientific and functional way. No sex for the few days preceding my ovulation, and then sex once or twice a day for the four peak fertility days. No sex when we felt like it, and too much of it when we were tired, on different schedules, wanting only to catch up on sleep. But we were diligent and determined and we followed the program. We would not fail through lack of trying. Every morning I took my temperature and recorded it on a chart, tested my cervical mucus and recorded that. Ted participated as much as he could, entering the figures on the chart, helping me remember all the things we needed to do to keep track of my ovulation cycle.

After a year I was still not pregnant, and I had entered an overwhelming world where I followed my body helplessly as it swelled up each month in a hormonal charge of nest building, readying itself for the fertilized egg, all hot and fat and active with preparation. Only to leak out slowly each time in a delayed and crampy puncture to my expectation. Each month became more painful as the hope rose higher and fell lower in a stormy cadence that I could not share.

I had begun to really want a baby—this was a new feeling—before, it had been a kind of abstract, intellectual idea. But now, I wanted to feel that life growing in me. It became painful to go to the supermarket because I could not bear to see other women who were pregnant. What these women seemed to get so easily was off-limits to me. In some part of my mind I thought, too, that having a baby would be a reason to take some time off from the crazy schedule. Perhaps it would be some time to focus on something to do with myself.

I couldn't explain to Ted the feeling I had when I saw a pregnant woman, or the feeling of failure and loss when I saw the blood spotting as I began my period. He was pushing for medical intervention and wanted me to go to the next stage of diagnostic procedures: a salpingogram to shoot dye up through my cervix and into the fallopian tubes, a laparoscopy to peer at my tubes through tiny slits in my abdomen, or a uterine biopsy. I wasn't ready for any of these; I mistrusted doctors and feared any kind of intervention into my body. So I kept my sadness to myself in order to avoid his "struggling" with me to start the medical procedures.

And in keeping that sadness inside, a kind of sullenness overtook me, a meanness of spirit as I tried to protect myself; a crazy quietness that shouted at the others, in silence, to leave me alone. All I wanted was closeness. It felt the same as my childhood home where, to protect myself, I had developed a meanness and selfishness in order not to go crazy, because my sister, who did not have these qualities, just blew up, went over the top, popped. Her core was transparent like a glass fish and everything went straight to the inside of her like rusty arrows cracking that delicate covering, and all of it got mixed up and mad. I, on the other hand, covered myself in a blanket of dark and bided my time until I could make good my escape.

Now, as then, I became depressed and closed in on myself. I began to make mistakes at work. It reminded me of my last days with the Intercommunal Survival Committee when, despite ten or twelve hours on the street, I could only sell two copies of the Black Panther Party newspaper. I was becoming paralyzed by my disunity and isolation.

Finally, in a flurry of anger and despair, I wrote an unguarded memo to P.O.O:

To: P.O.O.
From: Claire/NB25

I am clearly not thinking objectively right now. I feel deeply resentful whenever I am given tasks. I don't understand the purpose of the bakery, I don't like the way workers are treated there, and, above all, I still don't understand the level of disconnection that exists between cadre. I suggest I take a break for a couple of months to think over my commitment to the O.

When P.O.O. received this, he quickly arranged for an ideological "hearing," in order to determine what to do. Ted was to be there as well as Vida, Jerri, and the scowl-faced Debbie.

It was at this meeting I first discovered that only five houses down from 801, at 905 Sullivan, there was another O. cadre duplex. This address had been passed to me in a memo, and I was told to leave work early (I was still on second shift, while most of the other cadre worked nine to five) and ring the front doorbell. So I parked my car at my house, 801, and walked up the block to 905. It had obviously once been a single family home, but was now chopped into two; the rooms were small and dark, like 801, but much more rundown. Some of the walls were just bare sheetrock and tape. An old curtain separated one room from another. And the stairs were broken and dangerous. As I entered I saw Cindy, Nancy's mother, leave the lower apartment of the duplex. "Oh," I thought, "So that's where she lives. Well, at least it's close to Nancy." But it was unsettling to find that for a year I'd lived down the block from other cadres and had no idea. Secrets were certainly well kept.

I came into the dull, unornamented living room and sat on the one empty chair. Five chairs had been arranged in a circle, four of which were already occupied. Ted looked sheepish and sad, his sandy head bowed, as the three women cadres wrote preparatory notes in their notepads with a businesslike air.

Debbie opened the meeting, speaking quietly. "We are here to look at the contradictions in 25's practice, and to determine the correct conditions for her further development. There has been a significant amount of decay and stagnation. However, she has expressed an interest in taking steps to turn this around. She has also accepted that her memo to P.O.O. was subjective and did not move the process forward. The purpose of this meeting is to provide a struggle condition in which 25 may view her practice."

Debbie looked up at me. "You may begin," she ordered.

I was quite nervous, but I had already separated myself a little from the O. I knew that I wanted to take some time out, and I was willing to listen to people's comments, and I was also willing, on some level, to accept the "steps" that they came up with. But within myself, I was clear that I needed a break. I could not continue as things had been going. There was not enough there for me.

"I've been feeling very subjective and demoralized. I can't seem to understand why we spend so much time trying to run a business. What is it for? How are we organizing people? It's so disconnected from politics."

Debbie intervened. "I believe that's been discussed at some length with you—by Jerri and others. You've been told time and again that it will take getting involved in the practice in order grasp the essence. Perhaps you should focus more on what is happening in the PR with Ted."

Ted shifted in his chair at the mention of his name. The corners of his eyes drooped like a little boy on the verge of tears. I felt sorry for him, but I was angry too—he had left me in this mess, left me to "struggle through the contradictions" on my own, offered me little, if any support.

"Well, Ted thinks I've been wallowing in subjectivity. I don't think I'd call it that. I just know I've been feeling there are real problems here that aren't getting addressed. That's why I want to take off for a while, get away and try to figure out what it is that's bothering me. Step back from things for a bit. And there just doesn't seem to be any connection between me and Ted right now."

Debbie looked pointedly at Vida, who referred to her notepad and then spoke. "You seem to be concerned so much with yourself. You spend a lot of time wondering about why you don't understand things and how that affects your well-being."

I liked Vida. She got on with her own work, but she wasn't bitter and judgmental like Debbie. Yet now she was obliged to criticize me. She continued, tucking a thick shank of her black hair behind her ear. "You say you're concerned for others, but I think that's just your self-image. It actually appears that you are only concerned for yourself, that you see yourself as the arbiter of what is right or wrong. Yet at the same time you rarely bring struggle to other people? Can you say you've really internalized your assessment?"

Now Debbie joined in again: "You want some time off. Supposedly to help you think clearly. But you look at leaving like a shopping trip. As a jaunt. Not as a serious questioning of your fundamental commitment to the struggle, or as any reflection of your organizational discipline. The main issue that you have to deal with is your unwillingness to accept leadership, and the fact that you want Ted to follow you away from the struggle."

I glanced up at her. I didn't want to take Ted out of the O. But I didn't want to lose him either. That was why I'd stayed as long as I had. I felt comfortable with Ted; happy in a funny way. I had no family to go to, no community any more. God knows I didn't want to be cast out into the galaxies, a lost star wandering the universe, unattached and hopeless. But I had to try now to have this break, to move away. I knew what the O. was doing made no sense, and I could not accept it anymore.

Ted said nothing during the meeting. Jerri took notes, looking as if her mind was elsewhere, probably worrying about production at the bakery. It was agreed, finally, that I should move out as soon as possible from 801, find a room for three months and spend that time reflecting on my practice. Debbie summed up: "It has been said that, given 25's property of value is 'TAKE', or 'OBTAIN,' that if she does not struggle with her bourgeois side, then all she will do is to try to gain as much from any revolutionary organization she is part of as she can, and that what she gains will only be for her personal benefit, as a step up in a desperate attempt at personal achievement."

Debbie's lips grew tighter, the acne scars in her white and pretty face stretched. "If her motion is allowed to run its course, then the only logical conclusion is that she will leave the O. and not be satisfied until she has pulled 201 (Ted) out with her. This shows her fundamental lack of respect for the revolutionary quality of 201's commitment to struggle. 25 is to move out immediately and to remove herself from programmatic work. She is not to continue in the PR as it is based merely on an exchange of value. She must summarize and come to understand the meaning of the Internal Trans-formation Process."

The Demand for Purity

In the thought reform milieu, as in all situations of ideological totalism, the experiential world is sharply divided into the pure and the impure, into the absolutely good and the absolutely evil. The good and the pure are of course those ideas, feelings, and actions which are consistent with the totalist ideolo-gy and policy; anything else is apt to be relegated to the bad and the impure. Nothing human is immune from the flood of stern moral judgments. All "taints" and "poisons" which contribute to the existing state of impurity must be searched out and eliminated.

The philosophical assumption underlying this demand is that absolute purity . . . is attainable, and that anything done to anyone in the name of this purity is ultimately moral. In actual practice, however, no one . . . is really expected to achieve such perfection. Nor can this paradox be dismissed as merely a means of establishing a high standard to which all can aspire. Thought reform bears witness to its more malignant consequences: for by defining and manipulating the criteria of purity, and then by conducting an all-out war upon impurity, the ideological totalists create a narrow world of guilt and shame. This is perpetuated by an ethos of continuous reform, a demand that one strive permanently and painfully for something which not only does not exist but is in fact alien to the human condition.

. . . the demand for purity creates . . . a guilty milieu and a shaming milieu . . . he is expected to expect punishment—which results in a relationship of guilt to his environment.

Robert Jay Lifton, Thought Reform and the Psychology of Totalism

Ted/201 could not make love to me that night. We slept in the same bed, we even hugged, but after that he ceased to touch me. It was a part of his moral code. Since I was questioning my commitment to the O., then clearly I was questioning my commitment to him. There was no other way he could see it.

"How are you feeling?" I whispered to him as we lay side by side.

"I feel sad. I don't want to lose you. I feel so married."

"Yes, I feel that way too."

I was silent for a long time. Thoughts came into my mind, things I wanted to tell him, but I could not frame the words; everything had to be examined, and I rejected all the possible ways I could say to him, "I want you, but not this life." And as I rejected the phrases, I became more and more frightened and lost in my mind, in the black space where aloneness lives. I could not speak. We slept.

CHAPTER 16

Later I felt much stronger. I lay on the green shag of the living room rug, excited to be leaving, feeling a breath of freedom at last. I leaned on my elbows studying classified ads. After a few days I found a clean, light place—another duplex, but this time the other side of town, down in South Minneapolis. It was a livelier area: Uptown had shops and co-ops, a movie theater and young punks posing in leather on the street corners. It felt more like a city, and thus more like home to me.

I bought a black and white TV and moved it, along with my desk, bed and a mattress, to the new duplex. My mother's quilt accompanied me and again its red and white suns brightened up the monastic bedroom into which I moved. Here I was almost completely alone.

It was a relief to be away from the pressure at last: the twenty-hour days; the fear of the telephone ringing with a new assignment; the fear of being handed another memo, stapled into its envelope, containing a criticism or a directive; the pressure of having no privacy, of having every action or lack of action subject to review. It was a relief, yet I recognized my status as a kind of prisoner. I had removed myself, but I was still under discipline. Judgment was hanging above me while I went through the process of self-examination. I felt I was in a punishment cell.

I was not allowed visitors. Despite the fact there were no bars, no guard at the door, Ted did not visit me. He had told me, after my hearing, that I was an Opportunist, and that I must look at my practice and summarize it if I was to be able to continue as a revolutionary serving the people, rather than looking out only for my own interests. I accepted that Ted was behaving correctly, even though I missed him intensely in my solitary exile.

I did not think about the earlier visit from the F.B.I. I had pushed it to the back of my mind, assuming that leadership had done what needed to be done and that any kind of F.B.I. frame-up would be handled.

For three months I had only three visits. Debbie's was the first. Her phone call telling me she'd come that evening encouraged me. Perhaps she would sit and talk, and I could tell her what I'd been thinking about: the ups and downs I'd been through in my first two weeks away from the bakery, away from 801, away from Ted.

Her briefcase entered the room first: tan leather with brass grommets. She came straight from work and was dressed in a blue suit, stretched tight over her buttocks, which were large, out of proportion to her small shoulders. Debbie had a spark of brightness still left, and this she wore at her neck—a bright-red silk bow flopping over the suit lapels. I offered her tea, which she refused. She walked to my desk, set her briefcase down by my file cabinet and said, "If you'll bring a couple of chairs over, we need to go through your files."

"What do you mean?" I asked.

"Anytime you move it's a good time to clean house a bit. And it's a security issue to keep too many papers."

"But I need my papers if I'm going to summarize and think about my practice."

I felt icy; she was there, not to give me support, but to take my papers away.

"Just pull out your files and we'll go through them. You can keep any current things, but I'll take what you don't need immediately, and anything of an ideological nature, and then you should throw away old stuff."

She pulled out of her briefcase two paper grocery bags, unfolded them and stood them up. One we filled with what she considered "old stuff" and this she took to discard, and the other she filled with most of my "secure" papers. And then she left, taking the two paper bags with her.

After I put away the chairs and closed up my file cabinet, I lay on the futon mattress, the only other piece of furniture in the living room. I lay flat, put my hands over my head and buried my face in the dusty smell of the old futon I'd brought all the way from San Francisco. There was no one I could call. There was no one to talk to. Debbie had turned the key on my isolation. Like a jailer, she was herself jailed, but one critical step above me, because she had been given a key and the right to execute my sentence.

Every day I went to my machinist job. I hadn't told anyone in the shop that I'd moved out on my own—it seemed too strange to try to explain to them. My co-workers knew how happy I'd been with Ted, that I was a newlywed (even though I found that a strange identity to have taken on—it was my cover really; I knew I was a revolutionary, but to others I was a happy newlywed, learning the ropes of married life), and there was no way I could explain to them that I'd moved out because of disunity with my political organization. I lived a lie and talked little with them about my home life.

My shift ended at midnight, and I'd drive home to the little duplex, watch my black-and-white TV for an hour or so while I unwound from the noise and the fumes, the tension of precision work and the vindictiveness of my surly foreman. And then I'd sleep, sometimes peacefully, sometimes afraid: hearing strange noises and unable to sleep until early morning. In the mornings I'd wake, eat breakfast and then begin looking for work. I knew I had to get out of the machine shop, and I wanted to find a computer job—I'd been trying for a year, following P.O.O.'s directive, and now I kept up the effort.

On the weekends depression hit. I had nobody to see. Once the forty-year old, lantern-jawed man upstairs came to visit—he was my second visitor. He was divorced, took care of his kids part time and talked sympathetically to me about the difficulties of being separated. He sat cross-legged on my futon in the bare living room and preserved a pointed etiquette; as he told me later, the last thing I needed was to have someone chase me around the bedroom.

"You must be very lonely," this stranger said. "You never have any visitors—you should try to see some people, you know. It's not good to be alone so much. I joined Parents Without Partners—it's been wonderful. But you don't have kids yet do you?"

It was springtime, and I decided that, alone or not, I'd get outside, enjoy nature, try to recreate the sense of well-being I'd had in the California outdoors. It had worked for me there—to get out of town, find a safe place to be to myself in nature, to feel the quality of belonging that I had found sitting on a California hillside surrounded by the scrubby, smooth-barked madrone, the red dust of the hills dry and warm beneath my feet. So I searched the state parks, drove one or two or three hours by myself on the weekend, took myself on long walks among the maples and the pines, along the deer trails and the damp banks of Minnesota rivers. But I was afraid still, of snakes and bugs and rodents and men. I did not know the country and it was not as friendly to me as I needed it to be.

Then, finally, my third visitor: Ted came. He said it was to straighten out my health insurance. We had not seen each other in weeks. We greeted each other formally, got in his car, and he drove us slowly towards Lake Calhoun. I wanted to touch him but could not. He did not move to touch me. He talked as he drove. Not about his "programmatic" work, of course, that was too secure to talk about, even with me, but he told me about Julie: she had gotten pregnant a couple of months before, and he had just received a memo telling him he was to be best man at her and Bill's wedding. It was to be in July, the same weekend as what would be our first wedding anniversary.

"If you're back by then, you'll go to the wedding too. I guess it's kind of an organizational event. They've done quite a bit of study on the Cuban Family Code, and we've been reading Engels on *The Family*. I think your role will be to sit with Beth during the ceremony."

Ted didn't know Bill well, so it was strange he should be best man. But I imagined him in this role and felt warm. And I was happy Beth was getting a father—she needed that. I would love to see Julie getting married, I missed her so much.

Ted carried on talking, not looking at me, but watching the road as he drove.

"I'm going home to West Virginia for a few days right after that. It's my dad's sixtieth birthday, and they're having a family reunion. And I'm going to talk to grandma about loaning us some money to buy a computer for one of the businesses."

The idea of him going home without me hurt—I wanted to meet his family, to know where he came from. But I couldn't say any of that. Instead I just said, "Oh, well . . . that's good. That's nice."

Then there was a silence. He'd pulled up by the lake.

"I miss you," I said. I watched his hands, his tapered fingers on the steering wheel. He did not look at me.

"I miss you too. Have you been summarizing your practice?"

I felt then, at that moment, that I would go back.

I wanted to come back. I wanted to go to West Virginia with Ted. There was no question of having a vacation in the O.; we only traveled when there was a functional purpose for doing so, but somehow Ted had found such a purpose for his visit to his family and I wanted to go with, to meet them, to travel, to have some rest and a change of scene for a few days. I wanted to come back. I wanted to go to the wedding, to see Julie again, to celebrate her and Beth's getting a new family.

It seemed like going back was strengthening my commitment, once again, to the struggle, and I was going back to my marriage, to Julie and Beth, and to the closest thing I had to a community. I could be no use on my own. And I had discarded the ties I had left in San Francisco. I felt stranded; helpless and alone in that empty flat in South Minneapolis, wanting still, in a desperate way, to dedicate my life, to feel myself useful and not useless; to feel myself significant: in Mao Tse Tung's words, "heavy as Mount Tai" and not "light as a feather." I needed to make a difference. Otherwise, my epitaph would be, "She was nothing and she did nothing. Death just came and swallowed her, and no-one ever knew the difference."

The Dispensing of Existence

The totalist environment draws a sharp line between those whose right to existence can be recognized, and those who possess no such right. . . .

The thought reform process is one means by which non-people are permitted, through a change in attitude and personal character, to make themselves over into people. The most literal example of such dispensing of existence and nonexistence is to be found in the sentence given to certain political criminals [in Communist China]: execution in two years' time, unless during that two-year period they have demonstrated genuine progress in their reform. . . .

. . . The totalist environment—even when it does not resort to physical abuse . . . stimulates in everyone a fear of extinction or annihilation. . . . A person can overcome this fear and find . . . "confirmation," not in his individual relationships, but only from the fount of all existence, the totalist Organization. Existence comes to depend upon creed (I believe, therefore, I am), upon submission (I obey, therefore, I am) and beyond these, upon a sense of total merger with the ideological movement. Ultimately of course one compromises and combines the totalist "confirmation" with independent elements of personal identity; but one is ever made aware that, should he stray too far along this "erroneous path," his right to existence may be withdrawn.

Robert Jay Lifton, Thought Reform and the Psychology of Totalism

When I'd left three months before, I'd said that I would summarize my practice, and I knew I couldn't go back without doing that. I sat at my desk to compose my summary and stared at the paper. My mind would not tell me what to say about why I wanted to go back. I got up and walked to the kitchen, opened the fridge and pulled out some cheese, cut off a slice and ate it. I put the kettle on. Then I went back to the fridge and chewed on a cold lamb chop, holding the bone with one hand while I rifled through the fridge for something else to eat with the other. The kettle whistled, and I wiped my hands, closed the fridge door and made a cup of tea. Then I went to sit back at my desk.

What was I going to say about why I wanted to go back? For a week I'd been trying to write this summary. How could I translate that hunger for friends, community, and meaning into a structure acceptable to the O.?

I stared at the paper—the whiteness stared back, giving me no clues. Outside the street was quiet. Debbie had taken most of the other summaries I had—usually I would look at someone else's and more or less copy the format, figure out how they were using the "four-step method" we'd learned from Mao's essays, or the home-grown Program Summary Forms (parts one, two, and three) that P.O.O. had advanced. Most summaries were structured with a special numbering system, which changed without explanation every now and then. The current system was supposedly a precursor to computerizing our self-criticisms, so that scientific studies could be made linking patterns of practice with ideological weaknesses. One's practice had to be classified into the following areas, referred to by number:

100 Construction
200 (For some reason this number was unassigned)
300 Production
400 Administration
500 Mathematics
600 Political
700 Ideological
800 Organizational
900 Theory
000 Economic

I began by writing down the categories of my practice first. There was the work at the bakery (this fit into 300 for Production, although I had some confusion over whether it was also 800 for Organizational—what if I got it wrong?). I tried to be honest and wrote down the problems I had with the way the bakery workers were treated, their long hours and low pay, and I wrote, too, about what I'd learned there: how to organize work, computer skills, purchasing and dealing with vendors, administrative skills, how a business runs in its entirety. Okay, I thought, I have developed through this process, and I will carry on struggling with the organization about the parts I do not agree with—I will speak up and make my voice heard about the exploitation of the bakery workers.

The next category was the relationship with Ted, the "Personal Relationship." This was classified as Ideological, and, therefore, a 700, the most critical category and the one in which I generally put anything that I couldn't fit anywhere else in the system. I analyzed Ted's and my parents' relationships. His mother was crazy and his father looked after her. My mother was crazy and my father didn't look after her, although he provided her with children and money, and sometimes jokes. This I described as the basis for my and Ted's pattern where Ted was the stoic, stable, strong one in the marriage, and I was the "subjective," emotional one. My subjectivity was allowed to go unchallenged, I wrote, and I was left to wallow in it instead of Ted struggling to heighten the contradictions. Clearly I should not be allowed to do this anymore.

In any summary, it was necessary to discuss one's history. And so I recounted, again, how I'd aggressively pursued political organizations (600) and then left them when I ran into disagreement. I also remembered the quantity of study groups I'd started out of which nothing long-lasting had grown. I duly noted that I could not deal with prolonged struggle, with organizational discipline, with unified action in the face of a minority in disunity, and I noted my inability to accept leadership in a centralized structure (unless that leadership was my own). Clearly, if this was my past, then the future lay in overturning these things. I must become disciplined, accepting of others' leadership, and committed for the long-term. Certainly, any disagreements I had with the O. were real issues, but my development lay, not in "running from struggle" but staying and dealing with the issues.

Finally I talked about my father, my Dominant Influence. How I had inherited from him the drive for Personal Achievement, competitiveness, and personal opportunism. His male chauvinism, indicated by his role of intellectual superiority had ingrained in me a disrespect for manual work and practice and encouraged a belief that if I only thought enough I could work out the solutions to problems. The O. was teaching me that thinking, or theory, was not enough. I had to engage in work, in practice, in order to accomplish and understand anything.

After all this, I wrote of my desire to return to the O., followed by a long list of specific recommendations of more summaries to do, ways to work harder, plans to make, O. forms to fill out to monitor my practice, and so on. This last was 800, or Organizational—they were recommendations to strengthen both myself and the O.

I sat in my straight-backed chair, before the icon of my typewriter. I used to soar when I wrote; my mind would travel like lightning in the sky, great arcs of luminescence to connect the disparate events of my life. I would revel in thinking, climbing on an architecture built inside my mind. Now my writing forced itself into categories and steps and acronyms. My journal remained empty and blank. I could not think anymore, it was too hard. Every time my thoughts opened up and tried to soar again I could not find the category or acronym in which to fit them. And so, it seemed easier not to think. Thinking led to summaries and I hated these summaries, they blocked me in like four walls slammed up against me. If I couldn't think, then I simply wouldn't try anymore. It wasn't a conscious choice, just a conclusion.

Loading the Language

The language of the totalist environment is characterized by the thought-terminating cliché. The most far-reaching and complex of human problems are compressed into brief, highly reductive, definitive-sounding phrases, easily memorized and easily expressed. These become the start and finish of any ideological analysis. . . .

For an individual person, the effect of the language of ideological totalism can be summed up in one word: constriction. He is, so to speak, linguistically deprived; and since language is so central to all human experience, his capacities for thinking and feeling are immensely narrowed. . . .

. . . his imagination becomes increasingly dissociated from his actual life experiences and may even tend to atrophy from disuse.

Robert Jay Lifton, *Thought Reform and the Psychology of Totalism*

I had completed my summary. The street outside was sunny and quiet, just the occasional shout of one child to another. I had resolved my internal struggles once again. I went to a pay phone and called Debbie's number. The phone rang three times—her code—and then I hung up and called again. When she answered I said, "It's Claire. I have a summary. Can I meet with you?"

The Cult of Confession

Closely related to the demand for absolute purity is an obsession with personal confession. Confession is carried beyond its ordinary religious, legal and therapeutic expressions to the point of becoming a cult in itself. There is the demand that one confess to crimes one has not committed, to sinfulness that is artificially induced, in the name of a cure that is arbitrarily imposed. . . . In totalist hands, confession becomes a means of exploiting, rather than offering solace for, these vulnerabilities.

The totalist confession . . . is a means of maintaining a perpetual inner emptying or psychological purge of impurity. . . . It is an act of symbolic self-surrender, the expression of the merging of the individual and environment. . . . It is a means of maintaining an ethos of total exposure—a policy of making public (or at least known to the Organization) everything possible about the life experiences, thoughts, and passions of each individual, especially those elements which might be regarded as derogatory.

The assumption underlying total exposure . . . is the environment's claim to total ownership of each individual self within it. Private ownership of the mind and its products—of imagination or of memory—becomes highly immoral. . . .

The cult of confession has effects quite the reverse of its ideal of total exposure: rather than eliminating personal secrets, it increases and intensifies them.

Robert Jay Lifton, *Thought Reform and the Psychology of Totalism*

My recommendation to return to the O. was accepted. A week or so later, I received a memo from P.O.O. saying that I had, indeed, reflected on my practice, but that I should realize that "the revolution is not a dinner party." Maybe I could cut it and maybe I couldn't. Not everyone could. It remained to be seen, through my practice, whether I was going to settle down and be serious about being in a Marxist-Leninist organization. I resolved to prove myself.

CHAPTER 17

I was sitting at my desk when I saw him coming. He walked along the side-walk in front of my window carrying a big floppy bunch of peonies at chest height. They bobbed along ahead of him in abundant pinkness, and I smiled. Ted looked like a clown, the peonies flapping like oversized shoes in front of him as he made his way to my door.

He had never brought me a present before and I was happy. He came in, and we stood shyly, and then I put the peonies in water, and we hugged. Soon we were by my bed and then on it, making the love of people too long without. He said, "I'm glad you're coming back."

I said, "Me too, it's been hard here. I'm really pleased to see you."

We lay in bed smiling together. I moved back in the next week.

Julie was visibly pregnant for her wedding, her stomach protruding beneath a cream silk dress—but this circumstance seemed to fit her style quite well. She abhorred convention. Bill looked happy and uncomfortable in his suit. Beth was dressed up in a frilled party dress and ran excited circles around her uncles and grandparents. As planned, she sat between me and Ted for the service. Strangely, Julie and Bill were married by a minister in a church down in South Minneapolis. Later I found out that leadership had directed them to do this in order to form a strategic alliance with their parents, both sets of whom were involved in church mission work. There was also some discussion of this being the culminating "negation of the negation" (this being one of the dialectical laws) of their religious backgrounds, a double negative that they assumed had meaning for their ideological development.

After Julie and Bill exchanged their vows, Julie stepped back and Bill beckoned seven-year-old Beth to the platform. She came up shyly and stood by him while he knelt down to her height. He took her two small hands in his, his blue eyes looking in her brown ones and said, "I take you, Beth Winnie Preston, to be my daughter. I thank you for letting me join this family. I will struggle to be a father to you, to love and respect you and to earn your love and respect."

Bill turned to his comrades and family sitting on the hard wooden pews and announced that he would be legally adopting Beth and then the little girl added, almost inaudibly, "I take you, Bill, as my father."

She gave us a surprised and delighted smile as if she had only just discovered the full mirth of this arrangement, and then she raised up her arms and jumped up into Bill's. They hugged on stage and Julie joined them while the audience rustled with Kleenex and dabbed watery eyes. Julie then took center stage and stood with her legs planted firmly apart. She lifted her head and spoke.

"This song is sung to my dying, bourgeois side. I am glad to finally give up this stubborn independence so that I can be part of a new kind of family: a family based on mutual respect and struggle."

Her clear voice rang out, a capella: "I never will marry, I'll be no man's wife . . . I hope to stay single, for the rest of my life . . ."

A confused silence followed, broken suddenly by the organist who struck up a chorus that everyone knew. We all joined in and sang together: "This land is your land, this land is my land, from California to the New York Island . . ."

Afterwards there was a square dance. Cindy and the teenaged Nancy and Nancy's father, were there. Debbie was there. And then most of Julie's family. Julie and Bill even had a honeymoon—a short one, granted, but they went off to her family's cabin for a rare weekend off.

Soon after, Ted and I went to Wheeling, West Virginia. Ted had a big, noisy Jewish family, and I felt very shy at first. Later I came to love them and take them as my own family, but that first visit was hard. I tried to dress up nicely for them but I felt tight and constrained in my Minnesota-casual embroidered blouse and cotton slacks. Ted seemed tense with them too, except for late at night when we stayed up with his brothers and sister and they retold old stories and jokes about their growing-up until the early hours of the morning.

Ted's father, Sid, was a dentist, a respected member of the small Jewish community in Wheeling, and known throughout the town simply as Doc. Lorna, his wife, reminded me of a bat, blinking behind her butterfly glasses and constantly surprising me with her complete indifference to social norms. The first time I met her, the day after Ted and I were married, I asked her to tell me about him (of course she didn't know then how little I really knew about him). We were walking around Lake of the Isles and after a silence of some length she turned to me and touched my arm.

"I better not say anything, Alexandra, because I can't think of anything good to say. He was a playboy . . ."

We stopped walking and she paused. Then she looked up hopefully and said, "But he was always kind to animals."

I was speechless, and we walked on in silence. Ten minutes later she took off her sandals and handed them to Sid. Without a word she walked into the lake, her floral dress billowing up softly around her and she eased herself into a steady breaststroke, just her head and sparkling glasses lifted above the water, and she swam a good half mile clear across the lake. She left the lake just as casually and made her way towards us gingerly picking her way bare-foot and dripping along the asphalt path. Dealing with Lorna required an open mind.

Sid and Lorna's house was informal and with three bedrooms not big enough to house all of us. Lorna went off to bed early and left the rest of us vying with each other for sleeping space and for pillows and blankets from the short supply. As a married couple, Ted and I got some priority; we landed the thirty-year-old sofa-bed in the den, to which I conceded defeat half way through the night as I rolled out of its stranglehold onto the relative comfort of the carpeted floor.

After the party for Sid's sixtieth birthday, Ted and I met with his matri-archal grandmother, Hessie, and both his parents. Ted sat nervously on the edge of the floral armchair in Hessie's living-room while I, equally nervous, shared the couch with her. Hessie was the opposite of Lorna, a model of good manners and nineteenth-century grace. Ted and I had discussed my role earlier—I was to say as little as possible and let him do the talking. He began by describing a completely fictitious business that we were supposedly start-ing—a computer business. It didn't strike me, or him, as deceit; after all, we knew the O. had computer businesses, we had done work for some of them. Why did it matter if it was strictly our business, or the O.'s? We were the O. anyway.

Finally Ted put the question to her: "Grandma Hessie, Alex and I will need to make an initial investment of $5,000. And I hoped that you might be able to help us out with the financing."

Hessie looked unperturbed, listening carefully and sitting with her ankles neatly crossed. It was not the first time one of her grandchildren had asked her for money.

"How will the money be used, Teddy?" she asked.

"We need to buy a new computer. A Hewlett-Packard. They're technologically the most advanced now and expected to overtake IBM in the marketplace."

"And then what?"

"We'll develop advanced software on that machine, and then we'll market it to small businesses."

"Teddy, I don't know anything about the computer business. When I was growing up, we didn't even have radios yet. But I trust you. You've always had good sense, and you've always done well at anything you've set your mind to. As long as your father agrees it's a good idea, I'm more than willing to help my grandchildren with what I have."

Sid nodded in the background, looked up from behind his bifocals with a friendly grin, "Oh, sure, I'm confident in Ted. Always have been! And with a wonderful wife like Alex at his side, I'm sure things will go well. You know, when I started my Jerusalem artichoke business I learned that you have to invest. Have I told you about my artichoke delivery route yet? I get up at 4.30 every morning, and I've got *several* of my neighbors and dental patients signed up already. I harvest the sunchokes, bag and deliver them fresh, before going into the office. More Vitamin C than oranges. So, I know about investment."

As an afterthought he added, "Just make sure you pay it back when you can."

Sid went on, describing more of his ventures. We sat politely, listening.

Ted's grandmother was too elegant a woman to give us the check in person. But when we got back to Minneapolis she'd mailed it to Ted's post office box. He cashed it and forwarded the money, without question, to P.O.O. He had successfully completed his assignment.

After the brief summer interlude, it was back to work. I was now assigned to work full time at the bakery, to go to school at the Vo-tech to study purchasing and to quit my machining job, at last. For a while, my schedule eased up.

I continued with my customer service responsibilities and also took on the daily management of the bakery. Jerri helped me out over the phone from her computer programming job, and I reported to Debbie frequently. She was now general manager and kept an eye on everything I was doing.

Every few weeks Debbie would call me from work and tell me she had to leave town that afternoon. She would be gone for two or three days and then show up again as suddenly as she'd left. She would be almost cheerful when she got back. I assumed she was going to Chicago. I'd figured out, despite the extensive security measures, that a few O. cadres were living there. Other cadres seemed to go there every once in a while for meetings. In fact, Jerri had received a directive to move out of our duplex and I assumed she was moving there also. I was sad in a way, because Jerri didn't scare me as much as Debbie did, and I'd miss working with her. But on the other hand I was glad that Ted and I would finally be alone in the house—perhaps we would be able to relax with each other a little more without a third person in such a small space.

I had just fallen asleep a little after midnight when I was awakened by the phone ringing twice. After a pause the ringing started again—that was my code. I got out of bed to take the call.

"We need to get together. Can you make it tomorrow after work?"

We never said our names over the phone. Sometimes this made it hard when I didn't recognize who it was I was talking with. But Debbie I could always recognize, she spoke in a clipped voice, shorn of softness.

"Okay," I said.

"Six o'clock at the Steak House—we can get coffee there."

"Okay."

I went back to bed, starting to get wired and trying to figure out what she wanted. It was probably a new assignment for the bakery. It was hard to sleep, the meeting loomed up before me with the promise of less time, less sleep, more responsibility, more work that alienated me. But since I'd come back to the O. after my three months of "reflecting on my commitment," I had to put on a show of not resisting and of at least acting as if I understood what we were doing.

Debbie was already sitting in a booth at the Steak House when I arrived. We always chose restaurants that had booths, apparently for security reasons. I sat down. She didn't look up for a moment—she was finishing up some paperwork. When she did look at me, the corners of her mouth were indented into the whiteness of her cheeks, it wasn't a smile, more of a stretch of her lips, and she kind of raised her black eyebrows just a little, a small and rare sign that she was unsure of herself.

"It was suggested that we discuss the pregnancy process and share what we have each summarized this far about it. I understand you've done some study and research?"

At first I was relieved, this didn't appear to be a new assignment, and at least nothing about the bakery. But then my stomach tightened up again—had she been sent to put pressure on me about the diagnostic procedures I'd been avoiding? But from her tone and the words she'd used, I ascertained she just wanted information from me. Debbie was nothing if not direct and would have jumped straight to the point were she there to criticize me.

"Yes, I've done a fair amount of study. The first thing is getting the ovulation cycle figured out, making sure that you're having sex at the right time and that ovulation is not a problem. If that's taken care of you look at sperm count for the man. That's easy to diagnose, but harder to fix. If the sperm count is okay, then the woman has to start going through various procedures to see what the problem is."

I knew this stuff backwards by now, not that knowing it seemed to be helping me get pregnant. In an uncharacteristic manner Debbie lowered her eyelids and let her dark eyelashes rest on her cheeks.

"I've been trying to get pregnant for seven months. We think I might have a problem. My PR did have some problems with proctitis, and we are working on getting that cleared up, but we don't think that's the contradiction. And my cycle is regular; I've been tracking my ovulation for the last several months, and I am able to arrange to have intercourse at the appropriate time."

Now it became clear to me—her sudden monthly disappearances were obviously to have a rendezvous to try to get pregnant. Her PR must be in Chicago, where, by now, most of the cadres had been relocated. No wonder she seemed cheerful at those times! It was hard to imagine her making love, but now I tried, and it gave me a different view of her. Perhaps there was a way she could be loving, perhaps she saved it up for whoever he was.

"It's awful, isn't it," I ventured, "That feeling when you find out you're not pregnant yet."

"Yes, I do get subjective then—that's why I think it's important to get a more scientific view of the process. Of course, I was brought up Catholic, so it runs pretty much counter to my world outlook to look at reproduction in a scientific manner."

"Oh, I see. I guess your folks were French Catholics then? Where were you in the family? Have you had much experience with kids?"

"Sure," Debbie laughed shortly, "I was the oldest of ten children, so I spent most of my time looking after the others. I've wanted children of my own for a long time. It's only in the last year that I've been told it would enhance my development rather than holding it back. Before then I would have had too much value invested in being a mother. Now I'm able to be more objective, to see having children as part of developing the Internal Transformation Process."

This was the most personal information Debbie had shared with me in the couple of years I had known her. We continued talking about the various tests and procedures, and Debbie took notes on the things I'd learned, the books I'd read and the names of doctors who'd been helpful. We'd been there over an hour and had really talked; it wasn't the usual rushed run-through of a list of tasks to be reported on. I had often complained of the lack of real conversation in the O. and now I felt good that Debbie and I had finally approached communication. I didn't agree with everything she'd said, but we had talked and shared some of our experiences about trying to get pregnant.

She finally got up to leave, picking up the check from the table to work out the split.

As she rose, I said to her: "You know, this has been really helpful to me. I've felt so isolated going through this on my own. And Ted can only understand so much of it. I'd really like to get together again and check in with you about how it's going—just to give each other some support."

The change was almost invisible, like a flash freeze, water crisping to ice on its quiet surface. She locked a little and sucked her teeth.

"We'll get together if it's functional. Otherwise it'll just become an exchange of value."

She put her money on the table and walked out without saying good-bye.

I sat on in the dark booth.

Meanwhile the Bakery was going bankrupt. It was decided, after a couple of years of trying to get financing to make it an ultra-modern, computer-driven concern, instead to give up and close it down "gracefully." The concessions from the workers and the endless hours of free cadre labor weren't enough to make it economically viable. Our hold on the whole-grain market was being challenged by the established bakeries as they caught up to the "mainstreaming" of healthier eating.

It wasn't for lack of effort on our part. Debbie and Jerri, in particular, had spent long hours devising production methods and schedules, and writing loan applications to banks. But in reality, we were a day-by-day survival operation, holding our breaths each evening as the orders were tallied, to see whether we'd make enough sales that week to make payroll. (Of course, it wasn't "payroll"; the workers actually got weekly "dividend" checks.)

One of our last attempts was to register as a woman-owned business. This was supposed to give us some preference in the market—although it never materialized. We printed up an expensive three-color brochure depicting the various women principals. At the same time, we developed a sales kit: white bakery boxes were printed with red ribbons and filled with cellophane-wrapped slices of our various breads, mini-muffins and rolls, produced according to the salesperson's prospect list. A delivery service delivered the samples, and the salesperson followed up. This was based on the directive from P.O.O. to "depersonalize and proceduralize" the sales process. For a while, I had the misfortune to be nominated as the salesperson.

This was after Walt Johnson, the previous salesperson, had left the O. He was actually able to sell bread and had developed good relationships with several of the hospital dietitians of our largest accounts. But he had left, so I was told, because of his arrogance and his constant need to maximize his value. It was likely, I was also told, that such a person would become a police agent. I couldn't imagine Walt as an agent, although I had to agree he was arrogant. During his tenure in sales, he constantly criticized my work in the bakery. After the eight-hour weekend clean-up shifts that a couple of us would work, along with the thirteen-year old Nancy, he would walk around and wipe the window ledges with his finger. Holding up his flour-dusted finger he'd say, "Look at this! Is this clean? Doesn't the cleaning procedure cover this?"

Walt was a perfectionist and always found fault. Consequently he also started telling Jerri and Debbie how to run things, and presumably P.O.O. too. Whether he left or was expelled, I didn't know, but after he was gone I was told to take over.

Being a saleswoman was excruciating for me. I was still shy, and, while I could manage in groups after I got to know people, the quick social connections one had to make in sales were anathema to me. But out I went, in my new dress-for-success gray suit and my blue high heels, with a briefcase in one hand and the ribboned box of samples in the other. After one particularly bad encounter, I returned home and sat at the kitchen table recounting my frustration to Jerri.

"Oh, Jerri. I went down to the university to talk to the head of catering. He wouldn't let me into his office, so I kind of hung around in the doorway. He didn't remember I'd made an appointment with him and acted like it was weird I was even there. Then he got real aggressive with me and pretty much threw me out. I felt like a kid—it was so embarrassing."

Jerri didn't know much about sales work, but I could generally talk to her about things. She thought carefully before she spoke.

"Well," she said, in an apparent non sequitur, "Have you ever considered that shaving your legs might make you feel more equivalent?"

I blushed. I thought people didn't notice. I had never in my life shaved my legs, and I wore my slightly hairy legs as a badge of feminism, along with my lack of makeup or the other feminine accoutrements with which I had never been comfortable. I wore heavy, opaque hose with my suits, specially chosen so that the wispy blond hair on my calves could not be seen. But of course, as Jerri was my roommate, she'd seen me bare-legged. I was deeply embarrassed. I had to admit that the opaque hose troubled me—I knew this was a chink in my dress-for-success disguise. But shaving my legs seemed like such a submission to the ideology that women had to see their physical selves as faulty and scrape and paint and girdle themselves into the proper form.

In Berkeley I had celebrated the acceptance of women's physical selves among the Left and counterculture communities, and it was humiliating to have Jerri, someone I respected, and who was also clearly not into conforming to the stereotypes of women, challenge my personal physical care. Without her saying anything further, however, I knew she was telling me: It was my bourgeois personal independence that made this hard for me—that my proletarian side would happily shave my legs if that would make me a more effective saleswoman. Within the O., fitting in, conforming to the standards of the business world, was seen as a desirable trait. Personal style was always a negative. Style was to be functional, and, as the stage of the O. was developing enterprises to create an economic base, then our style should be subordinate to that goal.

I knew, without trying, that I would not be able to defend the hair on my legs. That weekend I bought a pink Lady Bic razor and ritualistically shaved my legs, nicking them several times in the process, the tiny veins of blood trickling down as I dried myself after my bath.

At night, in bed with Ted, I waited for him to notice as we began to caress each other. And, I had to admit, I had a certain excitement, felt "feminine" in an unfamiliar way as he discovered the new smoothness. In Berkeley I had learned to appreciate my femininity, even though I expressed it in a tomboyish way. I had a sweet, vigorous appeal that left me able to reject the face-painting with confidence. But now I accepted that this too was holding me back, and if I wanted to be seen as an equal in the business world, I would have to give up my rather childish principles and preferences and, in order to subvert the corporate culture, I would swim in the mainstream and work my way into the belly of the monster.

My sales figures did not respond, however, to my hair-free legs. Soon I was removed from the position with the criticism that I had not developed sufficiently in my ideological transformation to perform the sales function properly. I was relieved and, in comparison, didn't mind going back to production and purchasing.

I was now charged with manipulating our creditors on a daily basis: keeping the supplies coming in while stretching out our payment terms as much as possible. Every Monday my stomach knotted as the production workers and I waited for the Best Brands delivery. Would they deliver or not? Would they unload the flour and yeast, the frozen eggs and caraway seeds, the dough conditioner and sunflower seeds? Would they refuse the partial payment I tried to make every week and finally demand full payment? Luckily they kept supplying us—while other vendors cut us off, which would mean I would spend the day running around to grocery stores spending our petty cash dollars on enough of one ingredient or another to get us through the day's production.

I learned a lot at the bakery: crisis management (we were always in crisis), cash flow management, and I became a veritable expert at dealing with vendors. I knew when to sweet-talk them, when to threaten, when to take the offensive and when to apologize and bring my most middle-class of English accents to bear.

Eventually, the bakery closed for good.

Ted and Zack, two cadre who had been involved in the Bakery from its inception, spent the next year writing a summary. The Bakery had been the longest running of the O.'s economic programs—nearly everyone had worked in it at one point or other, and it, perhaps, had been the closest to succeeding as a business.

Their summary lauded the administrative and technological successes of the Bakery. It blamed our failures on the banks and the "stranglehold on capital" that they held. And its conclusion was that, although we had failed economically, we had succeeded in our actual goal, which was the ideological development of cadre. This last had been dictated by P.O.O., and Zack and Ted dutifully added it to their summary. I tried to share with Ted my cynicism about their conclusions and felt he agreed on some level, but the summary stood.

The last year of the Bakery had been very hard. We held on, doing every job in the place as the workers fell away, one by one. The end was sad: so much work had been put into the place over the years. But mostly I was relieved. Every time a project ended, or I was pulled off an assignment, I felt reprieved, my stress level dropping as my responsibilities slackened.

Finally, by a combination of luck and persistence I landed myself a computer-programming job. I was hired as a junior software engineer to program computer chips for Lee Data, a fast-growing, hi-tech company out in the silicon suburb of Eden Prairie. From spending my days arguing with vendors about flour prices; delivering bread in fourteen-foot trucks; subbing for the bench worker, the slicer, the sorter—all young working-class St. Paul blacks and whites; and running all the daily functions of the bakery, I now found myself in a gray cubicle with my own personal computer, surrounded by bright, mostly white college graduates who had stepped upon the hi-tech fast track, shielded from the quiet noise of their neighbor's keyboards by a productivity-enhancing white-noise machine.

I was undergoing another profound change in my public identity; posing as a college graduate while I'd actually left school at fifteen, I entered a new stage in my double life. At work I struggled to find my feet in the completely new world of software engineering, while in my secret O. life I continued to try to get pregnant and became involved in a series of new projects dictated by the beige, stapled memos that arrived from the leadership in Chicago.

CHAPTER 18

Television

1985. Helicopters again. This time flown by the Pennsylvania State Police who drop a firebomb on a Philadelphia neighborhood, burning down sixty-one houses and killing six adults and five children. Only two MOVE members survive out of the thirteen who lived together in the targeted row-house. John Africa, the dreadlocked leader of the armed group, is among the dead. He had refused to vacate the house when police appeared to arrest him after years of neighborhood complaints. MOVE has harangued the neighbors with hour after hour of speeches amplified day and night into the street; they have turned the house into a fortress complete with a rooftop bunker. The police chief who orders the firebombing is also black. There are claims that MOVE is a cult, but others say it was organizing in the community against police brutality. One way or the other, the police have the last word.

Ted and I received another memo from P.O.O. I noticed that there seemed to be at least two distinct P.O.O.s. One used a smaller typeface and wrote in a clear, readable style. The other, while using the same beige paper, had appalling grammar, spelled badly and made countless typos. The grammar bothered me—it made the memos almost impossible to understand. I wrote a note criticizing this and was told that yes, it was a problem, but P.O.O. had many priorities and proof-reading was not one of them. However, due to my criticism, P.O.O. would try to spend more time checking the memos for read-ability. The grammar did not improve, but I learned from this to identify which of the P.O.O.s was communicating. I had also tried to ask Ted or Jerri what P.O.O. stood for, but neither of them knew.

This memo, from the P.O.O. who couldn't spell, informed us of a name change. In keeping with our strategic direction of building an economic base by developing businesses, we would no longer be called the O. The new name was TJE Enterprises, which was now referred to as the Enterprise or, the E. This grated on both me and Ted; it seemed to make official that all political work was to be subsumed under the business entities. And it felt ridiculous to go about calling ourselves the Enterprise—it reminded me of Star Trek, or the Mafia. Of course, I wondered what or who TJE stood for, but again, given the need-to-know principle, I never asked.

During 1985 I recorded the following handful of journal entries:

What is this work that I do?
I've been stagnant, it feels, for years.
I can't think anymore. I hate to think or to summarize.

* * *

With Ted I feel secure.

* * *

My arms have been tingling. I worry.
I dreamed about Leonard this morning. He was marrying Kim. I looked at him and her, and he had loving eyes and I loved him still.
I was swimming, but I couldn't make any headway. Someone had to come and save me. I felt the tingling in my arms, and I had no strength. It was Leonard who came to get me.

* * *

These are dry years. Desert-like, thin and barren, staring reality in the face. It has been years since springtime.

* * *

Things are not good right now. In myself, or between me and him.
Beyond that, I cannot go. I stick there like in quicksand, letting the muck rise over me.

I am terrified and angry and tense with all this inside me. At work I feel better. But here at 801—I cannot call it home—I am protective, defensive, suspicious.

And he grates on me all the time—cannot touch me gently, without aggravating me somehow.

Oh, goddammit.

* * *

I woke strangely this morning. Like these years.

In the evening, after work, my steps drag—I don't want to go home. I feel my stagnation too much there. I feel the dullest and deepest pain I've known.

What is it?—like a steel casement above my head pressing down my ability into a little shell, an empty self.

I want to scream and throw myself across the room and feel that feeling of going over the EDGE like all these people I've known. I miss so many people I've loved and I feel starved for it. And I understand them—that feeling that I just cannot resolve the contradiction any more and my mind bursts with the strain.

Lyndall and Hatty and Joy. I have separated myself from them.

Only four of us remained in Minneapolis: Bill, Julie, Ted, and I. Everyone else had been moved to Chicago. It was now that I learned that the cadres in Chicago had formed a company called Dependable Computer Programs and had spent the last few years developing accounting software. This accounting system was introduced to the four of us in a memo, as the "Cadillac" of accounting systems:

> The scientific tools of the O. have been applied to its develop-
> ment and it has achieved a level of quality and scientific develop-
> ment as yet only dreamed of by other computer companies. The
> Minneapolis unit will market this system, along with Hewlett
> Packard hardware, as the premier system for mid-sized companies.

We were also to make contacts overseas, to attempt to form joint ventures to market the product. Bill was sent on a trip to India—he'd been born and raised there, of missionary parents—to make contacts through his old school friends. At this point, P.O.O. also became interested in my father's business.

Ted and I were encouraged to take a trip to England: a memo from P.O.O. instructed me to convince my father to bring me into his business, and to move his company into software publishing. This was the only way I would be allowed to visit my family again and so, despite my hesitations about the assignment (I couldn't imagine for a moment that my father would pay any attention to my opinions regarding his business), I accepted the task at hand.

My skirt and jacket felt uncomfortable as I sat in the restaurant across from my father. He probably hadn't seen me in a skirt since I was a teenager, and then it would have been the shortest of mini-skirts, not this staid, knee-length garment I now wore. Ted had encouraged me to dress professionally for this meeting, telling me my father would take me more seriously dressed this way. The very fact that I felt uncomfortable seemed to prove the point—I was changing my identity with my father, and change was, by its nature, uncomfortable.

We met in Bertorelli's, the Italian restaurant in London's Soho district where my father took me and my sisters as children when we came to his office; I used to come on weekends and earn a few shillings stuffing magazine invoices into envelopes. The result of my knowledge of his work life was a disdain and dislike for the business world. This was one reason it was so hard for me to engage in the O. businesses. I had worked hard to be away from that life, and now, here I was, embracing it, asking my father to let me into his firm. Only now it was for the revolution, and so I could swallow my pride; we weren't just trying to make money for individuals; we were doing this as part of a greater plan, to learn new skills, to fund revolutionary activity, to develop ourselves as cadre for the long haul.

In any case, as I sat, trying not to be a child in relation to him any longer, but rather a grown woman and a business woman at that, I felt a squeezing of myself. It appeared I had not moved through time, sucking on the same bowl of *spaghetti al vongole,* dripping the red sauce on my blouse just as I had always done. It was the same humiliation I felt at the business lunches I attended under one O. guise or another back in Minnesota. At those uncomfortable meals I spilled my food so badly that I'd get nervous at the sight of the menu until I learned to order, not the foods I liked, but those that I could eat neatly, with a fork, with no drips. Across from me, my father fed himself, an engine vacuuming up fuel, head down over his plate, his glasses removed to concentrate better on the fueling at hand.

I felt flattened, two-dimensional, and this served its purpose as I talked to him about turning his business into a software publishing house. He smelled a bad business proposition immediately and deftly changed the subject. I was relieved; I had done my bit, carried out the assignment, and thankfully been spared any further explanation of our plan. Yet the assignment had enabled me to see my family for the first time since I'd moved to Minnesota. The very nature of the assignment also allowed me to stop trying to make my father see *me*, to add the third dimension—that of my self—to our relationship. I was building a new identity with him, and so the old one, the constant need I had to try to show him what lay beneath the surface of my quietness, my good grades, my sudden changes at adolescence; that old identity could be left to dry up and rot naturally. It no longer concerned me, because P.O.O. had said that my father would only respect me on a business level, and this was what I was building. It didn't matter that he didn't see beyond the exterior—I couldn't tell him the underground truth of what we were doing anyway, or that I belonged to a revolutionary organization, but I had the satisfaction of knowing that this was so, and that my inside life had significance.

Secretly pleased that I had failed at plan A, I moved on to plan B a couple of days later. My father and my sister Lyndall had been fundraising for South Africa's African National Congress. I had proposed to P.O.O. that Ted and I work with them on this in the United States and P.O.O. had readily agreed. This was my real interest—it would be the first political work I would do in my five-year association with the O.

Ted and I arrived, more casually dressed this time, and so more comfortable, at my father's office. The secretary announced us and showed us into a large office, with full-length windows on one side that looked out on to the crowded sidewalks of Gower Street. The wall on the opposite side was covered with a miscellany of pictures: covers of *Running*, my father's latest magazine and pictures of him and his new wife, Sarah, in their running gear crossing the finish lines of races, or sporting winners' medals or standing shoulder to shoulder with the fit and wiry members of the veteran athletes' world. A picture of Nelson Mandela was displayed too, along with jokes and notes and other photos of old South African friends.

This time the discussion went better. I opened it, reiterating an earlier talk on the phone: "Dad, I mentioned that Ted and I wanted to help in some way with the ANC work. Either fundraising in the U.S.—there should be a good market there—or doing computer work. We'd love to be able to do something useful."

Here I felt much more confident. I knew what we had to offer, it made sense to me, and I wanted to do it. To do work for South Africa would help resolve the raw loss I still felt for the heat and color of Africa, and make my politics directly connected to that source of my desperate need to change the world.

My father sat on the edge of his desk, piled high with magazines and papers and his scrap-paper lists and scribblings of ideas. He nodded, thinking.

"Mmm. Yes. I'm sure that'll be useful. I talked to Dennis a little about the computer business—I'll give him a ring, see if they've made any decision yet."

Ted and I had read about Dennis Goldberg in the Guardian, the Left-wing paper I still subscribed to (though clandestinely, it was not approved reading in the O., being too theoretical, and not dealing with ideological issues adequately). Dennis had been part of the 1962 Rivonia treason trial; he was captured, along with other ranking ANC members, at an ANC hideout, a farmhouse in Rivonia, shortly before Mandela's capture. He'd served at least twenty years jail time, and had recently been released at the very beginning of the easing of things in South Africa, in the mid-1980s. There'd been some controversy because he had been sick, and had been forced to "renounce violence" as a condition of his release. The Left debated his integrity for a while, from the comfort of life outside of a jail cell, but the ANC had supported him, and now he worked full time for them in their London office, and traveled around speaking on behalf of the cause.

We met later that week: his eyes smiled from behind pebble glasses as he shook our hands warmly. He was endlessly pleased to meet another daughter (and an activist at that!) of his old friend Sylvester's, and referred to "home" constantly, with the assumption that for me, too, South Africa was obviously home. This was reward enough: to have the assumption of a common home without having to explain myself and my rootless relationship to geography. Dennis had no question, of course South Africa was my home, and of course I would want to help the struggle, precisely because it was home. I was welcomed to help: I was moved through the security checks quickly, because, not only was I South African, and so had an inalienable right to join the struggle, but I was also Sylvester's daughter which cleared me of suspicion immediately. I had been away from this home we shared as long as many ANC members—thousands having been exiled about the same time we'd left.

Dennis responded enthusiastically to our proposals and set up a meeting for us with the Logistics Department. They needed a computer program to help move supplies from Europe to the administrative and guerrilla bases in Africa. He would see if we could help with that.

Ted especially liked Dennis, as did I, but my shyness made it hard to talk to him. I felt such respect for what he had been through, and such inadequacy in myself. What could I hope to do, what could I offer? I would offer the little that I could, and hope that it would be useful—that would be my satisfaction. Dennis represented to us what we wanted to be: brave, dedicated, in it for the long haul.

Two days later I waited outside the ANC office on Penton Street; the eye of the video camera watched me as I watched it panning towards where I stood. I had already announced myself over the intercom, and some minutes passed before I heard bolts sliding and a key turning in the lock. A young African man opened the door and then locked it behind me. In the hallway, stacks of brown cardboard boxes overflowed up an already narrow and constricted staircase. A few of the boxes were open, and in one I saw folded clothes, in another exercise books and pencils. More school supplies—pens, pencils, paper, used text books—were piled on top of closed boxes. Some of the boxes were labeled "Solomon Mahlanghu School, Mazimbu, Tanzania," others were bound for Lusaka, Zambia.

I followed the young man past the security station where he monitored the split-screen video showing the front and back of the building—alert for the deadly terrorist attacks of the South African government. He picked a path through the precarious cascade of boxes, up the stairs to a third-floor room filled by two desks and an array of mismatched filing cabinets, still more boxes, ashtrays, dirty mugs sporting the black, green, and gold ANC logo, and two white men: Wolfie and Toine—both of whom worked for the Logistics Department. I had heard of Wolfie. He was well into his seventies, a small, owl-like man who spent a good deal of his time as a courier around London due to the fact that, as an old-age pensioner, he could travel free on London Transport. But what I remembered about him was a quote from Ruth First's book on her 180-day detention in the Marshall Square Police Station in Johannesburg:

> The large exercise yard had other diversions. On the blistering green paint of the yard door was the detainees' register. The first Ninety-Dayers had seen the scratched initials and cupid's hearts that decorated every blank police station's space. Next to "Edith loves Vic for Ever," Wolfie Kodesh had scratched "W.K. loves freedom for Ever."

I shook Wolfie's warm and wrinkled hand as I was introduced to him. Later I learned that for the past thirty years he had paid my entrepreneurial father an annual visit to ask for and receive a reliable and sizeable donation. In fact, it was this history that had led to my father and sister finally setting up the fundraising operation.

Toine rose to his considerable height to greet me, holding out both hands to grasp mine. He was younger—perhaps mid-forties, and he spoke with the strong accent of his native Netherlands. As a young man he had been a seminarian and had moved to South Africa to be a missionary. What he had seen there had led him to the ANC to which he had dedicated himself for decades already. Toine had strong features—a large nose and a high forehead broadening beneath thinning dirty-blond hair. His wide smile created deep creases on either side of his face. I was struck, as always, by the warmth with which ANC people greeted me—they knew me only through my family, but that created a welcome and acceptance that moved me.

Toine made tea, and then we sat at his desk while he detailed for me the Logistics Department's needs for their requisitioning and shipping system. Wolfie passed him a wide ledger with a mottled green cover. This was the existing system—it was Wolfie's job to transcribe all requisition and shipping transactions from Toine's order forms and invoices into this book. I was not allowed to look closely at Wolfie's meticulous cursive script, line upon line of it filling the book—these lines described, Toine told me, all the items sent from Europe (purchased or otherwise procured by Toine) to the bases in Africa. Toine said that these items ranged from airline tickets (he was the ANC's central travel agent), to the omnipresent boxes of clothes and supplies headed for the school in Tanzania, to computers and automobile parts. Years later, when the system was already installed and operational, and Toine called on me to fix a programming bug, I did see samples of shipped items; I noticed memos to ANC Executive Committee members and several shipments of gold wedding rings. For a time I convinced myself that this was simply code for a more deadly cargo—however, now I believe that, indeed, Toine was responsible also for the marital needs of the Congress.

I spent several hours with Toine defining the new system. He worked in a precise and knowledgeable manner, and when I left the Penton Street office and headed back through the gray London drizzle to the tube station I had solid and detailed information with which to begin developing the software on my return to the United States.

My father, sister, Ted, and I had also begun the discussion about fundraising; we drew out a sketchy plan and agreed to begin work on it when we returned to the States. We were to work with the New York office of the ANC, and we left England with the names of our new contacts: Enoch Gqomo, the New York treasurer, and Solly Simelane, the deputy representative at the United Nations. At last we were doing political work.

It was our final day in England. Ma lay in bed. Her head was hidden under the white sheets, her body just a mound curled up like a baby under the duvet. I put the cup of tea on her nightstand and stood at the side of the bed, my arms at my side, wondering what to do. Should I lean over and kiss her? No, she was turned away from me. I would not lean over that far. Just the top of her head, her brown hair was showing—what was there to kiss?

"Bye, Ma. Take care of yourself. I brought you some tea."

The olive green walls made me feel dark. I'd never felt comfortable in my parents' bedroom, which was now hers alone. Rows of Victorian portraits hung over the beds—who were they? The sepia-colored drawings of women in long ruffled skirts, sad-eyed women with ringlets easing past their ears, round-framed pictures of strangers peering over the bed in ordered elegance.

She didn't move or reply. I shrugged my shoulders and left the room, walked downstairs to the kitchen feeling empty and dejected. And as I crossed the kitchen to sit at the four-hundred-year-old refectory table that centered the house, heavy and immovable as history, I saw the spinning of a delicate flowered teacup, pirouetting past the bay window, duetting with a silver teaspoon as they flew in slow motion with the green of the oak trees and the garden lawn silhouetting their descent. Ted watched too. We turned to the window and looked down as the muted crash came—the corpse of the teacup littered the grass, the teaspoon lay silvery like half-buried Easter treasure.

Ted was open-mouthed.

"That was the cup of tea I brought her," I said. I closed my eyes and breathed deep, settling the sadness down into me. I didn't want it to come out now, we were on our way home, waiting for the taxi to take us to the airport.

It would be a year before she spoke to me again. Ted and I had visited my father. That was the mistake we'd made. I was not to have a father anymore. She was a re-writer of history, cutting him out of photographs, never mentioning his name, refusing to see mutual friends who still saw him, and becoming enraged when I saw him on my visits to England. She never forgave me for running away from home, and she punished me still. Whenever I most needed her is when she left me.

Ma used her arms when she was angry, and this I inherited. Those arms of hers threw plates and dropped teatrays in Sunday morning screaming fits aimed at my eldest brother and sister in their teenage years. Later, much later, when she was mad again, I had to pull her off my sister when she smacked her, over and over again around her head. And now, she'd risen from her bed, because I'd seen my father for a couple of hours the day before, flung open the window with the energy she found in her round and aging arms and thrown her rage at me. It was always like this when I left. Why should I expect anything different?

CHAPTER 19

On our return to Minneapolis a unit was pulled together to work on the Logistics program. P.O.O. named Suzanne, who I had never met, as the leader of the unit. She had just moved back to the Twin Cities from Chicago with Zack, to whom she was married, and their one-year-old daughter. Zack and Suzanne were in an arranged marriage, and they seemed like an odd match to me. Suzanne was all duty and function, whereas Zack, who I knew from the bakery, still found time to talk and read and smile. Bill was also assigned to the unit along with Betty, who I met at our first unit meeting. I recognized her as the surly-faced woman who had refused to greet me on my first morning in Minneapolis several years before. I was impressed with the longevity of the group members.

For the first time in the O., I had a role of some importance as the contact person to the ANC. The ANC's involvement was highly secure (a security measure that was, for once, justified), and when I discussed the project I spoke only in technical terms and never alluded to the ANC as the client.

Three or four times a week, we each arrived at Suzanne and Zack's apartment after work or on weekends for work shifts of several hours. We usually worked independently and alone, so we communicated, again, through memos. At the end of a shift, we spent at least a half-hour filling out summary sheets describing our work habits for the shift, the mistakes we'd made, responding to criticisms left by others, and, if we felt in a strong enough position to take the offensive, we'd leave a criticism for the next person.

At the end of this process, we did turn out a useful program for the ANC's Logistics Department, something about which I felt proud, and glad to have done, despite the isolation in which we worked. I had by now, completely submitted to this lonely way of working although I still didn't agree with it. It created a permanent state of tension in me—always apprehensive, wait-ing to get criticized, relieved when the criticism was for someone else, sad-dened when, on the rare occasions that I worked with someone else that the conversation was limited solely to the project at hand. It was only with a few people that this could be expanded a little in a tentative way.

Despite my role as the ANC contact, P.O.O. began addressing all cor-respondence about the ANC work to Ted. Then Ted would tell me what was said, or show me that part of his memo that was "open" to me, either cutting off the rest of the memo or folding it over so that I could not read it. I tried not to mind this, but I felt belittled; why could P.O.O. not communicate directly with me? Obviously this was because I was still ideologically weak, and this would teach me a lesson about my arrogance. It made me angry, but I knew there was no point in questioning it; all that would do would be to open me up to more criticism.

Another directive arrived. By now I was only getting three or four a year. I got direction from other cadres, or Ted, but rarely heard from P.O.O. myself. The software marketing work for the "Cadillac" of accounting systems had finally run out of steam, and now I was told to leave that program and start working with Bill and Jerri on the Youth Farm Program. Bill and Jerri had worked on this for years, taking inner city youth to spend the summer on a farm, working and learning about farm culture. Both of them were deeply committed to YFP as they cared about the kids, and it was the only program left that wasn't about building businesses.

Bill and I drove down to Madison, the halfway point between Chicago and Minneapolis, early one Saturday morning. We were to meet Jerri there for a unit meeting of the Farm Program. As we drove along the single stretch of highway that took us the two hundred miles to Madison, across the Mississippi, through the low, green hills of the Wisconsin Dells, and over more flat, endless prairie, Bill flipped open the glove compartment and pulled out a volume of Mao Tse Tung's *Collected Works.*

"I thought perhaps you could read out of this, and we'd have some dis-cussion while we drove—it would be a useful way to use the time." Bill was soft-spoken and left the idea as a question rather than an order.

"I really can't read in the car," I replied, taken aback by his request, "I'll get car sick."

He reached over and put the book back, resting it on top of the maps of Minnesota and Wisconsin and Illinois.

"Why don't you tell me something about yourself then. What's your background?"

Even though we had worked together on various projects for several years, we had never really talked. So we spent the next hours exchanging histories, in a careful kind of way. It was then that I discovered that he and Jerri had been married.

"What happened?" I asked, surprised to discover this connection between them. It seemed strange too, that they had worked so much together over the years. It must have been difficult to say the least.

"Back in '79 we left the O. for a year. It was in the period of the Intensification Campaign. Lots of people left then. We just couldn't take the level of struggle that was coming down. So we went to Denver—that's where part of my family was from, although none were there then. Jerri worked as a machinist, and I got a job as a hospital orderly, and we checked out the Left there. We realized that the Left hadn't changed much, still talking and debating and getting nothing done, and ideologically they weren't looking at themselves at all. So we decided to come back."

I'd heard about the Intensification Campaign, although I didn't know any details about it. I thought that was when Julie had left, too. Yes, I thought to myself, that would be about right, because she wound up with me in San Francisco in 1980. Bill continued, in a clear analytical voice, describing that period to me.

"We were split up when we got back."

I interrupted, "Why? Weren't you upset? Did you want to be split up?"

"We kind of knew it would happen. We knew when we decided to come back from Colorado that the identity between us was going to be challenged. I was upset at the time, in fact, it was fear of that happening that was part of why we left. A lot of relationships got broken up during the Intensification Campaign. But when we came back I could see how the relationship was holding us back. Particularly Jerri. We were too comfortable in it, and she didn't take as much leadership with me around, she needed to be independent of me."

He paused, and we drove on for a while. I looked out of the window, seeing the country to the east of the Mississippi for the first time, my eyes taking in the wide sky and the open fields. This was the closest I'd gotten to being out in nature for at least a year. But it was outside of the small car still, and inside was this story of Bill's marriage that filled the air as he explained it to me so reasonably.

"But what about you?" I said.

"It was a very subjective relationship for me. We couldn't move beyond that. Julie and I have a much higher level of struggle between us, and we've got an objective, functional relationship where we call each other on our bourgeois motions a fair amount. And we use the Dialectical Tools to look at our family. Not enough, of course, but much more consistently than Jerri and I ever did."

We arrived at the motel in Madison around noon, and I waited in the car while Bill went in to get the room number. Then we drove around the building and parked our car well away from Jerri's. Checking that we were not being observed, we made our way to the room and knocked on the door. Jerri answered it, stepped back from the door and let us in quickly without saying anything. Once we were in, she gave me a brief smile—we hadn't seen each other in the year since she'd moved out of the duplex at 801 Sullivan.

Even though it was midday, the heavy curtains were drawn as a security measure. The small table had been pulled up to the bed and two chairs were set up by it. Jerri's papers were spread out over one bed and the other was left clear for one of us to sit on. She was wearing a skirt. The table lamp and bedside lights shone a dim yellow light around the room. It was very dark inside, even though outside was a spring day with blue sky and black branches that, still budless, stood out in the clear air.

Now that I knew about Bill and Jerri, it felt a little uncomfortable to be sitting there with them. After a terse greeting the meeting began. The three-hour discussion centered on a major criticism of Bill and Ted's work in the O.'s clandestine print shop. This was the first I had been allowed to hear about the print shop, although I had guessed at Ted's involvement in it when he came home late some nights in greasy work clothes and with thick ink smeared beneath his fingernails. This would embarrass him, particularly at his computer programming job where he was very particular about his appearance, wearing shoes shined to a high polish, stylish ties and laundered, starched shirts.

Jerri criticized the print shop's work on the Farm Program's brochures.

"They'll all have to be redone. We're using these for fundraising. We can't send out this quality of work, it will destroy our legitimacy. You and 201," she addressed Bill, while referring to Ted's number, "will have to do a complete summary on overhauling the process at PSP."

PSP was the print shop's acronym and code name.

"Claire will join the PSP unit, and is to be trained in immediately. This will be a condition to introduce a new element into the identity operating between you and 201."

That familiar clutch of muscles grabbed my chest; Oh, god, I was being given yet another assignment when I hadn't even become accustomed to the Youth Farm Program work. I was already overwhelmed. I was dealing with my new job; starting to come to grips with my infertility and beginning to look at other options for building a family with Ted; I was working at the Youth Farm Program as well as working on the ANC projects. This was too much. I said nothing. I bowed my head and picked at the pink threads of the motel bedspread. Perhaps it would all just go away?

But it didn't go away. The next week I began work at the print shop. Now Ted and I would go together, after changing clothes from our day jobs as computer programmers, and head to the print shop. PSP was spread out between the basement and the garage of the O.'s childcare center. In the padlocked garage was an old offset litho press that was used to do glossy brochures and a huge power-cutter for sizing paper stock and trimming finished work. It was freezing in the garage. There was no insulation and only one electric heater. The first part of the printing procedure was for one of us to go in an hour ahead of the shift to turn the heater on. This warmed the garage up enough so that the ink would run properly, but not enough to allow us cadre printers to remove our gloves or coats. So in winter we fumbled with gloves, or blue fingers when gloves got in the way, and produced ream after ream of scrap as we went through the adjustments of ink and pressure and feed. By the end of our evening shift we may have set up the printer to run properly, but it would be too late to actually do the run. And so the machine would have to be cleaned completely, and we could only hope to duplicate our settings the next night to get out a decent run. Like so many of our O. projects, the printing was another exercise in amateurism, in the lack of respect for skill and specialization.

In the basement of the childcare center was a smaller offset printer, used for leaflets and other one or two-color jobs. There was also a full-size, ancient camera for shooting negatives. The basement was worse than the garage. When we arrived in the evening, we were not to speak to the childcare workers (who were generally non-O. people and had no idea the center was anything but a normal daycare center). They had been told some story to explain away the press in the basement and the people, like us, who came and went at odd hours. We would surreptitiously head down to the basement, unlock the door to the room containing the press and begin the shift. First the shift notes from the previous shift were read and analyzed, then we made our shift plan, and work began. As I knew nothing about printing, much of the time was spent explaining the press to me and having me read printer manuals. Then I would watch as Ted or Bill set up the machine. Again it seemed that nothing was accomplished in most of these sessions other than the creation of mounds of waste paper. Because the print shop was a closed program, we always left the shift with our cars filled with black garbage bags containing the scrap. It could not be left in the center's garbage cans in case the connection between the center and the Farm Program or the various software concerns was established—a serious security violation. And so, after the shift, at midnight or so, one person would stand look-out as the other flung the top-secret bags of scrap paper into the stinking dumpster at Cub Foods.

The worst thing about the basement press was that we had to work with the door closed. There was no alternate ventilation in the ten-by-twelve-foot room. After a half-hour the room was foul with ink and solvent vapors. I would remember my days in the machine shop and how I had struggled for ventilation, or masks, or less toxic materials, and now I was recreating the same unhealthy environment with no authority to which to complain. I was scared, too, because I was still trying to get pregnant. For a couple of weeks each month, I hoped and believed that a fertilized ovum was growing within me. Then, most of all, I panicked about the toxic fumes in that tiny stinking underground pressroom and worried for the health of the delicate cells that I imagined were dividing inside me. But we were not to open the door for fresher air because then the childcare workers would see us, even though the noise of the press already reverberated throughout the seedy structure.

I hated PSP. We could have sent any of the work we did out to a quick-print shop and saved both money and time. But when I raised this I was told that, again, the work was for our development and what we learned at the print shop was going to be used, in the future, to create an "open," commercial shop that would generate income for the O. I hated the chemicals, I hated the long hours when I was already exhausted, I hated the dead procedural-ization of the process, I hated the blurred, uneven quality of the work we produced, and, most of all, I hated the uselessness of it all.

Meanwhile, I was assigned to lead the Youth Farm Program teenagers in calisthenics during their orientation sessions—this was to prepare them for the

hard farm work expected from them in the summer ahead. The teenagers terrified me—I don't know why, other than that I had no experience with teens
and didn't know how to talk to them. During the exercises some of them giggled in the back of the gym, and I had to raise my voice to quieten them. The
session was videoed. The O. was beginning to be interested in video as a new
tool; our software programming walk-throughs were videoed, and cadres
were encouraged to buy camcorders on credit as part of the standard set of
tools O. members required. We were instructed to use videos in fundraising
for YFP. Apparently the video of me leading the exercises was shown to
P.O.O. because soon after Jerri forwarded a criticism from P.O.O. saying that
I was resisting the Internal Transformation Process by refusing to drop my
accent. Obviously my mixed British/South African accent, which, after fifteen
years in the States was still pronounced, was seen as an impediment to organizing rural Minnesotans. I tried to explain to Jerri that one didn't just drop an
accent, that it was a permanent fixture at this point. But she was just the mes-
senger and not interested in my justifications.

In addition to the pressure of all the O. programs, and my new job, Ted and
I were also well into the bureaucratic maze of adopting a baby. After two
years of tests and diagnostic procedures that finally presented us with the
choice between adoption or in vitro fertilization, with some relief, we decided to move ahead with adopting a child. Even though we both felt positive
about our choice, the decision to adopt nevertheless began a whole new and
difficult process of decision-making.

Once again we had dressed up—this time in what we imagined was the
appropriate attire of suitable parents-to-be. We attended an orientation at the
Jewish Family Services Adoption Agency, met with social workers and cleaned
our house for the anticipated inspection. Because the house was still held
hostage to function and function only, it lacked the decor appropriate for the
potential home of a new baby. Apart from the poster of Victor Jara that smiled
benevolently down on our sterile marriage bed, there were no other pictures
anywhere in the house. And so, as we had dressed ourselves up for the inter-
view, we adorned our house; we made a trip to the local library and checked
out four dusty landscapes from the Visual Arts section, and these we hung hur-
riedly one morning just before the arrival of a rotund and jaded social worker.

Not only our political life, but also our chance of having a child, now
rested on the success of our disguise. Another part of my life had been wrest-

ed out of my control; Ted and I now depended on a pink-cheeked matron from the agency to grant us this child for which we both yearned. Although the adoption inched forward almost imperceptibly, it did bring us hope: hope for this unknown child that already lived in us as the one we loved.

But in my O. work my internal resistance was back on the upswing. I felt myself cramped into a smaller and smaller space, sometimes, now, barely able to breathe.

Television

1986. Television allows us to repeat history as often as we wish. Slow motion, freeze-frame, instant replays. Images are examined and re-examined, and they burn a collective memory among the millions of private moments we each save, some to pass on to children as family lore, and others to be kept quiet forever in a personal shame.

A silver-and-white rocket, decorated with the nation's flag, streaks upwards into the blue, and, as the camera tracks the smoke and flame of its silent ascent, a momentary dissolve takes place. There is a delay in our senses and when three gaseous fistfuls of fire fly off in white-heat, we wait for the narrator to explain the silent image. The *Challenger*, fault of ice and an O-ring, has exploded within minutes of take-off, and all seven of its passengers instantly killed.

I imagine the moment—of dying without knowing you are dying. There is always the question—did they know?

When the letter bomb exploded Ruth across her university office—did she know? We assume, it seems to me, that it's better not to know. Is this a safe assumption?

I hear about the *Challenger* blowing up at work. The young men with whom I work leave their computer screens and gather in clusters around the radios that people have brought in to keep them company in the late-night overtime hours.

The day after the *Challenger* disaster, a meeting was called of all the software engineers on my project. A team from California was there, from a company that Lee Data had just acquired, and we were meeting as a group to confer on the design of System 2, the new communications controller that was to be our flagship product. Thirty of us gathered in the gray-carpeted conference room, twenty-six young white men, three Chinese men, and me, all seated around the shining conference table. Next door was the lab—a quiet, carpeted tangle of machines and cables strung out on metal racks and across the floor. Behind the multi-layered hum of computing power came the murmur of programmers discussing technical puzzles and the occasional shout of frustration or of laughter when the damn thing did-n't work again.

"Who's got the final protocol?" said Clay loudly to open the meeting, his legs splayed out as he leant his full weight back on the springy red workchair.

"It's here. We've taken the last bit for error-checking."

"No, that was reserved already! There's got to be some priority for the ack-nack routine," Chris shouted back, his lanky frame hunched over the table. The opinions flew among the over-confident white males as they bat-tled for intellectual territory with a certainty that demolished me. I sat quietly, half-hidden by Clay, my mentor. Sweat crept through the blue cotton of my unisex button-down oxford shirt; I couldn't keep up with the conversation or the arguments, most of the words were in a language that was still foreign to me, and I felt no right to stop and ask for a translation.

"What about diagnostics?" asked one of the California team. I still sat quiet, perhaps Clay would answer for me. The diagnostics piece of the proj-ect had been assigned to me, and I had no idea yet what to do with it. All I knew is that somehow I had to write a program that would be "burned" into a computer chip to sit inside the main box of the controller. When the con-troller was turned on, my program would kick off and run through all the memory, check that each byte could still remember its data, and then check all the communications ports, making sure the computer could send and receive. It had taken weeks for me to simply understand the task.

Clay turned to me, "Alex, what about the diagnostics, what's the design looking like?"

My face grew red. I could feel twenty-nine pairs of technical, masculine eyes on me and could not find a way to fit into the disputes; I had no opinion and was unable to pretend I did. "I don't know yet," I whispered, seeing the room and the eyes looking at me larger than life, unreal like a movie project-ed onto me. The pink mouths flapped, and cheeks were like balls of flesh, electric and moving with a life of their own. The table was still, or moving, I couldn't tell. I sat. I did not know how I could last through the meeting with-out fainting, but I did not have the courage to leave.

I heard Clay say, "We'll discuss it later."

The talk moved on to something else. I gripped my leather folder and did not move to wipe the glistening salt water from my forehead. The meeting ended, and I found my way to my cubicle, sat in my chair, put the folder in front of me and tried to breathe. I knew I couldn't cry there, but tears came from inside my back, stifled but running anyway. Clay and Bob came up.

"Are you okay, Alex?" Clay asked.

"Yeah, I just don't feel well." I didn't turn to look at them. I was afraid of losing control, so I sat rigid, looking down at my folder lying on the desk.

"I think I'll leave early."

Clay touched my shoulder, "System 2 meetings are enough to make anyone feel sick," he said sympathetically.

And I did leave, crying in the car as I drove home, feeling my body to be betraying me, going its own way into a cycle of shortened breath and heartbeats. It would not work, I was convinced, my body would break on me. What I had relied on with such casualness for so many years was now breaking. There was nothing I could do to stop it—if my heart decided to stop working, if its beat became irregular, as I could feel now, almost every day, it was beyond me, out of my control. All I could do was listen to it failing, and this I did, tuning in with every sense to the decay occurring without me, yet inside of me. If I stopped listening, surely then, that would be when it stopped completely.

I am dying, I realized.

But I kept myself functioning all week nonetheless. Until I started waking early. Sometimes at three or four in the morning. And then I would be cold. Freezing, shivering.

"Ted, Ted," I called him out of sleep in a half-voice.

"I'm cold, I can't get warm." My teeth were chattering so loudly he could hear them.

"Hang on, I'll find you some more blankets," and he rose from the bed and found a sleeping bag, a woolen blanket, a bedspread and laid them on top of me, one by one as I kept nodding my head for more.

"You can't still be cold," said Ted. He was angry and worried at the same time. Not knowing how to help, yet realizing there was a problem. I was shaking beneath the mound of covers, teeth clacking together like a skeleton. I wanted him to come under the covers with me, to warm me up as if I were a hypothermia victim. It was impossible for me to generate my own warmth. Or

I wanted him to fit heated blankets around my body, like they had done in hospital the year before, when I came to after my laparoscopy. There they had pumped my abdomen full of cold carbon dioxide and then pierced my skin through the navel and poked a tiny camera through on the end of a catheter to investigate the condition of my fallopian tubes. When I came out of the general anesthetic I was freezing too until one nurse finally brought out sweet hot blankets and stopped the cold for me.

Three mornings of this and Ted panicked. At five in the morning he called my chiropractor—who said, "Keep her warm." It was that morning that Ted told me to go to the ER if I needed to go.

After an hour my cold attacks would subside, and I'd get up, gray and drained, listening to the irregular thud th-thud th-thud inside, unable to tell Ted I knew my heart was stopping.

On Saturday morning I drove through the Lowry tunnel section of Interstate 94 in Minneapolis, giving a silent twelve-year-old boy a ride back to his mother's after his stint with the Farm Program, and my heart began to fail me again. Although my body appeared to be behaving normally, I felt as if it wouldn't obey my orders; I feared it would flail off on its own at any second, so I gripped the steering wheel, slowed down, breathed lightly so as to hear my heart sounds better and would have prayed if I had had any religious inclination at all. The square yellow lights along the sides of the tunnel flew past me at a speed I didn't understand; the boy next to me was like a terrible weight, a cargo beyond my abilities. But I got him home because I had to, and then I called Ted and then I drove myself—another interminable drive—to Hennepin County Emergency.

When the doctor finally saw me, he checked me over thoroughly, felt I had this or that, but couldn't find anything in particular and got ready to send me home. I was sent to the waiting area while they completed my paperwork. And among the slinged arms and crying children I sat there, until I got dizzy again and a nurse came by because my head was hanging down low onto my chest.

"Do you feel all right?" asked the nurse. She was kind, I remember her voice being kind. Ted had met me at the hospital and sat next to me, white, also, and his lips drawn to a thin and anxious line.

I looked up and couldn't answer, the lights were white behind her head. My mouth moved. No sounds came.

"Get her on the gurney!" Two orderlies grabbed me gently, like a child in their arms and laid me on the gurney in the hallway. I had become a priority all of a sudden. The nurse was taking my blood-pressure and a doctor was searching for my pulse. I was limp, giving over my arms to them, one to each, concentrating on the ceiling, the white lights above me and hearing the dull sounds of filtered life dancing a muffled dance towards my brain.

"Her pressure's dropped to the floor . . ." They talked with Ted, they leaned over me and talked to me through the muffled noise, "We're taking you up to Cardio. You'll be put on a monitor there—we need to figure out what's going on here."

Oh. There was something going on. But they were going to figure it out. Like in the movies, I was wheeled along corridors, in and out of elevators, without any desire to get up and say, "No, don't worry. I can walk." No, all I wanted to do was lie there and watch the ceiling roll by above me. There was something going on, they were going to figure it out.

Within an hour I was in a flannel nightgown, a drip running into my arm, the four cold plastic discs of the heart monitor glued to my torso and my heartbeat transmitting its wavy lines and its murderous thud th-thud to the green screen at the nurses station. I no longer had to listen for it. They could see it; my sad heart's sickness was on TV, they would look after me. I felt safe.

For a while, words left me—only pictures remained. There was a white pane. Light poured through. The light split into all its colors. The colors, in turn, became a deep, rich white. The luster of diamonds buried me, laying me flat and clean and empty. I floated in a drop of nothingness, but I did not fall. I was a note of music held in the air.

The light was intense and beautiful—not bright and sharp like the squinting of sunlight, but smooth, intensely relaxing, so my eyes dilated as with a drug. I was peaceful, lying without effort in the white bed, smiling as the square of light floated above my eyes, in my mind, around my body in perfect reassurance. This condensation of all color made me remember a stream in the foothills of the northern Rocky Mountains. There are places or moments of beauty that you never forget; they last a lifetime like small, unchiselled diamonds of memory. This stream curved through the mountains laying gold-dusted silt on its banks. Only one old gold-panner still lived there, living out the grandfather clause on his claim in the Trinity Alps.

I had been there in my California years. Spent a springtime week surrounded by wildflowers. On one silted bank of the clear cold river a tiny pasture of yellow flowers had grown up, grown so close to each other no dirt or green was visible, just a spread of yellow petals that glinted and turned together in the morning to follow the sun as it rose over the eastern rim of rocks above. The clear water slapped along the slanted bank, the flowered gold, the blue from the sky and the spotted green from the foliage dipping down—all these colors floated in the water broken up by the humped backs of the riverbed rocks.

I'd lain by the stream listening to the song of the water, catching tiny drops sprinkling on me, watching the shining yellow pasture, and every nerve, every sense, was warmed by the sun, was part of the mountained life, absorbed forever in memory and remembered, now, from a white hospital bed where the absence of color finally gave me peace.

A soft white sandwich lay by my hospital bed. I didn't want it, couldn't imagine the process of chewing or swallowing food. Julie came by with Beth. I stretched my hand out to them. I smiled. Beth bobbed up and down around the bed. I wanted only to rest and every part of me did so. Ted must have come and gone—I don't remember anymore. Jerri and Bill, both of them tall, stooped towards me, Jerri kindly wondering after me, "Don't worry too much, it's probably Ideological. You'll be able to struggle with it."

I didn't move. My spine pressed into the bed, my shoulders settled deep in the pillows. I would only face them but not raise myself, my mouth slack but smiling.

It came to an end. The heavenly interlude lasted no longer than twenty-four hours. They let me go the next day. The doctors had come by, showing me off to the young interns—I was an example of something, I never knew what. The heart monitor had shown nothing, the electro-cardiogram had shown no irregularities. They let me go. I had no one to help me anymore.

I wrote a memo to P.O.O. to inform him and to request a reprieve from my workload. P.O.O. replied, removing me from the Youth Farm Program, the print shop and the computer work. P.O.O. told me to look after myself.

CHAPTER 20

Then came my first child. Ted and I had made our way through the adoption process, and, after almost two years of waiting, we had finally been assigned to a child in Honduras. We traveled there; I held my baby in my arms, and he looked at me, all his three months of life open to me in those eyes that met mine and held my own. I continued being terribly sick in Honduras. I still did not know what was wrong with me, and I ached as I held my new son, in terror that I wouldn't be alive when we returned the requisite six months later to bring him home for good.

We left him after that one week that the Honduran government allows adoptive parents before the process continues its bureaucratic way. As we flew home, my heart ached for missing him and with the fear of never holding him again. I realized that I had to become better, that I had six months in which to recover if I was going to be his mother. The little baby boy who threw up more bottles of formula than he could keep down, the little baby who slept so delicately, his thin soft limbs already agitating to be on the move—I needed to repair myself or I would lose him.

I traipsed from one doctor to another after the hospital sent me home that previous year. I knew there was something wrong. My arms and legs tingled and felt numb and weak. My chest almost constantly hurt. And I would get these feelings of unreality that reminded me of being high on drugs. The form of things would change; colors became brighter, unbearably intense, pulsing with a life they shouldn't have.

I drove up Highway 100 coming home from work one day, gripping the steering wheel to keep the car straight. On my right was the shoulder and then the concrete barriers that bounded the road. My attention fixed on that gray line of concrete. It seemed impossible, then, to avoid crashing into it. It was so close, and it swerved as the road curved and then the cars to the left of me became animated—why wouldn't they steer into me? It was all so completely out of control! Any car could veer off its lane and shove itself into me. What was keeping any of it together?

For months driving became torture—before it had been something I enjoyed. I was a good driver. In fact, when Ted and I went out together I used to insist on driving because he'd totaled three cars already (he used to fall asleep at the wheel, usually after a string of double shifts where he'd get only three hours of sleep a night), and he'd either tailgate, or slow down to a speed illegal on the freeway. But now I took every chance I could to avoid driving.

I knew I wasn't well. I carried inside me everywhere I went this knot of fear, this packet of panic. And I went from one doctor to the next trying to get help.

Chiropractors administered tests and gave me lists of diseases that I would get if I didn't sign up for six months of treatment, give up gluten, change my cookware and quit my job. They threatened Alzheimer's disease, liver malfunction, arthritis . . . I had sense enough to stop going to them finally. But after spending that week in Honduras with bright, smiling Luis, I found Dr. Anderson, a neurologist who was my last port of call. I was scheduled for an encephalogram.

"All right, dear," the nurse said—plump and middle-aged, brittle, dark curls surrounding her face—"Just have a seat in the chair there, and we'll get you hooked up!"

She laughed as she said this to defuse the tension. I was looking at an electric chair. It was made of worn brown leather with straps dangling from the headrest. It was just like the picture of the Rosenberg's death chamber.

"Do I have to do this?" I began to panic. I had always hated doctors' procedures and tests and especially now, when my whole body was in a heightened state, I couldn't imagine putting myself into that chair and into their control. I didn't trust them at all.

"Well, dear," said the nurse, adjusting her polyester uniform that was bunched too tightly around her hips, "Dr. Anderson can't see you without getting some diagnostic information. It's really not so bad. We just take a reading of the electrical function of your brain. It doesn't hurt at all."

I let her talk me into it and tentatively sat on the chair, already hyperventilating. Another woman, younger and blonde, came in and sat behind me. She showed me the electrodes: red plastic discs on black cables with gold points at the end of them. These were attached to a machine pulled up next to the electric chair.

"I'm just going to attach these to your scalp, and then we show you some different patterns to look at, and have some lights going on and off. All you have to do is sit there and watch, the encephalogram machine will do the rest. I'll be right here with you."

She sat on a high stool behind me as I looked forward, hands clawed upon the arms of the chair. Her fingers pulled and parted my hair and rubbed Vaseline into the spots she cleared. The cold of the cream seeped down my spine, and down to a numb place in my calves. I couldn't pull away from her; it would be ridiculous and so I stopped myself. She took the gold point of the electrode and scratched into one of the Vaselined clearings on my skull. Okay, that was all right. There was the cold cream and a little scratch. Then she began to screw the point down. I could hear it scrape as she turned and twisted it into the top of my head. It sounded too loud, the sound traveling around my skull and down into my jaw, but I couldn't stop her. And on she went, screwing perhaps ten or twelve of those electric cables into my scalp.

"I'm scared of electricity," I managed to say at last, certain that the cables would send electric currents into my brain. I remembered Chris, one of Hatty's old boyfriends, one who had smacked her, and I recalled how he'd believed he had a radio receiver implanted in his head, and when upset he would rage at the violation of it. For the first time I empathized with him. This was unbearable.

It didn't stop. When the metallic scraping against my head was done (which I had borne only by remembering Hector and the little scars all over his small body, saying to myself, absurdly, "Imagine this is for the people, imagine that it is torture, real torture, and I would have to bear it then. Think how much worse it could be"), then the blond nurse turned out the lights and sat herself in front of me hidden behind a large cardboard square surrounded by floodlights. She turned out the ceiling lights and then switched one of the floodlights on and the black and white pattern on the board was illuminated, like an optical illusion pattern, or one of the pop-art pictures popular in the sixties—op-art, I remembered it was called, as I sat there, wired up, strapped in, chugging for breath as if I were in the last stages of a marathon. The white light held onto the board, and then the blonde nurse technician sent the black-and-white images on the board spinning and my eyes were sucked into the pulses of black and white with colors now popping out on sticks like eyeballs scaring me. She turned it off.

"We've got a baseline!" she said cheerfully. "We'll try once more now."

The smell of my own sweat rose up to me. She turned the floodlight on again, the board started up its nauseous swinging and then the other lights flickered on and off. The sweet blonde had started up a strobe, and all I could feel were the gold points pinned into my head and the tormented thought that she was directing electricity into my brain, even after I had asked her not to. I couldn't even see the strobe anymore, I felt obliterated.

Afterwards I was unstrapped and taken to wait in the doctor's office. My shoulders crumpled as I waited there. Dr. Anderson came in, very friendly, not much older than me. He was good-looking, gray-haired and slim, and he focused on me in a gentle but intent manner that made me fall immediately in love with him. He seemed to care.

He asked the usual questions: When did I get symptoms? What were they? What did I think was going on? He hammered on my knees and elbows, had me walk along a straight line, gave me tongue twisters to repeat, let me follow his reassuring fingers as they moved in front of my eyes. He thought, and he wrote. Then he looked up at me.

"The tests show your neurological function to be good. But I've noticed something. You seem to be sighing a lot."

As he said that, I sighed, deeply. Tears pricked my eyes and the back of my neck tensed.

"That usually indicates hyperventilating."

"But I thought hyperventilating was when you just take shallow breaths?"

"That's part of it, but then the sighing is an attempt to get additional oxygen. I think you may be experiencing panic attacks. The level of stress-related symptoms that you're having fits with that and they can all be caused by hyperventilation. I don't believe there's any physiological malfunction."

He explained to me the physiology of panic attacks: the accumulation of stress, the faintness and dizziness caused by irregular breathing, the so-called "second" fear that is generated from the developing physical symptoms and then the increase in shallow breathing leading to additional symptoms and fear. It was a vicious cycle, he explained, and the disorder had only recently had been understood by the medical profession. Treatment was through counseling and education. The prognosis, he claimed, was good, because we had caught it early; many people had panic attacks for years before being diagnosed.

It made perfect sense to me. Here was something concrete, that fit what I had been going through, that gave it a name and a treatment. I left his office armed with a bibliography on panic attacks and an appointment with a psychologist specializing in the field. I went straight to the bookstore, bought a couple of the books and spent the rest of the day reading. Yes, there it was, it fit perfectly. My relief was immense. I was sick, yes. I'd had panic attacks. And the books, with great sympathy and understanding, described all the pain and fear I'd felt and gave me easily understood ways of breaking the cycle of stress, tension, and second fear. It would take time, but now I had the tools I needed. And I wasn't dying. I would live to see my baby come home. I would live to be his mother. With tremendous relief, I saw the end of the blackness that had controlled me for the last year.

I began to go to the psychologist, and then to a panic-attack group where the fears of driving, of dying, of heat and cold, of being in meetings, of performing, of perfectionism, all were shared and understood by a disparate, suffering group who helped me back on my feet. But, of course, I kept my organizational secrets. The psychologist encouraged me to make more friends, to get support around the coming arrival of my child, to modify my schedule to get more sleep. I couldn't explain to him that the rules under which I lived meant I could do none of these things freely.

But I began to get better, and I learned that beneath the panic attacks lived feelings. Feelings about my work; about the O. (which I could not allow to emerge, only occasionally admitting to myself that I still did not understand the work and still did not like the way that things were done); feelings about my son, Luis, arriving; feelings about Ted's distance; feelings about my loneliness; about the lack of time and privacy in which I could be myself. Ted and I started to talk about this, and, for the first time in our relationship, we began to allow that there was room for the "subjective." In fact, as I pointed out, look what happened if we didn't allow room for it—look how sick I'd become. My illness had frightened Ted so much, and he had been drawn into it so thoroughly, believing almost as much as I did that I was, indeed, dying, that he was able to admit this entrance of feeling into our lives. From the bitter experience of the last year he too could agree that we needed to share that interior part of ourselves, even when it wasn't objective, ideologically sound, or part of our rising, proletarian sides.

This brought me back to my original set of beliefs that I'd held before joining the O.: that the subjective, felt experiences of people were as important a part of understanding history and the development of the world, as the objective statement of facts and economic laws. It dawned on me slowly how the O. had removed any of the subjective, that it simply wasn't allowed or acknowledged as having any value. And I had accepted that, and now knew that it was a clear part of the credo: that anything subjective was automatically tainted by one's bourgeois world outlook and so should be dismissed. No, the subjective was real too. My panic attacks had been as real as anything. My mind and my body had cooperated to make me so sick that I could barely function.

In my summaries I put it down to the stress of the upcoming adoption and my internal resistance to becoming a mother. This followed the line of thought that since my Ideological Form was Male Chauvinism, then obviously I would resist motherhood. My struggle was to embrace the new stage. But privately, in one of the handful of journal entries that I made during those years, I wrote a list detailing the conditions in the O.: the overwork; the lack of friends, of sleep, of family; the double life and the secrets.

There are two other entries from that year.

October 4th, 1986

I must forward a memo about going to the panic group and the psychologist. I will have to make it "objective." I will say that my neurologist referred me, and he said that many "effective" people get the same problem and that it helps to talk to others about it.

And what about Ted, when he struggles with me? Inside myself I want to curl up into a ball to protect myself and say "Don't hurt me." Then I can't hear anymore what he says, I am just paralyzed trying to block him out.

Why is it such a struggle for me to accept criticism?

Why do I think the criticism will hurt me? Why don't I see it as help? That's what Ted says it is—he says that only developing my rising side will help me get better. He says I have to look at why I always think I'm right, why do I think the O. is wrong, that leadership is wrong? He says that leadership has more experience than I and has proven itself in practice—and look at me, obviously I am out of control, and I can't even accept that—look at my panic attacks.

He pushes me into a corner, then I feel so trapped I want to scream, but I can't, so I lower my head and enter that protected place. I try to talk to him about some of my feelings but he just pushes me back in. It makes me want to totally close up, to back off, to leave.

October 20th, 1986
I am starting to be able to make the physical connection of the fear to the pain in my chest. Yesterday, trying to explain to Ted what my feelings were, I could feel the tension in my chest, how my breathing was all stopped up and how that hurt me. When I cried and felt myself and my anxiety, my chest relaxed and the pain eased up.

That's all that's in the journal, and there are no more entries for six months. But after I wrote those lines I wanted to read Sylvia Plath again. Leonard had given me a book of her poems in 1978, and in San Francisco I had read and reread them. She wrote of places and people I knew and feelings that I could at least imagine. Her book was still down in the basement, in one of the cardboard boxes labeled V that I had not yet unpacked in the four years I had been in Minnesota. Later that week, when I was doing the laundry, I pulled out my old book boxes and I unpacked them. Now that we had no roommates I could fill up the empty spaces in the bookshelves with the precious words that had lain lost and unread, unshared, for so long. I reread the poems of Sylvia Plath's *Ariel* and tasted the words that I loved:

I am the baby in the barn . . .
A vice of knives . . .
Viciousness in the kitchen/the potatoes hiss . . .
The hills step off into whiteness . . .
In a forest of frost, in a dawn of cornflowers . . .

I flipped through the words—my old friends. My favorite phrases: they were still there, just as they had been, dense and rich and passionate. I clutched her book to me as if it were a person, and I held the smooth white cover to my cheeks and felt its coolness, just like I remembered.

* * *

To: 201
From: P.O.O.

There will be a marketing effort to place NB's [the bakery's] highly productive data-processing system in South Africa. The E. will place itself and with HP hardware become a dominant force in SA's market. Only the E. will have the ability to take the productive experience learned through scientific practice and bring it to a realization of distribution in the world economy.

You should look into methods and contacts that Claire's DA [my father] might have in SA for positioning the NB software system. To note, it will eventually be rewritten to run on the HP 250, quality hardware.

I listened in disbelief as Ted read P.O.O.'s latest memo out loud. P.O.O. wanted me to get contacts through my father to market the bakery's software system in South Africa. This was the weirdest directive we'd had yet. What the hell was he playing at? I asked myself. It was one thing to focus on production and creating businesses to fund the revolution and learn administrative skills (I'd read the history of Lumumba and the Belgian Congo by now and was willing to accept the need for the incredible amount of work we all put into developing this), but this was going too far.

"Doesn't P.O.O. realize there are *sanctions* on doing business with South Africa. This is ridiculous," I said to Ted.

I hardly knew how to begin expressing myself. My mother had boycotted South African grapes and oranges from the time I was a four-year old, when I'd accompany her to the local market. The economic boycott of apartheid had been going on for my entire lifetime and in the 1980s, the ANC, after years of struggle, had finally become strong enough to force through sanctions in the United Nations. Within the United States, students and other activists had brought the boycott to universities and corporations. Sanctions were in full swing and were a powerful tool in the fight against apartheid; in the Reagan eighties, sanctions were one of the few clear progressive stands people were taking on a mass scale. The South African government was isolated and derided by most of the world. I could not believe that P.O.O., whoever he was, was suggesting that we break sanctions.

"Can you imagine me asking my dad to help us sell software in South Africa? He'd really think I was mad. Jesus Christ! I cannot believe this."

"It's probably just a mistake," said Ted. "Look, we'll write back and say that sanctions are on and that your Dad wouldn't break them. I can't really see how leadership could make a mistake like that, but maybe its part of a bigger initiative—you know, we don't have all the information about what's going on."

"I've got enough to know that you don't break sanctions. How's that supposed to develop our relationship with the ANC, for crying out loud. God. We're trying to build a working relationship with them. How are you going to explain that one away? 'Oh, Solly, don't worry about us breaking sanctions, it's just tactical. Really it's to fund the revolution so we can help bring the government down.' Give me a break."

Eventually Ted and I wrote a politely worded memo to P.O.O. reminding him that U.N.-sponsored sanctions were, indeed, in place and that we would jeopardize our relationship with the ANC if we attempted any kind of economic activity with South Africa. But it continued to stick in my craw and I started to secretly hope that Ted would see the hypocrisy and begin to talk with me more openly about the flaws in the Organization. But apart from agreeing with me and writing the memo, he raised nothing further about it. And I was still silenced. P.O.O. had told me, back when I'd tried to leave the O. in 1983, that all I wanted was to pull Ted out and turn him into a fat and happy bourgeois. In my mind, I could not, therefore, ever raise the topic of leaving the O., or even of fundamental disagreements with leadership. The initiative had to come from Ted or I would be fulfilling P.O.O.'s prophecy.

Up the street from 801 Sullivan, about five doors up, was 905. Since the cadres who'd lived there had all been moved to Chicago, Ted and I had been put in charge of the place. We were, in effect, the landlords. We found tenants, collected the rent and generally looked after the place. I don't believe the tenants knew that we lived on the same block—for the usual security reasons, they only had our work phone numbers. It was almost impossible to rent the place because it was so run down, so we usually ended up renting it to single black mothers on welfare; they didn't have many other options, and to us they seemed to be a better risk than young black men.

We always had trouble getting the rent. Rhonda was the last tenant with whom we dealt. She was twenty and had three children. She fit the kind of stereotype that the *Tribune* would have enjoyed featuring: poor single black mother, probably on drugs, and hanging out with unemployed black men. Well, what did we expect? We were renting out what was essentially a slum dwelling in a mostly black neighborhood.

Once I went over there to fix the toilet; it wouldn't stop running, and the water bills had finally gotten so high we'd decided to fix it. There was practically no furniture in the place, and the kids were all sitting on the floor in the empty living room watching TV with a man who said he was Rhonda's brother. He was obviously living there too, in violation of the lease agreement.

I checked in the kitchen to see how the cockroaches were doing—we had to have the place fumigated each month because the roaches were so bad. The cupboards were completely empty except for a box of dried WIC milk, the kind distributed by the government as part of the child welfare program. The fridge contained a baby bottle half-full of juice and some curdled milk. On top of the fridge were boxes of cereal: Froot Loops (they have to spell it like that because there's no actual fruit in them), Alphabits, Coco Pops. I wanted to cry at the barrenness of it all. But I fixed the toilet instead. And Rhonda, very defensive at this white woman in her house, refused to make small talk with me and showed me out as soon as I was done.

The next month, we were told to evict her as she quit paying the rent. The day she was to leave, we went up to the decaying duplex. Rhonda and her kids were gone and the place was trashed. The powdered WIC milk was dumped on the kitchen floor and cockroaches were already examining it. The frosted pink and green circles of Froot Loops were spread across the living room floor; pop bottles and used diapers intermingled with the cereal. Then I went into the bathroom.

I did a double-take, almost comical, like a Marx Brothers movie—something wasn't there. It was such an odd sight that it took me a second to figure it out. I stood staring at a hole in the floor, black and deep, sinking into the guts of the house and I put my head in my hands and thought, "What am I doing here? How did I get to be a slum landlord? Oh, the goddamn Froot Loops. Oh, the children!"

The toilet stool had been ripped out.

I wanted to weep again. This place was disgusting, but it had been disgusting when Rhonda had rented it: I couldn't believe what they had done, but I couldn't blame them either. Rhonda was communicating to me, her white landlady, in a language of complete contempt, one that I had not had to hear before. It was an act of rage and desperation, and I had been seen as the agent of their misery. No! I thought, I was just following orders, I will never do this again.

Later, we were told to develop a plan for improving the 905 duplex as an investment. We talked to realtors and city inspectors and brought in redevelopment specialists who had an interest in the neighborhood. All of them agreed on one thing: rip the place down, get rid of it, start over. It was substandard on every level, and the last remodeling job had divided it into tiny cell-like rooms with patched sheetrock. To tear it up, make it a single family home again, fix the stairs, the roof, the heating and the plumbing would cost more than the price of a new house. There was no way to make it work.

We realized that this was the context in which landlord-instigated arson occurred; we finally saw how people could come to that. It was sad to see housing become destroyed and then to see its effect on the whole block—it was an unsafe eyesore. We summarized the advice we had been given and forwarded it in a memo to P.O.O. We advised in the strongest terms possible putting no more money into the property but foreclosing it, or selling it, or letting it revert to the city.

P.O.O. responded angrily; we were giving up, he (I had now come to assume that P.O.O. was, in fact a "he," and that there was just one of him, not a leadership group as I'd been led to believe) told us this was organizational property, that our attitude disrespected the labor that had been put into it over the years and that if we could not deal with the assignment then he would gladly pull us off it and put someone else on who would show more commitment. Once again I found myself pleased to be demoted from a thankless task. Debbie was shortly to return to town, and she would be given the job.

Shortly after the affair at 905 I brought little Luis home from Honduras. It was a happy time. Ted arranged a small welcome in our cramped living room. Bill, Julie, Beth, and her new half-sister, Sally, came, along with Sara (another long-standing cadre I'd only just met) who had recently moved back from Chicago and been installed in 905 in place of the rageful Rhonda.

Now that Luis was home, my family once again started asking for a phone number or address for me. They had only had my post office box number for the past four years and were getting more and more anxious over my whereabouts. Ted and I requested that we be allowed to give them the number. The request was denied based on security. It was clear that there was something about 801 that required particularly intensive security.

Now that we were involved in the ANC work, and were to begin fundraising for them, Ted and I saw an opportunity to finally get out of 801. It wasn't as bad as 905, but it, too, was a stifling place to live: small, very secure, and with this pall over it that I didn't understand till later. We wrote to P.O.O. requesting that we move due to the security issues around the ANC work. The fundraising would require a more public presence, we said, which was in conflict with the security needs of 801. Thankfully, P.O.O. agreed we could move.

* * *

We were sitting at the kitchen table in 801 on a Sunday morning. Luis was down for his morning nap. Ted was reading the paper, and I was checking the classifieds, looking for a house or a duplex for us to rent. Two bedrooms, decent—we wanted somewhere nice to live. Especially now we had Luis. He needed room to play, to learn to walk.

"Hey, did you see this?" said Ted. He was reading the Metro section of the paper.

"I think this is someone who was connected. He's come back into town and given himself up to the police on some charge. It looks like it was to do with that drug killing across the street."

"Hmm. That's odd." I didn't pay much attention. Ted was always reading things about people he'd known, or noticing people at the supermarket that he'd read about. He had an acute memory for names and faces and close to an obsession about it—sometimes imagining that he knew someone just because he'd seen them on the TV.

"Here's a good place." I said. "Two-bedroom duplex in Golden Valley, big yard, attached garage. I'll go see it today while you're at the print shop."

I folded up the paper and went to get Luis who was making restless noises in the bedroom next door.

Chapter 21

Television

1989. A young man stands thin and small in the center of my TV screen, the square of his white shirt fluttering above loose black pants. An olive drab tank rolls towards him. This image I notice. What passes me by, however, is that later, hundreds of protesters are massacred in Tienanmen Square. Somehow I shut my eyes to it; perhaps it doesn't seem important.

Anyway, it doesn't move me. I have given up on China years ago, ever since Mao's death. I have held the position that the "Capitalist Roaders" have been restored to power in the form of Deng Xiaoping, and I hold on solemnly, maturely, I think, to what I see as Mao's correct line and I refuse to be shaken the way others are shaken by the turn of events in China. It's just like the Soviet Union, I proclaim. The law of Uneven Development—some advances were made, now it's someone else's turn. Don't look to China for anything more. I am determined not to be struck down by disappointment and cynicism in the way that my parents' generation suffered after the invasion of Hungary in 1956, or the exposés of Stalin at the Twentieth Congress.

No, I am very mature, dialectical. After Mao's death all hell had broken loose. I didn't choose, then, to wonder why. Nonetheless, the image of the young man does not disappear from my memory—it is stark; he seems alone, like a figure in the desert where the haze blurs the features of his face.

We moved to the house in Golden Valley, an older suburb adjacent to Minneapolis. For a year we lived in a rented rambler with two beautiful willow trees in the backyard that at least partially hid the freeway that roared by a hundred yards away. We had finally left 801 which had stayed empty for a few months until Dave and Debbie and their child, Sam, returned from Chicago to move in. It was only now that I discovered that Ted shared ownership of 801 with Kristin Olson, and this puzzled me: Was that why the FBI had come looking for her?—because she owned 801? And after all, didn't the FBI agent say there'd been a killing there? I couldn't put it together, but I was relieved to be out. With P.O.O.'s new directive, Ted signed over his ownership to Debbie, and we were clear of the property.

We were well into the fundraising work by this time, and the FBI was already on our tail because we used the name of the ANC (having been cleared by the London office to do this) in an ad in *Mother Jones* magazine. The FBI had responded to the ad immediately with a letter to us and to the New York office demanding to know why the ANC was soliciting for donations in the United States. This violated, apparently, their diplomatic status here. We pulled the ad immediately and began to rework the campaign. Finding our own legal representation, we set up a non-profit organization, the South Africa Freedom Fund. We learned the hard way that we had to create our own campaign here, within the confines of U.S. law and culture.

In England, my sister and father had organized newspaper campaigns in the name of the ANC. England did not have the intense paranoia of foreign organizations apparent in the United States. There they were free to use the ANC name, and use it they did. After a couple of years of work, they were running full-page ads in the national newspapers there—the ads made up of thousands of names of celebrities and other supporters. They built a kind of rolling campaign, where each ad would lead into the next, paid for by the previous contributors and culminating in these full-page spreads that were dramatic, simple and effective. Within four years, they had a lucrative donor base of 20,000 names. They raised millions of pounds for the ANC as well as contributing to the general positive profile that the ANC had developed in the United Kingdom.

Ted and I hoped to duplicate at least a small portion of this, and to this end we worked hard. We researched the other fund-raising efforts going on in the United States, we learned about direct marketing from my father and sister and from seminars and books, and we researched list brokers and bought, traded and tested lists. Together we wrote and rewrote letters and designed packages. We developed our own computer system to record results and automatically generate receipts and additional donor letters.

Another memo arrived. P.O.O. was obviously pleased with our ANC work, although he continued to slight me by sending all the memos to Ted. He congratulated us on our various direct-mail pieces and encouraged us to keep making further connections with the ANC. There was no further mention of breaking the sanctions; actually there was not even any acknowledgment of our memo replying to that, the idea was simply dropped. I had begun to notice this—that if I objected to an idea and said so in a submissive tone, then often the idea was quietly dropped. Not always, but often.

But this memo set me off again. There were two parts to it. The first suggested that we discuss with the ANC the idea of us setting up an adoption agency and working with them to place orphaned South African children in the United States. Again, my first response was disbelief. How could P.O.O. think that the ANC would be anything but insulted by this idea? There were so many reasons not to do this that I didn't know where to start. Ted agreed with me, again, that it was a bad idea, but with his usual need to be disciplined and accountable, he decided he would go ahead and at least ask about it. I tried to talk him out of it—I felt embarrassed by the whole thing.

The second point in the memo was that we ask our ANC contacts, Enoch and Solly, if they could get us any leads in Ghana or Mozambique for large building contracts, such as airports or government buildings. We knew, at this point, that there was an O. contracting company. This was the company that had worked on the interminable and poorly managed remodeling of the O's daycare center which Luis now attended. For over a year, the kitchen and entrance had been torn up, the inside walls replaced with plastic sheeting and months had gone by with no visible signs of progress. Just the week before, Ted and I laughed because a large construction sign had been erected at the center, and we'd finally found out the name of the company: Careful Construction. This hit our funny bone—Dependable Computer Programs and now, Careful Construction. I imagined a burly construction worker holding up his hammer in one hand and displaying his unscarred thumb on the other: "We May Be Slow, But We're Always Careful!"

Ted and I laughed, too, about the marketing prowess (or more specifically, the lack thereof) of our comrades in the construction and software divisions of the Organization. This was one of the places we could safely share our feelings about the O.—as long as we kept it humorous and did not edge into the dangerous territory of actually criticizing leadership.

So, the thought of the obviously inept (yet careful) O. construction company taking on large projects in Africa was clearly someone's fantasy. Ted realized that this was a bird-brained idea and not one to help us nurture what was still a very positive relationship with the ANC. We agreed that this was something on which we would not follow through, and we wrote back, yet again, politely declining this assignment and pointing out that the hugely divergent tasks and requests that were being put on the ANC connection would only defuse and undermine our efforts, which, so far, were having a small degree of success.

Solly and Enoch stopped by that winter to visit and check on the fund-raising project. Ted and I made them welcome in our home, showing them into the house in the lily-white neighborhood in which we now lived. I happened to know that the suburb of Golden Valley included only six black families in 1980, the year of the last census—this research having been done for yet another aborted O. project.

I made them a big dinner of lamb and roast potatoes and our lively Luis entertained them both while we ate. After dinner, the two of them sat on the couch, and we talked for hours. Solly told us about his family, who he hadn't seen in fifteen years since he'd fled South Africa during the Soweto riots. Now he was married and had a seven-year-old son here, but his mother and brothers and sisters still lived in Soweto. He worried about them constantly as they were harassed and poverty-stricken, and we listened as he told us his story and were moved to silence. Now Solly worked out of the ANC mission at the United Nations, and also traveled around the country speaking and organizing.

Ted asked, "Is Solly a common name in South Africa?"

"Hey, Ted, that's not my real name! Many of us who fled have had to change our names—they will still come after us, even now."

Ted and I felt a certain camaraderie now; we could identify with their code names—after all, we too had our own code names for security purposes.

Enoch worked in New York as an accountant and was the treasurer for the ANC in the United States. Both of them were warm and open and talked to us about the struggle and offered us thanks for any help we gave them. I felt they were the ones to be thanked, because they had given me this opportunity to help, the chance to do something real, for the one place in the world that perhaps I could call "my country." I was tentative about it though; I had left so young, I did not feel the right to call it my home. Yet when I heard South African music, especially the penny whistle tunes that drew for me pictures of barefoot African boys, their small fingers tapping out the melody as they danced with their feet in the dust—that was when I felt the music pulling at the emptiness in me with a remembered longing. I imagined the African dust rising under my own feet and in my hips I felt the sway and the resistance of the hot ground. For this I wanted to thank Enoch and Solly—for being there, for sitting on my couch in a Minnesotan suburb, for bringing a piece of myself into that white, snow-covered landscape.

We moved on to discuss the business at hand, our fund-raising work.

"The problem with the FBI is all cleared up now, isn't it Solly?" Ted said.

"Yes, yes. Don't worry. We must just be careful next time. We can't use the ANC name at all, okay? They just looking to get us on anything you know. There is a man in Washington—all he does is spend his whole day reading Left publications to check out this kind of thing. We will do a nice non-profit—we can use the Solomon Mahlanghu school in Tanzania—and do all our fund-raising for them. That will be no trouble."

"We need a signer for our letters, too. Can we use your name? Or someone on the East Coast?" I interjected.

"Nah! It must be an American. Or they'll get us again on that Foreign Agents Registration Act. Alex, you will be good. You're South African and American—you must use your name. And the donors will get to know you—after you've sent a few letters."

Ted and I had been worried about this. After years of keeping our phones and addresses secret from everyone—our own families having only just gained the privilege of having anything more than a post office box number for us—the idea of sending out tens of thousands of letters with my name on them was not only terrifying but would break the O.'s security. I searched for words to explain my reluctance to the two African men while, of course, not being able to tell them about our membership in the O.

"But Solly, it might not be a good idea for it to be known that I'm personally involved with this. I mean, you know what it's like here, look at the FBI, they keep such close tabs on people once they put their names out there. You know, we were thinking we could get a celebrity—Harry Belafonte, or someone like that—to be our signatory. A big name would really make a difference to the campaign."

"Yah, yah. Of course. We'll get you a celebrity, but we can't wait for that, and besides, you have to have someone consistent, and that's you Alex."

Solly started to sound annoyed and continued sharply, "I don't know what you're afraid of, there's thousands of people putting themselves on the line in much more serious ways. There's really no problem here. Anyway, we'll talk to Harry Belafonte for you, I see Harry a lot in New York, and he always helps us out. And then I'm sure we can get Arthur Ashe or Danny

Glover. Danny did a big speech for us out in Berkeley. He told me he'd do anything for us."

He looked at me more kindly then. "You don't need to be afraid, Alex. We're not in Soweto here." And he gave a big smile.

I felt embarrassed at having brought it up. I did not want them to think I was trying to protect myself—it was the Organization's security I was trying to shield. In fact, there was nothing I wanted more than to put myself on the line for the ANC, for the cause; this was meaningful to me, this was work that mattered, that made me feel that *I* mattered. But I couldn't start my speech about the U.S. repression, about COINTELPRO, about Fred Hampton and all the others; after Solly's stories I couldn't make it seem so simple.

We set up a bed for Enoch in the study, and Solly slept in the living room. After they showered and breakfasted in the morning, we continued the meeting for an hour or so. That was when Ted brought it up.

"Say, we've talked over the years about doing some things around adoption. You can see we'd have some interest in that, what with our experiences. And we're very concerned for children's welfare. Do you think the ANC would have any interest in working with us on setting up an adoption agency?"

Enoch looked up, his deep black brows furrowed. "Huh? You mean in South Africa? Most of the ANC kids go to Solomon Mahlanghu School— yah, we've had a lot who've lost both parents."

"Um," said Ted, "Actually we meant here. I mean, if there are any kids who need homes, and we could arrange to find good homes here for them."

Enoch and Solly looked at each other. I wanted to sink into the ground. It was humiliating to be forced into this false position. Perhaps in my other work for the O., the bakery or the print shop or the Youth Farm Program, I did not understand what the programs were about, or their history, or what we were supposed to be developing, but this, this I knew. I knew what needed to be developed, and I understood the politics of it. And three times now we'd been given completely foolish directives, that if we'd followed would have destroyed our credibility. As it was, it was being considerably strained.

"The ANC is looking after the children, comrades," Enoch replied seriously. Almost as an afterthought he added, "And this is a very white city, isn't it?"

Ted tried to recover. "Oh, it was nothing really, we were just wondering, that's all."

I hoped they put it down to our being adoptive parents. The thing we had really noticed about our work with the ANC was that they were not that interested in what we said or suggested, but if we actually did concrete work for them, like the software programs we'd written, then they didn't fail to show appreciation. Clearly they'd had a lot of experience (and they talked to us about this) with Leftists who talked about supporting them, but who never actually did anything tangible. So Solly and Enoch rolled over our peculiarities and accepted that we were dedicated and serious and could be relied upon to do what we said we would do.

And we did. I put my name to the fundraising letters—we did finally get Arthur Ashe, and the actors Ruby Dee and Ossie Davis to sign also and they were helpful and cooperative knowing nothing about us other than that the ANC had said they should work with us. We never did succeed in getting Harry Belafonte although we tried for the next two years. We finally reached a stalemate when he insisted on a signed request from the president (meaning Mandela, who was free by then) and we gave up when it became clear that the president obviously had other priorities to attend to.

CHAPTER 22

Television

1989. A young man in jeans and a black jacket crouches on top of the wall. It seems as if he rips the chunks of brick off with his bare hands—I see no hammer swinging to help him. He is silhouetted there like an animal, tension sprung in his body as his arms hurl out the man-made graffiti'd rocks.

"No!" I'm shouting (but silently, inside myself). The young man reminds me of myself—when I was twenty and vigorous and sure, yet casual about the things I discarded.

My stomach is acid and sick. "No!" my voice repeats and repeats. There is no audience, just the television flickering its images, the rock and roll of history, a strobe of events I cannot control.

Dan Rather, square in his belted trench coat, moves to center screen. He stands, immobile, impassive, holding a piece of the wall—perhaps one of the pieces that returns to America, a souvenir to sit on his polished coffee table.

"They can't let it happen," my voice continues. I think of Mia, Ted's great-aunt, who is ninety-three years old and soon to die. Ted and I still visit her at her retirement home. She tells us stories of her last days in Vienna where she taught music at the Workers' Cultural Center and lived in the Karl Marx Hoff. Her husband was in the resistance, but she never tells us much about this. One day she was pulled off a tram by the police. They demanded of each of the passengers, "Do you have any Jewish blood?"

Mia is a tiny woman, fair-haired—she could have passed had she wished, but she stood up to the police and announced in a strong voice, "I am 400 percent Jewish!"

She explains the dry joke to us as she did when she turned to the startled onlookers that day, "400 percent Jewish—all four grandparents!"

She was forced to her knees and made to scrub the sidewalk that day, surrounded by the good people of Vienna.

Later she tells us of her escape on the train with her son. Only her husband, son, and a niece who was sent to a convent in Scotland, survive the massacre that was to come. The rest of her family are ashes left by Hitler's killing factories.

"They can't let the wall come down." It's not that I wish East Germany to be preserved, it's just that I can't bear to see the two Germanys reunited. I have a fear lodged deep in my gut. I see the dark hair and the dark eyes of Anne Frank staring out at me again. My insides are collapsing in on themselves. "Doesn't anybody understand?"

No one seems to talk about it. There is a wall of silence and forgetfulness. Who will break this down?

Other young men in jeans and black jackets, with balaclavas pulled over their white, white faces burn down the houses of Turkish immigrants, killing women and children. They beat Algerian workers on the streets. African students report their fear to those who will listen. Jewish cemeteries are desecrated. American fascists send the German youth forbidden Nazi paraphernalia in the mail.

The wall is coming down. I turn the television off.

Debbie and Dave had a strange relationship to their children. They loved them, you could tell that. You could see that in the way that Debbie crouched down in her business suit to take little Angela in her arms and hold her. You could feel the love she had for her daughter. Like the red bow at her neck, she had the color of love left in her, but it was strange how it could exist only in the thin and diagrammed lines of their belief system.

It was a hot summer's day in Minneapolis. I stepped out of my air-conditioned car onto the sidewalk in front of 905 Sullivan where I was to give Dave a memo. I saw him and his son Sam coming up the street from 801— they lived there now they'd come back from Chicago. Jerri had told me that people were moving back now because the center of the struggle was going to be here; that Minneapolis, being an "idealist" city, was going to be more suitable for the mass organizing towards which the O. was working.

"Now cities are idealist!" I thought cynically to myself. I could not imagine what mass organizing was going to take place; there was an inertia to the activities going on in the O. that I could not imagine transforming into political work.

I watched as Dave and two-year-old Sam made their way up the street, little Sam balancing a red plastic wheelbarrow on his head, running under the scented lilacs that drooped over a neighbor's wire mesh fence. The smoky smell of barbecue made me shift my head like an animal, lifting my nose to better get its direction, the smell emanating from a sawn-in-half oil drum. This was North Minneapolis' preferred barbecue, a tradition imported from the South, from Mississippi or Alabama, from where, only a generation or two before, the Twin Cities' small black population had arrived.

Sam hopped and ran up towards me, turning under his wheelbarrow, watching the sunlight streaming through it and making patterns on his tee-shirt. Dave came up from behind him, tall and lanky, his arms rolling a little stiffly by his sides; he was dressed in jeans and a workshirt and carried a three-ring binder that, I imagined, contained his PS01s, 2s and 3s on the remodeling of 905. That is what they spent each weekend of that summer doing: working with Betty and Sara, who'd also been moved back from Chicago and were now installed in 905 where, with the collective remodeling work, and the help of the construction company, they would create "use value" from the decrepit slum.

Dave was Jewish: dark and hirsute, his five o'clock shadow started early in the day and darkened his long face even more. He had a slightly hooked nose and brooding, hooded eyes which sometimes could be kind, but more often were pulled deeply back into himself. He'd come into the O. with Ted when both had dropped out of Brown University, the Ivy League college they'd attended in the early 1970s. Ted's mother thought Dave was the handsomest man she'd ever met, which I thought made her a woman of unique taste. Yet I think it was his eyes she must have been attracted to, and the hidden sadness that made you feel there was a person of great feeling under there. Mostly, though, he reminded me of Eeyore, his gloominess was of such a deliberate and unrelenting kind. I'd even been driven to criticize him once for never smiling. I said it drew attention to him at the daycare center rather than keeping him incognito, which was the goal. After that, when he met me at the center after work as each of us were picking up our children, he would acknowledge me with the slightest nod and then his eyes would look to the floor and a strained grimace would cross his face. He and Debbie seemed to be a natural fit: the laughter had been squeezed out of them by life in general, not just by the O.

The day was warm and beautiful when I met them at 905, and I smiled and bent low to wave at little Sam as he came up to me, and I stood back up to greet Dave, but he had other things on his mind as he approached us, moving with a focused certainty towards his son. Sam still had the Fisher Price wheelbarrow up on his head.

"A nice hat!" I'd joked to him as he sang to himself and turned beneath the sun, gripping the yellow handles with his strong toddler's hands and watching the red sunlight playing with the shadows.

"Sam," said his father gently, as he caught up to him, towering lankily above the child, "That's not how we use a wheelbarrow is it?"

They were heading to 905 to do "production." Production was what Dave and Debbie valued above all else, and two-year-old Sam was expected to participate in every kind of production, spending his weekends working with his parents at the childcare center, where Debbie was now the manager, or working on either of the houses at 801 or 905. Production was the key to development in their view.

Little Sam ignored his father at first. He shut his eyes and made noises in his chest trying to save the sunniness in himself, and he turned faster and faster and sang some more until his father caught him by the arm and brought him to a standstill.

"Sam!" repeated Dave in Eeyore's gloomy voice, still holding Sam by the arm, "Show me how we use a wheelbarrow, please."

And little Sam pulled the red-and-yellow plastic toy from his head and set it right side up on the sidewalk. His face turned sad, and he wheeled his wheelbarrow, wobbling, up the sidewalk to do "production" in the stinking, roach-ridden shell of 905.

This time I was the one who could not smile. I handed the memo over to Dave in silence. But I could not erase the scene I had witnessed, and I turned it over in my mind, again and again, as I drove back to our house with its own abundance of lilacs falling upon the sun-room windows.

I wanted to get back to my Luis, to hug him and to make him hats out of everything: paper bags and boxes and lilac leaves and imagination. I could not imagine forcing him to use tools "properly" at the age of two. He was exploring and inventing and learning from everything, and this was what I wanted for him. I remembered how it felt, to crouch on the sidewalk on a hot summer's day, feeling the warm concrete under my toes, the sun on my back and watching a line of ants make their cooperative journey between home and work. I remembered the fascination of the details and the epiphany of color, wherever it was found: a ragged green spear, grown huge in the view of an ant who must circumvent the grassy obstacle; or the electric blue of a favorite tee-shirt that seemed to reflect my own intensity; the pale shades of gray showing through the tree branches that I watched from my child's bed in London, the spaces of gray making pictures of African girls with corn-rowed hair, or of giraffes with waving necks, or a street of squat motor-cars traveling in the sky. I remembered the multi-colored jewels of sand that ran through my hand as I sifted it, hot and inches from my eyes, laying on the beach in Italy where I'd studied, too, the red flowers blooming behind my eyelids closed to the midday sun.

Luis gave me back my childhood, and I loved him for it, watching him as he ricocheted from excitement to contentment to anxiety and fear in moments, from safety to frustration and back again.

The image of Dave, his big hand gently restraining Sam from the sunlight and the colors, stayed with me. It wasn't a serious incident, but it troubled me, and I did not yet know why.

Ted and I agreed on child-raising in nearly all respects. We had a laissez faire approach, and with Luis we learned that he had arrived complete: a lively, imaginative, social boy who could keep himself busy forever. We realized early on that we could not change these basic temperaments of his; what we could do was to allow his strengths to flourish and to help him learn to manage his areas of frailty, his fears and his sometimes overwhelming passions. We even found child-development books that supported this, and we read them eagerly and Ted forwarded the titles to P.O.O.

We also realized that this view did not fit into the O.'s ideas of child development—which was that children were either Idealist or Metaphysical, had Ideological Forms, just like adults, and bourgeois sides which had to be struggled with while their proletarian sides were encouraged. We could see that the two philosophies didn't coincide, but we felt we were contributing to the O. when we wrote up our thoughts and sent them to P.O.O. Meanwhile, Debbie and Dave had a whole different approach. The books that they studied, and which were required reading for all O. parents, were from the Eastern Bloc. One, from the Soviet Union, discussed the importance of inurement: for instance, keeping the windows open on the coldest winter days to build up the children's immune systems. Ted was rather attracted to this idea, but the double-digit sub-zero realities of our Minnesota winters defied its actual practice. He also liked the book's idea of not over-stimulating children with endless after-school activities and expectations, and I thoroughly agreed with this. The other book was written by a Czech. Both books were long out of print, and dog-eared copies had been passed from one O. member to the next as the children came along.

The Czech book seemed to contradict the Soviet one and was composed of detailed exercises to speed up the child's development. Theoretically one could teach them to talk at an earlier age by walking around the room with them from early infancy pointing to objects and giving their names. Likewise, one was to create homemade gyms and run the babies through exercises morning and evening. Ted and I read the book but failed in our discipline to set these required conditions. In spite of this, Luis learned to walk and talk quite adequately.

Dave and Debbie had also developed a means of quantifying child development using a Lotus spreadsheet. They created an Observation Form (OF) which we were all mandated to use on a daily basis. Ted and I only used this form sporadically and mostly felt guilty that we were not implementing the Observation Form Process, as it was known. In the long term supposedly this process would be marketed by the childcare center and make lots of money.

Dave and Debbie were convinced that this was a scientific application of the laws of dialectical materialism, and they "cured" their son, Sam, of not staying in his bedroom at night by a combination of the rigorous use of the OF's (complete with computerized Lotus bar charts, pie charts, and histograms), with the decidedly low-tech method of guarding his door and holding it closed every time he tried to get out, while he screamed and kicked at it from the other side.

I know this because during a study session, which they led, they used this example for us—the accompanying charts shown with a quiet, understated kind of pride in their work—to illustrate the benefits of the OF process.

Some years after Walt (the former bakery salesman) left the O., he sent Ted and me a letter from San Francisco trying to tell us that the O. was a "cult of personality." He listed P.O.O.'s various aliases, including what he claimed was his real name: Theo Smith. But as neither Ted nor I had met P.O.O., or knew who he was, this didn't make much impact on us. Ted forwarded the letter to P.O.O. for instruction on how to deal with it. We received a curt note back: "Return the letter to sender." Ted promptly did so, and this effectively put it out of our minds. P.O.O. did not even use Walt's code name; he had just become the "sender."

Television

Christmas Day 1989. The little box shows us a courtyard. Pale white or gray, a small courtyard with indefinable shapes lingering in my memory of it—are they benches, or people standing by the walls, or guards? But the guards' uniforms are darker, they stand out. They come into the courtyard with the two black-coated figures. Nicolae and Elena Ceausescu, wearing heavy wool coats and white blindfolds. By the back white wall of the courtyard, they appear disoriented, their heads and necks moving in circles like turtles, perhaps looking for light beneath the cloth of the blindfolds.

A silence. I don't hear the sound.

He crumples at the knees, his body falls. Then she, too. I imagine that their heads must smash hard, top-heavy, on the concrete or the stones of the courtyard floor, but I don't hear a sound. Anyway, it doesn't matter. They are dead.

We receive images of the babies. Three or four to a crib, and though they look like babies they are actually four, five, six years old, but so wasted and stunted with malnutrition and disease that their bodies have never grown to full size. These pictures are gray, too. There is no color in the nurseries, or in the faces of the children. These are the children who were immunized with dirty needles, thousands of them now infected with AIDS.

Childless Westerners desperately try to adopt the uninfected ones.

There has been no abortion allowed for twenty-four years. Women have been forced to bear babies who have been murdered, slowly, by the State. "Policy" has killed these children. Ceausescu, behind the walls of a nation's isolation, has taken his power and strangled the people.

How many tears were shed when his head smacked the stone floor of the pale gray courtyard?

CHAPTER 23

For a cadre of underground revolutionaries, we lived a remarkably quiet life in those years. There were moments when I almost felt happy. My baby daughter Ana had arrived, bringing the same wonder and relief as had my son two years earlier. Ted and I had moved from the suburbs back to the edge of the city and lived in a gray clapboard house with black shutters, shining wood floors, a small square of well-kept grass and an occasional view of pink-streaked clouds that stretched beyond the neighboring houses as the sun went down.

P.O.O. was noticeably absent. For over a year, there were no memos at all. In our relative contentment, we chose not to question this. However, we did feel impelled to "move forward the program" in some way and felt we should take the initiative and, in the absence of direction from leadership, figure out what to do ourselves. We embarked on a lengthy summary of our experiences both with the many failed O. programs and with the fundraising and logistics work we'd done for the ANC. By this time the fundraising work was winding down, and in the following year we were to close down the project completely. Despite our best efforts, we were only breaking even and were unable to raise any significant sums of money. Americans, we noted cynically, seemed more willing to give money to animal rights than to human rights. Dolphins, apparently, presented less of a political stretch than South Africa's children.

The conclusion of this summary was that we should attempt to build a successful business: one that would learn from the failures of the past and actually be robust enough to earn money to build a base for further activities. Knowing as we did, the computer world, and having marketable skills in that area, it seemed obvious to start there. Our long-term goal was to do international development work where we would provide computer assistance to various developing countries. Between ourselves, we agreed that we would only work with those countries we understood to be progressive. Without saying so out loud to each other, we were guarding the project against the possible demands of P.O.O. where he might suggest working in some dictatorship such as Guatemala or El Salvador.

P.O.O.'s long silence allowed us, indeed, to begin thinking again. The long-standing contradictions within the O. and in P.O.O.'s directives began, more and more, to demand my attention. Just a little window of light opened in my mind. I was getting more sleep than in previous years; I had more control of my schedule than before, and with the children's arrival we now had implicit permission to have a certain amount of fun: playing at the parks, listening to music and singing, even seeing our families a little more than before. A degree of normalcy crept in and with it tentative spaces in which to think and compare and sort out the frenetic, blurred and deadening experiences through which I had tumbled in a kind of numbness or shock.

Within a year, our new computer consulting business had begun to make a steady profit. We held to our tactics of keeping other O. members out of it so that we could avoid the mindless bureaucracy and proceduralization that seemed to kill the other O. programs. We also upended the O.'s Cultural Revolution approach to organizing by assigning each other, and the few people we employed, to our areas of strength and by encouraging initiative and ownership. The O. had always accused people of "inflating their value" when they did well at things, or of "accumulating exchange value" if they cared "too much" about a given project. Objectivity was paramount, followed by the Maoist concept of "Red and Expert," which actually translated to a generalized contempt for any expertise at all.

We were clear that our approach ran counter to the O.'s but we felt we could prove the efficacy of our methods and in doing so contribute to the O. Ted wrote up everything we did and forwarded our business plan, profit-and loss-statements, and monthly summaries of our progress to the still-silent P.O.O. As we began to make money, Ted decided to pay his grandmother back the $5,000 we had borrowed and previously sent to P.O.O. some years before (and about which we'd heard nothing since). Although we had not paid dues for a while, we fully expected that at least part of the profits we were generating would eventually be "centralized," although such a request never arrived. As leadership's silence persisted, we figured that no news was good news and carried on.

* * *

It was a bitterly cold day in February—too cold for new snow to fall and the piles of dirty city snow already fallen were crisp and peaked with an ice crust which squeaked and crunched as I walked from my car to Julie's house. I buried my face in the soft black collar of my plaid lumberjack's jacket and hunched myself up to make as small a target as possible for the frost-biting air. I delivered a memo to Julie from Suzanne—observation had informed me that the two of them were now running the daycare center, along with Debbie. Given our relative success with the ANC work I had finally been promoted to the responsible position of O. postal worker: I delivered memos from one cadre to the other but did not yet have sufficient development to deliver them to P.O.O. himself—or to know of his whereabouts or actions.

I stood in the doorway of Julie's dingy, cramped kitchen which was in the sorely-needed process of being remodeled, presumably by Careful Construction.

"I can't stay long—I've got to pick up the children," I said as I handed her the stapled envelope.

Julie looked at me; she was excited, bouncing up and down on her toes as she tossed the memo, unopened, among the tools that lay on the table.

"I just heard on the radio!"

"What?"

She blinked a couple of times in her owl-like way.

"I just heard it—Mandela's being released. Tomorrow. Did you hear it? Nelson Mandela is going to be free!"

"Mandela . . ."

I knew it was coming. But it didn't sink in right away. I had been exhilarated when the ANC had been unbanned just a short while earlier, but hadn't been able to convey the import of that fact to anyone around me. But now, Mandela was to be free . . . I couldn't stay and talk with her about it, but I gave her a hug. I didn't quite know how to take the news in.

As I drove home through the stark black-and-white landscape of a northern winter, I said her words over again, "Mandela is going to be free . . . Mandela is going to be free . . ." After twenty-seven years. Then it was like a key turned in me also; in my chest a space opened. From a place as long as my life, all kinds of connections fit and freed themselves, and I wept in relief and pain and completeness. Yet I felt connected to the millions who right then, at that moment, were also in a physical condition of release or joy or hate or pain as they considered the news and let the life of emotions that his jailing had meant to them rise up and be felt.

I thought of Robyn, my childhood friend. She had lost her mother, Ruth, to his jailers' letter bomb—blown up in her Mozambique University office. Her father was really gone from her, too, bearing a heavy load of responsibility in the struggle. What was the mix of feeling the news brought in her? I could not imagine the complexity of her knots. But for me it was the closing of a circle: Mandela's imprisonment had been a constant for so much of my life; Robben Island was a kind of landmark to my own existence. Mandela was to be free—the historical momentum of this was personal to me in a way few other events had been. A phase, a historical period that I was a living part of, was over.

The next day I woke early and with Ted and the children went to the basement to watch his release on the television. Again came a crush of longing and happiness and loss inside my chest. I was riveted to the screen. Ted took on the shushing of the children, while I tried to explain to them the meaning of this elderly African man's twenty-seven-year sojourn in jail and the world's exuberance at his release. That night Julie, Bill, and their children came over with a bottle of champagne. We toasted Mandela and the ANC and put on a scratched recording of the ANC anthem, "Nkosi Sikelel'i Afrika." Out of tune, and losing half the words, we sang along. I felt lonely again, to be without any other South Africans, and though with friends, I wanted to be surrounded by black and brown and white bodies, singing the anthem in choral strength, where the melody and words pass on from one to the other and where so many fists are raised that mine would just naturally join them.

Our lives, however, continued as before. In the mornings, Ted or I picked up Zack and Suzanne's two children and car-pooled them along with Luis and Ana to the O.'s daycare center. There I always felt a dragging inside me as I left them off. Despite the so-called remodeling, the place was bleak, and apart from a core of two or three, the rest of the staff turned over so fast I never learned the new teachers' names. A final depressing note was the new "state-of-the-art" computer system that had recently been put in by Suzanne and Debbie. Instead of signing the kids in on a sheet of paper, I now had to check each one in on the computer, but in the typical O. style, the computer was out-dated and interminably slow. It took ten minutes each morning to get the children signed in; the O. had taken a simple thirty-second operation, computerized it and created a barrier of frustration for the parents and a deterrent to actual contact with any of the teachers (the latter consciously done—for better efficiency). It was a Kafka-esque experience—to wait there each morning staring at the hopeful "Working . . ." ("But I'm not!" I wanted to shout) that blinked ever more slowly on the screen as the database of logged-in hours grew.

The back rooms of the day-care center were low-ceilinged and dark, with mildewed mustard-yellow carpet and the stains of years of taped kid art spotted all over the walls. Boxes of unused supplies were heaped up in corners. Old notices, procedures for cleaning, mealtimes and staff notices, were peeling off bulletin boards. Here and there were brighter spots: the hamster cage or the science table strewn with rocks, seaweed and bleached bones—someplace where one of the teachers had made an extra effort. But the overall effect was that the place was a dump, and despite the endless hours of volunteer work that cadres put in at nights and weekends, it had been that way for years.

Only the new front office was clean. Here the staff notices were freshly printed and stuck firmly to the cork boards. Here Debbie, Suzanne, and Julie spent most of their "free" time managing the center, presumably led by memo also. Although perhaps P.O.O.'s silence extended to them too—who knew? Here Debbie's famous memos to the low-paid staff would appear for them to appreciate when they came to work in the mornings:

To: ALL Staff
From: Center Manager
Re: Staff Accountability

Staff have been failing to follow the sweeping procedure as outlined in the staff manual. THERE IS NO EXCUSE FOR THIS. Accountability will be ensured through APPROPRIATE CONSEQUENCES. Center Staff will now fill out the attached Daily Accountability Form to be co-signed by shift leaders.

For six dollars an hour, not many teachers would put up with being treated like this, hence the high turnover. But there was a core of longer-term teachers who had been with the center for several years. They were three young white women, Becky, Denise, and Karen, just out of college, who had a gentle and loving manner with the children. These were the teachers with whom my children had grown up, who kept the center running day after day.

One day I discovered that there had been a "purge" at the center. Julie had been criticized and kicked out of management. Karen, the head teacher, had been demoted to night-shift teacher. This was clearly intended to elicit her resignation, which it did. Becky and Denise resigned in solidarity with Karen. This I only found out later, my first indication of any changes being Luis' report to me:

"Mama, I don't want to go to daycare anymore."

"Sweetie, why?"

"All my teachers have gone. I don't like the new ones."

Once a week or so Julie and I walked together at the North Side YMCA, climbing up the steel spiral staircase to the old wooden track that circled the ceiling of the gym. The North Side Y was dilapidated; this was the inner city, a place where a Y was most needed yet where the Y had the worst facilities. Despite previous edicts against "social exchange" Julie and I had begun to exercise together; things were still pretty loose and besides, if anyone from the O. asked what we were doing, we could always make a case for exercise being "functional."

Julie and I used this time to talk, tentatively, with each other. It had been years since we'd had this kind of time together, and we slowly edged closer, testing out the waters of what we could safely discuss. I brought up the latest events at the daycare center.

"Why did they fire the teachers?" I asked. I knew she had been pushed out too, but I didn't dare approach that directly. Inside I was seething at being left so powerless to help Luis and Ana adjust to the new situation.

"I tried to stop it. Karen was a good teacher. They forced her to resign—Debbie said the center was going through a major overhaul. She told me, 'You can't put new wine in old bottles.' Of course I'm being blamed too—even though I had to clear all my decisions with P.O.O."

"It's just like the bakery," I replied, "It's always the workers' fault, never management. The only way they see to solve problems is to purge people—just dump them."

She nodded. We marched around the track, speeding up now to rid ourselves of some of the anger we both felt, our arms pumping and faces scowling.

Later that night I talked with Ted.

"How can they do this? How can they dump three teachers and not even tell us? What about the kids?"

"Yeah, I'm worried about Luis too. He was attached to them. It's hard to leave him there in the mornings with no one he knows anymore. I don't know what's going on over there. But Suzanne wants us to put in some time—we're supposed to come up with a plan to redecorate the place—she wants us to meet her over there on Saturday."

"You've got to be kidding!"

"No, I got a memo earlier."

"I'm sorry, there's no way I'm going to do any work over there until someone has the courtesy to tell me what's going on with the staff. We're parents, for crying out loud. What do you think?"

"I agree—we should have been informed. I don't mind doing the assignment, but I agree that there needs to be some struggle about the process."

I called Suzanne.

"I need to talk to you Suzanne. I need to understand what's going on at the center. My kids go there, and as a parent I have the right to know what is happening with the staffing and why decisions are being made in this way."

"Alex, you'll get a letter next week. Someone is writing it up and will send it out to all parents."

"But Luis is going to daycare Monday. What am I to tell him? Why can't you tell me now?"

"You're being subjective Alex."

"Damn right I am. I feel subjective. You know what Luis is like. This is a big deal when all three of his teachers are gone at once and a bunch of substitutes are dragged in. And nobody has the common sense to tell the parents. I'm not going to do any work for the center until somebody talks to me about what's going on."

This was a direct threat, and Suzanne understood it immediately.

"This is an organizational assignment," she stated coldly, "It has nothing to do with your criticism."

She remembered then that she was using "closed" words over the phone, and then I got the response I was eliciting.

"I'll be right over," she said and put the phone down. I stood there shaking, and Ted looked up at me from the kitchen table where he'd been listening. I relayed to him Suzanne's half of the conversation.

A short time later, Suzanne sat across from me on our living-room couch, her large white thighs spreading out from her shorts. I shouted at her, "You can't do this to people. What about the other parents. You've got a handful of brand-new teachers who don't know what they're doing looking after fifty kids. How can you wait a week to tell us? Did you think no one would notice?"

I was so upset for Luis and Ana, and at being run over again and again, only this time it was affecting my children in a way that I knew I would never accept from any other daycare center. I told Suzanne this, who was obviously conflicted too, because she was dedicated to her children, and she knew what the staff disruption did to the kids. But she had her Organizational persona to maintain, and she stuck by the need for Organizational Discipline as the panacea for all problems. She pursed her lips, folded her arms and listened, interrupting to say, "It has been planned by leadership. It's a temporary problem to address the fundamental contradiction at the center. Leadership has carefully planned the transition."

"Including Becky and Denise leaving? And leaving parents in the dark so they have no way to prepare their children?"

"We didn't know Becky and Denise would leave."

"Well think about it then—why did they?"

"They have their own internal issues to resolve."

"No! They were protesting! They're trying to tell you something—they're telling you it's unfair."

She licked her lips. "That's your interpretation."

Ted sat back during the meeting, tipping the rocking chair slowly back and forth, his brows pushed together and his lips thinned out in anxiety. But it was as if he were an observer and Suzanne and I were the ones fighting. He knew the turnover was bad, and probably done for stupid reasons, to cover up the management problems, but he wasn't as angry as I was and was certainly less willing to bring it to the point of refusing to do the assignments. I didn't know exactly what he thought or where he stood, although it seemed as if he agreed with me. But I had long accused him of saying "Yes" to me in our arguments and then showing his actual position by refusing to carry out what he had just agreed to do.

Finally I said I would continue with the decorating assignment and that I would work to find a "principled and objective" way to raise my criticisms of the center. Suzanne had responded to me by coming over and had at least heard me out. She said she would try her best to ensure that the children would not be adversely affected by the changes at the center. So, after she left, Ted and I talked again and decided to do an honest appraisal of the center and write up a summary and criticism of the problems we saw. We realized we'd complained about the place for years and kept it between the two of us, and now it was time to raise it to the level of an organizational criticism.

Using the analytical experience we'd gained in writing the ANC summary and in developing our new business plan, we wrote an accurate and consequently subversive critique of the daycare center. Even more dangerous was our introduction which stated that the elements in the criticism could just as easily have been applied to other programs, such as the bakery, the software marketing companies, and so on. Ted was not willing to say we were criticizing the organization's methods as a whole: one of the cardinal rules of the O. was that criticism had to be specific and targeted, which meant we could criticize particular programs or individuals, but not the organization itself.

There were times, during our writing of this document, that I felt happy and excited, and I recognized a strange feeling from years before, from my life in California. The feeling was that of engaging in analytical, critical thinking. Ted and I were actually trying to look at our real experience and draw conclusions from it, rather than stuffing the experience into pre-arranged forms and categories (700: Ideological, 500: Administration . . .). We had begun this with the ANC work and continued with the business planning, but it was really with this criticism that I could feel those faculties kick back in properly. We both felt the pleasure of it, the sense of control and empowerment that came from naming our experiences and saying clearly: this is where it worked, this is where it failed. For hours, we worked over this critique. I felt we were starting to grasp something important, something concerning the O. as a whole. I was sure we were making a real contribution to the O.; if others could understand what we were saying, things could really change and the O. could get a new lease on life and finally begin to organize in a dynamic way.

Our fundamental thesis was that, in order for a given project to be successful, people had to care about what they were doing. They had to be internally motivated. Otherwise the result was what we had already seen so often: mechanical following of orders, inflexibility, lack of creativity, lack of taking true responsibility, and a resulting failure of programs. With motivation, people could truly move a program forward, take responsibility for it and cease to rely on leadership's approval for every nickel-and-dime decision. Boiled down, our critique amounted to an opposition to the deadened, mechanical, blind carrying-out of someone else's orders. We wanted to release people's creativity and energy to develop dynamic programs, coordinated by the larger Organization. In our view, cadre had become devoid of initiative, and this had to be restored at all costs. Initiative was only possible when people cared about what they were doing. Otherwise it was a completely abstract proposition, and no amount of correct analysis could breathe life into it.

"Ted, we've got it, you know!" I announced, once we'd completed our paper. "Don't you see that this is the organization's main contradiction? I know this is right—it could be such a significant change for the O."

I welcomed back that long-forgotten tension, the rush of intellectual adrenaline into my body that had been a staple in my pre-O. years. We had nailed it. We were describing something that was true. I committed to myself that I would see this thing through; this would be one time where I would not step back and let them tell me it was my ideological problem.

Again Ted seemed to agree with me. He typed up our paper in his neat and structured manner and forwarded it to P.O.O.. But it's strange how I can't remember his voice anymore, or any of what he said in those discussions. I remember what I thought and felt and even the gestures I made as ideas came pouring out of me for the first time in years. But I cannot remember his contribution at all; not the sound of his voice, nor the look on his face. It's as if an eraser came and rubbed out his essence, leaving just a sandy image of him sitting back in his chair, his hazel eyes turned down at the corners and the sad look of a lost little boy on him. It disturbs me that I can give him no voice, but that is how it is. I suppose it is a reflection on myself, or him, or both of us.

The things I do remember, and cannot forget, are the times when he failed to speak. The times when he left me to drift alone in the cold waters of fighting the O. These times, when I knew him to be annulling his own beliefs in his silence, these times, when he held on to the unfaltering assumption that the Organization had the right to everything, these times, when he could not raise his eyes and say, "Well, I think . . ." these are the times that I cannot erase.

"Why?" I want to shout, "Why didn't you stand up for me if you could not stand up for yourself! Every time I tried, you left me alone, and you were proud of doing so!"

And then I sigh—but without relief or release—because I know why; because I know that he was scared, even more scared than I, and that his courage had been stolen by the O.

CHAPTER 24

Perhaps it was having children that highlighted it for me that year. Maybe my daughter brought my girlhood fears back to the surface; although, to be clear, this terror was never forgotten, though I wished many times it had been. Instead it was stored in a corner of my mind and sometimes at odd moments, but nonetheless regularly, the images would suddenly present themselves and cause me to flinch. Still now, so many years later, I jerk my body away from the threat, even though, at that time, when I was eight years old, I had not moved a muscle. Now the memory seemed to take up a larger space in my mind and demand my attention.

I was secretive about my decision to seek counseling for this old hurt: I told Julie and Ted but made them promise not to tell any other O. members. The O. condemned therapy as bourgeois; I was not going to risk judgment or interference. But I could no longer physically bear the state in which the memory remained in me. I wanted it gone. In the office of a kind and attentive young social worker I recounted my story.

I remembered the dark man; thin, a white-shirted ghost at the bottom of my bed. A strange, white-shirted, dark-faced ghost who I noticed when I woke up in the middle of the Italian night, in a hotel on our way back from vacation. I rose into consciousness, and the first thing I realized was that there, at the end of this strange bed in this strange hotel, with my sister still asleep in the bed across from mine, was a man who didn't belong, who was looking down at me, and I closed my eyes because I knew something was very wrong. It was deep in the middle of the night, and everyone else was still asleep except for me and this man with the white shirt and the black trousers and the small black mustache.

He moved quietly to the side of the bed. I must have drifted between sleep and wakefulness for a time, because I cannot remember him moving. But then he was there, at the side of the bed. And the bedclothes came down.

I remember his hand on my body. I closed my eyes. And then I stopped breathing. Because if he is doing that, I reasoned, then he must also want to kill me. If he knows that I know that he is doing this to me, then he will undoubtedly want to kill me. He will silence me. He will move this hand away, and he will bring the other hand around and he will reach over my face and perhaps he will put both of his hands around my neck, or he will take the pillow and put it over my nose and mouth, and either way, he will squeeze the life out of me. If he knows that I know.

I will stop breathing. I will close my eyes. I am dead. I am dead. . . .

And then he moved away. Silently, like a boat shifting in the wind at night, the ghostly white shirt floated over to my sister's bed. And now my eyes were crimped open as I watched him lean over Hatty's bed, and fear punched up into my throat, knocking and knocking at me—he will do it to her, he mustn't do it to her. I know he is there, and he is going to do it to her and I mustn't let him, but I can't do anything. How far is it to the door?—but I can't reach it, and maybe he's locked it, and where is my mother? What room is she in, and I will be in the hallway, and he will come and get me and grab me and squeeze me onto my knees and kill me there. I can't let him touch her. I don't know what to do. I don't . . . I can't . . . he will . . . not her, no. No.

Then he left.

She was spared, and so I was spared. I lay deadly still for a good time longer.

Then I got up and crept to Hatty's bed. "Hatty, Hatty," I whispered. She woke up. I pulled on her arm. I could barely speak, "Hatty, you've got to come. To Ma, to Ma."

Together our bare feet crept through the darkness and over the wooden floors, and we turned the brass doorknob and navigated our way through the little twisted hallway, and we found my mother's room, where she was sleeping with Lyndall, and when we got to her bed I put myself inside her arms, and I wept for minutes before I could tell her what happened.

But I could never really describe it to her. My mother told me I should have screamed. But I hadn't known that. It was no comfort to tell me what I should have done.

All I wanted was a bath.

And this I remembered, detailing the scene until the flinching shrunk to a manageable tick. My therapist offered me a useful metaphor: that I could let myself down into the well of darkness that frightened me so much, but that I had a lifeline—I could imagine a rope that led to somewhere safe, and I could go as far or as little down into that well holding onto the lifeline, and whenever I needed to come up again, I could just pull on that rope. So I did. I faced my fear without the physical cringing; I walked into it, in a manner of speaking, with my eyes open. I talked about what happened, recalled all the details, and I held on to that rope, knowing that with it I would not fall off the edge of the world.

Ted helped me early on in this work. He held me at night when I could not make love with him. He was understanding when I explained the flashbacks to him; when I told him that what made me feel safe was to be held close. I began to feel that the thorn that had festered in me for so long was being excised and a sensation of relief moved into the open place.

Things continued to change for me in the O. Ted and I were summoned by the sullen and unsmiling Dave to discuss our criticism of the daycare center. Dave greeted us in his gray-carpeted living-room. He and Debbie were living in our old duplex at 801, and had remodeled it yet again. He pulled out a copy of our paper; I could see from my spot on the couch that several sections had been highlighted in yellow. We spent the next two hours discussing these sections.

"Who wrote this sentence?" he demanded, quoting a highlighted phrase.

I was puzzled.

"We co-authored the document." I replied.

"Yes, but there's always a Dominant Aspect. Who wrote about these criticisms being applicable to the Bakery also?—who initiated this idea?"

I was silent. Ted reached over to look at the paper, to make sure he understood what was being asked. Dave tried again.

"Ted, is this your thinking?"

"Well, yes, I kind of agree with that."

"Kind of?"

"I suppose I wouldn't have exactly put it that way if I'd written it on my own."

"So then it was Alex's phrasing?"

"You could say that."

"Do you agree that this is an organizational criticism, or is it just a critique of the center?"

"Just the center—that's the focus," Ted said.

"No—it's as it was written," I jumped in. "We clearly said it reflected problems in the Organization as a whole. And I stand by that."

I could see the manipulation so clearly this time. As the session continued, I watched in a paralyzed horror as Dave coaxed Ted into retracting any criticisms of leadership or the O. as a whole. Generously, he allowed the specific criticisms of Suzanne and Debbie to remain. Ted withdrew his support of the document as a whole, while I folded my arms and held on stubbornly, knowing that this was a turning point.

Ted and I could not speak about it. Where we had previously gradually reached out to each other over the walls of organizational security, Ideological Forms and Use Value, now those walls had been reinforced again, sending us each into a personal silence and a subtly spreading distrust.

An envelope addressed to him came soon after. It was from the daycare center, and I immediately became suspicious—why would it only be to him? It was an invitation for him to be on the "Advisory Board" of the center. Ted was being wooed again by P.O.O. Unfortunately P.O.O. knew how to appeal to our basest emotions, and, in this case, Ted was being given acceptance, the illusion of importance in being asked for advice, and of course, he was being separated from me as I was pointedly not invited. I made a few sarcastic remarks about divide and rule to Ted, but he did not respond. It was working, he was feeling important again and needed by the O., and this was more compelling to him than any alliance between the two of us.

About the time he got his invitation I got another, quite different missive. I received a message that there would be a "discussion" with me concerning the content of the criticism we had written. I understood what this was—it was a hearing. Julie told me she was to have a hearing as well. Debbie and Suzanne would comprise the hearing committee. I became very anxious about this and had about a month to dwell on the anxiety between the time of receiving the memo and the appointed time of the actual hearing.

Soon after this Ted started to go off to meetings at Suzanne's house without me. This had been standard practice in the early days, that we each had our separate "secure" projects, but it had been years since then. In the last few years, we always worked together and knew exactly what each other was doing.

My therapy, meanwhile, was reaching some kind of natural conclusion. I had begun talking about my fear of taking responsibility for what I believed in and how my fears had been magnified by the experience of being a powerless child waiting for a man to throttle me. It was as if I were in a permanent state of alarm. This understanding made sense to me. I talked to Ted about it, and then, too late, realized he must have told Debbie and Suzanne.

He came to me after one of his meetings at Suzanne's house, and he said, his arms folded across his chest and his best O.-criticism expression on his face, "Have you looked at what you are getting out of this therapy? It seems that you aren't talking about the abuse anymore. Have you looked at what value you are starting to get out of it?"

The edges of my body got cold.

"What are you saying, Ted?"

My teeth clenched, and my hands rested on my hips.

"What I'm saying is that I think it's time you stopped."

I felt an unfamiliar anger. Ted had overstepped a boundary here, and this time I was ready for it, convinced, finally, of my right to protect myself.

"I don't give a damn what you think. This has nothing to do with you. This is entirely *my* decision. You have no idea when I'll be done. How can you tell me, you who have never looked inside yourself, how can you know when I will be done? Don't you dare try to take this decision from me; this is for me to decide and nobody else."

I knew what was right, and I stood up for myself. I knew that he'd been put up to this, that he'd told Debbie and Suzanne I was doing the therapy during their secret discussions where they were trying to figure out what had happened to me, why I was beginning to be so insubordinate. And of course it proved to them that any kind of outside influence was negative; after all, look at the effect it was having on me. They were right, of course, and I was right to have kept it from them up to that point.

The sad thing was, I realized then that I could no longer trust Ted, that he had chosen his side again, and that if I was to continue to become stronger and clearer on what I needed that I would not be able to share it with him, except in our usual indirect ways,. They had succeeded in pulling him back in, while I was headed for my hearing the next week. A distance had found its way back into our relationship, only this time it was also coming from me; I would no longer share with him my doubts, my sorting out of the years in the O., my tortuous interior debate. It would only be "centralized" and used to manipulate me. I was going to have to work it out on my own.

* * *

Sometime that summer, we'd received a scathing criticism from Dave and Debbie. They hadn't been back long, but we could feel things shifting since they'd returned. It was a kind of tightening up: things we'd done previously in a casual way now made the little hairs on the back of my neck stand up. For instance, the previous year, Ted and I had taken up the habit of having Beth babysit our kids every Sunday morning while we went for a working brunch at one of the new downtown bistros. It was during these leisurely Sunday mornings that we'd worked up a detailed analysis of Luis' development, summarized our experience with the ANC and developed our business plan, not to mention drafting the childcare criticism that led to so much trouble later. These were creative, productive times where we worked well together and built a closeness into our partnership. But now that Dave and Debbie were back in town, I used to get nervous going to and from our bistro breakfasts, knowing they would never set foot in such places, and I worried that they might witness our Yuppie backsliding. It became like that again: I had to watch my step because if I didn't I could be sure that Dave and Debbie would be watching it for me, and reporting it all in brief but functional memos to P.O.O.

Their child, little Sam, went to the daycare center with Luis. They were both active, imaginative kids and were drawn to each other immediately. Every day one of them would ask to visit the other at home. Finally, after some pushing from the five-year-old Sam, Debbie agreed to let them play together, and for a few weeks we exchanged visits at each house. I liked Sam: he played with the exuberance I was used to from Luis, and he didn't demand too much of me, which meant I could enjoy extra time with Ana. One day Luis came home from little Sam's.

"How was it Luis? Did you have fun?"

"Yeah," replied Luis, typically laconic about his outside activities.

"Well, what did you guys do?"

"Dave made us play cards with him. It was okay."

Dave was playing with them? That seemed odd to me. And cards? It had been a glorious summer day—I couldn't imagine Luis and Sam spending that time playing cards. But I understood once I read the criticism delivered to Ted and me the next day.

To: 201, 25
From: 204, 301
Date: 8/17/90

Over a period of time, a number of observations of your practice have occurred that indicate to us a low or deteriorating level of ideological awareness on your parts.

1. Your response to the changes occurring at Eastside [the daycare center] are expressed as a fear of negative effects on L's [Luis'] development, due to the disruption caused by the changes. First off, what is objectively happening is the supercession of the old by the new. This is always characterized by struggle and disruption of the old ways of doing things, of old identities. You did not seem concerned that the old at Eastside was characterized as a lack of consciousness of struggle to develop the children.

2. When M. [Dave] asked T. [Ted] what the basis of your initiative to encourage the identity [friendship] between Luis and Sam out of school was, T's response was that the identity already existed, and that L. wanted to see S. He said he hadn't observed much about the content of the identity. (In fact, he had seen them play together a number of times). Claire later added that it was good for Luis to be around older children who he couldn't manipulate. Neither response represents a serious analysis of L's social (600) development. Do you have such analysis?

We observe that when they get together in a free play condition, imaginative play—in particular Ninja Turtles—dominates. We don't think this is of developmental value for S. at this stage. Is it for L?

A concrete analysis is needed: who is the Dominant Aspect? What content does each bring to the identity? What possibilities for development exist, and under what conditions? The answer to these questions would provide a direction as to how we should structure their friendship, or if it should be encouraged at all.

It is our position that O. children should not be encouraged to relate to one another outside school unless there is a concrete developmental reason to do so. To do otherwise, makes unnecessary, externally observable connections, and fosters a low level social/family identity among O. members.

We see:

A) Metaphysics: recommended actions based on superficial or no analysis: a conservative response to the process of change (Second State of Motion) now underway at Eastside—either you didn't conceptualize the process of change/struggle at the Bakery or you are not re-applying that understanding to Eastside.

B) A social rather than ideological relation to other O. members.

Our position is that the attempt to build the identity between L. and S. outside of school be suspended pending 1) an analysis of their identity by you and recommendations based on that analysis and 2) a response to this criticism.

It was so cold. Dead really. Granted, I was no fan of the Ninja Turtles, but that's what all the kids at daycare played—it was a national obsession among five-year olds, and I wasn't prepared to outlaw them nor to define what Luis should and shouldn't play (beyond some basic house rules such as "No tying up living creatures"; "Mom and Dad won't buy you guns"; and our version of non-violent conflict resolution: "Use your words!"). The idea that we would prepare an agenda for the kids' play sessions seemed completely ridiculous—the kids were capable of figuring out what to play quite adequately on their own.

I did not agree with the criticism at all. Ted responded to it, diplomatically agreeing with certain of the points, while refuting others. Whatever we may have thought, however, Luis and little Sam were no longer allowed to play together.

They do not believe what I believe. They don't want what I want. They're not fighting for the same things at all. I want children to be able to play, to imagine, to be free. Debbie doesn't. She doesn't want this at all. Her freedom and mine—they have nothing to do with each other. What do we share if we don't share at the very least the same goals?

Another shift. A critical one, a small incident—but it raised questions that I could not ignore. What was the end to which we were working? What was the end to which everything else was subordinated? And perhaps, finally, did the ends justify the means? Out of meanness, coldness, rigidity, and a lack of life, was it possible to build fairness, beauty, and freedom?

CHAPTER 25

My journal starts again after a four-year break. The preceding five years fill a scant twenty pages. And then there is the turning of a page, one frail leaf of the mottled composition book, and into this familiar and balletic flip-flap of a single sheet of paper disappear the last four years, where not a word was written from that inside place, the dark interior. The discussion within myself, that I had logged since puberty, had slowed like a glacier at first, and then had quit completely. Given up. Surrendered. It had been the easiest thing to do.

These years are documented, instead, by memory; by the growth of Luis and Ana; by summaries, discussion forms, observation forms, criticisms; by memos to and from P.O.O. and 203, 26, 24, and 310, to and from Ted, Bill, Julie, Jerri, Debbie, and Suzanne: all code-names for the people who inhabited my life. These years are documented by incorporation papers of failed businesses; by adoption and naturalization papers; by stacks of printed materials rotting in the basement; by promotions for the ANC fundraising; brochures for the failed software companies; articles of incorporation for joint ventures in India and Mozambique that were to sell software, export cashew nuts, or work with church groups to make corn grinders out of bicycle parts. Acres of failure—only the bright lights of my children shining out as real and true. And, less bright, but still real: the growing financial success of Ted's and my consulting business (the only profitable venture in the O.'s long history) and, finally, and more importantly, the ANC work, the only political work I had done in ten years.

It was with a feeling of relief that I returned to my journal, smoothing its pages, finding comfort in its openness, its structureless white pages.

December 21, 1990
  Yes, this is the right book to write in. It is mine.
  I have had such a desire to be creative, to have friends and family. To not be alienated any longer. To be free to refind myself.
  There is a black hole that opposes the feelings and ideas in me.
  I am loosening my allegiance. There is very little to which to have an allegiance. I am tired of feeling guilty, of not having clear human contact, of preempting criticism and of being afraid to talk to others for fear of conspiring.
  I don't know what is in me anymore. Even my political life feels like it has died. All that "clarity" I used to have.
  Of course, I must remember, it is a world-wide problem.

Julie and I met at the YMCA on a Monday night. I rested my foot on the locker-room bench and pulled tight the laces of my running shoes.

"Oh," I let out a sigh, "I've got my hearing coming up. That's bothering me."

"Me, too. I'm worried about mine. They're going to try to decimate me over the childcare center. But you know, it wasn't mine and Kristin's fault that things were so stagnant at the center. We tried over and over again to shake things up, and we weren't given any resources. Any time we started something that was working, it was pulled out from under us. There was always some kind of bullshit."

"So what was the problem then?"

"I don't know. Conflicting positions maybe? Like around the construction—different priorities? I do know we weren't *allowed* to succeed."

"Tell me about it. That's what Ted and I saw when we did our analysis—a distinct pattern of failure. I mean, that's why we started the business—to *prove* it was possible to succeed. And we have, haven't we?"

"Yeah, I think it's great."

We swung our arms, warming up now as we circled the track. My shoulder was stiff, and I pulled my head over to one side to loosen it.

"I don't know how to stop being so worried about my hearing."

"What are you worried about?"

"I'm worried that I'll want to jump out of my chair and punch Suzanne or Debbie on the nose. I just don't have the tolerance for it anymore. I'm not willing to have them put me down again, but I'm scared that they'll push me. I don't want to be pushed into anything before I'm ready."

"Maybe you should look at your internal before the hearing. What you think the different aspects are that are going on. What are you reacting to? What buttons are they pushing? That kind of thing."

"Yeah, I guess."

Our New Year's party was small and sad. The previous two years most of the cadre in Minneapolis had come to our house where we hosted a big turkey dinner and let all the kids play together. They were close to normal holiday gatherings. Being the O., all the children had to prepare summary books of the year. But even this was a positive thing as they shared collections of captioned photographs of the year's events. Then the adults did a round-robin in which they each summarized their lessons and struggles for the year. Other than this obligatory summation, these gatherings were some of the most human moments I shared with other O. members.

But this year, after the childcare fiasco, tensions ran high between myself, Ted, Bill, and Julie on the one hand and Dave, Debbie, and Suzanne on the other. Ted and I decided not to host the event and instead just had Julie and Bill and their kids over. I had wanted to invite Jerri, too. She was among the several cadre who'd come back from Chicago to the Twin Cities the previous year, and she'd brought Anthony with her, a man she'd met there and with whom, quite out of character for the O., she was allowed to have a relationship. He wasn't in the O. and knew nothing about it, yet Jerri and he had moved into 801 Sullivan to live in the upper duplex, above Dave and Debbie. She also started working with Ted and me in our computer consulting company, and she and I were now on a project together. As before, I respected her abilities and found her relatively easy to work with; she had none of Debbie's judgmental dourness.

I wondered how Jerri managed to keep her involvement secret from Anthony; it must have been hard. It was because of him that she could not be invited to an O. gathering. And so it was just the four of us: Ted, Bill, Julie, and I, who sat desultorily around the table after the kids had gone to bed, and, still following the O. format, took turns looking at the past year and looking forward to the future.

"I've been very troubled," I started. I leaned my elbows on the wooden kitchen table and rested my chin on my hands. "I'm reevaluating my position in the O. and looking at where I do and don't have unity with it. There have been many things this year that have accumulated, and my resistance is returning with a vengeance. The ANC's unbanning and Mandela's release were the high points of my year. I learned a lot from working with the ANC. I learned the value of practical work, with real goals and real results, and now I'm questioning so much of the O. work that I've been involved with. I question the Internal Transformation Process; the whole concept of the development of cadre always being held up as the central thing. I question the lack of summarizing of the many failures. And I question, most of all, the lack of criticism and independent thinking. My position in the O. is very tenuous right now. One way or the other, it will be resolved this coming year."

My shoulders sagged after my speech. Bill and Julie gave equally gloomy summaries (once again, I cannot remember Ted's words), and we ended the evening solemnly, staring at the center of the kitchen table as if we were visitors at a séance wishing for the word to come from the spirits. It did not, and we began the New Year with the backdrop of Eastern Europe crumbling and the struggle in South Africa blossoming, though still drenched in blood.

I knew then that I would not last out the year in the O. Yet somehow I felt that Ted was still with me.

New Year's Day 1991

I must re-evaluate my role. This time I am no longer "me" but more of a "we." Like a turtle, now I carry my house around with me—no more the free-wheeling me who can move at will. Now I come with my family: the children and Ted. What happens must happen with them. Despite the troubles with Ted, we must fight to stay together. We mustn't let them pull us apart.

It takes me back to when I was fifteen—all I ever wanted was to be part of something, to have a role, to be of use. How will I make a contribution?

All I ever wanted was to be a good person.

I have come full circle back to my thoughts of my pre-O. days. My belief in the unity of the subjective and the objective. I can no longer agree with the O.'s destruction of the subjective side of things, people, feelings. It has been fundamental and constant, this disunity of mine. I must redefine my role.

> Study: "Retool my brain"
> Exercise: "Retool my body"
> Create: "Retool my soul"

Television

Back in the basement watching the news at strange hours. For three days I sat while the Gulf war played out, and the pictures of TV reporters in Israel struggling to put on monstrous gas masks frightened my daughter.

This was TV verité, the camera tilting and shaking so you knew a camera was there with a scared human being operating it. And the reporters talking, not to the camera, but dropping their words anywhere into the room while they struggled to listen through earpieces to a producer's voice that I, in my basement, could hear better than they. Bombs streaked through the sky behind them, and Ana, only two, gripped my legs and mewled, while I thought of a mother and daughter in Iraq, or in Israel, hiding in a shelter and feeling the thud of bombs as the daughter clutched and whimpered like mine.

That week there had been an anti-war rally at the University. Ted and I went with the children. We discussed whether it was appropriate to go or not; perhaps it was breaking O. discipline—but at that point neither of us cared that much. There had been no memos or discussion about the war, so we pretty much just decided to do as we pleased. It certainly seemed appropriate to us to demonstrate our position against the war in the face of the hundreds of jingoistic yellow ribbons going up on lampposts around our neighborhood.

Ten thousand people trudged through the January snow to be there. It was as if we had all come out of a deep sleep. Where had ten thousand people appeared from?

There were some students, but most were our age or older, many with children, who cried or misbehaved if they were young, or who took it in very seriously if they were older, reminding me of the demonstrations I had attended as a youngster. People who hadn't seen each other in ten or fifteen years waved each other down, shouted a greeting, gave hugs. Ted spotted several people he knew from the co-op days and pointed them out to me—though he would not approach them: that would clearly be a violation of O. security. We saw Bill and Julie and their two children; a couple of people from the neighborhood; people we knew to be local activists; people we didn't know at all, but who just looked familiar because they were, to some extent, like us. This was the generation of the 1960s come back out to its familiar stomping grounds, but grown now, with responsibilities and children.

It was like watching the cockroaches rushing across the floor at night when one steps into the kitchen and turn the light on. Turns out we hadn't disappeared after all.

January 18, 1991

Julie says, to look at my internal. What I find is a desire to regain my drive to contribute. It has been killed in me. What I find is my complete lack of answers. I used to have so many, and now I cannot even think about the questions anymore.

January 29, 1991

Julie says, "Use your brain." She says I have a good brain, and I must use it. This phrase rings and rings in the brain of which she speaks. I have a brain. I will use it. I will use it.

I feel the beginnings of movement. Ted is seeing things quite differently since his meeting with Debbie and Suzanne. He appeared to have some unity with me, but since that meeting with them, he's shifted. That's okay. This is a decision he will have to make himself. He will have to learn to think independently sooner or later. He is separating himself from me. I can feel him doing that. Perhaps this is what he needs to find his own thoughts again.

I must create some space so I can start to think again. And I must stop the self-censorship. That is the first thing that has to go. If it means I keep my journals under constant lock and key, then that's what I'll do. I must have the space to think freely.

The political (and ideological) isolation has been extreme. No study. How can we develop the objective aspect without study? Study is the means to grasp the patterns of the world into which our subjective falls. Without study the subjectivity of some (or one) simply becomes dominant—it announces itself as objective. And what is objective cannot be questioned.

No discussion. Intense "compartmentalization" of people. No discussion of: Panama, Grenada, Perestroika, and Glasnost (we could use a little), reunification of Germany, Tienanmen Square, South Africa, Nicaragua, the situation in the Gulf.

Isolation within our nuclear, or sub-nuclear families.

Contradictory and false emphasis on "Security"—we're not supposed to "make unnecessary connections," but when it's convenient all the connections in the world get made—for God's sake, all our kids go to the same daycare center. It's not real security. It's just to isolate people.

And the answer to every question or challenge is: "It's for your development" or, "It's a conscious condition." No. Not so. Not any more, for so many years, to isolate and deprive people of so much. There is another story here.

And my role? To take responsibility. To take on the struggle. To be clear and principled.

All these ideas that have been put out for so many years with no reason, no overall strategy. WHY? What is the secret?

CHAPTER 26

The next time Julie and I met the sound of a referee's whistle and the squeak of sneakers echoed off the shining wooden gym floor, bouncing off the concrete walls as a group of black men from the neighborhood yelled and passed and dribbled a basketball below us. We needed to talk, and this was our talking time, and so we walked next to each other which was always a problem on the narrow track because the people who were jogging had to make their way around us. We were always turning and getting cricks in our necks to see if someone was catching up to us, and if someone was, then we fell back into single file for the time it took one of the sweaty, bouncing people to make the detour around us. A fifty-year-old white policeman dressed in regulation navy blue shorts and gray tee-shirt usually exercised at the same time, and, every time he lapped us, he was offensive, pushing into us or muttering or outright swearing at "bitches who block the track," while we watched the sweat spreading into a black triangle down the back of his tee-shirt below the pink wrinkles of his well-exercised neck.

We talked again about the child-care center. All the mistakes that had been made. I talked about the bakery and the mistakes made there. We talked about Dave and Debbie and how they dealt with their kids and our disapproval of their rigidity. Julie agreed with Ted's and my analysis of the center, although we didn't show her the actual document—this would have been breaking the security rules. Even talking in the way that we did, we realized was on the edge. We knew we would be in big trouble if it was known that we were discussing our programmatic work.

"I need to sort through what's going on," I said. "When I got that criticism from Debbie about Luis and little Sam, it stopped me in my tracks. I thought: the kind of world they're hoping for is not the same as what I want.

I want a free world, a place where kids can play with each other and have fun and have food enough to eat and a decent house to live in, and the love of people around them. Dave and Debbie want to have complete power over their children; they want to force them into a mold of their choosing. Our two worlds will never meet. What am I doing? We struggle and struggle and we're not even struggling for the same end."

Twenty Northside women replaced the basketball players on the gym floor below us. They were white and black, thin and fat, dressed in baggy sweats or skin-tight Lycra with stream-lined luminous details. Funk and R & B and hip-hop boomed out from a boom-box as the muscular aerobics teacher coaxed her motley class through the Y's Keep Fit program. This was the class Julie and I took together before we needed to talk more than we needed the body-toning. We strode around a lap or two while the music pulsed up to us and the women below kicked their multi-colored knees up as high as they were able.

"Someone needs to start talking about the problems in the O. Look at what's going on in Eastern Europe—I mean we haven't even discussed any of that. Surely, as a Communist organization," (here I lowered my voice, the policeman was only a quarter of a lap behind us), "We should be understanding what's going on in the rest of the world. We never talked about Tienanmen Square or the Soviet Union. It's always because there are 'other priorities'—it's crazy—no-one's talked about any of this for years. Then if you try to raise any of this, you're accused of anti-Organizational organizing!"

For a few moments we walked fast and silently until Julie spoke again.

"I'm ready to talk about it," she said quietly. She kept walking, picking up the pace still more, her chin lifting as she marched around the track.

"I'm ready to talk about Randy."

I turned to look at her.

"Who's Randy?" I asked, feeling my breath more acutely. I walked faster to keep up with her. "I've heard his name, but I've never met him—who is he?"

"He's leadership. There are some problems there."

I kept silent. No one had ever used a name before when they talked about the O.'s leadership. This was clearly a huge security violation. I didn't want her to stop talking, so I stayed silent, giving her space to continue.

"And you're right, Alex, there has to be some criticism. Actually, if that's what it has to be, if that's what it takes for there to be any discussion, I am ready to start organizing against the O."

The policeman was jogging safely ahead of us now. I stopped, out of breath, and looked at Julie. She stopped too. She had a crinkled, ironic smile on her face, but her eyes were serious. She flipped her graying braid over her shoulder.

"Bill and I have already started talking," she said.

And I knew immediately what she meant: they were breaking security, they were talking about what they really felt about the O., in the way I had tried to with Ted. I couldn't stop myself then. Tears started rolling down my face. I'd waited for almost ten years for this, for someone to lift up the bell jar, to say, "I'm in here too, and I think there's still life outside." I turned to her and hugged her, her warm breasts, that I had hugged so often, softening up to mine. The relief was a completely tangible thing: there was a way out. What I had waited for in my protected little space for so long had finally arrived. I had tried to do it on my own, that time I left after my first year—but I had been unable to. But now I had Julie, and Bill: together we were going to stand up and get the hell out.

I held her hand. I did not think about the future, I did not think about what it would mean and how we would get out, but I knew that I was no longer alone. Julie had broken the silence and taken that one step towards me.

The pink-necked policeman thudded past us, disciplined and blinkered, annoyed again by our irrational and anarchic behavior on the track. I wiped my eyes dry with a corner of my tee-shirt, and the two of us laughed at him like teenagers as he cursed his way past us.

Julie was willing to organize against the O. and so was I.

Three chairs were positioned in a triangle in the big, bright, carpeted attic of Suzanne and Zack's house. This was Suzanne's office, which also doubled as their children's play area. A big doll's house from a grandmother sat at one end, the red-and-yellow plastic trucks and bulldozers of their boy were piled into another corner. We sat by a desk that held Suzanne's obsolete computer and boxes of floppy disks.

Tight-lipped, pale-skinned, fat-assed Debbie sat by the desk, her white knees pressed together. Suzanne moved slowly in a bovine-like way and sat herself on the next chair after pointing me to my place.

The hearing. I had steeled myself for this, been through fear and anxiety, but now I felt prepared. They were just two white women, approaching middle-age, women I'd known for years. I felt myself separate from them, pulled in with my fists curled, ready for a fight. I would not let them get me on the defensive. I would stand up for my role in writing the criticism of the childcare center.

Debbie was in charge, and she opened the meeting, tapping on the sheaf of papers that lay on her lap.

"In light of your recent practice, there has been a review of your assessment. Originally you had been seen as Metaphysical, but, with additional information, it can now clearly be stated that you are an Open Idealist."

This wasn't what I'd expected. But then I realized it was exactly what I should have expected. There would be no discussion of the childcare center, or of my ideas about it, or my criticisms of the O. I should have known. It would be turned back on me (well, that I *had* known) and this was how they were choosing to do it.

For ten years, when challenged about my practice, my work or my ideas, I'd had to summarize and present self-criticisms based on my Ideological Form being Open Metaphysical. There was a whole structure that came along with that, which was now second nature to me. As required, I had "internalized my assessment." I had even prepared for this hearing by looking at how my "Metaphysical side" had influenced the paper I'd written, my relationship to Ted, and so on.

But the gray matter refused to shift. I was Metaphysical—I had accepted this aspect of my essential character structure. My brain had congealed in this structure and the dirty gray coldness of it would not, could not, do an about-face after all this time. I sat, my leg crossed with my foot up on my knee and my arms folded over my breasts.

"You're an Idealist. You are no longer seen as Metaphysical." Debbie repeated.

My mind simply rejected the engagement. Why are they doing this to me?, I thought. I shuddered a little inside, letting the words bounce off my brain. The knots in my stomach ratcheted up a couple more turns. "Don't let them manipulate you," I instructed myself, "The stupid fuckers." I repeated this comforting phrase over and over again inside myself, encouraging these words to replace the old voice, the voice that had whispered to me all these years: "I hate myself, I hate myself, I want to die—give me a place to hide . . . I hate, I hate . . ." Now my voice was impatient and contemptuous but not yet given to public expression, even as it bolstered me, giving me an advocacy I needed in my trial without jury.

Finally I spoke out loud: "How did you come up with that one?" I asked, looking up at them, from one to the other. This time I couldn't keep the note of sarcasm from my question. "You stupid fuckers," the private voice kept on.

Suzanne took up the response. Her face was open, and she looked pleased as she leaned forward towards me.

"I felt so stupid!" she acknowledged, echoing the voices. "When it finally came out that you were Idealist—well, I didn't understand how I could have missed it all these years. It was so obvious as soon as I stopped to think about it!"

My internal voice stopped talking for a while now and began simply to laugh. It wondered who had screwed up so bad to give me the wrong assessment for all those years. But at least now it was finally clear! The grayness still wouldn't move.

"You've always wanted so many connections. And your social side, all this talk about wanting to have input into things, the way you insisted on seeing me about the daycare center. The years, really, of being so fixated about being isolated, and not being able to see the materialism of O. practice. You always talk about feelings, as if somehow, feelings had the answer. This is so clearly Idealist—I really don't know how I missed it."

Debbie took over.

"The important thing now is for you to look at this new assessment and to review your practice. You don't have to respond right away, but you need to take some time to reflect on it. We understand this is a big change for you, but once you internalize it, it will bring clarity to you on your practice."

My companionate voices fell into silence and in their absence a hook of self-doubt worked itself back into me and the old voices whispered, "Maybe you're wrong. Maybe you'll have to sit again, stare at the blank sheet of paper, and fit your life and your feelings into the bourgeois mannerisms of the Open Idealist, or the codes of conduct of the Open Idealist, or maybe you'll have to reread Cornforth's *Dialectical Materialism* or Mao's *On Contradiction* and squeeze yourself into that tiny space that they've created for you."

The hook scratched at me, but I had entered a kind of psychological freeze, a protective hypothermia of the mind and soul, and this dull coldness prevented a further hemorrhage into doubt.

We carried on talking. I agreed, for the sake of moving the conversation forward, that I would "think about" the new assessment, although I was already sure that, despite the hook, I would not let it move me from my course. I stood my ground.

"This is what always happens," I said. "Whenever a criticism is raised of the organization it's always turned back on the person making the criticism. It's always their ideological problem. I knew this would be an attack on me—

that we wouldn't discuss the criticism at all. How can there be co-operative and constructive discussion in this climate?"

Debbie smiled. "You see, there it is—there is your Idealism coming out. You want so much to have a voice, an impact, and yet look at your practice. What have you ever summarized from that? You see, you want that social connection of group discussions, rather than looking at what the Productive Forms of Association are."

I stared at her shoes. I didn't even know what that last phrase meant, and it dawned on me how little I actually understood of the capitalized pronouncements that had defined my life for the past decade. Finally I looked up and met her chocolate-brown eyes. I realized I had to break the direction of communication, they were trying to push me back into the bell jar. Silencing me with their magical language and deflecting my questions were part of their weaponry; I had to resist, keep myself present, keep my self outside of myself in some way, meeting them, showing them that I wasn't scared. And so I looked at her, and my looking at her directly like that scared her in turn until she lowered *her* eyes and continued in her monotone, but now looking at my shoes.

Nonetheless, she continued. "The Internal Transformation Process is the special contribution that the E. is making to the world revolutionary movement. This is the key unity that we have. The programs we have been involved in have been targeted to this goal: to developing our scientific knowledge of the Internal Transformation Process."

"But what about real life?" I countered. Here was where my work with the ANC gave me strength. Their work, their building, their reality had touched me. The ANC had been unbanned the year before. I had celebrated that news, going to work in a delirious happiness the day I heard it and, dropping my usual computer consultant mask, had told my co-workers about it and about the reason for my singing and humming through the historic day.

The ANC had shown me SOMAFCO, the school in the Tanzanian bush that educated and supported children whose families had been decimated by apartheid; whose parents were either dead or were full-time activists, or soldiers, or workers in the struggle. In SOMAFCO they built their own school out of mud and corrugated iron, had support from around the world, had a nursery named after Ruth First, Robyn's mother. SOMAFCO's graduates went to colleges in Europe and the United States to learn agriculture, science, medicine, and law. The children of SOMAFCO created culture: murals and songs and theater and stories. They struggled with a constant lack of resources, and yet they had love and strength and beauty. Oh, of course, I romanticized it, but I knew that there was something real that I had witnessed in the ANC that bore no resemblance to our years of dullness and mean-spirited sacrifice. I knew that the soldiers of Umkhonto We Sizwe suffered the same deprivations as other soldiers, and already stories of abuses in the military camps were beginning to surface, but they *had* fought, they *had* threatened the power structure, they *had* a function beyond a purely theoretical one.

And the greatest lesson I had learned from them was that they judged people by their practice, by what they could offer the struggle against apartheid, not by the words or the promises that were made.

I knew that the ANC was involved in union activity throughout the country, had neighborhood organizations, political organizations, clinics, nurseries, publishing facilities, all those things I had wanted to build in my early years in California. Granted, our place in history gave us no historic mass struggle within which to organize—but to settle for the Internal Transformation Process? The only results I had seen in a decade of a patient and soul-destroying suspension of disbelief were the atrophying of an organization and that of my own mind and abilities.

And, to cap it all off, the ANC had parties. They danced the township hip-swinging jazz of the *kwela,* and they raised dust with the militant *toyi-toyi.* They celebrated. Some even had holidays. They fell in and out of love, they had children who were good or bad, they fought with each other, they had political infights and names and slurs for each other and often, great love and respect under the layers of gossip and intrigue. And something had worked. They were winning.

"What about real life?" I repeated. "When will any of us be developed enough by the ITP to actually *do* anything? When do we "engage in practice" for it's own sake? When do we study? When do we organize? When are cadre developed enough to be let out to do the things that cadre are supposed to do?"

My voice was rising. I was no longer trying to listen, to fit my thoughts into the scheme that was being proposed to me, I was speaking out even though I knew that I would not be heard.

"You should review your history. How much have you studied of U.S. history?" Debbie interrupted me.

I was familiar with this one. This was always brought out to silence me: the fact that I had spent the first eighteen years of my life outside the United States, so, therefore, I did not have the right to speak. P.O.O. had often used this in his criticisms of me, and before now it had been effective. But, in fact, during my San Francisco days, I had spent years studying the history of the United States. I reminded Debbie of this. She was unimpressed.

"You should know then, what happened with the petty bourgeois women's movement, the first one, the movement for women's suffrage, and their alliance with the Abolitionists: they betrayed the cause of black people in this country. The current women's movement did the same. Look at the Women's Union in the seventies—they had the opportunity to take a class stand, but they chose their own class privilege as usual. They betrayed their black sisters. Until the Left in this country takes stock of their internal ideological weakness, this will happen again and again. The people with privilege will never cease to betray those without. This is what you are leading up to: you will betray the only force in the white Left that has consistently been using the Tools to dismantle bourgeois ideology. You say how much you've learned from South Africa, but you will betray that struggle too by your opportunism and individualism unless you accept the need to deal with ideological issues."

Debbie was angry now because she realized that she was losing me. She must have been frightened—how would she explain her failure to P.O.O.? What was *her* ideological weakness in being unable to successfully struggle with me?

I fell into that place in memory called déjà vu. The white guilt trip. I had never heard it so clearly spoken in the O. In fact, most of the O.'s papers did not refer at all to all those iconic phrases: Third World Leadership and White Skin Privilege, and so on and so forth. Instead, the O., (in its literature of ten or more years ago—I later found, with a shock, that nothing new had been written since then) had focused on people's class backgrounds and the need for whites to organize in their own communities (hence the food stores, the union work, the child care center). For so many years I had steered clear of white guilt politics. In fact the apparent lack of those politics was what had attracted me to the O. in the first place. It was strange to hear it coming from Debbie's mouth, as she scolded me and ordered me to reread my history of the Suffrage and Abolitionist movements.

I uncrossed my legs and set both feet flat on the floor.

"At this point, I don't believe that I have unity with the O. on the primacy of the Internal Transformation Process. I am working on what I do believe. What I see is that my criticism of the daycare center is getting no response. And that there is no discussion of what is going on in the world. I will tell you that I am seriously re-evaluating my relationship to the O."

Suzanne frowned. She was genuinely upset that I was not accepting the "struggle." We had almost become close in the previous year, when she had been bedridden during her second pregnancy, and I was one of the few people who came to see her, and listened to her when she was depressed and encouraged her to share her feelings. She wanted me to change. At that point I think she saw me as a wayward child and wished that I would see the light. It was so clear and obvious and helpful to her, especially this new concept of me as an Idealist.

She looked up and asked me, "Please think about it. Look at your motion as an Idealist and see if, perhaps, that wouldn't help to clarify things for you."

I didn't reply. The meeting came to an end.

The hook was still in me, but fading now, like a shadow, or a stain, and I stood in the snowy cold outside the door of Suzanne's house shaking my head to relieve the pressure and hunching my shoulders to ease the ache that the echoes of their voices stirred in me.

I would not think about it. I decided that on the way home, before I saw Ted. The issue of me being an Idealist was moot—maybe it was true, maybe it wasn't, but that was not what I had to deal with now. What I needed to deal with was the actual practice of the Organization and the work that I had done over the last ten years. Was this what and how I wanted to contribute, or not? Was the O. effective or not? Was there room for open discussion or not?

I would think about the questions I had raised and not get sidetracked by their mantra. But it took a physical effort to resist the grabbing of my mind that their words attempted—the hook would catch me, then loosen, then catch again, but I kept pushing it away and shouting down the hating voices when they rose up against me.

At the house Ted greeted me coldly. He was waiting there to struggle too.

"Are you going to look at your new assessment?" he asked as soon as I entered.

"No, not right now," I replied. I was exhausted and just wanted to go to bed. Ted leaned against the kitchen wall as I hung up my coat, his arms crossed over his chest. He looked down at his feet and then raised his eyes to meet mine.

"Do you agree that it's important to take a look at it? To struggle with it?"

"Well, that's what I'm not sure about. Right now I don't think it's what I need to be looking at. This time it's not a question of my ideological problems. I'm trying to bring out a criticism of the Organization, but apparently that's not going to be allowed."

I realized now that his meetings earlier that week had prepared him for this, and he was playing out his role. His job was to struggle with me, to get me to agree with the new assessment. But I was already clear that it was a red herring, a diversion to keep me off-balance, and I wasn't ready to give into it. They were playing the wrong cards with me. What had worked before was not going to work now.

Ted continued quietly, "I think you should look at it. There are people with considerably more experience than you who are putting this out. It's known that you want a response to your criticisms, but it's leadership's job to lead, not to respond to every cadre's momentary frustration about this or that."

"Oh Christ!" I exploded, shoving a kitchen chair out of my way. "And where has leadership led us, Ted! What have we built? Look at the failed businesses. What structures do we have? Look at the cadre—I mean look at us all! If we're not developed now, when will we be? No one takes initiative, no one thinks creatively about what they're doing. There's been no study, no plans put out. Look at all the things you've disagreed with over the last few years. Has anything changed?"

"I think there's some change happening. But that's not the point. The ITP is what is primary, and it's not our job to second guess every decision that's made, even if it has some personal effect on us. We don't know the whole picture, so how can we have the basis to criticize what's being decided?"

"Listen to yourself, Ted! What about criticism-self-criticism? Isn't it your job to criticize bad practice? Who else is going to do it?"

"I'm sure people are summarizing their own practice. When did you last do a summary? You are not even willing to look at your new assessment—how can you have the basis to criticize others?"

"Oh, God, this is ridiculous. I've told you, I'm re-evaluating my relationship to the O. I'm not clear at all what I think of the ITP. The questions have got to go beyond this. And you should think about it too, what are your *own* thoughts? I'm going to bed."

I went upstairs and stopped in the children's bedroom. Luis lay on his back, so beautiful, and I kissed him, feeling his sleep-calm touching me. I pulled up Ana's covers and watched as her mouth sucked on her thumb; she made a complete circuit with that thumb, some kind of self-sufficiency that was part of her core. I tucked her doll in closer to her, feeling the nostalgic pull that sleeping children exert on one's heart and quietly left their room for mine.

In bed I felt safe. Even edged over to one side as I was, so that I would not have to touch Ted when he finally came upstairs. This time I was going to block out his questions and his criticisms, this time I would not let them sway me. I was beginning to know that I was right, and they were wrong.

In bed I could nestle in the covers, keep warm and let my dreams sort out the mess for me. Sleep became a necessity then, as I recovered from the years when the nights were too short, when I did not have time to dream. Not having time to dream is the same as not having time to think. Because dreaming and thinking are two sides of the same coin. And when I don't have time to dream, I ache, I feel uncomfortable deep in me. It's as if things haven't time to settle, they remain jumbled, they don't get an ordered place in my brain in which to fit. It is as if dreaming were a way to sort, a way to put things into memory so you can find them afterward. Your very own Random Access Method, a kind of personal hashing system goes on, where the strangest mnemonic connections are made, and the pieces of life are stored accordingly. Without dreams a part of me is lost. My soul is scattered.

I needed to see Julie. Or Bill. They would help me remember my questions and stand up against the voices.

CHAPTER 27

Monday: back at the YMCA.

"Randy?" I asked, "Is he black?"

"Yeah," said Julie.

I looked down at the basketball players, the young and middle-aged black men from my neighborhood, laughing and playing and cursing each other for a blocked shot or a foul. A faceless picture of a black man became Randy for me.

"Is he P.O.O.?"

"Yeah," she said.

"Oh. I see now." I had never met Randy, never known who P.O.O. was. Now it started to fall into place. The reverence for him. The unspoken allusions to black leadership. The one person Jerri knew who had, indeed, been "transformed." The memos: those talismans that ruled our lives. Yes, it was becoming clear to me now.

"Did you know him?" I asked.

"Yes. I met him at the very beginning, in one of the food co-op study groups—that's how I got organized. It's just been the last few years that I've really worked with him though."

"Was he the man I saw at your house that time—when you were building the add-on for your kitchen?"

"Yes. Why did you think of that?"

"There was something about the way he was avoiding eye contact. He was leaning on the shovel—you were both digging out the foundation I think and I came by to drop something off and I said, 'Hi' and he looked at the ground and didn't say anything. It was odd. I just remembered it, that's all." I paused.

"And Kristin's kid, the little girl at the center—is that his kid?"

"Yes. Poor kid. I feel sorry for her."

I knew Kristin had a baby, and the baby had a black father. In the back of my mind, I'd wondered for a while who the father was. Another piece fell into place.

"There aren't any other blacks in the O., are there?"

"Not that I know of. There was one woman, Mattie, years ago when we still had the co-ops. But she left. She was always in trouble—she had kind of strong opinions about things."

"How strange . . . So that's P.O.O. How weird, all these years I've been in an all-white organization run by a black man. I never imagined it. Is there anyone else in leadership?—I mean, other than the hatchet men, Dave and Debbie."

"I don't think so, I've never dealt with anyone other than Randy. And his lieutenants seem to come and go, depending on who's in favor at a given time."

So. Randy was P.O.O. Randy was leadership. Randy was the father of Kristin's kid. Randy was the guy who did the construction and remodeling, he was the P.O.O. who wrote the unintelligible memos, he was the one who wanted to break sanctions on South Africa, he was the one who'd told me and Ted to get married and *there was no one else?* It made perfect sense, in a crazy kind of way. For years this blank non-person of P.O.O. had been the center of my life, and now, here he was, with a name (granted, still a code name) and almost a face (I couldn't remember it well, he'd avoided my eyes, but I could see his posture, leaning on that shovel in that hole in the dirt) and an identity—someone that Julie knew, after all, and now was able to talk about. So, maybe I'd been trapped by white-guilt politics after all. Certainly Randy's color must have been part of the charm. And even though I hadn't known him, it appeared to me now that I'd been sucked in, too; seduced somehow by a ripple effect of the white guilt I'd tried so hard to avoid.

Julie and I dressed in the locker room among the joking and teasing of the women from the aerobics class, and, while she traded greetings with them in her relaxed way, I kept quiet and felt shy and out of place among the women wiping the sweat from between their shiny black breasts.

Wednesday: at the Y. again. "Tell me about him then. It feels strange—why didn't I ever meet him?"

Now that P.O.O. had a name, and a partial face, I wanted the details. Ten years of not knowing gave me an unbearable curiosity.

"I remember being struck by him right away, in the first study group. He didn't say much, he just observed, but he had this very wise, quiet expression as if he knew a lot more than he let on. He carried himself with confidence but not with arrogance. Charismatic, I suppose."

Julie continued, "I met with him a couple of times in Chicago—about the software business. It was odd, because he took Bill and me out to nice restaurants for those meetings and talked about good wine and music and so on. You know, that was when no one went out anywhere nice, but somehow it was okay if it was with him. It was fun, I remember that. It was a break, anyway, from the daily grind.

"And I know he was in jail once. For about a year, when Kristin was living with us. She visited him there. I never knew what for—but I thought it was some kind of welfare fraud. I remember wondering how leadership could do something stupid like that."

Another piece began to slip into place. This I couldn't quite believe, but it fit didn't it?

"Julie," I lowered my voice and bent my head towards hers as we circled the track. I was scared and my breath was catching.

"Julie, do you know about . . . a murder?"

She turned to look at me.

"What?"

"There was a murder. At 801."

"What?" Clearly she'd never heard about it.

"I was home one day, back in '82, right after we first got here, and the FBI came to the door asking for Kristin. I didn't even know who she was until a couple of years ago. So I told them I didn't know her, and that I wouldn't talk to them and the guy says to me: 'You'd talk to me if you knew there'd been a murder here!'"

"So what happened?"

"I was told there'd been some problem with a drug dealer in the neighborhood and Jerri told me to see a psychologist—kind of a defensive measure, I saw it, to keep the F.B.I. from harassing us. But the weird thing is that a couple of years ago, right about when you're talking about, Ted noticed an article in the paper about someone who he said was 'connected' coming back to town to give himself up to the police. I just wonder, that's all. It seems like too much of a coincidence."

"And then everyone started getting moved back to town, right?—from Chicago. God. I don't believe it. It couldn't have been him! But he *was* in jail then. And the connection with Kristin . . ."

We left it there for the moment. Julie was struggling with this new twist—after all, she knew the guy. To me he was just an abstraction, one for whom I had lost almost all respect over the years.

"Who was killed?" she asked.

"I don't know—Jerri just mentioned this drug dealer—I assumed that's who was killed."

It was so hard to talk to each other. Each conversation was an exercise in how far we could go, tentatively testing the waters, seeing what the other person knew, what they were willing to talk about without veering too far off into anti-organizational practice. Even though Julie had announced, in her brash and defiant way, (a part of her I hadn't seen emerge in years) that she would organize against the O., she wanted to do it in the right way, in the principled way—but after so many years in the O. we now had to find our own way into an acceptable definition of "principled."

Now the piece of the puzzle that was the murder had been turned over, though not yet put into place, I began to have a new phobia that I did not recognize. A reflexive fear of black men took hold of me. At first I confused it with racism, but it wasn't that. It was that I had this shadowy image of P.O.O., the man who had so tightly controlled my life, and I did not have a face for him, and so, every black man that I saw: in the mall, or on the street, or playing basketball in the Y, caused me to cringe. Like a woman who fears men after a rape, I shrank in anxiety from any black man I did not know.

The following Monday: at the Y. "I don't want to factionalize," started Julie. "But I'm clear that things can't continue the way they've been going. We've got to bring struggle to the organization and to leadership. The thing is, how do we do it in a principled way?"

We stretched our legs on the rail at the top of the spiral staircase. Julie waved to a woman she knew from the neighborhood who was already on the track.

I launched in. "Being principled is bringing the struggle out. Keeping it to ourselves is definitely not principled. But there's no use bringing it out to Randy. Haven't you noticed how people just seem to disappear when they leave? Whatever happened to Walt, or Vida's husband? One day they're here and then all of a sudden you realize you haven't seen them for a year or so. I don't think there's any room for discussion, we'll just get smothered. We've got to be careful, if he finds out we're talking we'll be kicked out and not have a chance."

I told her about the letter Walt had sent to Ted and me, the one we'd returned. And she, in turn, told me how Walt had written a resignation letter criticizing the O., how he'd come home from work that day to find the locks of the duplex where he lived changed and all his clothes dumped out on the street. All the cadre who'd worked with him were told he'd become an Enemy Force. After all those years in the O., he was left without a home, and with no chance to speak with his old comrades.

Through these discussions, we began to make our way out. More talks on the track at the Y. Then sometimes meeting secretly, Bill, Julie and I, at a restaurant, or at their house, in their newly remodeled kitchen. I covered up my frequent absences from home by explaining to Ted that I was redoubling my fitness efforts and attending extra aerobics classes at the Y. Bill continued to run with Ted once or twice a week, and to feel him out and see if he would come with us. But by now Ted had retreated all the way back to his O. persona.

"I trust leadership," he told Bill, "I've dedicated my life to this organization, and I'm not going to give up on it just because it's going through a difficult time."

He used his experience with the ANC to explain this—which taught me that one can use any experience to justify almost anything; we were each using the ANC to justify our opposing positions! He, that the ANC had worked so quietly, in exile, for so long and had had the patience and commitment and integrity to build a solid base and that cadre had not given up just because the going got tough. I, on the other hand, used it to prove that they actually did things, that they didn't simply turn in on themselves and purge themselves of the Original Ideological Sins. The result was that little communication happened. I carried on meeting with Bill and Julie, he with Debbie and Suzanne, and we lived for a strange couple of months in a state of denial. We looked after the children, slept together still, even joked and worked at the business while a subterranean rift began to engulf us from below.

Ted refused to acknowledge that Randy was the sole leader—he still had an image of the leadership being some kind of collective based in Oakland. Where he got this idea, I don't know, but it was common in the O. for each person to carry his or her own, unspoken (it being forbidden to talk about) vision of how things were, and this was easy to do as we had so little information as to the actual reality.

In our clandestine meetings, the three of us agreed that the Organization was seriously adrift and that only struggle with it would move it back on course. Through these discussions, I began to learn more of the history of the O., bits of which I'd known before but never really the whole picture. (Of course, the whole picture is still not known.) And now I learned Randy's real name (among the five or six aliases he used over the years): Theophilus Smith. As fictional a name as one could imagine, but apparently the one under which he went to jail.

Now time compressed, or expanded, split up into shards of intense experience. Things do not come in a sequence anymore. It is more a collection, a kaleidoscope of images. Color re-enters, and breath. And thought.

Julie, Bill and I met almost daily. We wrote a long and detailed analysis of our experience in the O. We used all the O. terminology and the analytical structures, from Worksheets to PS01s to Four-Step Methods, to figure out what was wrong with the O. itself. Despite this reliance on the very "Tools" that had trapped us, we were using our own minds; the structure and the forms were not enough anymore, without the rest of the controlling paraphernalia, to prevent us from looking clearly at the last ten or fifteen years of our lives.

Eventually we came up with a statement: that the O. had become merely the organizational reflection of Theo Smith. He controlled everything and everybody, he allowed no criticism of himself, he was behind all the irrational decisions and the constant stream of failures. We began to discover another theme: that of thinly disguised violence and threats. We looked back at all the times cadre had ever tried to criticize the O., or Theo, and noted with growing dread that each time they had been silenced.

We sat in the bright, pleasant space of Bill and Julie's remodeled kitchen and told the grim stories each of us knew.

Kitchen Stories

In 1976 a group of cadres challenged the O.'s focus on the ITP and demanded they be allowed to do the work for which they had joined—that is, community organizing. This launched the Two Line Struggle between the O. and the New Reactionaries, as they became known. Groups of cadre in good standing were sent to each of the Reactionaries' houses. Each cadre wore dark glasses. Some carried baseball bats. Others carried cameras. The cameras were to take the Reactionaries' pictures, somehow that was supposed to threaten them—more likely the dark glasses and the baseball bats sent the appropriate message. An official order of expulsion was read at the doorstep, and if it was an O. house, then these so-called paramilitary units entered the house and bodily threw out the offender followed by their belongings.

Bill had been on one of these raids and wore his dark glasses and felt righteous and proud that he was defending the working class and proving his seriousness. I laughed to imagine him decked out as a revolutionary bouncer. Bill was one of the gentlest people I knew and one who I was sure wouldn't have known how to fight had a Reactionary actually reacted and fought back against the violent ouster.

In 1979, the Intensification Campaign had exhausted and frightened many O. cadres. Some left, like Julie, because they feared enforced separation from their children or lovers. Others couldn't cope any more with the twenty-hour days and the constant tongue lashings, punishments and committee hearings for petty failings. Still others couldn't tolerate the continued insistence on unquestioning acceptance of leadership. Some rebelled against the boxing matches. Bill also left, driven close to suicide by the pressure of that time. These cadres were denounced and labeled as the Eighteen Resisters. Supposedly they had engaged in an Ideological Conspiracy to undermine the correct line of the O. They had become, therefore, agents of the Bourgeois State and were to be shunned. In an Orwellian gesture, many were officially expelled, even though they had already departed voluntarily.

Years later, when Walt was dumped out of his house (and after Bill had returned and been rehabilitated), Bill made the serious security error of letting Walt back in to pick up his remaining possessions. For this act of consorting with the enemy, Bill was made to write a lengthy self-criticism. Soon after, Bill made another, unrelated security error—he gave his employer his home phone number. For that he was thrown out of the house where he lived with Julie and his two daughters, one of whom was a newborn. During the first six months of his youngest daughter's life he was not allowed to live with her as atonement for this error.

I remembered how Ted had sent Walt's letter back to him. Somehow sending the letter back meant it had never existed. We did not think to save a copy—that would have been insubordinate. We followed orders, even I who rarely agreed with them. It does not matter, in the end, whether you agree or not; what matters really, I have discovered, is what your behavior is. If you change your behavior enough, the belief system is largely irrelevant.

Another story: Stephen, an O. member I never knew, had broken his leg and been in the hospital. No one came to visit him. Perhaps it was to teach him a lesson: that to break one's leg was clearly a reflection of unresolved ideological contradictions, so he should be left alone to reflect upon his "internal." The isolation of weeks alone in hospital proved to be the last straw for Stephen, and he quit the O. After he got out, he was hobbling along on crutches when he ran into Richard on the street. Richard confronted him about his resignation, threw a punch that bloodied Stephen's nose and literally knocked the crutches out from under him, leaving him lying injured on the sidewalk.

What had lived in our minds as righteous defense of our Organization, we now began to see in a different light. Now that we were talking to each other and putting some of these stories together, we could begin to discern the patterns. These were not isolated events, mistakes by individual cadre who could not control their bourgeois motions—no, the intimidation was real. The message was clear—if you leave, leave quickly and quietly or watch out!

We all learned the lesson: there was to be no communication with ex-members. Leaving the O. was betrayal of the revolution. Someone who left deserved nothing but sharp struggle and to be put out of our midst without discussion. The O. operated on the principle of Unity, Struggle, Unity—but we had to remember that struggle was absolute and harmony relative. This meant that we should expect to more or less constantly be in a state of "internal struggle"—and that this was good, because it meant one was developing, moving forward in the struggle to transform one's internal contradictions. People who couldn't deal with the level of internal struggle required for a revolutionary departed as failures, either weak and pitiable, or, if they left trying to raise any criticism, then they were anti-organizational and never to be trusted.

We would need to have courage to leave with our heads held high, to make our criticisms publicly to the organization as a whole. I thought of other ex-members slinking off silently, not saying a word until the last moment and moving off into a new life, scared, ill-prepared and isolated. Some left feeling suicidal, many left feeling they had failed the Great Cause, that they could not "cut it" as revolutionaries and that they should disappear into civilian life carrying their shame with them.

Early on in our discussions we decided we would not be driven to this. Julie had left like this the first time, had slunk off, back when I'd met her in California. Bill, too had tried leaving. They'd come back, humiliated, to be accepted back, after lengthy self-criticisms, into the "revolutionary process." We knew that this time we had things to say, that we must organize a space for ourselves in which we could say them. The lessons of the dark glasses and the baseball bats were not lost on us. Now we would use the security measures that we had practiced for so long to protect us, this time, from Theo.

"Do you think he'll get violent?" asked Julie.

"I don't know," said Bill, "But I've seen him close to it a couple of times. When he was working on our house—these two black guys, Cliff and Michael, had come to deliver the concrete for our garage, but Theo and I had dug the form too deep so they had to go back and get more concrete. Theo got mad and told them it was their fault and Cliff talked back. So Theo went and threatened him until Cliff, a big guy, stood up and said, 'Go on, go on! Try and hit me.' Theo backed right off and left.

"Then another time one of the workmen asked him where he was going— because he was always going off in the middle of the construction work, and he'd act all secretive about it. My neighbor, Jackie, laughed and said, 'Oh, he always acts like such a big black revolutionary, but he's just running off to be with some white woman!' Theo grabbed a crow bar and went up in Jackie's face, but Jackie came right back with a hammer in his hand and Theo just ran off again."

Bill's stories, and the shadow of the murder, chilled us into a certain precision. We would plan our way out, every step of the way. We would not be pushed, kicked out onto the street, we would not disappear in shame, we would speak out and take the measures we needed to defend ourselves against physical or psychological attack.

For this reason, I could no longer trust Ted. I loved him still, and I still believed he would come out with us, but I could not afford to let him turn us in. I worked in secret on the documents that would explain our leaving, keeping the files on a floppy disk and carrying it with me, too afraid to leave the documents on the computer's hard drive. I didn't feel angry at Ted then, just sorry for him that he could not break out of his world enough to listen to what I was trying to tell him.

CHAPTER 28

March 1st, 1991
Codify the responses: Because everyone will have them.
1. Fear—physical fear. He will come to get me in the night.
2. Passivity—I'm alone. I can't do anything. It's hopeless.
3. Uselessness—I am nothing. I'm a useless person.
4. Depression—What's the point? What options are there?
5. Loneliness.

This is what's happening to me, and to Bill and Julie. It's the fallout, the unmooring, the process of stepping out of the field of power(lessness).

The analysis was clear: Randy (we still called him by his code name) had all the power and was squelching and exploiting the rest of us. We began to see how much we had been side-lined, our strengths turned against us all these years. Bill and Julie felt that the first step, the "principled" thing to do, was to confront Randy and see if he would accept change and share the power: they proposed an elected leadership collective. I had no belief that Randy would ever share his power—he'd had it too long and too completely—but I agreed that Bill and Julie could at least try to talk with him. Our plan was to first try to organize the people we thought might come over now. Then we would talk to Randy, and if he wouldn't negotiate we would put out our position papers to the rest of the cadres and resign.

We did assessments of who might stand with us. Ted, we decided, sadly, would not. We could not count on him not to tell Randy what we were thinking. He was too damn loyal.

Meanwhile, I had been talking to Jerri for months about this and so had Bill. She and I worked together every day doing computer consulting for a local software company, and so we talked often. I could sense her softening, questioning behind an enormous wall of denial and fear.

Betty and Julie worked together, too, consulting for another business; by now most of the remaining cadres were programmers and worked for one consulting company or another. Julie talked to Betty as they car-pooled to work out in the technology suburbs of Eden Prairie. Betty listened attentively and acknowledged much of what Julie said: the uneven distribution of power, the problems with the programs, the lack of political work and so on. Jerri and Betty, we agreed, were ready to be approached.

Julie and I met with Jerri at Jacob's, a restaurant near the daycare center by an industrial section of the city, next to the Mississippi. We met for breakfast, the place smelling of the smoke of last night's dinner customers, and dark with the musty-red of a bar in day-time; a place designed to be comfortable and warm at night but in the daylight revealing all its dust and stains and smells.

Jerri was thin and taut. She and Julie had never gotten along, but they were now both my friends, as much as could be in the O. I mediated, I suppose, between them in their discomfort at having both had the same husband, Bill.

We sat and pulled out our papers and passed them to Jerri. She read them intently and then listened to us explain, watching us with a nervous, pale face.

"I'll think about what you're saying. I agree with your observations of the problems but not with your conclusions."

These conclusions were to shift the power away from Randy/Theo; to review our practice; and as a group to plan the future of the O. democratically. But she wasn't ready to leave the O. with us, although she continued to talk to me as the drama unfolded.

Julie met with Betty also, and this was less successful. Betty got angry, refused to ride to work with her anymore and cut us off completely. She said, "I know times have been hard in the O., and mistakes have been made, but I've got faith in Randy. Sometimes these conditions are set on purpose. It brings something out of you that you didn't know you were capable of. I don't always understand what he does, but I'm going to follow Randy—maybe it *is* blind faith, but I'll follow where it leads me."

There was no one else to talk to then. We did not think anyone else in Minneapolis was ready to leave, and the others were in Chicago—we didn't have addresses or phone numbers for them, our connections always having been mediated by the secure internal mail system.

One night Ted and I made love. The love of people who know each other well, who have a certain routine with their bodies; one which mostly satisfies, sometimes disappoints, sometimes takes both to a happy closeness. This night my body felt his, and my thoughts dissociated. I held my arms around his back, pulling him closer to me and I thought, *This might be the last time—I might never hold him again like this.* Perhaps he felt that, too, but he did not know.

Television

1991. Over and over and over again we see Rodney King try to rise up from the ground, his empty, open hands covering his head, and the cops raise up nightsticks above *their* heads and bring them down on him. They kick him. He tries to rise, they beat and kick him. The video of this black man being beaten by L.A. police is repeated four, five times a night on national TV. The videotape is TV within TV. The videotape is a witness that the whole country witnesses.

Rodney King's face is bloodied and beaten and stares out from the screen and the front pages of newspapers.

"We waited for two hours, he never came," said Julie. Bill and she had been to the daycare center, where Theo had his office on the second floor. They had sent a memo earlier, via Kristin, to ask to meet with him, and he hadn't responded. So now, in order to be principled and not to go to the others before giving him a chance to respond to our criticisms, they were trying to catch him at his office to speak to him. Bill knew he worked there at night, so every night for the last three nights they set up a vigil parked in their car in the street outside the daycare center.

"What do we do if he gets violent?" Bill had asked. We'd talked about this for hours, trying to allay the generalized terror we felt, frightened that he would lash out at our insubordination. Finally Bill decided, "If it means I have to fight him, I will—I'll punch him—then we can run."

Now they were back at the house. We drank tequila. The tension sweated off us as the golden threads of liquor wound down the tightness in our necks, hands, stomachs.

The next night.

"We waited again, two hours," said Julie. "He's usually there every night—I wonder if he's avoiding us?"

"How would he know to?" I asked.

"Betty. I'll ask Betty. Maybe she told him."

And she had.

One more night they waited, and then we heard about the memo that labeled us and Jerri as "The Gang of Four." This we laughed about—tension-releasing belly-laughs. Betty had turned us in, and we were being accused of anti-organizational activity, the worst of crimes, the crime that would lead directly to our expulsion. But by now we knew we were psychologically *out*, because we could read this and laugh and not be affected. However, it meant that now we had to move without hesitating. We had to get to everyone before we were cut off, before they were ordered not to speak with us.

That night, after the kids were asleep, Bill and I drove to Zack and Suzanne's. We would tell them first. We parked in the driveway off the alley, walked through the yard with the kids' climbing frame and the big cedar pots in which Zack had planted asparagus ferns and blood-red geraniums. He had a love of flowers and literature that I shared, and I had always been able to feel the humanity left in him. We thought Zack was with us but wouldn't come out because of Suzanne, who was clearly not. It was March, but I remember it being warm, like springtime. We knocked on the back door.

"Hi!" said Zack, surprised—it was after ten o'clock.

"We need to talk to you and Suzanne for a while," said Bill. Zack looked quizzical, but not hostile, and let us in.

He called Suzanne, who peered at us, gave a tight, small smile from behind her glasses, and we all trooped up the stairs and sat back in that gray-carpeted attic, but this time we made a circle of four chairs, not the uneven triangle of my hearing. Bill sat his big, soft body on the chair; his hands were shaking a little, but probably only I noticed that. He handed out the papers we had written. He asked them to read.

As he read, Zack's leg started bouncing up and down, his knee jittering in a startling way. Zack always did this when he was nervous; I remembered it from years back, from bakery meetings, from meetings about child develop-ment—everyone noticed it and was disturbed by it—except, it seemed, for him. His heel was drumming away like a convulsive. This was almost his only response. We had touched something in him; he wouldn't come out now, but he wouldn't be the same either. A little bit of light had been allowed to enter.

Suzanne bent over the paper. She tried to hide her face, to compose her-self, but when she brought her head up she was flushed. I had rarely seen such emotion in her—she was normally white and placid, stonewalling any kind of feeling that might crop up. But now she was angry red; her legs were apart a bit, aggressive. She would not talk to me or acknowledge my presence. Perhaps because of our struggles over the daycare center she decided that I was the enemy, the ringleader. She acted as if she had been forced to sit in a room with poison, with a satanic force, with traitors.

"This is disgusting!" she managed to spit out to Bill. "How can you write this? How can you do this? Why do you want to destroy the O.?"

She was almost crying with anger.

Gently Bill replied, "We're trying to bring principled struggle. These are our observations. We only want a forum in which to discuss them."

We tried to talk to her, but she could not listen. Zack said little, but he couldn't stop his leg from bouncing. He frowned, very distressed.

We left, exhausted. Back to the safety of the kitchen at Vincent Avenue. Open the bottle of tequila for me, the bottle of whiskey for Bill. He was drink-ing a lot of whiskey now, I'd started to notice. His eyes got red and watery—I remembered that from my old friend Tracy at the machine shop. I decided not to worry about it yet.

Zack. I wanted to reach out to him. I wanted to hold him, to hug him. "Zack—it's okay, let it go," I wanted to tell him. Zack felt like a friend. I had laughed with him, talked to him about books over the years as we worked together on O. projects. He was open and warm, and we had had a gentle attraction between us, based on a human feeling that we allowed. I hurt for him, felt his struggle almost physically under my breastbone.

Meanwhile, Julie had been to see Kristin to announce our resignation and to show her our position papers. She came back after us and reported in, very sad. She felt close to Kristin, bonded with her and wanted her out. Kristin had been polite enough, had listened respectfully to Julie and, like Jerri, agreed with the observations but not with our steps. Julie knew she wouldn't come out: Theo was the father of her baby, and beneath Kristin's blond, big-boned, labor-lawyer confidence there was a battered woman—whether physically or not, we did not know, but her spirit had been broken, much like the rest of us, only perhaps more intimately.

Julie screwed the caps back on the bottles of liquor and pushed them back into the cupboard.

"Okay, you guys, get out of here. You better go tell Ted."

My face fell. I'd been going on adrenaline up till then, but now I felt myself cave in. I didn't want to leave Julie. I felt like a small child. She hugged me. Bill smiled and gathered his papers, looking at me a little shyly as I emerged from Julie's embrace.

We drove separately through the spring night to my house where Ted was home with the children. We'd decided, Julie, Bill and I, that it would be best if Bill and I talked to Ted, rather than me alone. That making it a political difference rather than a personal one would be the most principled thing to do.

I remember we woke him up because he came downstairs in his torn tee-shirt and underwear, his hair sticking up in that way that made me laugh— I liked to ruffle it on purpose sometimes, to laugh at him in a loving, teasing way. We sat in the living room: Bill in the rocking chair, Ted in the blue recliner and me on the couch. Bill gave him the paper and introduced the subject, repeating that we were trying to be principled but that we were committed to getting this information out in the open and discussing it with people.

"We'll be forced to leave without having a chance to state our position," said Bill, "Everyone who's left before has been hounded out without an opportunity for discussion—so that's why we're here. To make clear to you what our disagreements are before Theo clamps down on us. We've tried to get him to talk with us but, he won't. Alex, Julie, and I are resigning. We know that Theo will expel us in the next day or two anyway, and we want to have some control over how we leave."

I spoke next, appealing to Ted and feeling a weighted sadness in my chest, "It's a political difference, Ted. It's not a personal one. I can't continue in the O. anymore—the power imbalance is too great. I have to move away from it and find my own way again. But I don't want to leave you. I want us to stay together, to allow each of us to have a different relationship to the O., but for our family to stay together. We can work something out. I don't want us to be split over this."

Ted was sunk down in his chair, his long, square chin touching the reddish-brown hairs of his chest. His eyes darted from one to the other of us. He must have known already that something was up. Clearly he did, but perhaps what was surprising to him was that we were organized. He looked so frightened. But he spat out a curt, contemptuous comment: "You think *you* are capable of leadership."

Otherwise he was dismissive and ice-cold.

"Obviously you haven't looked at your Idealism yet," he said to me. He took the paper from Bill, but he barely read it and then ended the discussion.

"If that's all," he said through white lips, "I'm going back to bed."

And he climbed the stairs slowly, holding our paper by one corner, dangling it from his long arm. I said goodnight to Bill. Sympathy came to me sadly from his eyes and he left.

He met Julie back at their house and together they paid the last call of the night—to Dave and Debbie, who took the papers from them at their doorstep but would not let them in.

I went to work the next day, floating again in numbness. Dressed in my tailored blue suit (I had learned my own corporate elegance by now) I met Jerri and told her we'd left. March 23rd became a day I would never forget, a day I celebrated like a second birthday. I was *out*. It was an eerie feeling to be out, yet still completely entangled in an O.-built life. Jerri and I sat in the cafeteria talking. She was supportive but careful.

That night Ted went out late, after the children were in bed. While they were awake we had avoided each other, using the children as buffers. At one o'clock in the morning he returned, came into the bedroom and stood in the doorway.

"Are you awake?"

I was a light sleeper, and very anxious anyway, and this woke me up immediately.

"No," I replied absurdly. But he insisted.

"We need to talk."

"Right now?—I'm asleep, I've got to go to work in the morning. It's past one o'clock."

He got a nasty edge to his voice, "You didn't seem to mind getting *me* out of bed last night."

I realized I could argue this, it was only 11.00 when Bill and I had woken him, but I was too tired to fight it and understood that he had his O. duty to perform here. So I woke up, dragged on my terry-cloth robe and met him in the living-room, me on the couch again, him in the blue leather recliner.

"Are you serious about this?" he asked.

"Of course I am. I've been trying to talk to you about it for months. But I don't want it to affect our relationship. I still believe we can have a relationship."

"But you've betrayed me!" He looked shocked. I think he probably was in some kind of state of shock.

"You've betrayed the very basis of our marriage, of our family."

The words came out of him hurt, twisted beneath this veneer of control and rationality. But he was also carrying through a directive. This I could sense. He had an agenda to present here. But he couldn't unmix it from his shock and the position he'd been put in, stretched on a rack between me and the O., or, more accurately, as I began to understand, between me and Theo.

"No!" I said. "Our marriage is not just the O. It is also the children, our histories, the jokes we have, the life we've experienced together, the ANC work we've done, the business we've built. You can stay in the O. You don't have to choose. I'm not making you choose. I'm just saying that I'm not in unity with it anymore. Unless there are some moves to broaden the power, to allow people to speak, to deal with the questions that people have had for a long time about what we're doing."

His elbows rested on the arms of the blue recliner, his hands holding up his notepad; his eyebrows were deeply furrowed, his lips thinned to a pale line above his chin. His cheeks were even more sunken than usual, and he was as close to crying as I'd ever seen him.

"You *betrayed* me. Do you want to know what I felt when you and Bill told me that crap last night? It was like someone who's been cheated on—like you and your lover came together to tell me you were cheating on me. You went behind my back, and you planned this, and you've betrayed me and the children. It wouldn't have been so bad if you just left, or took a leave of absence to think it over, like you did before. But you *planned* it. And you planned it with *them*."

"But Ted, that's the point. Most everyone else who's left has left with their tail between their legs, in shame, feeling they couldn't cut it. We refused to do that. We wanted to be principled, to share our position with everyone and not be silenced and ostracized before we had a chance. I still want to be with you. I'm not leaving *you*—it's the O. I'm leaving. I love and respect you. I'm not leaving *you*."

Later, it must have been 2.00 A.M. by then, his agenda came out. He shifted, again, into a reasonable tone, but it was firm, like he was laying something down that would not easily be refused.

"I think we should go away together next weekend. To a bed and break-fast in the country. Just the two of us and then we can talk through this stuff. I want to understand your position more clearly, go over the paper and so on, understand what your questions about the O. are. Suzanne and Zack can look after the children. I think it's important you have some time away from here."

At first I was scared by this, certainly suspicious. I feared being taken away, isolated. But I realized then that I was quite strong enough in my posi-tion, and that with Ted I could hold my own. Of course this was an O. idea, because he wouldn't otherwise have offered up Suzanne and Zack's baby-sit-ting services quite so casually, or a weekend in the country, for that matter. I knew this tactic—the velvet glove approach—they would try to isolate me from Bill and Julie and then be nice to me, listen to my questions, throw me a bone, so to speak. But it had gone too far this time, I was clear it wasn't going to work. I suppose I hoped that the time alone would allow me to talk to Ted more, help soften the tension that was straining our relationship, help him to understand why and how I came to this point.

"Okay," I replied, "But I'm not prepared to discuss my assessment. If you think it's a time where you can try to turn my questions against me again and force me to look at this Idealist nonsense then I'm not going. If it can be an honest conversation between you and me, then I'll go."

We agreed on the next weekend.

Of that trip I remember little. We weren't able to talk to each other. He gave me copies of Mao's pamphlets, *On Resolving Contradictions amongst the People*, and *A Dialectical Approach to Inner-Party Unity*, but I couldn't read them. He talked on and on again about my betrayal and his belief that I was just being influenced by Bill and Julie. I tried to talk to him about Theo's dic-tatorial power, about the way we had all given up our own initiative, our own thoughts, our feelings, to him. But he could not hear me and was contemptu-ous again of the idea that I thought I knew better than "leadership."

Mostly I just remember an arbor in a garden somewhere. A bench and the wicker framework of the arbor with new leaves, translucent green, just beginning to emerge from a gray and twining vine. All that spring I was capti-vated by the emergence of life; I took on the work of the buds, inhabited the lilac's metamorphosis, cried over the sticky buds that greeted me from the ends of a chestnut tree.

We returned to Minneapolis with nothing resolved, but I carried inside me an unfolding; a dull, hardened shell was sloughing off, taking with it the years of tension, and I felt my *self* breaking through the layers of dirt under which it had been buried for a winter of ten years duration. Every morning I visited the lilac bush in my back yard. I touched the mint-green leaves, stroked the tight, tiny bunches of budlets and, as they started to open and their quiet gray trumpeted into an other-worldly lavender, and the perfume radiated all of a sudden one sunny day, my tears watered the laden ends of the shrub's branches. The glory of color and heat and new life kept me from going under.

I had always told my children, when they asked their children's questions about God and who is God? and do I believe in God?—I used to tell them, "I believe in People." Now I told them, "I believe in Nature." I noticed that this was a political change for me, for I had lost my faith.

I felt myself in the lilac; nature was there to tell me that winter ends and spring begins and I, too, was beginning again. Every morning, rain or shine, I visited the lilac, bowing my face into its purple sprockets: this was my meditation when the dirt was lodged in me and through the coming months when the dirt had to be faced. The love of my friends and the miracle of a Minnesota spring returned me to the land of the living.

CHAPTER 29

We talked only to the children. It was excruciating. The children were confused, but accepting as young children are. What did they know different?
We circled each other silently. I waited for a move; Ted was out often at
meetings with . . . Theo? Suzanne? Debbie?—he no longer told me. I was
out just as often seeing Julie and Bill as we helped each other through the psychological tempest into which we had thrown ourselves. Knowing that Theo
had never been neutral to people leaving his sphere of control, I waited for
the punishment that he would deliver.

I decided to go to England: to break the tension, to rest, and to talk to Lyndall,
someone outside of the O. Ted and I needed to get away from each other. He
encouraged me to go, which struck me as odd. But he would not let me take
either of the children and although this hurt I decided not to fight it. I didn't
want there to be any more fighting beyond the issue of me leaving the O.; I
didn't want to give them any excuses for making things more antagonistic than
they already were.

The day before I left the phone rang, and I picked it up.

"Hello, Alex?" I heard Suzanne's voice and tensed up.

"Yes."

"I have a message from leadership."

Okay, I get it, I thought to myself, it's from Theo. I'd never heard from
him before except by memo, so this call was fairly extraordinary, but somehow I had half expected it—that there would be some scrambling to get me
to stay, or at least to make sure Ted didn't leave.

"What is it?"

"He says you can meet with him this afternoon to discuss some business opportunities in the U.K." she said self-importantly, sounding proud that she was carrying this summons to me.

I was stunned. After more than ten years of nothing but anonymous memos stapled in those magic beige envelopes and now, now when I had left, he was prepared to meet with me? For a moment I couldn't understand how he could be so stupid. Did he really think I would be impressed?

"You must be joking," I managed to reply. "You must be fucking kidding . . . Tell Theo this, Suzanne: I've left the O. There's no telling me what to do anymore. Got it? I've left!"

I hung up on her and stood in my study shaking. That he could imagine I would talk to him, that he thought he could still pull the strings! *I had left.* He better believe it. Ted better believe it. This was not something I had decided lightly—to jeopardize my family, my life—I had left the goddamned O., and I was *never* going back.

April 14 1991

At the airport, waiting to go to England.

Luis cried saying good-bye. I went to the bathroom and cried too.

I don't like that Ted is keeping him.

I like less the fact that it feels like it's over with him—at least for now. If he stays in the O. I don't see how he can be allowed to stay with me.

I go between numb and awful.

Right now, numb.

In the wet spring of England Lyndall took me to the moors, and we walked, ten, fifteen miles a day. We walked, and I told her ten years of stories, the secret life she had known nothing about. Lyndall listened and did not judge, and at night she helped me into hot baths and fed me and laughed with me when I was able to laugh.

After the moors I stayed in London, sleeping on my mother's living room floor. I tried to tell her an abridged version of the story.

"What are they?" she asked shrilly, "Trotskyists?"

For her generation of Communists, Trotskyists were the ultimate form of evil, so this was her way of trying to understand.

"No," I sighed, "But that'll do."

Later I tried to confide in her again.

"Ma, I'm scared to go back."

"What do you mean?"

"I don't know what's going to happen when I go back, but I know it's going to be something awful. It's always bad when people leave. They're going to do something bad to me."

I wanted her to hug me. We could still hug, my mother and I and I wanted to feel her soft arms around me then. But she recoiled from me and said sharply, "What sort of group *is* this? How could you have been so *stupid!*"

I ran from the room. I never spoke to her about it again.

The day I got home from England, I was welcomed back by the children who wrapped me around with tears and hugs. Ted was silent still, leaving the house again that evening for another meeting. After I'd put Luis and Ana to bed I wandered around the house, ill-at-ease and anxious, trying to understand what would become of our family, this odd collection of humans who'd found each other by chance, it sometimes seemed, but who nonetheless loved each other and were, despite it all, a family.

On Ted's desk I found a memo he'd left out. It was dated March 24, 1991—the day after I'd left the O. It explained a couple of things and warned me of others.

> To: Ted
> From: P.O.O.
>
> 1) Bill, Julie, and Claire have created a condition of which there is no solution. Looking over their past histories, all three are undeveloped organizationally. . . . There is indeed a social unity among the three of them—what is the political reaction of this unity that have been directed at the POO. An investigation will be made into their unity of reaction.
>
> The political implication is that they have made a one-hundred-and-eighty-degree turn. History has shown that whenever anyone makes a one-hundred-and-eighty-degree turn politically, she/he stands alone. Before any conclusions are drawn, it is important to find out

from Claire by walking through concrete problems that are of such magnitude that lead her to co-author the paper with Julie and Bill. I will suggest that you and Claire take a weekend trip out of town to look at where she is coming from and where she thinks she is going.

2) Regardless of the outcome of your discussions with her, Claire's name should be taken off the computer business. It shouldn't be deconstructed, it must be transformed.

3) There will be a name change of the company. The transformed business will sell shares of stocks to members of the O. Coming on board will be Debbie, Suzanne, Jerri and maybe four others. But the first step is to get Claire's name off, or to transfer the assets to a new company. If by chance Claire, in the course of time, realizes the political nature of what she is saying and takes steps to change her views, then she will be given a share in the new company.

4) Claire is an idealist opened form with an associative identity with men. Her productive form of motion is transposition. If and when she thinks she can't transpose one functional set of identities to one place or another, then, we can expect irrational behavior. She isn't a person who will make a concrete analysis of concrete conditions, for this she needs you or Bill or some other theoretician.

The mix of emotions on reading this material was intense: laughter at being free, finally, of it all; fury at Theo's manipulation and pronouncements; adrenaline as I got the information that I needed to understand Ted's actions during our recent weekend; and lastly, a deep and lingering self-doubt: was I transposing?—whatever that meant. How was I to deal with all the ways Theo had defined me over the years? Was any of it true?

The next day, Ted said we had to have a meeting. It was a lovely day: sunny and warm. He said he'd take the children to Suzanne's, and he took them both: tiny, strong Ana, only two and a half years old, and sparky little Luis, not quite five.

Perhaps someone else needs to write this part. I have to write it with my eyes closed, my fingers typing by touch out on the keyboard, my head waving in a kind of pain, eyes shut, like Stevie Wonder, or the Ceausescus, the blind-folded turtles.

My heart and my head fall together in a giant kind of hurt. It's too much, really. Trembling. He sent them off as if they belonged to him. ". . . Your children are not your children, they are the sons and the daughters of life longing for itself, they come from you, they are not of you, they belong not to you . . ."* I always loved that song, it spoke for me and for my children. Bernice Reagon through the years gave me music I could live by and still do. ". . . Little brown boy with straight black hair . . ." this was the song of Luis that I sang years before he came into my life. ". . . in the circle, we'll make a little room for him."

Ted took them. We sat in the living room. All my mind's pictures of him now are of him in that chair, slouched down, his legs apart, his arms on the arms of the chair, elbows bent out. He says to me, "You will get out of the house. You will leave the business."

Okay, I thought, Okay. These are things I could expect.

"What about the children?" I say.

"The children will stay with me. We can arrange a schedule when you can see them."

My arms. My arms. Up from the ground like thunder when it's so close you feel it underfoot, this is what they call a blind rage. I'm in a blind rage. Can't you feel it? Can't you? On my feet at the same time my arms go out. Don't wait. There's a teapot on the table. My cup. A teapot for my tea—it's going over the brown mahogany table the heavy coffee table that we chose together when we bought this house, and we needed a coffee table it's heavy and it's rounded on the corners and it carries a white teapot now and my arms are part of my feet the ground carries me up the coffee table satisfies me with heaviness of thick round-ed wood, damn you I throw it over and the brown stream of cold tea sloshes out over the carpet, damn you Theo, damn you Ted, this will not pass.

> *Your children*
> *are not your children*
> *they are the sons and the daughters of life*
> *longing for itself*
> *they come through you*
> *but they are not from you . . .*

---

*The words of Kahlil Gibran were put to music by Bernice Reagon.

Ted jumps up. He is white.

I pick up my sandal now. He's half way across the room, beginning to look like—it's dawning on him maybe that this is real, it's not a game or an abstraction. His hands are patting the air down as if to calm me.

NO, YOU WILL NOT DO THIS. THEO WILL NOT STEAL MY CHILDREN TOO. The sandal goes flying at him. He runs out, this karate black-belt husband of mine, he runs out into the sunny garden. I see him standing helplessly by the tulips.

You won't ever do this to us, I whisper. I'm strong as a fucking mountain.

I walk the four blocks to Suzanne's house, having picked up my sandal from the sunroom. Waves of light, the blue sky, the anger of green spring leaves carry me along in a current of chemicals. I'm the mother who picks the car up off an injured child. I'm the bear who ravages the face of a stranger that comes too close to the cub. I'm the lightning of God that strikes in a blue vein of illumination.

Luis and Lily are playing on the red climbing frame, and he runs to hug me, happy and energetic. I hug him to me then leave him outside with Lily while I go into the house to find Ana. Suzanne is there, pasty and stolid.

"Where's Ana!" I demand.

Suzanne turns from the sink where she is doing dishes and gives me a greeting that isn't a greeting, just a purse of her lips and a look to evaluate me.

"I'll get her, she's napping in my room," she replies in a high voice. I'm horrified. I feel like she's trying to be cheerful, or polite, or something completely foreign to what the occasion demands.

"No! I'll get her," I say and rush into the bedroom, where, there she is, my beautiful baby, dark curls and thick black eyebrows moistened with sleep sweat as she sucks her thumb, the most beautiful child—I ache and grab her up, fast but gentle, I'm the bear remember. I hold her to me, I want to engulf her in my body to keep her with me, to protect her. I love her so much. She stays sleeping, fitting her head into my shoulder, her warm legs wrapped around my waist, her thumb still sucking, sucking in her mouth. Suzanne is by the door watching me.

I am acid.

"You're a good mother," I say. "How can you try to take these children away from me?! I'm their mother! How can you do that!"

She moves, it seems to me, in slow motion, like a whale at the zoo, round and round in an artificial tank. The words come bubbling out of her, slowly, deep like a record spinning too slow.

"You," she says, and now I've got Luis by the hand, one hand holds Ana, the other holds Luis, I have them both, my children . . . "You," she bubbles out in a deep drone, "You were the one who left the Organization."

I hate Suzanne for a couple of years after that.

Often, when Ted was asleep, or in the bathroom, or just out of the house, I went through his briefcase. Keeping a sharp ear open for his sounds, I lifted the flap of the expensive black soft leather bag, quietly pulled open the zipper and looked through his manila files. Sometimes I brought out his calendar, an elegant business calendar embossed in gold with his name: this had been one of our marketing devices for the firm; our customers each received one at Christmas. The things I found were extraordinary. I copied the memos from Theo and saved them. I tracked Ted's appointments with his custody lawyer: he was indeed attempting to begin proceedings to get custody of the children. I felt a humiliating guilt about spying on him, but I did it anyway. I would never try to take us through the tragedy and randomness of the court process, but I would defend myself to the last if Ted did. I understood that my actions were ultimately self-defense against Theo. The more I knew about what Ted was being told and about what he was doing, the more intelligent I could be in my response.

A memo—dated April 4, 1991—ten days after I'd left.

To: T
From: P

In the last memo to you, it was indicated that C's WOL or ideo-logical form of motion (IFOM) is transposition. This form can directly transpose one concept or thing from one place to another place irrespective of conditions. The productivity of this form of motion is essential as in the case of all IFOMS. All forms of motion have limitations if taken by themselves. . . .

The memo went on and on like this for a page, complete gibberish. I could not understand it—and I was only a couple of weeks out of the O.—it could not be that I had lost the language so fast, yet the truth was, it made absolutely no sense at all.

After attacking me again for an inability to "stay with anything for any length of time until I got pulled into the orbit of the O." (and this one still worked on me—Theo always knew this was my weak spot, my feelings of inadequacy because of the many moves and changes I'd experienced in my life) he went on:

I will proposed, I think it is a workable solution, that she move to the UK and set up a business that will tie in with the business here. You can commute periodically. For a period of time you should stay there to help her set things up and come back. In this way we will be in a position to do work in South Africa. To be clear, there are other ways and connections. It can be foreseen that if she stays here the family unit will breakup in the course of time. . . . To be clear what is being looked at is the preservation of the family unit in a principled way while at the same time giving C. room to do her thing without the risk of political confrontation. Maybe she can move to another state. Over a period of time, she will become less of a problem for all concerned. Under such a condition, the children's well-being can easily be worked out of course some temporary adjustment will have to be made, once C. is gone.

This memo took my breath away. The words, "Of course some temporary adjustment will have to be made" and "over the course of time she will become less of a problem for all concerned" kept running through my head, my heart, my muscles, and I would seize up in a terrible biological kind of anger. Theo was going to get me out of town, separate me from the children, until I either capitulated and rejoined the fold, or faded into the no-man's land of being an ex-member of the O.: a non-person, a non-mother, of course no bother to anyone anymore. Over the course of time my children would adjust to being without a mother—I would become less of a problem to all concerned . . .

After I copied the memos (using the copy function on our fax machine to create slippery duplicates of these documents), I'd leave, if I could, right away for Bill and Julie's and rage to them. Although then I didn't show them the memos, didn't even tell them I was looking through Ted's stuff; I felt too guilty about it still, though I knew it was something I had to do. If Ted was trying to get custody of the children, following Theo's orders, then I had to fight with everything I could. I would never let Theo destroy us like that.

Often Ted just left things out too, perhaps in a kind of Freudian carelessness. One time he left the notes of his meeting with his divorce lawyer requiring a list of my deficiencies as a parent. He had listed only the fact that I did not get up easily in the morning. This was, indeed, true: I am still slow and crabby for an hour or so after I wake. My children would be the first to witness to this failing of mine, but come now—was this grounds for losing custody? At least this gave me a good laugh, one I needed in those days of cloak-and-dagger machinations. Another note from Ted's lawyer advised him against seeking sole custody of the children: "It will be very difficult if she's offering you joint custody—you cannot expect much more than that." And even though I raged, also, against Ted, I knew that it was Theo I was really fighting, and the memos proved this beyond a doubt. Ted had no idea what to do, he was in shock, he was tied in so deeply to the O., and at that point all he could do was stay loyal and follow Theo's orders. I felt sorry for him, and I also knew how hard it had been for me to break away, and for whatever reason it was that much harder for Ted.

Yet another memo to Ted from P.O.O. included the following:

There is a valid concept of revolutionary sex-love that emerged from the height of the anti imperialist movement. This concept will continue to be valid in times of great movements when there is total and complete political unity.

The Tactical Sexual Relationship was formed as an instrument to help filter subjective feeling in personal relationships that needed objective principled communication. Here the Tactical Sexual Relationship was used to remove the behavior of sexism in its interpersonal political form.

Now, many years after the great success of the implementation of the Tactical Sexual Relationship, we now come to a different stage as is a very different situation in ideological needs.

P.O.O. will recommend a Conditional Sexual Activity, (CSA), with someone (there are several persons who might have an interest) to help you get off on the right foot, maintaining objective clarity with Claire. I first suggest for this CSA, Suzanne. A CSA with Suzanne can help overcome subjective idealism. Reactionary metaphysics just hates material dialectics. This should get you off to a good start.

I wondered how Ted would respond to that one. Yes, I felt sorry for him all right: I knew his sexual interest in Suzanne was non-existent, and surely he was feeling the same pain as I was about our relationship. He must be in some kind of mourning—and here Theo was trying to order him into sleeping with Suzanne.

I'd finger these papers with a kind of dread, then, if Ted wasn't home, steal upstairs to the fax machine, pull out the staples and copy the memos. I felt Theo then, prying inside my life, working Ted with his manipulations, and Ted, less and less blindly as time went on, following his directions, being the good soldier, almost until the end. I slid the poisonous directives back in the briefcase, my heart jumping in my chest, pulled the zipper carefully shut, being careful, too, to keep things in the order I'd found them. I got good at this, checking what was piled on what, which paper was next to which, before dismantling what I needed to track Theo's tortuous tricks.

For years I'd respected Ted's "security"—I would never have looked at his closed work. Or he mine. Yet, in all those years I never kept a journal, mostly out of the fear of discovery, where my thoughts would be bared, naked and incorrect, for someone to seize.

But I had an enemy now—someone who wanted to destroy my life, and I would do what I needed to protect the children and myself. Perhaps this is the part that could never be mended. The rift that grew and grew and never healed over. But I had the ammunition I needed and I defended myself. I believe that Theo had no real idea what he was dealing with. How, after all, could he understand a mother's love?

CHAPTER 30

Kitchen Story

In 1976 Julie and Matthew helped organize the O.'s takeover of the People's Warehouse. The warehouse was the central distribution hub for the rest of the co-ops, and the O. decided it should belong to the "people," not the bourgeois hippie forces. Matthew, an ex-member of the O. we have recently contacted, tells me the story.

A full-scale battle campaign was launched, planned in secrecy, with Theo at the helm. It culminated when two dozen O. cadres entered the warehouse late at night while Theo covertly directed operations from a nearby phone booth, fielding calls from a designated cadre and giving minute-to-minute instructions.

A few anarchists, knowing that the O. was about to make a move, guarded the place (though lackadaisically: they were stoned and sleeping it off on bags of oats when the attack came). They tried to resist but soon fled in the face of baseball bats, lead pipes, and anonymous faces behind dark glasses. The O. was victorious, and the cadres settled in for the night, perhaps on top of the very same oat bags. Later that night, Bob Paulsen, Theo's first O. recruit, shook Matthew awake. A couple of drunk co-opers were yelling from across the street, and Bob Paulsen and Matthew, still groggy with sleep, ran out to deal with them. Matthew grabbed a baseball bat to confront the Enemy, swung it at his drunken target, and the man-made heaviness thudded through muscle and bone and broke the hippie's arm.

It didn't take long, after the O.'s takeover, for things to fall apart again. The "hippies" set up a new warehouse and organized a boycott that eventually shut down the People's Warehouse. But the fight had put people firmly on one side or the other. Friendships, even marriages broke up over it.

During the boycott, the O. worked briefly with a black co-op worker, Joe Lawrence, to distribute the surplus food before it rotted. Bob Paulsen and Joe drove to the poor neighborhoods of the north and south sides and gave out free potatoes off the back of Joe's pickup truck. At some point an altercation occurred between Joe and Bob, and Theo instructed the diminutive Bob to beat Joe up, which he later unsuccessfully attempted to do, receiving the worse end of the fight in the process. Shortly afterwards, Joe's truck was fire bombed. Two O. cadres, not connected with the fight, had been assigned to the task. It was their last O. assignment, for they left immediately after: the violence was getting too much for them.

I wonder to myself about the stories that haven't been told. The secrets still kept.

Ted and I lived together for another two months, looking after the children but almost never speaking to each other. Finally I said I could no longer share a bed with him. From that day we alternated—one in our bed, the other on the sleeper downstairs. This way it was fair: no one would have the advantage of keeping the marital bed. But even this was too intimate a connection. Ted, however, still busy preparing for a legal fight, refused to move out until he was certain this would not affect his effort to gain sole custody of the children. Bill and I met with him once more, and, with Bill serving as witness, I gave Ted an ultimatum.

"Give Theo this message. Tell him that unless he lets you go into mediation with me on the custody issue, unless that happens, I will spill everything I know. It will all come out publicly: the history of the O., the petty crimes, the tax frauds . . . I'll tell it all. I'm not letting our family be dragged through court. Tell Theo he better back off."

I was beyond fear in some way and had come to the conclusion that the only way to deal with bullying was to stand up to it. And it worked. A few days later, we sat in the mediator's office and finally reached a temporary shared custody agreement that enabled us to make, as the mediator termed it, "the physical separation." Ted moved out in June to live in Zack and Suzanne's attic. At the same time, we also mediated a split of the business, each of us taking half the contracts.

When Zack and Ted moved out his half of the furniture, Jerri sat with me as a buffer (we had agreed she was the most neutral party). I remember it rained that day. As Ted moved the couch and dresser and chairs, I followed behind sweeping up the dust and rearranging the remaining items to fill up the newly empty spaces. Later Julie came over, and we drank tea together in the sparse but spring-cleaned living room. Despite the emptiness (especially during the times the children were with him) it was a relief to have Ted gone. Although I continued to work with Jerri to finish up a software contract, I now felt I was really out of the O. I no longer had to watch my movements or edge myself around Ted.

One morning when the children were with Ted, I read the paper, feeling quiet and relaxed. A small advertisement caught my eye. The heading read: FREE MINDS. I thought of my lilac bush, the way its shadows cast into the sun-room, how my little happiness each day was to walk over the few feet of damp grass to stroke the lilac's leaves, rub my cheek on the purple blossoms and let the scent surround me.

FREE MINDS. How I celebrated pushing away the funnels that had squeezed my thoughts so dangerously for too many years. How I reveled in the spark of synapses pursuing themselves at random until the organic patterns of nature were revealed to me. My mind felt open, spacious; I was like an adventurer, a voyageur standing at the edge of the plains looking out to the horizon of my own free mind. Sometimes I closed the curtains, put on music I'd loved and danced on my own for hours. Now, folding back the newspaper, I read on: "Combatting Cult Mind Control—author Steve Hassan speaking Wed. June 20th."

"Cults? Mind Control . . ." I repeated the words to myself. Something connected. I didn't know what. But I tore out the ad and saved it on the counter.

Later I talked to Bill and Julie. They didn't say much—except they didn't think the O. was a cult. Still later Bill asked me about it. Was I going to go to the speech?

"Oh, we've missed that," I replied. "But I was thinking of calling them."

"Well, why don't you?"

"I don't know. Perhaps I will."

Later still, I did. A woman answered the hotline. She was abrupt but said she'd send me some materials and recommended Steve Hassan's book. That week I got her package; the materials mostly referred to religious cults. But one sheet described the eight criteria of mind control developed by Robert Jay Lifton in his research on Chinese Communist prisoner of war camps.

This is what I read:

The Conditions That Lead to Mind Control or Brainwashing:
Altered Consciousness and Ego Destruction
    1. MILIEU OR ENVIRONMENT CONTROL:Purposeful limitation
of all forms of communication with outside world.
    2. MYSTICAL MANIPULATION: The potential convert is convinced
of the higher purpose *within the* special group.
    3. NEED FOR PURITY: Only by pushing toward perfection, as the
group views goodness, will the recruit be able to contribute.
    4. CONFESSION: Verbalizing all past imperfections. In all religious
cults, public or semi-public confessional periods are used to get members to
verbalize and discuss their innermost fears and anxieties.
    5. AURA OF SACRED SCIENCE: Implicit in this concept is the idea
that the cult's laws and regulations and rules are absolute and, therefore, must
be followed automatically.
    6. LOADING THE LANGUAGE: In each cult—a new vocabulary is
invented, confusing well-known words with their own new meanings. A
developing philosophy of pat and trite clichés.
    7. DOCTRINE OVER PERSONS: Past experience and values are of
no value in interpreting the new cult morality. The value of an individual
member is insignificant compared to the value of the group.
    8. DISPENSING OF EXISTENCE: The sharp line a cult draws
between those who will be saved, the cult members, and those who are
doomed to hell, the rest of the world!
    When attempting to relate these conditions to any belief system, it is
wise to remember that many apply to everyday situations in everyone's life.
BUT when many or all of these conditions are:
    1. Present at the same time
    2. In an intense religious (political/personal growth/commercial) group
that stresses separation
    3. With intentions that are deliberately kept unknown to the potential
convert
    . . . then "Ego Destruction" is in process.

It fit for me immediately. This was what explained what had happened
to me. Here, reflected in this poorly duplicated sheet of paper, were all the
things that had been done in the O., that had successfully trapped us for so
long. The isolation, the goal of "transforming" ourselves into perfect proletar-
ians, our confessional self-criticisms, the so-called "scientific methods" we

used that were so blatantly unscientific, the crazy language that made less and less sense to me each day that I lived outside of its realm, and, finally, the "Dispensing of Existence": that if you weren't in the O., then you were nothing at all.

I read the rest of the papers greedily. It was as if a trap-door had fallen open inside of me and I was falling through, holding on to these papers, clutching them in each hand as I fell out of my old world and into a new one. "Okay! I get it now!" I cried as I made my descent. "He used me, he used every one of us—he took all the details we told him, and he used these to manipulate us—he used our desperate longings, and he wove them with guilt into an invisible noose that has strangled us all . . ."

There was never any question for me but that this described the O.; we were a far closer match to a religious cult than to political organizations like the ANC, or the South African Communist Party, both organizations I had admired. Although soon I also began to understand the overlaps: the dangers of many of the political groups I'd been around; how many, it turned out, had these traits also. A continuum of power and control existed, and the expediency of mind control was a slippery slope down which many groups slid.

I drove to Julie and Bill's. Spread the papers on their kitchen table. Then I was surprised: they didn't share my understanding.

"We weren't a cult," said Julie.

"The O. started out trying to do something right. It just went bad. That happens. Theo got all hung up in a power trip," said Bill.

"No!" I argued. "Look at this stuff. The O. started out like this—as soon as it turned in on itself. And that happened right away—look at the warehouse struggle—there were already secret groups and plenty of weird stuff going on then. It wasn't just the last few years. It was from the beginning."

This was too painful for them. We didn't talk about it much more at first. But, meanwhile, I went ahead and ordered Hassan's book and read it through the day it arrived. Here, again, was my experience described—and this guy had been a Moonie! There was one footnote concerning a political cult out of the Bay Area: The Democratic Workers Party. I made a note to myself to investigate that later; perhaps we weren't the only political one . . . perhaps we weren't just the bizarre anomaly that people believed. I had always had the belief that no one's experience is unique, that we are demographic grains of sand on a beach, making up a landscape with our subtle variations, but each story having its neighboring story, a link with others, a shared history, that, seen together, stepped back from the microcosm of personal experience, can make a picture, a map, of the winds, the rocks, the oceans that brought us to this moment, here where we stand.

I hung on to this; that we were not alone, and because of that fact our experience had something to offer others. This is what kept me going during those months of despair: others had suffered this, were still suffering, and out of our despair would come understanding that could be distilled and wrapped and offered as a gift.

I knew Julie was in distress because she called me at work and asked if she could bring me a sandwich so we could have lunch together. She worked far on the other side of town, in St. Paul, and we never got together for lunch, so I knew something serious was going on.

I left the computer conversion project I was managing. Jerri was still on the project, and even though she had not left the O. this gave me hope, because her continuing to work with me went against everything she should have done given I was now a Class Enemy. Before I left, I gave the young programmer who worked for me his instructions for the afternoon, and then I took the elevator down a couple of floors to the lobby of the shiny new building in which we worked. Here there were pristine, manicured plants with towering white flowers surrounded by a display of new educational computer games that this client of ours produced, all lit with the natural light afforded by a three-story glass atrium. It was a beautiful building, I liked working there, but it was surreal: to move between the two worlds—my high-powered blue-suited consultant persona in a jagged rift with the cult survivor in the throes of divorce, custody proceedings, and a battle of wills with a crazed psychopath. Locked in this battle, I was intent on saving the souls of my friends, among them Ted and Jerri.

My lunchtime visit to Julie was just another show in the series of heightened events that took place that year. I pushed the blue glass doors open to the daytime sun, sighed as the sunlight hit my body and got into my car.

Five minutes later I pulled up in my Toyota and walked towards her. Julie was in a gray suit. She sat, waiting for me, on the grass between the parking lot and the lake. It was warm outside, and she had picked a spot under a young maple tree so that we would be shaded. Her shoulders were rounded, her posture sad.

"Hi, love," I greeted her and sat by her side. Of course, there were two brown bags—she nurtured herself and others with food, and no matter how upset, she would not forget the lunch she had promised. All around us, but far enough away for privacy, sat other business-suited and shirt-sleeved office workers eating their lunch on this beautiful spring day.

"What's the matter?" I asked.

We both sat like girls, how you have to sit when you wear a skirt, with both legs bent at the knee, ankles joined primly off to one side. I picked up her hand and held it. She started to tell me a story I had not known.

"Beth has been asking about her father, Jefferson, again."

"Yes."

"I don't know what to do. I've done something terrible."

"Tell me."

"Remember when Beth was about eight or so, about five years ago? She was asking a lot about Jefferson then. She was thinking about being black, and she wanted to know about him: if she looked like him, what he was like, what kind of music he played. Bill and I wrote up an analysis of it."

"I remember that. Wasn't that when Theo said, 'People are like flowers,' and she should blossom into whoever she was, that color wasn't the main thing?"

"Yeah. He also said that the contradiction with her birth-father needed to be resolved so that she could move on."

Her face was pinched as she said this, and she ducked her head a little. I squeezed her hand. I loved Beth. Even though she had grown into a taciturn and defended teenager who I had not found a way to approach, we had a remembered closeness that belied the current distance we both felt. I would never forget my years of mothering her in Oakland, and then, in Minnesota being her surrogate aunt, sharing her childhood as I waited for my own children to arrive.

Julie shut her eyes, squeezed out the next words as if she would do anything to hold them back, to have them not be true, but they came out thin and tight like metal sliced against itself.

"He told me to tell her that Jefferson was dead."

"And was he?"

"No."

I was silent and then I asked, "Did you tell her he was?"

She nodded. She looked up at me, crying now. She said, "I didn't want to, but we did . . ." She was sobbing. "Bill and I, we did an analysis, and he thought it was right, and I couldn't figure out why it wasn't and so we told her her father was dead. She was only eight years old!"

I grabbed Julie by the shoulders, and we held each other under the shade of the pale green maple tree. I felt such hatred for Theo and such love for Julie and such intense despair for Beth. The lake glinted blue-gray in the background, and I couldn't imagine how life got to be like this where someone had stolen this beautiful child's birth-father from her.

Eventually I brought out Kleenex. We blew our noses. Stayed holding each other. I stroked Julie's hair again, letting her head lean against my shoulder. That feeling of unreality surrounded me again, the top of my head felt like spinning off, leaving no boundary between me and the rest of the world. But Julie needed me and so I managed to sink back into myself as I felt her breathing coming more calmly now against me.

She said, "That's not all."

"Go on."

"Theo told us to tell Beth he was her uncle."

"Her uncle!"

"Yeah, that he was Jefferson's brother."

"Oh, God." This seemed almost worse. "That's like Jim Jones, that's disgusting. It's completely cult-like. Jim Jones—remember—of Jonestown, where all those people killed themselves and their kids with Kool-Aid. He made everyone call him 'Dad.' Theo really did that?"

"Yes. For the first couple of years he kind of spent special time with her—he'd take her to basketball games, come over to see her every couple of months. But he lost interest in the last few years."

Julie crumpled up again, and I too.

"What are you going to do, Julie?"

"I have to tell her. I can't believe I did this. I lied to my daughter. I let Theo tell me to lie to my daughter—about her *father!* I can't bear it."

"You must get yourself ready to tell her. You must find a way to feel all right about yourself when you tell her."

"Yes. I'll go to a family counselor. That's what I've been thinking. I need to tell her soon, but I thought I could talk it over with a counselor first, someone who might help understand how she might react. Then I was going to offer to take her to Mississippi—I've got the name of the town where his kin live. We can try to find him if she wants."

"That's a good idea. Yes, that's a good thing to do."

"She never liked Theo, you know. At least not after the basketball games stopped. She used to ask if he was like her father. I never knew what to say."

We left the sandwiches uneaten.

Julie moved fast when she'd decided something, and by the next week she had seen a counselor, told Beth the truth about her father and located Jefferson's sister in Mississippi.

Jefferson's sister told them the news over the telephone. Jefferson really was dead. He'd died just a month earlier, of lung cancer. He had still been working as a musician in Chicago. Theo had succeeded in stealing Beth's father.

Beth, of course, was distraught. She could not understand how we could be considered adults—how could people who loved her do this to her? She kept to herself in a pain that she would not let anyone else reach. A couple of months later, she and Julie did visit Mississippi, and there Jefferson's kinfolk opened their arms to young Beth with unlimited love. But Jefferson was gone from her forever.

I wanted to kill Theo. I wanted to feel him suffer as I wrung my hands around his strong neck and smashed his head against a wall, his death coming soundless but bloody. I had never felt such hatred before: he had picked inside the life of people and taken what was theirs.

CHAPTER 31

Julie found the clippings. She went to the library—I couldn't do that, I get nervous in libraries, there are too damn many books. Julie went to the library, and she looked up the name Kyle Ray in the newspaper index. We had found out by this time that there had indeed been a murder. Matthew had confirmed the story and given us the name of the victim: Kyle Ray, a local disc jockey. Even with this information Julie and Bill remained unconvinced of Theo's involvement so Julie went to the library to confirm it for herself.

Afterwards she called me up, and then she came to my house. It was summer, and she sat in the living room on the little blue love seat. Her face was puckered up a bit as I gave her a hug, and she sat down facing the sunroom window. Her face was dark. She looked at me and said: "I've got the clippings."

Julie who was stoic, (we joked and called her the Earth Mother, she is rooted and grounded and earthed and all the rest of it) she reached into her bag and pulled out the clippings, five of them, paper-clipped together, copied from the micro-fiched newspaper, with her distinctive writing on each page systematically giving the date and the name of the newspaper on the shiny photocopied sheets. I took them from her; I reached over towards her and took the packet of clippings, and, as she gave them to me, her hands moved up to her face, like a baby's; her hands curled into little fists, and she pulled her shoulders upwards towards her head, and the hands came up by her cheeks, curled like a baby's. And then her gray eyes shut, and her shoulders were almost up to her ears, and she was crying, silently, tears of pain.

I didn't have the pain, but I felt hers; it was tangible. Julie didn't cry often, at least not with me. But her hurt traveled over to me, and I moved in and put my hand on her leg and stroked her and whispered, and then I

295

reached up past her twisted shoulders and stroked the smoothness of her hair that was pulled over her skull down to where her braid began.

"He did what he was supposed to," she said. "He did just what black men are supposed to do—he killed another black man. That's what hurts me most. He did what the system wanted him to do."

Her arms moved across her breasts, and she held herself and looked up at me through wet eyes, the tears holding to her lashes.

"He was just trying to make it—the young guy—he was at university, he was a DJ at KMOJ, the community radio station. He was trying to make it. And Theo killed him. That's what I can't bear."

Her mouth twisted up, her face red with crying, and I wondered what her pain was really.

I brought her tea. Warm and sweet. I picked out for her my favorite mug—the one I got from the ANC office in London: it had a picture of three African women dancing in the ANC colors of yellow, green, and black, and it pronounced, "South African Women March For Freedom—ANC Women's Section." She calmed herself, sat back and sipped her tea while I read the clippings that told me what I already knew, in my heart, anyway.

Tribune, June 25, 1980—written at the top in blue ink, in Julie's hand-writing. Then:

FOX TRAP DISC JOCKEY FOUND SHOT TO DEATH
Staff Writer

A disc jockey for the Fox Trap Disco and KMOJ-FM radio station was found shot to death Tuesday morning in the vacant first-floor apartment of the duplex where he lived.

Police have not found a suspect in the shooting of 23-year-old Kyle Steven Ray, 801 Sullivan Ave N.

Ray was shot once with a large-caliber gun. According to the Hennepin County Medical Examiner's Office, the bullet passed through one of Ray's arms and lodged in his chest.

An anonymous caller . . . [Who was the caller, Theo, or Kristin or Debbie?] . . . told Minneapolis police early yesterday that a man had been shot at 801 Sullivan Ave N. When police entered the house at 5.10 they found Ray, who was wearing a tan running suit, laying facedown in the living room . . . [the living room where my son took his first steps, the living room with the green shag rug of the house I lived in for five years] . . . *of the first floor apartment. No murder weapon was found. The last person seen in the duplex was a workman* . . . [Theo is now just a humble workman, like Jesus—he would have liked that description] . . . *who had been remodeling the downstairs apartment* . . . [Careful Construction!] . . . *according to Captain Gerald Shoemaker of the Minneapolis Police Department's Homicide Division. Police have been unable to locate the workman, Shoemaker said. Neighbors said the workman had been coming to the house five days a week but did not go to work yesterday morning.*

Ray lived with his younger brother, Brian, who spent Monday night at a friend's house across the street from the duplex. They had planned to move out of the house today.

Ray had been scheduled to do his KMOJ show at 2:00 p.m. yesterday. He had been at the station since 1979 and had regular shows on Tuesday and Thursday afternoons.

He also was emcee for several local concerts and the head disc jockey at the Fox Trap Disco. He was scheduled to graduate this summer from the University of Minnesota with a major in communications.

The Rev. Emmanuel Harrell, who also worked at KMOJ, called Ray "lovable and outgoing. This is a great tragedy for the Twin Cities and the north side, where Kyle spent most of his time."

Another friend, Pat Jones, described Ray as "a quiet person. He wasn't violent at all. He didn't have any enemies. He was just a nice guy."

There will be a benefit for Ray tonight at the Fox Trap. Proceeds from the $2 admission charge will be given to his family.

Tribune, July 1, 1980

POLICE SEEK SUSPECT IN DEATH OF DISC JOCKEY

A second-degree murder warrant has been issued in connection with the shooting of a disc jockey for the Fox Trap disco and KMOJ-FM radio stations, Minneapolis police said Wednesday.

The warrant is for Edward Louis James, 34, aka George James. [Ed, George, Theo, . . . Randy, P.O.O., CL.—how many names did this man have?] *Police listed his address as 905 Sullivan Av. N.,* . . . [Where Zack lived, where Debbie lived, and Nancy's mother, Cindy, and Mona, another O. cadre, and now, Betty and Sara and each of their children.] . . . *a block from the residence of Kyle Steven Ray, who was found dead June 24.*

Lt. Steven Strehlow of the Minneapolis Police Department's homicide division said James remained at large Wednesday. . . .

Twin Cities Courier, July 3, 1980

MEMORIAL SERVICE HELD FOR KYLE RAY—3,000 ATTEND.

This clipping is dominated by a large picture of Kyle Ray wearing a gray suit and tie. It reports that the North Side community came out in force for his funeral.

Kyle Ray becomes a real person as I read. Twenty-three years old. A man building a career. Someone people on the North Side loved. The punch gets me in a kind of slow motion, until I'm without air, unable to speak. Words fail me. What can I say?

In 1980, I think, well, that was just a month after I returned to San Francisco, after that first trip here. So when I was first here, when I lived with Stan and Ted and worked at the bookstore, then this hadn't happened yet, everything was still "normal." Then he ran, ran to Chicago—and all the memos and the phone calls to Julie and the messages when we were still in California, came from him while he was in hiding in Chicago. The F.B.I. . . . they were involved because he'd crossed state lines . . .

The next set of clippings were dated 1986—that's when we'd already started the ANC work, and were done with the more ridiculous of the computer projects.

Tribune, December 31, 1986

FUGITIVE IN SLAYING CASE SURRENDERS AFTER 6 YEARS.

After six years on the run, the man charged with killing Twin Cities radio disc jockey Kyle Steven Ray in 1980 turned himself in at Hennepin County Jail Tuesday. [Remember that morning at breakfast, Ted said someone had come back to town. Was this the article he'd read? What the hell did he make of it? He knew there was a murder then, but he never told me?]

"I just wanted to get it over with," Edward James said yesterday after being released on $15,000 bond. . . .

"I wanted to get it done with, but it hasn't weighed on my conscience. I am innocent."

Neither he nor his attorney, St. Paul lawyer Douglas Thomson, would say where James, who also is known as Theophilus Grant Smith, has been hiding, except to say it has been in the United States. [And now the real name: Theophilus Smith. How do we know it's real? What makes a name real?]

"That was about the time that Ted asked his grandmother for $5,000? 1987, right?" I said to Julie.

"And Bill and I came up with $7,000 about then, supposedly to buy another Hewlett Packard computer. It must have been for his lawyer's fees— or bail. I wonder who else was told to give money?"

And he must have needed a considerable amount, because his lawyer was Doug Thomson, one of the top defense attorneys in the state. Apparently he earned his fees well: Theo was only sentenced to a year in the workhouse with ten years probation. That left him with seven years' supervision to go, by our reckoning.

Julie and I sat in mourning, for Kyle Ray and for ourselves. For our children. We sat silent. Julie had known Theo, unlike me—I had only seen him, from the corner of my eye once, digging in the dirt at her house, and recently a couple of times at the daycare center, not really knowing it was him, but having some feeling that probably it was as he refused to meet my gaze in a way that's not normal for a person who has nothing to hide. For Julie I felt that this was the moment when the horror seeped in; it was not a political difference anymore, this was a difference in humanity, and we sat and thought, each to ourselves: this was the man we followed, obeyed, trusted with every decision.

Here began the process of identification. Theo, Ed, George: he was the one who murdered. We were like the green shag rug, the silent backdrop drenched in blood we could not see: unwilling participants, blind, fooled, manipulated in ignorance. It is a hideous burden to have been drawn into a circle of murder you have not committed, a murder that is the opposite of all you have tried to do for decades, all that you have put your heart, will and mind to doing.

Perhaps time will let the burden go.

Julie got up, we hugged again. She left the clippings with me—I would copy them. I needed to have these documents.

We became a triangle. Steady and bonded and free-wheeling like a parachute team holding hands in a blunted circle and spinning down through the sky in a free-fall. Bill and Julie were indistinguishable to me. I'd go over to their house in some kind of panicked state and want to see either one of them—it didn't matter, then, which one it was. Or I'd call up and speak to Beth, who had the teenager's monopoly of the phone: "Is your Mom or Dad home?"—and be grateful, and relieved whichever one of them it was.

We held on, held each other up. One or other of us was always in need. Bill would get scared a lot and cry at the kitchen table, his blue eyes reddening as he contemplated first the loss and then the violent possibilities of Theo's reaction. Julie and I would shore him up, literally encourage him: "Have courage, Bill, it's okay to be scared, but we're brave too."

This was when the fears were at their peak.

Bill knew enough to feel threatened early on. He'd seen that mean, violent streak in Theo and was scared by it. Finally he got a baseball bat and placed it by the back door in case Theo should ever come for him. We encouraged him, "It's okay, Bill, Theo has more to lose than us by getting violent. Besides we know he's only been violent with black men before this—our whiteness and middle-classness will be helpful now—he daren't go after any of us."

We said this, too, to encourage ourselves. We talked through the fear over and over again. He would not come after us. It was one thing to kill a young black man, the police would not waste much time over that, and indeed, had not, until his family and the North Side community finally raised an uproar to force a more aggressive investigation. But us, no, Theo could not afford to go after us; besides, he was on probation—he couldn't risk trouble. We convinced ourselves, almost, of this. But still, Julie told us how she came home every day relieved to find the house still standing—her fear was that he would come and burn it down. She imagined her children caught in the fire, but she would not let the fear control her, and we just kept talking it out.

I was afraid nights, mostly. I'd wake at three in the morning, my heart racing and my whole body on the alert, listening to the house sounds, convinced that Theo was inside, waiting beyond my door for me to fall back asleep. It's odd how I wasn't scared when my children were with me, but when they were with Ted, then the nights terrified me. During the hardest times, I was also scared in the daytime. Every car that drove by the front of my house, or behind, down the alley, could carry Theo and a gun. I imagined a rifle, or a shotgun and the car slowing down as it passed, letting loose a volley through the windows, spraying glass and bullets through me, and then Theo's foot on the accelerator speeding the car up to disappear into the city streets.

Julie, meanwhile, would get depressed, feel the almost hopeless emptiness of leaving the organization that had been her home for fifteen years. She became paralyzed at times and then Bill and I in turn encouraged her: "Julie, you're strong, you're powerful, you are the one who got us together, you have such a gutsy organizing ability—it's just that it was never used in the O.—it was too threatening to Theo to use it, but it's a beautiful part of you."

And sure enough, Julie provided us with our best slogans of that time: the Talmudic "If not now, when? If not you, who?" and "Randy is not the O.; commutative law, the O. is not Randy" (even though this was wrong, it had the element of acknowledgment of all our selves in its formulation).

When Julie became paralyzed, Bill and I lifted her, metaphorically, by the elbows and gently set her on her feet and told her she had strength and beauty—now use them. We told her we loved her, and we did.

As for me. I had the weight of my disintegrating family on me; the weight of Ted's hatred and disdain, of the struggle with Theo for Ted's soul, and for my children's safety and well-being. Ted and I were continuing the legal mediation proceedings, trying to work out the permanent division of the children's schedule, the business, the house, our possessions. Ted was still living in Suzanne and Zack's attic and was holding on to his O. beliefs; but under the benevolent guidance of our silver-haired mediator, and the realistic assessment of Ted's attorney, he was starting to loosen from Theo's hold enough to resist the pressures to remove me from the children's lives.

I would come to Bill and Julie's house from these mediation sessions wrung out, wrenched apart and exhausted. They would sit me at the long wooden table in their kitchen. I always had the same seat, the one at the head of the table, near the french doors that led out to the new deck. I sat there while they brought me tea, good tea, milky, strong and sweet, the way I liked it. I would sit, fending off their dog's affections and let loose the day's burdens. Then we would eat. The children: Beth and her younger sister, and my Luis and Ana, would come in and out noisily, being yelled at often, the youngest being held and cuddled often also.

And I would sit among them, comfortable, resting and wanting to be cuddled also. Then they would encourage me: "Alex, you're doing the right thing; you are looking after your children. We admire you, you are strong and brave."

We sat then, on the deck in the evening sun, eating Julie's bean soup, or my couscous, or Bill's curry and washing the good food down with beer and red wine. We held on to each other. Julie and I continued to have our walks together. We hugged. Hers was the only physical affection (apart from my children) that I had in those months after Ted left me.

Every Wednesday we ate together, and often saw each other at other times, the weekends, and so forth. But Wednesdays were reserved for us, and later the others who came out. We ate and drank, and we combed through the years together. First we made a timeline of all we could remember. We listed as many of the illegal doings of the O. as we knew. This Bill turned into a document that we stored: one copy with an old friend of Julie's, and another in a safe deposit box. This was to be our security in case of a threat from Theo. The document opened: "This document has only one purpose, to prevent physical violence against our families. Unless such violence occurs, this paper will only be seen by the three undersigned individuals."

We listed what we knew of tax evasions, of personal manipulation and of misappropriation of funds from one of the programs to another. We had worked out that the Bakery, the Youth Farm Program and the daycare center had all been used at different times to funnel money through—to what ends we weren't entirely sure. We listed the threats and the intimidation, the bare facts of the murder.

Together we analyzed the history of the O., bringing together what each of us knew and had never talked about before. With paper and scissors and tape we arranged the chronology as the pieces fell into place. Bill had learned more about the early days from his talks with Matthew. We traced the events from 1973 when Theo first met two co-op workers at the Winding Road Farm, a hippie farm in Wisconsin, through the details of the murder to the final flurry of our exit.

According to Matthew, Theo, AKA Randy, was a student activist in SNCC in the early sixties. Then he worked in a catfish co-op in Mississippi—that's where he was from. Somehow he wound up in a kind of revolutionary migration to Detroit and got involved with the Black Workers Congress, a black communist organization. Then he claims to have been in RAM, the Revolutionary Action Movement, and then—and this is the bit no one really understood—he showed up in the early seventies at Winding Road Farm. It was this unexplained appearance at the hippie farm in Wisconsin that led us to speculate about Theo's possible involvement in COINTELPRO—perhaps he'd been a provocateur for the FBI? Maybe he'd committed previous crimes and this was the deal he'd made? Many government agents were recruited that way after all. We could come up with no other logical explanation for why a self-professed black revolutionary ended up organizing the white hippie Left of the Twin Cities. But there was never any proof of this hypothesis.

Theo met Bob Paulsen at the farm, and he was the first member of Theo's circle. Together they started organizing study groups in the co-ops. They put together an intensive organizing campaign. Paulsen was the one who did most of the public work as he had the connections to the people in the co-ops.

Theo's study groups discussed Marxist theory in the context of the co-ops. Those people who showed any interest in the study were talked to about discipline and being serious about the struggle. They were taken aside and given special attention. The new recruit would be invited to a secret group: they weren't supposed to tell anyone about it and right away people started getting trained in this idea of secrets—that this was necessary for security. This wasn't hard for activists to understand: in Minnesota, anyway, it was just a year or so after the massacres of the AIM people at Wounded Knee, and COINTELPRO was in the headlines and so on.

No sooner had a recruit reached this higher, secret, level then they also started to get criticized. Those who came late to study groups were lambasted, subjected to intense criticism and then made to make an on-the-spot self-criticism; and it was assumed you knew how to do this, so there was always this feeling of trying to feel your way in the dark, knowing that if you hit the right note then you would be let off the hook, but until then you were on the hot seat in the middle of this kind of brain-numbing silence. There was this pattern, then, of praise/punishment, leniency and assault: build up your ego, then break it down in front of a group of people. These were classic cult techniques.

People wanted desperately to make change, they wanted leadership, they wanted to be taken seriously. Theo knew too well how to use this.

About 200 people went through those study groups. Then Theo started another campaign which did much to destroy the Twin Cities Left. (That is not an understatement. To this day, people in the Left have intense bitterness around some of the things that were done then.) He came into this situation like a chemical catalyst and divided the Left in an explosion, leaving people, relationships, co-ops, and organizations destroyed in his wake. This destruction led further credence to the COINTELPRO provocateur theory.

The Co-op Organization (or CO, as the O. was then called) tried to take over the co-ops—in the process they split them up and eventually destroyed many of them. The CO would supposedly direct the co-ops to "serve the people" (meaning the working class) rather than the petty-bourgeois hippies. This had some appeal to co-op activists, and Theo was able to mobilize them around this goal. He proclaimed the "hippies," or, actually, anyone who wouldn't go along with him, the Enemy. People were being divided into those in the CO, and those outside: the Enemy.

In the midst of this was the takeover of the People's Warehouse, accomplished with the O.'s scare tactics. Mostly people didn't get physically hurt, but Theo had an eye for the theatrical and a gifted hand when it came to creating an atmosphere of fear. Alive and Truckin', the agit-prop theater, was split too. Ted was involved in that, and he and other CO members were told to "appropriate" all the props, the theater's musical instruments and so on. After they destroyed that theater, of course they didn't create a new one—they had just proved they had the right line and the fruits of their appropriation rotted in our basement for a decade. This was typical of the other splits. Before the O. Ted loved that theater, he loved performing; he was a clown, a juggler, generally a ham. That's how the O. worked: people were turned against the things they loved most. That's how they were supposed to prove their commitment, their seriousness about being revolutionaries. It was part of the great sacrifice for the People. Many other groups were either split or taken over: the New American Movement; the Women's Union; the Car Shop; Vietnam Veterans Against the War. The Elizabeth Blackwell Health Center for Women, a collective born out of the women's movement, was taken over by the O. and subsequently staffed solely by men, a quintessential O. move, which rather effectively ensured its rapid demise.

By 1976 the Co-op Wars* were over and the hundred or so people left in the CO went all the way underground. The so-called Mass Purge expelled fifteen cadre who were still trying to do actual community organizing. Things got very tight then. Now it was called simply the O. (supposedly we'd grown beyond the co-ops—well, we'd destroyed most of them anyway . . .) Everyone lived together in various duplexes around the city. But Theo shuffled people around in those duplexes like a juggler himself. You could not get close to anyone—for a few years no one stayed in the same place for more than three months. Around this time Theo introduced the Assessment Process and the Internal Transformation Process. He used these 'Tools', as they were called, to begin breaking up people's relationships. By 1978 Theo announced the Intensification Campaign to once again ideologically purify the O. after a group of cadres started to raise criticism and demand more democracy.

The physical punishments started up during the Intensification Campaign. We listed what we knew of these incidents. Ted got beat at least once. People were set up in boxing matches with each other—supposedly to increase ideological struggle—Theo would often set men against women in these boxing matches, particularly people who'd been in a relationship. Bill broke Jerri's rib in one of these matches. Slapping or paddling became normal punishments for infractions of discipline or for "disrespecting" the Organization. Bill was paddled for burning the frozen vegetables and thus endangering the safety of his household. Nancy, the teenager who'd lived in the upper duplex of 801, was smacked with a ruler for failing to wash the dishes on time. Zack was forcibly subdued by three cadres and paddled for failing to adjust the bakery schedule for a holiday weekend.

The physical punishments didn't last much beyond this period, but the fact that people were so numb already that many accepted this as normal and right meant that Theo's control was consolidated to a frightening degree. Discipline was truly internalized at that point and physical violence became redundant.

Most of the O.'s co-ops and the other programs fell apart during these years. The ones that weren't destroyed by the splits were driven into the ground soon enough by Theo's "leadership." He always said the purpose of

---

*Some of this history is also documented in Craig Cox's *Storefront Revolution*, published by Rutgers University Press, New Jersey.

the O. was not to run small businesses (although that's what he would keep starting up again later), but was to create a revolutionary organization that would build ideological unity and develop cadre who had worked through their bourgeois inheritance. This "ideological struggle" was the main thing on which we focused for all those years. What political organizing had been done? When we looked back, all we could see, after the destruction of the co-ops, were years of unsuccessful attempts to build small businesses, along with a much greater success, on Theo's part, at isolating and controlling a handful of semi-comatose cadre.

Bill was the historian, he wrote down the facts, spent hours transcribing dates and places and typing up what we had discussed. I was the one who pushed us to go beyond the confines of the organization, back into the outside world, to look at our experience from the outside with new terminology, with a new framework.

Bill, Julie, and I worked through this history together as we tried also to piece our lives back together. No one else could understand what we were going through. We could hold each other's hands, look into each other's eyes and say, "I know the terror you are going through. I know the black emptiness you are afraid of. I know the courage it is taking to trust yourself. I know the beauty you see as springtime unfolds itself and you within it. I know the doubt and the despair. I know, above all, the loss of all those years."

We laughed too. We laughed until we cried, often as we sat at that kitchen table, with the children and the dog, and the children coming in angry sometimes: "Be quiet! You're laughing too loud and we can't hear the television!"

We looked sheepish then, but couldn't be quieted because we hadn't laughed like that, belly laughs, for years, and we carried on laughing at the tragedy and the absurdity as it began to unfold before us and the dark, black humor was the best kind of humor of all.

We were a triangle. My children came to the house often. They played and fought with the other children and the dog. Climbed up on a knee—they didn't much care whose, but they knew that here was love and laughter and perhaps some tenderness. Often I stayed late when the children were there and then I'd drive them home after they'd fallen asleep. One time, after a night of too much tequila, Julie wouldn't let me drive home and called me a taxi. I never got seriously drunk, but she was cautious and motherly. These are the nights I remember. Struggling, half-tipsy, to carry the two children into their beds. One at a time I'd carry them through the dark, up to the back door, fumble for the key and deposit one on the couch. Then back to the car, or the taxi, for the other, repeat that and then get each of them up the stairs and onto their beds. Take off their shoes and socks, pry off their pants and tuck them in, safe, into their beds, kissing the warm, still cheek of Luis, and brushing the hair from Ana's eyes, trying to kiss her gently because she was the light sleeper and batted at me like I was a fly if I bothered her in her sleep. Then the love for them overwhelmed me, and I felt them tucked in my heart, and I was certain that I would protect them and make them safe.

Then I could go to bed too, and, even though I was happy and comforted by the two other sides of this survival trio, I would put myself in my double bed, curl up under the white covers and cry from the depths inside of me, years and rivers of tears and regret, letting out the repressed self into the open again, it spreading in salty wetness across my pillow, saying, "Me. This is me, and this is the pain it takes to be myself again."

In the morning, I'd find both kids in the bed with me, and we'd wake to sunshine and birds singing and breakfast in the garden.

Bill and Julie and I kept each other alive. We trusted each other. We relied on each other. We held each other up, and we helped each other learn to love ourselves; we helped each other through the voices that told us to hate our insides, to be scared, to disappear.

CHAPTER 32

I passed the book *Combatting Cult Mind Control* around. Slowly, Julie and Bill came to find it helpful—to see the O. as a cult. I had begun going, sporadically, to the Free Minds meetings, finding much support and understanding there. They were gentle, this odd collection of people, never pushing, but sharing their stories and asking after me in the kindest way, offering every now and then a delicate insight, a view of my shattered self that empathized with the depth of a shared experience. They made me feel that I was not crazy. They understood the weightlessness I was feeling, the struggle with Theo in which I was engaged as I tried to help Ted and to protect my children; they understood the night fears, the terror of retribution. Perhaps most important, they understood the loss and the humiliation—the lost years, the shame of being conned, the knowledge of psychological rape.

Early on, I took Julie and Bill with me to one of the larger meetings; ten rows of chairs were lined up in a dark, wood-floored church hall. We sat, the three of us, toward the back, heard the introductory remarks and then listened as people began to introduce themselves. There were ex-members of various cults—mostly religious, but some came from the personal growth cults: Lifespring; the Forum; a nameless group about the size of ours. A couple of ex-Moonies attended. There were family members of people in cults: a woman whose husband was getting into Scientology, parents whose children were in the Minneapolis Church of Christ, others with a child in a survivalist Christian Right group. Even a couple of current cult members were there to find out if their groups were destructive and to find out what a cult really was. The meeting was rounded out by two ministers whose ministry was to help people in cults, and others who'd had experience with cults as members or family-members years ago and who had since devoted much of their lives to this education and support work.

It was Bill's turn to introduce himself.

"My name is Bill. I came here tonight with my friend Alex and my wife, Julie," he motioned to us sitting next to him. "I've recently gotten out of a political group. We think it was a cult."

Then Julie's turn. She was wearing jeans and a open-necked shirt, and was sitting uncomfortably on the folding metal chair.

"My name is Julie. I was also part of this group."

She stopped, she didn't want to say more. Now, strangely, people began to ask questions—this was odd because usually any of the Free Minds volunteers left a person to speak at his or her own pace, knowing the difficulty of putting people on the spot who have just come out of a group whose whole purpose was to have one continually on the spot. But this was something new for them: they had never had people from a political cult in their midst, and we represented a new part of the world of mind control. They wanted to know more.

"Where is it based, this group?" asked a young woman.

"Here in Minneapolis," Julie replied quietly.

"And what's the leader's name?"

It was asked innocently enough. But a silence descended on the three of us. We all looked down. I touched Julie's leg, saw Bill reach to hold her hand. We stayed silent a moment longer. I looked up and saw people turned in their chairs to us, looking at us with concern and curiosity, but without blame or malice or judgment. I didn't know what Julie would do.

None of us had ever spoken his real name in public. This was the big secret. This was "security." To give his name in this room of strangers—people we had never met, whose politics we didn't know, whose motives we did not understand. Julie looked up then, her mouth drawn down at the corners.

"Theo Smith," she finally said.

The people in their chairs continued to look, but kindly. Julie's eyes watered, she shook quietly next to me, a tear dropped. And I too, felt my chest send messages of release to my eyes, my face reddened—I put my arm around her.

After a moment someone said, "Is that the first time you've said his name in public?"

Julie nodded her head.

"Is it frightening?"

"It's very frightening," Julie said.

"He's violent," I added, hoping to explain the fear.

We had turned him in, blown his cover. Later we would talk ourselves out of our fear, going over and over how no one in that room would have cause to go to the police, or run into Theo or anyone else still in the O. It would be all right. He wouldn't find out. Of course, we all three understood at that moment another part of his intense control over us. It was liberating to say his name in that roomful of people who could quite well understand the fear involved. But how do you explain the fear entrenched in a secret that has driven your life? For years "security" considerations had defined our actions: where and when we used the phone, who knew where we lived, who our friends were, how and where we met and talked with other cadre. All this was to protect the revolution. Even though we knew now that it protected only Theo from the consequences of his crime, the speaking of his name went against decades of conditioning—were we sure it wasn't a betrayal of our principles? This doubt co-existed with the physical fear of Theo's revenge to create an inward tension that gnawed at us. And this inner tension was precisely the feeling that the veterans in that room could understand.

Sitting in the kitchen again. Bill and Julie had built it. It was good for their development. Funny thing that any kind of remodeling was good for one's development; Cultural Revolution stuff, manual labor and all that. When Ted and I bought our lovely house, ready to move into and left in beautiful shape by the previous owners, Bill criticized us—there was no need for any remodeling, how then would we get our development?

Theo had helped build their kitchen. They were supposedly raising the value of the property but, of course, to pay for Theo's labor costs and for the materials (which payments he handled, Julie always suspicious of the exorbitant cost, and being viciously criticized by Theo for her suspicion) they had to get a loan, so the mortgage and loan combined were now way beyond the possible market price—largely because of the neighborhood. That's the system—it doesn't matter how much work you do to a house, if the neighborhood is "wrong" (and that usually means black) then you can't sell, or only for a pittance.

The O.'s houses started off as dollar houses—bought for a dollar from the government in an incentive scheme where the buyer promised a certain amount of work and improvement on the property. This was one of Theo's many get-rich-quick schemes (all of which failed, to my knowledge). But supposedly Julie and Bill's house was "improved"; Theo got several thousand dollars for the work, even though it was shoddy work. (Bill had told us how Theo once put a crowbar up in their black neighbor's face because the neighbor told Theo the work was shoddy and made suggestions as to how it could be done right.) With the shoddy improvements then, the house was still a dump. A nice, new, big kitchen, but the rest of it was slum-like: falling apart; small, dark rooms; dangerous stairs and so on.

The satisfying thing was using that nice, new, bright kitchen, courtesy of Theo, to debrief and to recover. First just the three of us: Julie and Bill and I, then the others: the ones who had left years before who we found again and brought to the kitchen; the others who began to leave after us as we supported them with our new knowledge; the ones who visited from California where they'd been driven after a terrible feeling of failure at leaving, or after being terrorized by beatings to ensure their silence. And then there was the youngest one, Nancy, who'd been raised in the O. She was now a young woman, and we told her, sitting around that kitchen table, that her parents had been in this organization, the O., for most of her lifetime. She had never known there was such an organization and consequently had never been able to understand the strange and repressive environment in which she had grown up. We watched as her face changed with the same moment of horrific epiphany that we had all been through as the jigsaw pieces fit together to reveal the sordid image. For her it laid bare the whole of her life, the life she was a child in. Her anger spilled like acid over us all, but we kept our arms open for her as she flailed at us, and we listened to her as she made meaning of what we had told her.

We gathered there, over the months, around the pine-wood kitchen table that Nancy's father had made years before, and had left with Julie after one of his Theo-directed moves from one apartment to the next. We sat and ate and drank and talked.

Kitchen Story

Matthew was in the O. for eight years, had met his wife in the O. and somehow had managed to marry her without Theo's involvement. But in the early 1980s he rebelled. His wife and he wanted a child, but as they loved each other, they began to get clues from the O. that they would soon be confronted and forced apart like so many others. Together they left, their relationship, at least, intact.

Matthew was beaten on his way out. He had gone back to his old apartment to pick up belongings he'd left there, and he found a welcoming committee: Betty and three other cadres stood at the door to the apartment waiting for him with baseball bats. He turned and ran when he saw them, and they gave chase, catching up to him on the street, surrounding him as he curled up on the sidewalk protecting his head with his arms. Betty had the assignment of beating him—she was instructed to hit him on the head with the bat—but later she told us she couldn't do it and tried to hit him as lightly as she could on his body. He remembered this too—laughing finally, at the kitchen table—after years of private fear.

"She couldn't bring herself to hit me hard! Thank God for Betty!"

Matthew can laugh, but he also understands something about grief. Soon after he left the O. his wife became pregnant—they had a baby girl. One morning when the child was just two years old, Matthew woke to find the still body of his wife lying lifeless beside him. She died in the night of heart failure. He was left alone with his baby daughter.

In the O., Theo told the remaining cadre that Matthew had killed his wife. Matthew, said Theo, removed his wife from conditions of struggle and development in the O. and had, therefore, ideologically murdered her. This is the phrase Theo used. It was passed among the remaining members like a curse. Some people believed it to be true. Others were left with an indefinable feeling that terrible things would happen to those who left.

This we do not laugh about.

Soon after Ted moved out, Matthew called me. It took a couple of months after Bill contacted him for Matthew to trust we were really out of the O., that this wasn't some complicated machination to manipulate him again.

I was lying alone in bed one night, reading *Combatting Cult Mind Control* for the second time, when he called. I had met him once, years before, at a South Africa fundraising meeting. He didn't remember this, but he called because Bill had told him about me, that Ted had left, and also told him what we were learning about mind control.

We talked for an hour. He understood what it was to lose someone. He asked me questions that brought me to the verge of tears, simple questions like: "How are you feeling?"

He said, "You're brave. It's very frightening to leave."

I knew that he understood the fear. I considered him brave—that he admitted his own fear.

I said, "I lie awake at night sometimes and the dishwasher turns on and I lie sweating in terror thinking the noise is Theo, and I wait for him to turn the doorknob slowly, to open the door and appear in my bedroom."

"Yes." he said. He paused, then: "As for me, I'd like to put a stake in his heart. I was scared, too. It passes. It will take time. It took me a couple of years to get back on my feet."

I groaned to think of a couple of years like this.

"Life is good," he said, "Life is good on the outside."

He was about to get married again. He had done interesting work in the last few years. At the end of our conversation he showed his trust and gave me his phone number.

"Call me if you need to."

After he hung up, I lay on the fading red suns of my familiar quilt and wept with gratitude.

Later he thanked me; the concepts of mind control and the laughter of the Wednesday dinners helped him resolve some of the old, bitter heaviness that he had carried with him for so many years. Even though he had been out so long, the O. had not been out of him, and this was the gift we offered.

Every lunchtime, Jerri and I left our work on the software project and for an hour walked around the summer suburbs, under the weeping willows, past the lawns greening under their sprinklers. We talked. I gentled her along. She reminded me of a young horse sometimes—a sensitive, high-strung thing whose eyes would glisten with fear, and she'd back away from me, hardly meaning to, but unable to fight the instinct of fear that had been bred into her.

I walked by her side. We talked.

Slowly, very delicately, she began to drop hints. She talked about the anger that Theo had when she began to see Anthony, the man she lived with (they were an exceptional case—Anthony was not in the O., and did not even know of its existence, yet somehow Jerri was allowed to be with him). She told me how Theo made her scrape tile off the floor during one of their "developmental" remodeling projects and refused to say one word to her the whole three days they worked on it together. She told me how he began to ignore her in meetings. That she sat there with Debbie, or Suzanne, or Dave, and he would not greet her, would not acknowledge her when she spoke, would not meet her gaze at all.

"I wondered what I had done wrong," she said. "I thought there was a lesson I needed to learn. That if I thought enough about it I would realize what he was trying to teach me—that he was doing this on purpose for my development."

"Did he ever tell you?" I asked.

"No. You know how it was—you were always supposed to figure it out for yourself."

"Yes, I know," I said, remembering the blank sheets of paper that I'd stared at, trying to figure out what to put down, trying to second-guess what my ideological crime had been so that I could then create the proper confession. "And what did you think you had done wrong?"

Her eyes looked sidelong at me. She spoke softly.

"I thought maybe he was jealous of Anthony." She paused. "I mean—Theo and I—we were in a relationship."

I thought to myself, "Ah—yes, I knew. I knew she had something else going on here." I felt inside a terrible empathy for her.

"How long?" I asked. She didn't answer directly.

"It started a long time ago. It was after a meeting, in Chicago. He asked if he could stay the night. I didn't think that's what he meant."

"Did you want him to?"

"I didn't even think about that. It was—you know—him asking was more like telling. I thought he needed a place to stay that night. But then he went to my bedroom. He took off his clothes and lay on the bed. I did too. I didn't really know what to do."

I held my breath. We walked. It was warm. The smell of cut grass, marigolds, tomato plants, filtered into the scene that played out in my mind. This must have been the first time she had told anyone this. I felt it in my body. Now she was beginning her exit from the O. She was starting to tell the secrets. We walked together, and I meant to send her every message of love that I could. I wanted her to feel surrounded by comfort—I knew the feel of a frightening man.

"He started, you know, doing things to me. He just made me lay there while he did things. It felt so . . . I thought, what am I supposed to do? Then he told me I needed to learn how to have sex without emotions. That that was my problem; I got too caught up in my emotions, and that was why things didn't work out with Bill."

"But I thought you were told to split up with him?"

"Yes."

"I'm sorry." I was sorry. I thought to myself, sex without emotions—I felt it as rape. Jerri who is such a feelingful person, so delicate, so loving, so hurt. What it must have taken for her to lay herself down and allow his body in hers, to say to herself, "This is for my own good." And then to dissociate, to remove her emotions, whatever they were.

She lived alone in her apartment in Chicago—he told her to do that. No one but he ever came to it in the five years she was there. He never took her out. He simply came to her when he wanted—just showed up, assumed her assent. She had given everything else, why not her body?

One day, I gave her a ride home. She was living in 801 Sullivan then. She was so close now, she was almost out, but something was holding her back. She could not yet make that final decision. I dropped her off at her house after work. Then I remembered I had something in my bag and thought, perhaps this is the right time? I felt a little cruel, is it too hard to do this to her?—she had such terror in her thin body. But I called her back.

"Jerri! Did you ever hear about the murder?"

She looked at me sideways again. "No. What do you mean?"

I wondered—she'd been my contact when the FBI had visited 801 and tried to question me. She was the one who'd told me to go the psychiatrist with the phony story about FBI harassment. Did she really not remember all that? Later I was to discover this was common. People had an uncanny ability to, perhaps not erase things from their memories, but certainly to push them aside, to set them behind a curtain of fog, to put them in a compartment where none of the normal connections would get made.

"There was a murder here—at 801."

She turned to look at the house in which she lived, her eyes sad, her shoulders hunched up as she cradled her briefcase to her body.

"Theo did it. He went to jail. I've got the clippings here from the paper . . . I thought . . . maybe you'd want to see them?"

I held out the sheaf of papers for her, the stucco building of 801 in the background. I was shivering, I felt like I was bringing the criminal back to the scene of the crime. She took the clippings from me, a certain disbelief on her drawn face. She looked at me, and I felt guilty, perhaps I shouldn't have done it? But I wanted to push her off her equilibrium, and this was only the truth that I was offering her, not a manipulation, not deceit, just the facts, and she took the clippings and folded them into her briefcase and walked away into the house in which a man died and poured his blood on to the floor at the hand of the man who penetrated her without emotion.

CHAPTER 33

Kitchen Story—or—The Revolution Will be Televised

We tell the story of the potty-training video. That's right. Potty-training for the Revolution. Actually, this was an advanced use of the Internal Transformation Process. Using the tools of the ITP, the video proclaimed, one could both ease and speed-up the process of training small children in "urinating" and doing their "bowel movements" in the appropriate place.

My daughter starred with Debbie's daughter as the cooperative poopers. Then there was Charles, the resistant metaphysician who was "unable to make the connection" between his poop and the need for a potty.

One Wednesday evening, for a change from our usual kitchen routine, a group of us viewed an actual copy of the O.-made video. There were the girls, patiently pulling down their pants and sitting nicely on the pot, copying the "eh, eh," sounds that an invisible Debbie, out of sight of the camera, was coaching them in. "Eh, eh," was a sound supposed, according to our 1950s vintage child development book, to encourage elimination. Charles, recalcitrant, was shown throwing a tantrum as the camera attempted to keep his thrashing body in focus. The voice-over (Debbie's), intones his problem: "This child is a *realist*. Realists face the problem of disconnection. With correct potty-training, this potentially life-long limitation can be corrected at an early stage in a child's development."

From the blurred images of Charles' rage, it did not look as if they were having too much success correcting his "realism."

In between scenes a yellow cardboard sign was held up with scene titles such as: "First Stage of the Process," and then, imaginatively, "Second Stage of the Process."

317

It is painful to watch, but humorous, which makes it at least bearable.

The video was to be marketed, intended to make a profit for the O., and, to this end, Debbie and Dave toted this product around to day-care organizations trying to peddle it as an educational tool. I believe this was yet another failed business venture. Perhaps their next one would be more successful: a pre-school soccer training franchise . . . apparently also for the Revolution.

It was 9.30 at night and the children were with Ted. I was alone in the house when the phone rang.

"This is the operator, I have your parties on the line for Mr. Brodsky's conference call. Will you please hold while I connect the call?"

"Okay." I sat pressing the phone receiver to my ear. The operator connected me to a nine-way conference call with all of Ted's immediate family. I had requested this meeting so that I could explain to them what was going on. They couldn't understand why we were breaking up—and with such bitterness and antagonism. As a youngster, Ted had been the Golden Boy, his mother liked to tell me, and since our marriage he had come closer to his family, and we were now the Golden Couple of the family; our revolutionary cover was so deep that we had seemed to them to be the most normal and well-adjusted of the children. They could see we liked each other and got along, so they could not fathom what had destroyed our marriage this way, and why Ted had fought to keep the children from me.

I'd already talked to Hy, Ted's younger brother and my favorite among my in-laws, and explained to him as much as I could. Now my challenge was to give them a thumbnail history of the O. and a crash course in the methods of mind control. I needed them to help Ted, to help me, to help my children. I knew that they loved us, and I, in turn loved them, felt like they were real family to me; more of a family, in some ways, than my own.

"Hello, this is Sidney." Sidney was Ted's father; he had already visited us in an attempt to stem the tide that was drowning our family—but this was before I'd learned about mind control or thought reform; before I could explain why Ted was being so recalcitrant and punitive. Now I had valuable information that explained it. Through Hy, I had asked the whole family to read *Combatting Cult Mind Control*, which described so well the knot of forces, coercive and seductive, that had been the O. for me. In a week, the third annual family reunion would take place—a relaxed but chaotic week by the sea—and I wanted to prepare everyone for this time they were to have with Ted.

"Let's do a roll-call," said Sidney, relying on his World War II years of military training. "Lorna and I are both present."

Ted's two married brothers and their wives announced themselves, followed by his sister, her husband and, finally, Hy.

"Alex, will you begin? We want you to know that we are all here supporting you, and we're listening," said Sidney.

"Okay," I said. I straightened out the notes I'd worked on for the last week in preparation for this. I would try to tell them everything—except for the murder, I wanted to spare Ted's mother, so this I had only told Hy.

"I'm going to take you through some of the history of the O., and then I'll describe something about mind control and cults and try to show you why I think that the O. is a cult and how that's affecting Ted's behavior."

"I knew he was in a cult fifteen years ago!" exclaimed Lorna, but Sidney shushed her.

"We must let Alex speak and then we can each have an opportunity to respond after she's done."

I began. I spoke out through the telephone wires to these nine other people, people whose lives were familiar to me but from whom most of my life had been hidden until now. I felt I was speaking out into the depths of the night sky, but I imagined them each sitting in their living rooms, spouses on extension phones in bedrooms—they were listening to me in Massachusetts, Rhode Island, West Virginia, while I sat, alone, in my empty house in Minneapolis.

As I began, the cat jumped down from the other kitchen chair with a quiet thud and ambled over to rub her side against my leg. Her gray tail lifted high in the air. This was the cat I bought for Luis the day Ted moved out—not, certainly, to replace his father, but to fill up a little of the empty space with the movement of a new, soft creature. The tabby cat walked, back and forth, against my leg and then jumped, again, back to the chair to rest.

"Later," I said, "I'll talk about what we can do—really, what *you* can do—because Ted cannot speak to me, he can't hear anything I say—I've become the devil for him and only make him defensive. So really, it will be up to you to give him the help he needs."

I paused for a breath.

"Okay, Alex," said Hy gently.

The weeks of kitchen stories allowed me to piece together a history of sorts, which I recounted. I described for my scattered, unseen audience the strange history of the O. as it disintegrated into the final handful of members it held now. I told them how I had worked my way out with Bill and Julie and how Ted had been pulled back in. And then I walked through for them the eight points of mind control and how the O. had used each of them: the breaking down of people's identity, then their reconstruction in Theo's image; the control of our time; the permanent exhaustion; the isolation—above all, the isolation.

Every now and again as I told this story over the next hour, I heard Hy who had taken on the role of the assenter; he "hmmm'd" and "uh huh'd" and sympathized his way through my tale. As an actor he understood the importance of an audience, and he gave me an anchor among those scattered breaths that received my words in emptiness. At the end, we discussed how to help Ted. We arranged that his brothers would meet with Steve Hassan, the cult exit-counselor in Boston, to get advice about how to educate Ted about mind control. I had already spoken with Steve several times and had sent him a stack of material on the O. and about Ted, and he had helped me understand how to help him in a respectful way.

We discussed the need to build trust with Ted but at the same time to start talking openly about the O., to break the mystical hold that the security rules had for him. I gave them information about the O. that they would introduce to Ted to help break down the magical aura that surrounded it; information about Theo's sexual activities, his criminal past, the various violent incidents we knew about, his Jim Jones-like insistence on being Beth's "uncle."

The exit-counseling methods they would use included talking about Ted's pre-O. life, the things he'd liked to do, the friends he'd had, the goals he'd had. They would push him to compare the O.'s rhetoric with its actual accomplishments, try to present him with the O.'s flagrant contradictions, discuss also the good sides of the O. experience, what Ted had learned so that he could minimize, perhaps, the terror of the loss of those years that the rest of us had experienced.

His family would learn enough about mind control so they could point out to Ted where and how he had been manipulated and controlled. His mother and sister were skeptical. They did not want to plan this intervention; they felt it was another way of trying to control him. I insisted that was not so, that their goal was only to get him to think, to give him factual information and to allow him some space to think critically after years of the cult-induced "thought-stopping" to which we had all succumbed.

Finally I was done. They each said good-bye. Hy said he would stay on the phone a while. When the connections had quieted and only his voice remained, he said to me, "You're incredibly strong, Alex."

I looked out of the corner of my eye to the cat. She was curled up around herself. I missed the children. I could not reach the cat to stroke her. "I know," I said. "I've had practice." I wanted to say to him, "I'm so tired of being strong. I don't want to be strong anymore. I want to collapse, to have someone take care of me. I cannot face it, doesn't anyone understand? I cannot face holding up the children and myself and Ted. I want to be like this cat, fed and rested and curled in upon myself for years."

But instead Hy and I exchanged words of love and caring. I put down the phone. I was spent.

The family took it on, though. They laughed, later, that they'd used reverse mind control on Ted, using sleep deprivation by keeping him up until 3.00 each morning talking and laughing, remembering and challenging—and then he'd be woken at 7.00 by the kids, ready for breakfast and then the beach. This was the method Hassan called "low-stress exit-counseling." My sister who (along with my father) also played her part in reaching out to Ted, called it the "drip-drip method." It would carry on for months after the vacation: more information being doled out to him; more challenges to him about the secrets; more communication to break down his isolation.

Ted stayed in the O. for the time being, and he still refused to talk to me, but he did at least begin to listen to his family.

Finally Jerri came out. She announced it to me almost casually one day: she'd decided to leave, but she wouldn't give her resignation until she'd figured out what to do with the house. She was now the official owner of 801—having been directed to sign a contract for deed for the property some years previously, and having put many thousands of dollars into its remodeling by . . . yes, Careful Construction. She needed to find a way to untangle herself from that situation before she made her resignation known to Theo, and to Debbie and Dave who lived, supposedly as her tenants, in the lower duplex of 801.

Right away she told Anthony, who had known nothing of her involvement in the O. Now he heard that the leader of this group had served jail time for killing a man in the house where they lived. That the victim had "disrespected" Theo and thus given good enough reason for his demise. Anthony took this incredible story involving the woman he had been with for four years and out of his shock built a Leonardo Da Vinci-like mechanical barricade made out of hefty two-by-fours which swung into place each night, solid, to protect the flimsy stairwell door they shared with Dave and Debbie. This and a baseball bat by their own front door were to prevent Theo's rage from exploding in that house once again. The ghost of Kyle Ray haunted them. Downstairs was where he'd died, the bullet ricocheting off the muscle of his arm and pounding its way through his heart. Despite our rational assurances that history would not repeat itself, they lived in a state of terror for some weeks while they planned a legal and financial way out of the property Jerri owned.

The love that that first core of us built, and the growing understanding of what had happened began to spread out like sunlight over the months as we built a kind of haven, or a secret garden for the others who started to come out, one by one, in their own terror, from the O. Betty came out in September and joined us hesitantly in the kitchen. Her blind faith had finally run its course. Then Zack left Suzanne, and he was out also, although desperately burdened, as I had been, by the O.'s bitter attempts to keep his children from him. Finally Mona and her husband (another of Theo's arranged marriages), who'd received the paper we'd mailed to them in Chicago, came out also. Ted, however, stayed on doggedly through those months.

Those who'd left years before began to find in us the expression of what they had never expressed, the description of what they had felt but never named when they were completely isolated, carrying their secrets in a hidden fear. One was a man who'd married after the O. and for ten years never told his wife about that time. Another had fled the state for several years in fear for his safety. Others had simply refused to discuss it, hoping that time would blank out the memories and humiliation and self-accusation.

The Wednesday night meetings got bigger, louder, carried on a tide of laughter, and tears sometimes too, but now the tears came less often. At a certain point, a person finds there are no more.

Kitchen Story

I hear about another form of punishment I'm grateful to have missed. Zack tells us about a committee hearing in the late 1970s held to review the practice of two cadres, Linda and Steve.

I imagine her long full breasts falling down her ribcage, unsupported by a bra, the fistful of curls covering her pubis, her comical bellybutton, the muscles of her arms outlined by shadow. Her head, of course, hanging down— even if it wasn't, then her eyes ashamed, trying to escape inside herself. Or him, and I'll say now, I knew neither of them (although later I was to discover someone I'd known who'd had the same treatment). I imagine him with glasses and fair hair, a pale, skinny body—well, he wouldn't have seen much sun for the last few years. I wonder where they undressed? In the room in front of everyone? Or in another room, and then they were to make an entrance, naked?

It was punishment. For crimes of ideology. To strip naked in front of the committee was supposed to expose you—strip you down to your ideological essence, I suppose. I ask the people who were there to look at this now and acknowledge it for what it was: humiliation, shaming, a form of sexual abuse perhaps. Later I talk to Ted—he'd witnessed one of these—and asked him how he felt. It took a long time, many questions, to get a reply from him. Finally he said, "I didn't want to be there. I was relieved it wasn't me."

And so, to make sure it would never be him, he behaved (and this, of course, was the desired result), kept a low profile, didn't create too much conflict because, look, this is what could happen. He too could be standing in a room full of his "comrades," stripped naked, his penis dangling helpless before him and his audience. I wouldn't have wanted it either.

It made me wonder how I could have joined such an organization. I used to say: But I joined late, after all the craziness—I missed the boxing matches, the paddlings, the stripping naked, the small acts of violence that created such a large terror among the Left here. Perhaps I wouldn't have joined then, but it was the same organization, they still arranged marriages, lied, punished (perhaps in slightly more subtle ways), required that one seek permission for almost any act in one's life. If I separate myself from the woman whose nakedness was turned into a fist to the jaw then I have not understood my own message. And it is this shame, induced through these acts of terror, that keeps the stories from being told.

As my freedom expanded before me in a delirious way, I felt Ted slipping from my grasp as a drowning person slides from the tired grip of the rescuer. I was losing him.

When I began to go to the secret meetings with Julie and Bill in the tense weeks before we left, I don't think he knew. One time I giggled as I told him that Saturday morning I would be going to aerobics, again, for the third time that week, with Julie. This was our cover. This from me, who could barely drag myself to exercise once a week and suddenly I was the most enthusiastic attendee of aerobics, and I giggled at him, because I was sure he must realize what was going on, but he just looked at me through his glasses and smiled, sort of shyly and that made me feel even more sure that he knew, and that on some level it was okay with him, that I didn't have to keep it a secret anymore.

He had been my best friend. Even though we could not look at each other when we made love. It violated the boundaries that defined our relationship to get that close. And when he took his glasses off, his eyes were different, his face was different, he didn't have the look of confidence that he wore in the outside world. Ted kept the space between us always. He did not want to look. I could not. There was a space between us that held us together all those years as it kept us safely apart. Instead of looking at him, I would touch his body or, I spoke to him, as best friends do, over cups of tea at the kitchen table, both of us safely myopic behind the reflective lenses of our spectacles.

Ted was my best friend for all those years. We went out together for cappuccino, we stole away to secret, though short, vacations. We shared joke after joke after running joke that only long-time friends can share, especially with the common history of our liberal Jewish upbringings adding a kind of generational texture to our jokes.

Endearments. Generally the things people are embarrassed to say in front of other people. Only "darling" much later, when we were struggling to save our marriage. And "darling" had become a plea, a desperate attempt.

He wouldn't touch me in public either. I wanted to walk down the street hand in hand, or arm in arm, in a comfortable kind of closeness. This didn't suit him; it embarrassed him, even though his parents did it, or perhaps because of this. Again, it was only towards the end that began to change—he took my hand as the first sign of rapprochement after the months of shunning, but then it was when his brother and sister-in-law were with us, out walking among the fall leaves at the Arboretum, and this time I was embarrassed that he should choose to make such an intimate gesture, his first move towards me after the cult-induced separation, in a public place, with our relatives present and watching.

He was my best friend. We worked well together. We built a family—under some duress, I might add. We built the ANC fundraising organization. We built the consulting company together. We had a way of doing that: dividing the tasks according to our strengths, making analyses and strategies together.

We were each other's best friend, in a friendless environment. But we never opened each other's skin. Only when my skin exploded through force of the pressure of our constrained lives—only then did the insides come out, and then he was forced to deal with me.

But, generally it was about containment and limits and love within those limits. I will say now that his limits were closer in than mine and that his fear was greater, and his loyalty to the leadership was the rope that kept us both tied to the O. for so long. I had severed that rope. And it meant acknowledging that Ted might hold on longer than I and that I was casting myself off without him, holding tightly to my children as I launched us off into the boiling waters of the unknown.

Through Ted's visits to divorce lawyers and his pronouncements that he would gain custody of the children; through the nights of terror in my bed and the days I spent writing up household budgets to ensure I could support the children and myself; through the dead days, weeks, months of speaking to Ted with him averting his gaze, never able to look at me to face the truth of the O., the murder, the sexual exploitation; through all this I held on, fighting an absolute struggle for survival which I would not lose.

And I didn't. But the price was high.

Kitchen Story

Nancy—she was the one raised in the O. Her parents were still in—they lived in Chicago with Vida, another O. woman. Nancy says: "Sabrina! I *hated* Sabrina. Remember when I had to live with her and Ted. Oh, God. Ted was all right. I hope he comes out. He used to play basketball with me. You know we shared a room—I was only eleven, and he was a grown man! I'm glad it was him."

"You shared a *bedroom* with him?" I ask.

"Yeah! Weird. But not as weird as her. I was like this little kid, and she caught me looking at a fashion magazine one time, and maybe I asked her about makeup or something. Anyhow she got really mad. And she was *scary*."

Zack interjects. "Everyone was scared of her. She was this tiny woman, but talk about powerful. She was one of the lieutenants for a long time."

Julie adds, "Something odd happened though, didn't it? She left really suddenly. She had that kid, too—Solomon. Then she was pregnant again, and all of a sudden she just disappeared. God, I wonder what happened to her?"

"We should try to find her—see what happened. I bet she knows a hell of a lot of dirt," I say.

"It was his child she was pregnant with," says Jerri.

Nancy gets a little exasperated at us. She is trying to tell her story.

"*Anyway*, she starts going on at me that women are exploited, and I shouldn't be looking at those magazines, and, you know, I really was just this little kid. This was a *fashion* magazine, right. I didn't know anything about women's oppression or anything. So she rips the magazine from my hand and orders me to go down to the Tom Thumb and get a magazine that'll teach me all about women being exploited. This was ten o'clock at night—it was dark—and we lived down by Dale. That was a bad neighborhood."

Nancy is angry now—her cheeks are red, flushed and her red hair is swinging in front of her eyes as she talks to us.

"She sent me down there on my own and told me to buy *Hustler* magazine. I wasn't even old enough to be allowed to buy it. It's not *Playboy*. I mean *Hustler* is *gross*. I didn't know what it was, but they sold it to me anyway. Sabrina was weird. Scary. How can you do that to a little kid? I didn't know why I was supposed to be going out alone at night and looking at this gross magazine."

Nancy's stories always quiet us. She has none of the ambivalence that most of us still feel, unable to jettison, overnight, the decades of our life that were dedicated to this kind of perverse activity.

I offer up another story.

"There was this strange stuff about sexuality. I mean when Ted and I got married, we did this whole worksheet on our sexual practice. It was supposed to be some kind of scientific way of approaching our relationship."

We all remember the Worksheets: multi-page forms where cadre were to lay out all aspects of the contradictions in a process. The forms had a hypnotizing effect—it was so hard to understand how to fill them out with their

Aspect A's and B's; Principal and Non-Principal Aspects, endless columns of numbers with which to categorize each problem, and all this interspersed with unexplained mathematical symbols garnered from Set Theory and topped off with quotes from Mao Tse-Tung. The Worksheets demanded endless detail, and it often took months just to fill one out completely.

Julie gets up as the others rest back in their chairs to listen; she fills up our glasses with wine.

I continue: "The first thing was, when I was still trying to get pregnant—I did this flowchart, a flowchart mind you, on the process of getting pregnant. It was so pathetic. Here I am, I always hated doing flowcharts anyway, and it says things like, 'Pregnant? Yes/No. If yes, Stop. Else, have sex.' Oh, God."

Most of us in the room are in the computer industry, thanks to the O., and there is a chorus of laughter as we imagine this document.

I'm remembering the scratchy little penciled boxes I'd drawn for this particular exercise, bending over the paper like a schoolchild as if my grade depended on it. I start laughing, holding my stomach as I bend over again, my forehead resting on the smooth golden pine of the kitchen table, and the tears are leaking out of my eyes as I laugh and laugh. Betty comes over, laughing, and holds me by the shoulders because we all know that, thank God, we can laugh because there have already been so many tears of grief.

The laughter slows to the occasional bubble. I finish my story.

"And then . . ." I say, gasping a little for breath, "And then, we decided, on the same logic, I assume, that Sabrina was using with Nancy—we decided that an important step in our sexual practice—to fully understand the relations of domination and subordination between the sexes, and to explore the nature of the economic exploitation of women and sex—got it everyone?—well, the step for that was to go to a porno movie together. So down we go, to Alexander's old place by the bakery, and we sit there, the newlyweds, doing our homework, surrounded by the smell of stale sperm and me with my peripheral vision working overtime to catch the jerks jerking off around me."

This starts off another round. Zack is sputtering. He's holding his hands between his knees, like maybe he's protecting something, and he's banging his feet up and down on the ground.

"No, no!" he laughs, "Tell me more!"

"That's all. We sat through two movies—it was a double bill that night. Of course I had lots of fantasy material after that for my sexual life—perhaps it wasn't such a bad step after all . . ."

We wipe our eyes on paper napkins.

CHAPTER 34

I go to a Free Minds ex-cult-members meeting. A group in a church. A few chairs, the circle of recovery, now a staple of American life. How many of us have sat in that circle? The replacement for a damaged community, where a new community forms in anonymity to weld back together the humans who have been thrust centrifugally from their roots, their families, the places of their birth. These circles in the basements of churches are places that describe the bonds of a particular life, that notice the community of experience that brings these tired souls together.

"My name is ___." Some give last names, some don't.

"I was a Jehovah's Witness for forty-five years," says a man who's about sixty; he's gray and balding and round but handsome, with strong eyes. "I've been out three years. I come here to see old friends, to help people who are coming out now. I want to offer support because I understand what it feels like."

Next to him sits a young woman with pink glasses and straight yellow hair. She says nothing for the two hours we are there. Another young woman, pale, with bobbed, pale hair and big, tired eyes, sits next to her. She speaks:

"I came up from Tennessee to visit a friend. Two people from Free Minds flew down last month and exit-counseled my whole group. I've been in it since I was three years old. We woke up at four in the morning every day. I had to work in the fields. I'm sorry, I feel so much emotion . . ."

She can hardly talk. We are silent with her as she collects herself.

"I've been out a little while, but when Bruce and John came down, I couldn't hold back thinking about it anymore. For years I didn't think about it. I drank and did drugs and went to AA. Now I've started, I can't stop the thinking. I don't know who the real me is. There was no me before. I was just a little baby. This is all I've known—my whole life was in it. Our leader was a woman, she said she was God.

"Sometimes it's good to think about it and piece it together and discover bits of who I am. But when I cry, I wonder how long I'll feel this way."

She cries, silently. My throat tightens. I want to tell her that even now I can find myself in the beauty of the black-eyed susans in my yard, that sometimes I can focus on the moment, on allowing myself to open up like the leaf-petals of a flower. But I'm silent—I'm new here, I don't really understand.

"My name is ___, I was in the Boston Church of Christ for a year. I got out a year ago. I helped my wife get out. I am still trying to understand what happened to me. I cannot pick out clothes to wear in the morning. I don't know if I believe in God anymore."

I am frightened by the number of people here from religious groups. But later I discover many others from the so-called "personal growth" or political groups—some well-known: EST, the Forum, Lifespring, and other small groups like mine, led by charismatic leaders who stumbled onto this formula of control.

We continue to make our introductions.

"My name is Alex," I introduce myself. "I was in an underground communist group for ten years. I got out three months ago. I think it was a cult. My husband is still in it, and I want to help him get out. I'm trying to understand what happened to me."

The topic for today's meeting is Truth.

We talk about the Truth.

"We had the Objective Truth," I say.

"No," says a young man in torn jeans who wears a single gold earring. He tells us he was born into the Jehovah's Witnesses and walked away last year. He is only seventeen and has left his entire family behind. They are shunning him.

"No," he repeats, "We had the Truth. When we greeted each other we'd say 'How long have you been with the Truth?'"

A middle-aged woman from Christ's Household of Faith in St. Paul, grimaces, "No, no, it was we who had the Truth. We had the Holy Way and God's Truth, and that truth was dictated by our leader. The same leader who made us beat our babies. Spoil the rod and spare the child—that was our Truth."

Mr. Farrakhan, I think to myself, also claims to have the only Truth. Truth is a potent commodity, apparently there is only one of it, and the owners each claim a monopoly.

A young woman talks about her emptiness inside. She cries. She gave up her music for the eight years she was in her cult. She was in leadership, she tells us, she was a "victimizer." I look at her and think of Debbie. I feel sorry for Debbie under the hatred I still feel.

Another woman is trying to leave her husband who is in a white supremacist, Right-wing fundamentalist cult. She is scared to leave him in case she loses her children. Her husband says she is "an unsubmissive wife." She wants to be a good wife, a submissive wife, but she knows she has to help him out of this thing. Her small daughter is with her and lays her head on her mother's lap. She looks up at us, sucking her thumb. Her mother strokes the little girl's soft curls, holding her, protecting her, while she tells us about the True Race, the Truth of White Supremacy, the ideology of her husband's group. Last week, she tells us, she threw his books, all the group's materials, out on the front lawn.

"I told him I never wanted to see that stuff again. But now I don't know what he's going to do."

I am amazed at the company I now keep.

I leave the meeting. It's a dark summer's night. I cross the empty parking lot; it's so lonely. I look up at the black sky—the sky starts spinning, I feel completely dazed, in another place. Time and breath stop. I keep looking at the stars. My head is buzzing, black like a starless darkness. Knowledge is too much light, and my head is aching with knowledge. I cannot believe. My feet are on the asphalt, it gleams in the light. A deep breath. I am breathing in the night. One foot after the other, I walk to my car.

This is the feeling of unreality. Of being shattered. I cannot encompass it all; the rest must overflow, past this numb, speechless brain, run off in excess like a waterfall. This is all I can take tonight. No more.

I go home and sleep, stunned. My brain, in the morning, has a hangover of comprehension. I have joined another world. I'm a survivor again. These strange once-religious people have understood, and they, too, have felt it: the two voices, the pressure cooker, the stifling of one's voice, the anger and resentment, the strength of oneself becoming doubt, the beauty of oneself destroyed, hidden, turned inside out, recast as sin.

Kitchen Story

"Who else did he sleep with?"

"Not me, thank God," I answer. "I always wondered about that—I mean, why he asked me to send a picture of myself. Thank God I'm not photogenic!"

Zack says, "I'm pretty sure he slept with Sally, and then there was Frank McCollum's wife. I know they slept together."

"And we know about Kristin, and Jerri, and Sabrina."

"He must have slept with Debbie—I just feel it, he must have," I say.

"I did once," volunteers Mona. She and her husband still live in Chicago. They've been up to visit us a couple of times. They've already joined Forum, a personal-growth cult; Mona's position is that everything in life is a cult. However, in the cult-recovery world, this is known as cult-hopping, a phenomenon that happens to some of the people who don't process their experiences and learn the details of how mind control works. Nonetheless, they are quite as glad as the rest of us to be out of the O.

"You did? That must of been weird—how'd that happen?" Julie asks.

"We'd had one of those meetings in Madison—some technical writing issue about the accounting package. You know we'd booked a hotel room and some folks had come from Minneapolis—Jerri, you'd been there, and others of us had come down from Chicago, me and Suzanne had come together."

Mona doesn't seem too bothered by this, she's telling it like it was a funny story, a one-night stand, nothing much to be made of it.

"It was late at night. Everyone else had left, and I was getting ready to go, and he just suggested I stay. I didn't see why not, so I did. But I thought it was kind of strange. It was almost like, I was there, so he might as well fuck me."

We sigh a collective sigh and move on.

"Anyone else?" asks Julie as we pursue this unpleasant inventory. She continues, "Well, I know he slept with Charlene. For quite a while actually. Even though she wasn't in the O. She finally dumped him; he was getting controlling about her kid, and then he just came around when he wanted sex, and she couldn't deal with it anymore."

Julie rests her chin on her hands, her elbows leaning on the kitchen table. Charlene had been her best friend through high school and their early twenties, and Julie had dropped her cold, like the rest of us had done with friends and family, on instruction from leadership. Friends were bad, they represented "social unity," one of the more serious ideological errors.

We finish the evening with reminiscences of the TSRs (Tactical Sexual Relationships) into which Theo had ordered people. This was his favorite method of breaking up couples—"breaking down their bourgeois identity," he called it. When I later began reading the memoirs of people who'd lived through the Cultural Revolution in China, I found we were not so unique in this. Well, TSRs were strictly our own, but the wrenching apart of lovers was a well-worn story. Love, as George Orwell told us decades earlier, is mightily subversive.

One day, in the kitchen, Betty said: "He came to Chicago right after . . . after the killing. I think I was the first person he saw there. He was different than I'd ever seen him before—dressed in fatigues and a black beret—like a Panther you know. Before he was so low-key, in jeans and flannel shirts. But this time he was shaky, very scared and jumpy.

"He told me what happened. He said this guy had disrespected him. They had a fight, and Theo thought the guy had a gun. So he ran to a drawer and got his gun. I don't know why he had a gun in that house; he wasn't staying there, he was just working on it. He got the gun, and he told me, 'I was pistol-whipping him and the gun went off.'

"I asked him, 'How could that happen?' and he just looked at me— remember how he would look?—and he said, he kind of rose up out of his nervousness, he switched it off, he looked at me and he said, 'You'd never do that for the class struggle.'

"He said it with such contempt. So, I didn't ask any more questions. He told me to unload his stuff from the car. He wouldn't go down to the car. He didn't want the cops to see him, I suppose. Me and Bob got all his stuff out."

Betty's brown eyes hurt with the telling, still afraid of the secret.

The gun went off. If you pistol-whip somebody with a loaded gun, then the gun might go off. I saw the fight happening, replayed in my mind's eye. In the living room of 801 Sullivan, where I'd watched my son learn to walk, the blood carpeted over by then with new, cheap green shag. History remodeled. I could see history now, as it had really been: the young Kyle Ray, arms sprawled out, the gunshot through his young, black chest, his body falling through the air.

And then Theo, in the costume of a revolutionary, shaking and sweating on the run, telling the story, inventing reality as he went, building a reality of armed righteousness and feeding it to Betty. No, indeed, she could never have done that for the class struggle.

Kitchen Story

Betty: "I was trying to adopt a child. Theo said he knew a way to adopt a child—I think from Mexico or something. I can't remember now. He told me he needed $7,000. I gave it to him, and then I never heard anything more about it. When I asked him, he said I'd better learn my lesson—this was a lesson for me to learn to take care of my finances better.

"I did think he was crazy then. But then I still believed in him too—I thought it was just something going on with me and him and that he'd get over it. That he'd been hurt, damaged in prison and that he still had so much to contribute to the struggle. I really respected what he had to offer. I believed in the ITP. But after that, I did look after my money. I never let him have any more. I did learn a lesson from him, like he said.

"Although before, all those years I was in Chicago, when I was working for Dependable Computer Programs: he must have made tens of thousands of dollars off me then, because I was contracting, and he was billing me out and paying me maybe a third of what he billed. And he lied to me and didn't pay any of the withholding taxes, so I got stuck with a bill from the IRS, and I'm still paying that one off."

The next week Betty brought over a paper grocery bag. It was heavy and wrapped around with gray duct tape that had been peeled off and then replaced, leaving the corners hanging a little from the paper.

"I've had this for years," she said. "When I moved into 905 Sullivan I was told to look after it. I decided to open it last night."

Her face had a green tinge to it.

I took the bag from her.

And now I sit here typing out the insides to an anthem that has followed me all these years, something that stayed and could not be drowned out, only muted. The sounds of Victor Jara and his "Anthem to the People," the only tune I ever really learned—I could pick it out on the piano, me, the tone-deaf one. Or play it on my recorder, soulful and tinny like an Andean song, played on the mountains in the thin air.

> *Llevantate y mirate las manos,*
> *para crecer estrecha a las hermanos,*
> *juntos iremos, unidos en las sangre,*
> *Amen, Amen . . .*

> *Stand up and look at your hands,*
> *stretch out your hands to your brothers and sisters*
> *so you may grow.*
> *All of us together, united by blood,*
> *Amen, Amen . . .*

A grim bag of tricks, that's what Betty gave to me: notes, all kinds of notes from the moment Theo called Kristin, and Kristin called Debbie at work. Kristin and Debbie's handwritten notes, and pounds of court transcripts that I pull out of the paper bag, tell me how Debbie rushed from her programming job, telling her boss some quick lie (this we'd all done, was a skill we learned—how to disappear in the middle of a shift without getting fired) and met with Kristin and Theo at Byerly's, the supermarket restaurant. Already, so soon, still in shock from the murder, he had instructions for them.

Imagine the adrenaline. He can't be helpless and ask for help. He is the leader and must tell them what to do; they are incapable of acting independently or giving an honest and intelligent opinion on what to do in this crisis. No, he must work it out—what a responsibility to carry. He tells them, "Call the police, Kristin—arrange with your brother, he works for the State Attorney's office, go to the house with them and explain to them that this happened."

And then he constructs, with imprecision, because that is his style, and he is, not to be elitist but simply accurate, uneducated and cannot put a simple sentence together on paper—he constructs a scenario that it is up to Kristin to make believable, first to her brother, who will help her because he is her brother and loves her and trusts her and assumes there is some reason for her behavior (the way we all assume there is a reason for Theo's behavior, for the directives that do not make sense, for sudden changes in direction that cannot be explained rationally, but are acceptable once you also accept the "need to know" principle, which turns out to be a principle that is used largely to keep people out of the know, and to allow one figure to dominate and dictate for what amounts to generations at a time). He constructs a story of a recalcitrant tenant (later they will try to posthumously vilify him), asking for trouble, though perhaps not to be murdered.

Piecing together these documents, I'm like an investigator. I discover they wanted Kyle Ray out of the house; they wanted it to be an O. house, and he wouldn't move. They try to build a case to evict him. There's a list of his crimes: he left his bicycle in the front porch where it wasn't supposed to be; he used the washer/dryer—serious violations like that. Since when, I ask myself, is murder an acceptable means of eviction?

In these few moments at the restaurant, only minutes after the murder, Theo tells Debbie to take his truck. This will later cause problems in court; why is this white woman given his truck? Why not his girlfriend, Kristin, also a white woman and legal owner of the house in which the murder occurred? I am reading all this in the transcripts of the various court appearances and this question causes a lot of anxiety among the prosecutors and the police—it is not a normal arrangement familiar to them. It would fit if Theo was a pimp and Kristin and Debbie his hookers, but they've never seen hookers as well-grounded and educated as these two: one is a law student and the other a well-paid computer programmer; clearly these women do not have a financial need, and there is no sign of drugs. What the policemen don't understand is that they *are* prostitutes, but prostitutes of power, paid in self-esteem and self-belief; they would give anything to Theo, he has taken their selfhoods entirely and held them hostage, and without knowing they are imprisoned they give of themselves night and day to his madness. The policemen in Minneapolis have not run across this kind of mind control before. In California it would be more easily recognized. California is the capital of cults, and there the memory of Jim Jones still sets people's hearts afire with grief at the lives lost: the greatest Electric Kool-Aid Acid Test, the women and children sacrificed at the feet of the great god, not too far from the ancient Mayan bloodstones, where the blood of women and children was collected also, but thousands of years ago in another time.

But in Minneapolis the only model is black pimp and white hooker, or black man and white battered woman, or a black man with a happy white woman, married, or not, with beautiful brown, loved children. All of these are commonplace in Minnesota and well-understood by law enforcement. But the two financially secure white women, the confusion of property, the awesome dedication and loyalty, the brick wall of hostility to the police, this is a formula they cannot identify and in that the trail goes cold, left to the FBI when it becomes apparent he has crossed state lines.

The FBI found white men also involved—obviously not hookers, no appearance of being gang members; they are far too middle class and sincere for that. And the white men are able to alert their families and prevent the leaking of information from that source. The families (nice, white families, doctors, dentists!) say nothing, say they know nothing, but more than that, offer up a kind of prideful silence, that they know nothing, but believe in their wayward children, that whatever it is they are caught up in, they are the kind of parents always to think the best of their children. That, after all, Zack and Matthew, Bill and Walt, were always the first to think of other people, were do-gooders really as they grew into adults. They will believe the best of their sons, no matter what should happen to them.

The FBI runs into a dead end, so I learn from these peculiar archives. There is no trace of Theo before 1972. He has no known identity, beyond a stint as a carpet-layer working out of a small town in Mississippi. They have only a faded picture of him with a small black boy we assume is his son. Surely the FBI could figure this thing out? They must have had hundreds of cases of power-mongers, of cults, of organized crime. It is surely all the same: decent people, or not so decent people, trapped and manipulated by a con man driven by the need to control, to inflict pain before pain is inflicted upon him. It is not a new story, or unique.

Perhaps it was too small. After all, no drugs, clearly no strength to the organization. And a handful of benign programs traceable through Kristin and Debbie: a small and scruffy childcare center, likewise for a health-food bakery. Nothing too much to get excited about.

And the victim was a young black man. Important only to his community, to the North Side. Not worth bothering about. Hardly at all.

I find in the dusty bag of tricks a carbon copy of my report of the first visit by the FBI to 801 Sullivan where I lived, the duplex where the murder had occurred, unknown to me, three years earlier.

To: P.O.O.
From: Claire.
Date: 2/1/83

An F.B.I. agent came to 8xx [our sophisticated code to protect the identity of the house]. About six-foot, 165 pounds. Mustache, dark

brown hair. Blue or black tailored overcoat—possibly with a dark
red short scarf. Age: early thirties . . .

I am taken aback by the familiar typeface of my long-abandoned electric
typewriter. The documents are making my hands dirty. I have to stop for a
while.

How things do come around.

CHAPTER 35

I've got the rest of the bag of tricks. The O. used all the systematic, proce-dural methods they knew to try to smear the victim of Theo's rage. The first thing they did, after Theo fled, was to steal Kyle Ray's papers and personal belongings from his apartment—because, of course, Kristin was the landlady and had access to 801. Among the stack of files in the grocery bag, I find a fat manila envelope filled with these bits of Ray's life. Strangely, one of the accompanying files contains photocopies of each of these items. I imagine Debbie at an all-night copy shop surreptitiously copying these fragments of evidence they're collecting to deny to themselves, as much as anyone, Theo's culpability. But here in my hands I have the originals. Most of these items are wrinkled and aging—after all they've been hidden away for fifteen years now in this manila envelope. Only looked at a few times, by Theo and Debbie and, finally, me.

There is a photo-copied page with the words: *"PARTY TIME 4089 Clinton Ave S."* handwritten about thirty times, as if someone had been assigned to write lines as a punishment, but clearly, this was for fun.

There is a court document, inviting someone to appear on a case of aggravated forgery.

A surrender of driver's license form.

A pink form headed "Office Memo," requesting Kyle Ray to call a Dave Brown on Aurora Ave. re: employment.

A formal letter from the Minneapolis Public Schools indicating that, due to a shortage of credits, Brian, Kyle's younger brother, would not graduate into twelfth grade that year. In addition there are computerized report cards indi-cating an astonishingly high rate of absenteeism and a failure in every class. Also, a check stub from Delaria's Kitchen showing twenty-five hours worked

338

in a week-long period and net earnings of sixty dollars. He will work but apparently won't go to school.

There is a letter to Brian from his mother. The envelope is pink with a design of hearts, flowers, and doves on the outside, even where the address area is. His mother's return address is L.A. She moved there not long before, the letter reveals. Her writing is a flowing cursive. The letter tells him that she doesn't have much to say, but she misses him and hopes he is well.

A scrawled, handwritten note:

> Brian
> I told you, don't give my phone number out, and you did it again. Some dude called here very impolite for you. Next time you're moving out. Also take out trash tonight!

More stuff from the state—the unemployment office, receipts . . .

A blue examination book for Kyle Ray on the subject of criminal law— the grade is B+.

Two photos of a newly walking baby. The baby is standing on the out-door-carpeted front steps of a porch.

A light-blue invitation. On the cover are a white man and woman danc-ing in evening dress—circa 1920s style. Inside it says:

> Super D.J.
> Demands Your Presence
> at
> 801 Sullivan Ave, No.
> 1.00 am until.
> For Champagne and Hors d'oeuvres
> April 30th, 1980
> BIRTHDAY

There is an old, cracked photo of an attractive young black woman holding a long-stemmed wine glass. Her eyes are all you can see of her face, they are inviting, looking straight at the camera. A piece of old tape is still stuck to the photo.

A small notepad, something has been spilled on it, so many of the hand-written ink messages have smeared. In the space for "Name" on the cover can be discerned, "Super DJ—Kyle Ray." It contains names and numbers and notes. Some seem to be notes for his radio show—announcements of events and the like. An address for a theatrical lighting company.

"Final Notice of Gas Shut Off"—from the Minnesota Gas Company.

A form letter to Lavada Watkins from the Hennepin County Welfare office regarding her request for assistance for Damage Deposit.

A pink receipt for a cashier's check.

An envelope containing several blue Pillsbury pay stubs for Lavada Evans. The pay stub shows a $1.00 deduction per pay period for the United Way. I remember how hard it was to refuse those forced "charitable" deductions at work. They make you fill out a form with everyone's name listed on it and your deduction is made public. Even as I resented it, I still gave, like Lavada, $1.00 per pay period. Regular rate: $4.645 per hour. Amount for the two-week period: $360.00. So, she was working full time.

Ah, here's something I recognize immediately. A half-sheet of plain white typing paper like so many memos I received in the O. It's the carbon copy of a typed note and it reads:

Kyle—
Renovation work will be done on both floors of the house. You will have to move out by May 7th.
Kristin

I find it interesting that the note is not dated. I wonder, when Kristin wrote that note, what she imagined for the future? Or Kyle? That this was the beginning of his last journey, the start of a story that ended with a fight, a pistol-whipping with a loaded gun by the man who captivated Kristin. "I was pistol-whipping him and the gun went off." It went off and it shot Kyle through the shoulder and ricocheted, (off a bone?—no, from the muscle, the autopsy report said—they kept that, too. It's in a file somewhere here . . .) and the bullet went through his heart, and then he died.

This is odd. There is a photocopy (must have been made by our comrades) of a package of rolling papers. It's an elegant art nouveau package. On the sheet of paper is photo-copied both the front and back of the package— whoever copied it opened the package and spread it out on the copier. There is a picture on the front of a bespectacled man reading a newspaper at a Parisian café table covered with a checkered cloth. He is looking up from a newspaper entitled *Revue Scientifique*. In front of him is a small cup of coffee—a *café exprès*—and a glass of water. He is smoking, of course, and a long, curled plume of white smoke rises from his cigarette. The words "Club Cabaret Width" are spelled out in letters that curl inward blackly upon themselves.

I turn the photo-copy around to read the words on the back of the copied package of rolling papers—the text is adorned on either side by art nouveau curlicues resembling the shape of a harp. I start to wonder what color the original packet was; here I see only white, black, and gray. The text reads:

> *Hand made Club papers*
> *have no additives. So pure*
> *fibers entwine when wet and*
> *leave no ash when burned.*
> *They are light as a*
> *butterfly's wing.*

I wonder if I'll find the actual papers here.

More party invitations. One of them announces:

> *"NO RIFF RAFF, you know who you are."*
> *A champagne party—all night—Happy Birthday. Disco by Kyle Ray,*
> *Billy Bump. Hosted by Franchel Batton.*

Well, the guy was a D.J. This was his job, after all.

A glossy four-by-six photo, in a cardboard display, of a young white woman. It's a studio photo, or it could even be a high-school photo. She looks to be in her late teens. Brown wavy hair, a gold chain around her neck, plucked eyebrows and sweet brown eyes. Her shoulders are held well back, and her head is turned to the camera with a small-mouthed smile. No name, no note on it.

Now there are stacks of printed invitations for various private discos. This is obviously a whole sub-culture of which I am completely ignorant. The common theme seems to be Kyle as D.J. and the availability of free champagne. The image of Johannesburg shebeens comes to my mind. Not that I was ever in one, but I feel as if I knew them because the shebeen was well documented in the South African literature of the fifties and sixties and in the songs I grew up hearing:

Back of the Moon, boys,
Back of the Moon boys,
Back of the Moon is where the folks unwind!

As a child I had hazy images of the Back of the Moon as a secret place bathed in pennywhistle music and the soft, silvery threads of moonlight that existed behind the painted door of a stage set. It was only as I grew older that I discovered that the Back of the Moon was the name of a township shebeen, probably only the name and the music romantic. I didn't imagine the smell of beer or of *skokiaan*, the spittle of drunks or the shoving of fists flailing in an alcoholic haze. What stayed in my memory were the pictures in our family album of wild *kwela* dancers, swinging their hips dangerously around the dance floor and the wide-open African laughter I grew up with, along with the jive and jazz and the richness of color.

A note. Perhaps written by Brian:

Kyle call J Cotton at home
She wants a ride to the fox trap at six o'clock.
6-22-80

That was the day before Kyle's death.
A full-page ad for a disco:

Let's get serious—Disco Tour 1980
Featuring: Kyle Ray, Billy Bump, Pharoah Black, Jerry Burley, Jimmy Harris, James Brown. $3.00 advance. $3.50 at door. Oxford Recreation Center.

Wait a minute, is that the Jimmy Harris of Jimmy Jam Harris fame? Probably. He made it—one of the country's most successful record producers now.

On the back of one of the full-page invitations—notes in pen:

1. Tornado Watch. 40—60 degrees tonight. Low to mid-60's. High 80 degrees. Showers tonight. Mostly cloudy Fri, Sat. Keep your eye on us to [illegible]. Tickets. Toots concert Sunday night.

An almost empty address book—only four or five addresses in the whole thing. At the back is a section to record birthdays. There are the following entries:

April:	Leila Ray 1 year old April 24, 1978
May:	Kyle Ray *My Daddy*
June:	Lavada's birthday June 4. Leila's mom.
July:	Russel Taylor, Karms Ray, Aunt Pauline.
August:	Snooky 770-5778
September:	Grady.

I'm nearly at the end of the pile. The last sheet of paper is just names and numbers, it's grimy and crumpled.

I stuff all the papers back in the envelope. I'm getting good at this—I didn't cry once. And I don't feel the dirt invading me: the dirt of someone else's life, as ended by Theo, and then these paper pieces of it ransacked and stolen from his apartment and kept, away from the police all these years and used to build an offensive against a dead man. The best defense is always an offense. That's what they say. And that's exactly what Theo and his high-priced lawyer did: took all these documents and built a "case" claiming that Ray was a pimp, a drug dealer, and so on and so forth—generally a "bad element."

True or not—did it imply a vigilante death sentence? Does the fact the victim did not have a pure character entitle Theo to end his life? These are questions we've gone over time and time again.

Then there is the evidence of his community, the 3,000 people who attended his memorial service. Like most of us, perhaps Kyle Ray had some good in him and some bad. Perhaps he had a big ego. And one thing Theo couldn't stand was to be out-ego'd by someone, especially a black man. I can see him going to get that gun, brandishing it to show Ray that he could no longer disrespect Theo. But Ray was a man of the streets—he'd been around. The fight. Theo has flipped—gone completely over into his psychotic hatred. Pistol-whips the guy (this is giving Theo the benefit of the doubt—after all, it is his story that he pistol-whipped him). The gun goes off. That'll happen with a loaded gun, won't it?

Among the court transcripts and the newspaper clippings and the legal research on similar murder charges and all the rest of the debris that surrounds me now, I pull out of the grocery bag a memento of Debbie's, some evidence of her role.

According to Debbie's notes, written in her neat, controlled handwriting (the pages have been pulled out of a tiny notepad, they are held together with a large paperclip, which has left rust stains in the shape of itself on the first and last page of this collection), this is what transpired:

> *Contractor—sympathized* [what the hell does that mean?]
> *Contacted me at work (10.00). Saw him at Byerly's by where I work. He told me he was working—& K. renewed conflict—K came down the stairs—HAND IN POCKET, had an attitude. Ed* [AKA—who else . . .] *sensed there was trouble—(I'd called lawyer re: trespassing today).* [Well, they were trying to kick him out, weren't they?]

Debbie's notes continue:

> *Given K's nature—what I mean: NO RESPECT—sent notice of certain limits given construction work and all went totally disre-garded—busted off lock on basement door 2-3 times, used wash-er-dryer, parked car in back, blocking truck, late parties, urine all over hallway, gambling table, tough scene.*
> *Ed* [you know who] *thot K. had a gun—Ed had a gun in kitch. drawer—K. kept following him around, yelling at him while he worked, cursing. K. had hand in pocket all along—threatened Ed repeatedly.*
> *"I'm gonna put an end to this shit"—provocative—*
> *Ed asked him why did he busted open basement door?*
> *K: "I don't wanna deal w/ that shit."*
> *K. cursed more &* [here the words "physically threatened" are crossed out] *moved toward Ed. Ed managed to get away from him to get his gun, when he got gun, K. grabbed Ed.*
> *Scuffle*
> *Ed was trying to push Kyle out of apt and gun went off, hit K. in arm.* [Not what he said to Betty, later, in Chicago. What about the pistol whipping?]
> *Ed called info—asked for ambulance. Operator kept insisting his name—he said Ed James & then tried to help K. (tore open his shirt, or something)—*
> *Then K. stopped breathing & Ed got scared &* [the word "ran" is crossed out] *took off.*

(He was in his truck & said something about Canada) [This must have been someone's bright idea—a red herring to steer the cops away from Chicago?]

That's when I saw him last. He said he'll stay in touch.

B. went home [Bonnie was Kristin's code name.]

A new page:

dead 10-12 hrs —
detective Hartigan

blood on stairs

9.00—B.M. lvg address 801 —

Kyle.

Another page. In pencil—Debbie writing still, her writing smaller but more untidy:

I get clarity when it's put out, explained, but don't sustain it when get in the real conditions.

CHAPTER 36

Journal Entry

September 6, 1991

> *Offer up my self*
> *Lose my self*
> *Find my self*

That Halloween, Ana dressed up as Batman. She was now a three-year old with intense brown eyes, thick eyebrows and the muscular body of a natural athlete. The black costume with its yellow bat emblazoned on her chest lit her up, transformed her, as she wished, into something all-powerful. Luis was a purple-caped Shredder, an evil hero with a sword, a scabbard, and a foil-covered helmet—but he was too thin, and his smile too wide to properly frighten us.

    We trick and treated for a while. Ted had come to the house—he was easing up towards me now. At the end of our tortuous mediation sessions where we untangled every piece of our shared lives in preparation for divorce, at the last session, he had finally said he wasn't ready to set a date for the divorce, but that now he would go into marriage counseling with me. I was stunned. But I accepted it, too. I didn't want to lose him, to lose our family. And I had a mission to save him that meant that while he was still in the O. I didn't have to think about much else—didn't have to think about the future, didn't have to jump into the rebuilding of life that I could not face. Saving him had become my one drive. That and learning to have fun again and enjoying beauty.

And finally, a week or so before Halloween, he had moved towards me, holding my hand in that embarrassing moment in the park with his brother and sister-in-law. He could not speak words of mending to me. He could only show me how he felt with this inarticulate gesture, one which disturbed me because it left so much unsaid.

Later he'd asked me to dinner at the little house he'd rented. The kids were bubbly, delighted to have us together at one table. They laughed and played, and we loved them together and put them to bed in the temporary room he had set up for them after he'd moved out of Suzanne and Zack's attic.

The children slept. In the living room, Ted and I talked. He'd been reading Vigotsky, a Soviet philosopher and linguist—a kind of Soviet Noam Chomsky. This was an intellectual domain in which Ted had been interested through his own initiative, and it was his way of asserting some independence from the O. (I did not know at the time that Vigotsky provided the theoretical underpinnings for another Left-wing/psychotherapy cult: the New Alliance Party.) I encouraged his interest, was pleased he was starting to think again, could sense him feeling his way out of this terrible black corner into which he was painted. And then, clumsily, like a high-school boy on a date, he moved towards me and kissed me and soon we were tangled back together in a physical embrace.

But part of me was gone. So much had separated us I could not fall together again as before. I let him make love to me. I was his medicine, an embrace to return to, a softness on which to land from his great fall. But for me? It was an empty arrival, though I tried to welcome him back.

In the morning we returned to our old house for breakfast. And then it began to snow. And snow. It did not stop snowing for twenty-four hours and the snow piled up, twenty-four inches of it in one of the heaviest snowstorms ever seen in the Twin Cities. So, of course, Ted stayed over that night in the house we used to share. My red quilt with its fiery suns covered us again. The children had small goldmines of Halloween candy, and they had us together. That night they slept like cubs in a cave, safe and warm, protected.

The next day the whole city was snowed in. But this was the day I was to meet Steve Hassan the exit-counselor. This was some months after I'd been in touch with him, after he had met with Ted's family, and now he was here on other business, and I'd arranged to meet with him to get more advice on how to help Ted.

"Absolutely no travel advised," the radio and TV repeated all morning. "Only emergency vehicles should be on the road. All taxi services are canceled."

Here I had Ted and the two children with me and Steve due to arrive at the airport. Even though Ted was still in the O., I had been clear with him that I was becoming involved in the cult-awareness movement. I told him the near-truth, that I had to pick up an acquaintance at the airport. Despite the unrelenting weather, he seemed to accept this with equanimity. Anyway, it was the kind of thing we always did in the O.—going out in conditions no one else in their right minds would brave—only now I wasn't doing it for the Revolution, I was doing it for Ted. He helped me dig the snow and ice out of the driveway, and, with a couple of neighbors pushing the car, I managed to get on the road.

I remembered back to my first year in Minneapolis when I was the customer-service representative at the Bakery. There was a huge storm again—this time in spring, an April storm. That was when I lived with Jerri and Ted in 801. We all worked at the Bakery then: Jerri was the manager and Ted was in charge of personnel. No one could get to work for their shift, but Ted and Jerri decided the Bakery must open, that this was our duty as committed cadre—bread would be baked! So the three of us trooped down the middle of Olson Highway, wrapped in layers and layers of clothes, the entire city silent around us, our footprints cutting a lonely trail down the deserted freeway. Three cold little humans, doing our duty. Somehow we got to the Bakery that day. And we baked bread. Even tried to deliver it later in the day. Of course, only a handful of our accounts were even open to accept delivery. It was only as the snow cleared the next couple of days that we discovered that every other bakery in the city had shut down for the day; that our efforts, though heroic, were foolish.

So here I was again, ploughing through snow against all the warnings of the authorities. I made it to the airport. I found the tall and skinny Hassan and drove him across town as he huddled in his seat, wearing only a thin leather jacket and a narrow scarf against the cold. With a Minnesotan's savvy and my own brand of determination, I hauled that car through ice patches and snow drifts and parked at the top of the hill by Bill and Julie's place, explaining to Hassan that I would never make it back up the hill if I took the car down there. He was shaken when we arrived, having put his life in my hands—he knew from his own experience what recovering cult members were going through.

At Bill and Julie's we sat around the table and drank tea. I explained Ted's current situation: the week spent by the sea with his family, them surrounding him with love and asking hard questions until the early hours of the morning. And how I'd showed him, recently, the clippings of Kyle Ray's murder and his casual and enraging response: "It doesn't seem that significant." I recounted our hours, first in mediation—that bloody dissecting of our lives—and then his agreement to do marriage counseling. I told him how the counselor seemed to understand a good part of the cult issue and kept Ted focused on making his own decisions within his own ethical framework, while I sat there, resentful and hopeful at the same time, wanting attention also, but giving over my lesser need to Ted's greater one.

And then, this month, Ted's reaching out wordlessly to me. I still remembered Hassan's early words to me: "Are you sure you still want to be in this marriage? You know, most cult marriages don't work once you're out of the cult." Then I had answered, almost instantly, "Yes, I'm sure. We have a good marriage."

That was before, though. Now? I still wanted Ted out. I mostly wanted him back with me, although I knew there'd be problems. But problems were something I was used to dealing with. It wouldn't be the bitter struggle between Theo and me that had marked this period.

Hassan sat at the table, Bill on one side of him, me on the other and Julie sitting across from us. He leaned his leathered elbows on the table and talked, and then he leaned back, and his hands made talmudic patterns in the air as he talked. He was casual, not worried.

"He's on his way out," he announced. "It's just a matter of time. Don't push him. Just let him have time. The most important thing is for him to make his own decision. But it sounds like, given he's seeing you again, Alex, that he has. I'm sure that can't be allowed easily in the group. He must be taking some flak for it. Keep doing what you're doing."

I wanted something more. Some medicine. Some psychological trick that would break the spell. But I trusted Hassan, too, and so I accepted this, tried to relax, tried to let things happen as they would.

Kitchen Story

I tell the others about rummaging in the lockbox in the basement after the scare with the F.B.I. coming to 801, the time we were told to clean out our files and lock up any "closed" documents.

Now, sitting with my ex-comrades at the kitchen table, I find out what it means to be paddled, because more than one person there has either been paddled themselves, witnessed such an event, or actually meted out the punishment. Zack tells of fighting off a group of people (Ted among them) and then finally submitting as they pinned him to the bread bench at the bakery, pulled down his pants and beat him with a one-by-four. His crime? He had forgotten to change the production schedule for a holiday shift. It wasn't the pain, he tells us, that bothered him so much, but the depth of the humiliation. He thought about leaving the O. after that, he says, but he didn't. His logic was that nothing much worse could happen after all. If he could take that, he could take anything.

Ted's crime, Jerri tells us, was that he'd met a woman in a math class and, from what I later piece together (from the tone of his voice the few times he ever mentioned her to me), he had fallen in love with her. This was before our marriage.

Somehow Jerri found out that he was seeing a woman not in the O. Perhaps he was forgetting his assignments, or making security errors— maybe he stayed out all night too often, and Jerri began to ask where he had been. In any case, it came out. He had never told me about the beating— only that he'd had to write a self-criticism and break off the relationship. Years later he would still say that breaking up with her was the only fair thing to do.

I remember wondering at that; wondering what he felt about it, if he still cared about her? For the truth was, he had been paddled for it. By whom? Jerri? Debbie? Dave? He had loved a woman—and for that been beaten!

In the kitchen, among the talking, the laughter and the wine, I work out the dates and realize that it was shortly after this that he sent me that first letter introducing himself. Ah, that must have been another Method of Correction—I can almost hear it: "Develop a Personal Relationship with an O. cadre based on mutual development." I catch my breath at the thought of what that meant to our marriage, our love. He had been beaten for loving. Now maybe I could see why it was so hard for him to meet my eyes, to let me see inside.

Just after Christmas, Ted moved back in. I kept Bill and Julie away from him. He still saw them as the enemy, the betrayers. He hadn't left the O. yet, but we had agreed to disagree, and we had the children, after all, and our history to bind us together. Occasionally we talked about the O.; I trod delicately, using what I knew of exit-counseling techniques to try to keep from getting angry, to keep him from being defensive, to encourage his open thinking, and to discourage his thought-stopping. But it was very hard. He didn't want to think about it, and he didn't trust me enough to explore his doubts.

I returned to my practice of monitoring the memos in his briefcase. Until he got all the way out, I felt it necessary to keep tabs on Theo's influence, and I stopped feeling guilty about my eavesdropping. I discovered that now Ted had been directed to investigate a new computer product: Smalltalk. This was an "object-oriented" computer language; once again, the O. was hot on the heels of the latest buzz-words in the industry. Even Ted was able to see the humor in Theo's idea of putting the Internal Transformation Process on Smalltalk so that . . . what? They could export the computerized ITP to third world countries? Sell it to childcare centers? I didn't know the long-term plan, but there surely was one.

It was a strange period. We were happy, all of us, because we were back together—a family. But Ted couldn't talk. We still talked only about the children or about work. Nothing else.

Every morning I drove the children to the daycare center. I hated going there. On the one hand, I had my new-found life and liberty. The freedom to choose what I would do, the clothes I would wear—so many choices I could make now. I could find my own style again. I could go to movies I wanted to see without needing a justification. I began to read again: a voracious reading of novels, of memoirs of ex-communists and socialists: Doris Lessing; Arthur Koestler; George Orwell; Chinese authors who had lived through the Cultural Revolution; books by people who had been in cults: Scientology, therapy cults, EST. I was stunned by the reflection of myself I found in these volumes as vast landscapes of experience unfolded before me, deep and rich in detail as good books are supposed to be.

And then, here was daily life: trying to re-establish a relationship with Ted—with whom I could discuss nothing of this richness that I was re-discovering. And driving back, so to speak, into the jaws of the O. every morning, taking my children into this day-care center where I had to face Suzanne or Debbie, glaring at me in silent condemnation, amid the years of depressed history of that place. Ted still insisted the children go there, and I had decided this wasn't the fight I wished to engage; the most important thing was for him to freely make his own decisions again. But it was at some cost to me, though the children were indifferent; they knew nothing better.

I had pulled myself out of the O., and yet here I was, still stuck in it, returning daily to have my nose rubbed in its mess.

One day I walked the children into the building, holding each of them by the hand. We stopped by the coat hooks, and, as I stooped to unzip Ana's jacket, I saw the curly brown hair and the sad-eyed smile of young P___ . I looked up, expecting to see Kristin, her mother; instead I saw a short, stocky black man in a leather jacket standing across the room. The muscles around my ribs locked up, and my breath tightened.

"Ana! Luis! Get your coats off!" I took them by the hand again, fiercely, and decided to stand up straight, to look him in the eye. I recognized Theo by context and by the faint aura that had alerted me before, that day he leaned on his shovel at Julie's house. He heard my voice and its distinctive, mixed-up accent, and by that recognized me also, as, not just another day-care mother, but a departed member of his rapidly dwindling flock. He turned away immediately and sidled off, swiveling his eyes to check me out with his peripheral vision, and then left by the back door so he wouldn't have to walk by me. (He must have been a master at peripheral vision—always looking out without letting anyone else see in.) I stared after his leather-jacketed back as the children pulled on my hands. He seemed to me to be all hunched over, his head pulled in on a short neck, like my memory of the Ceaucescus: a blind turtle startled from its hiding place.

My recognition of his fear did not diminish my own; I knew how he could act when threatened.

Perhaps he went up to his office—Julie had told me how he had used some of the day-care center's grant funds to build himself an office on the second floor of their building. From that day on, whenever I went to the center, I looked up to the second floor to catch a glimpse of him—Theo, the man who had silently ruled my life for ten years. And now, every time I left the center, I cursed to myself—he was up there where he could look down on us—as ever, in a position of power. He could see me, but I couldn't see him. How long would it be this way?

I would walk to my car with my head held high; he would not steal my dignity again. I would get in my car, drive around the corner and then break down, turn the radio up full blast to muffle the sound of my screams as I raged and cursed until my throat ached.

"I hate you, Theo! You bastard! You are POISON, SHIT, CRAZY—

Motherfucker! Son of a bitch!" I struck the steering wheel over and over again. Then, I would sit exhausted, take a few minutes to compose myself and drive the rest of the way to work. There I went first to the bathroom to wash the tears from my face and try to cool the swelling around my eyes. Then I could go to my office acting simply as a project manager—nothing unusual about *my* life.

I was trying to give Ted the space to make his decision about the O.— one which, even to me, now seemed inevitable—it was just a question of how he was going to find a way to leave without too great a loss of face.

The end came soon after. The situation was becoming intolerable to me, the rage I hurled out in the upholstered shell of my Toyota was beginning to spill out elsewhere. I had run out of patience with Ted.

I borrowed a video, *The Wave*, from one of my Free Minds colleagues and one night after the children were in bed, I turned it on and sat on the cat-scratched couch to watch it. Casually, I suggested to Ted that he might be interested in it. He wouldn't sit by me on the couch, he couldn't pretend to that permanent an interest, but on his way through the room he stopped, leaned against the door jamb and then watched, intently, for the next half hour or so.

I first saw *The Wave* at a "walk-aways" exit-counseling that Nancy and I attended, put on by one of the ex-cult member support groups. *The Wave* is based on a true story. A history teacher in California tries to explain to his class how Hitler rose to power and wielded such influence over so many. The children are horrified by the stacks of bony bodies shown to them in the movies of concentration camps.

"How could people do that to each other?" they want to know. Some are crying. It is too painful to believe that this really happened. They want to know: "Why? How could this happen?"

In a sincere effort to answer their questions, the teacher studies Hitler's methods and, without informing the children, begins a pedagogical exercise. He forms a club in the school. Only certain of the kids are allowed to join— it's exclusive: they are specially chosen and praised. Everything within the club is secret; they mustn't tell the outsiders because the outsiders cannot under-stand them or their purpose. When one of the children tries to step out of line, he is immediate in sharp reproval—a reproval with the shadow of a physical threat behind it. Students are told to cut off their relationships with the non-members. They are not to listen to their parents but only to him. They have their own language, their own symbol (the Wave of the title), their own uniform and salute. They chant their slogan: "Discipline, Unity, Truth!" over and over again at the beginning of each meeting. They begin to feel proud as they become, indeed, disciplined and united. The teacher keeps them busy, overloaded with club activities, that seem, from the outside, to have no purpose. He tells the students in the club they are transforming themselves, helping each other, helping the school. They are becoming strong so that their club and their school will be strong also. When questions are asked, he confuses them with convoluted answers that turn the question back on the questioner and end up being challenges to their loyalty.

One of the students, a slender, brown-haired girl, begins to fight back. She realizes what he's doing and that he's gone too far. The teacher has become drunk with his own power—all these children are following him blindly. The experiment has gone out of control. The girl confronts him and turns him in to the administration, and after some resistance he agrees he will end the experiment—his way.

Finally, he organizes a culminating event, the special goal towards which they strive, a rally where he will reveal to them the great truth for which they have all been working.

Hundreds of the club members convene in the school auditorium, all uniformed in their light blue shirts and wave-embossed armbands. The young lieutenants that the teacher has appointed (the elite within the elite) lock the doors. Two large projection screens hang on each side of the stage. The teacher leads them in their chant: "Discipline, Unity, Truth!" and then steps to the podium.

"Today," he announces, "I will tell you that we are not alone. We are, in fact, part of an international youth organization. In schools all over the world, Wave clubs like ours have been organizing for Truth, Strength and Purity."

The students gasp, turn to each other, finally, applaud. They are so happy! This wonderful thing is, after all, bigger than themselves!

"And now," the teacher continues, "We have a message from our Leader . . ."

The students quiet down until there is complete silence. The projection screens turn bright with the projector beams that travel over the heads of the blue-shirted youngsters, who lean forward, eager in their chairs, waiting for the revelation of the one who will lead them. Through the dusty lightbeams, images begin to appear—it takes just a second, that's all—then there he is, the unmistakable black mustache jerking and quivering above the mouth that is shrieking at an adoring audience. The camera pulls back as his arm shoots up in the air, past the slick, sideways part of his hair, and there is Hitler, larger than life, his fingers pointed like a dagger in that poisonous salute.

There is silence, then a burst of collective grief as the students break down in anger or despair. It's a lesson taught too hard. They understand, now, the answer to their questions, "Why? How?" but they have been damaged in the process. They have put their *selves* into this experiment. They hurt inside. Some, the trailing credits tell us, will carry permanent reminders of their unknowing participation in this dangerous exercise in mind control.

I was with Nancy when I saw this video; afterwards as we walked the corridors of the empty church building, I turned to her. She was generous and full of feeling as she held me in her young arms and let me cry. Yes, fascism was the end result of my life's work to become a revolutionary. The others in the exit-counseling had moved away respectfully. Bruce, the counselor, has seen this reaction before.

But now, it was months later, back in my living-room. The video ended. Ted stood impassive. Then he left the room. God knows what he was feeling. I followed him out.

"How are you feeling?" I tried.

He shrugged his shoulders. Then looked at me. "That was a true story?"

"Yeah."

"Hmm. I don't see that it's got that much to do with the O."

Goddamn him! *You are so fucking stubborn,* I thought to myself, *I know there is feeling under there.*

A couple of days later, the phone rang. It stopped after two rings. Then it rang again. Oh shit! Oh *shit!* It was years since I'd had that sickening feeling, counting the number of rings of the phone to see if it was for me. We hadn't used the code for years—but of course, now that I wasn't in the O. and Ted was back living with me, apparently the O. felt moved to use it again. God knows none of them wanted to speak to me.

The phone was still ringing so I picked it up. Suzanne spoke: "About the meeting tonight . . ." she said, thinking, of course, that I was Ted.

"This is me," I interrupted. "Why are you using that code? Do you think

I don't know it's either you or Dave or Debbie who's going to call. What's the big secret? Is it going to kill you to have to hear me say, 'Hello' and pass the phone to Ted?"

She said, "I discussed it with Ted," and hung up the phone.

Ted came home from work, as dapper as ever in his well-cut suit, a gray-beige to suit his sandy hair, his shoes shined to a high-black polish. I turned on him as he came through the door. "What the *hell* is going on? What's this bullshit about using code rings now? *I'm not in the O. anymore.* So that stuff isn't going to happen in this house! Just get it out of this house!"

I felt a hysterical tickle rise in my throat. Goddamn them, they're not getting inside my house anymore!

Ted put down his briefcase—he looked surprised—I had been so patient and understanding recently. Where had this sudden rage come from?

"I'm sorry. I'll tell her not to call. I didn't realize it would upset you so much."

"I don't fucking care if she *calls*. It's the bloody *code* crap I can't deal with. It's so stupid. I know who they are. What do they think? It's just a control trip to make it so bloody mysterious—don't you see that it's part of building that magic aura that no one is allowed to question? It's all so mythical, magical! I don't know what you want to call it, but it's nonsense—it has no meaning. *Think* about it, for Christ's sake!"

"Okay," he said, "okay," backing away from my anger, moving upstairs to change his clothes.

The phone rang again, twice. Then again. I picked it up and shouted, "Who is it!"

The phone clicked, and the dial tone droned in my ear. I picked up the receiver, dialed Suzanne's number. She answered, and I shouted into the phone: "Don't you ever fucking call here again like that! Never! This is not an O. house anymore . . ."

I was ready to go on for a while, but she hung up.

I didn't know why this little detail got to me, but it did. I stormed around the kitchen slamming food and frying pans around. Ted had been back in the house for two months now, and we were still playing these games. It had been a year since I'd been out of the O. and I still had to deal with it, every day, through him. Enough.

The next day Ted was gone late. He got home after a meeting—I assumed with Suzanne. "I got into trouble over that call you made," he said.

"*Well?*" I was belligerent. That whole week I was simmering, just waiting for things to set me off. I knew Ted didn't want to be in the O. anymore, couldn't be, really, as long as he was with me. But he couldn't make that final break.

We sat in the TV room. His long, thin fingers picked at invisible scabs on his arms. Then he turned to me. "We decided it would be best to take the children out of the day-care center."

He announced it with a certain confidence, knowing how it had troubled me to go there every day, perhaps sure I would be relieved.

"We? . . . Who the hell is *WE?*"

It was like he'd lit a match in me. I was beyond the self-control I'd held onto all these months, letting him go his own way, go through his own process. It was back to the kids now and a certain entity: "WE," was making the decisions about them again, and it was a "WE" in which I was not included.

I stood up, bouncing on my feet like a prize fighter ready for the next round. "Who the hell is WE? You and me are the only WE who are supposed to be making decisions about our kids. How dare you come in here and tell me where they're going to daycare! Who has decided this?"

"Suzanne and I met. We decided it would be best."

"It's NOT HER DECISION! Don't you get it? It's *our* decision. Oh, Christ! I can't take it anymore, Ted. I just can't take it."

I couldn't believe that, after so long, he could still be doing this.

"It's got to stop. Are you getting out or not? It's not going to work like this anymore."

I slumped back on the couch, sunk my head in my hands, felt the tears trickling down the sides of my face. My shoulders were crumpled. I could not hold them up anymore. I couldn't hold us all up anymore. No more.

The next day he told me he was resigning from the O. He had one remaining task: to teach Suzanne how to run the print shop. I laughed curtly at this: "How long is it going to take to do that?"

"No, she used to work there. I've just got to update her, that's all. Then I'll be out. I want to be principled in how I leave."

I did not have the energy then to celebrate. That came back to me later. And then I was happy. My family was together again. Theo had no hold on us anymore. Together we could explore this strange future; like Rip van Winkle we could finally wake from our long sleep and taste the pleasures and the complex ambiguities of the world outside.

CHAPTER 37

Jerri lived through her own terror in these months. She became pregnant and had a miscarriage—her second. She did not sleep. Her body went haywire. She told me of driving her car and wanting to just shift the steering wheel, to plough into the freeway divider. She told me she didn't really want to die, but yet she thought about it all the time. She just didn't want to feel the pain and the fear and the anxiety anymore. I told her truthfully, "I know how you feel."

It took months to disentangle the property dispute at 801. Every night the barricade was swung into place. There were days at the lawyers; negotiations by memo with Dave and Debbie, who at first refused to either buy her out or move, claiming that 801 was socialized property and she should just leave. At Theo's orders, she had put over twenty thousand dollars into 801—at the very least she wanted her name off the mortgage so she wouldn't be liable for it anymore. The negotiations went around and around in an absurd game, but Jerri held her ground and finally they signed, agreeing to buy it from her for a small sum.

The day before she moved out, Dave knocked on her door.

"There's a memo for you in the basement," was all he said.

She walked down, saw the envelope lying on top of the washing machine. The memo was not dated, had no name on it. She picked it up and read this:

> You have committed ideological murder, killing your baby girl through an abortion process. Why? Only to continue your romantic relationship with Anthony?
>
> You don't have to worry, you will not be going to jail for what you did. But in some point in the future, you will be appre-

hended by none other than your own practice. One can never beat their own ideological practice—no one.

You did not have a miscarriage as reported.

People must have a choice. But this was not a legal choice.

You and all of your friends are eating out of the bowel of white racism. You and all of your friends like that of your big brothers and sisters, the white imperialist class, have sucked the blood of black labor for the betterment of your owned personal life style.

You and all of your friends are ideological racists, the shared belief that whites are totally superior to people of color. This was your motivation for going overseas when you were a college student. There wasn't anything you did of value when you were there except create problems for yourself and others. No person of color should never trust Zack again. He is a running dog for the white imperialist class of racial exploitation. He always had class contempt for people of color.

The main reason some of your friends have children of color is to personally preserve the capitalist ideology of white superiority. One of your friends fraudulently took the sperm of a poor working-class black man just to have a child of color to prove herself worth in relative superiority. She and her friends and family have a long history of misusing men of color.

What else can explain the natural ease and willingness to drink from the political cesspool of Jim Crowism.

There is a truism: you are what you eat and drink. This is why careful, planned steps were taken to clean house of all the nasty white trash that had accumulated. Race-based politics is a very sure way of getting you and all of your friends fuck up real quick!

What skills you and your friends have as the means to make a living is due totally by the conditions and resources provided by . . .

Time determines the truthfulness of action. The physicians who ripped the hell out of one of your friend's reproductive organs were right. Their position is that this person was unfit to be a natural mother (according to their record). Today we can say that their position is so very true. She had group sex with six men all at one party and in one night, a common practice before she requested to be transformed. She will continue to have her mind in between her legs for the rest of her life. Sex is all that she knows how to hold on to.

*Another one of your friends have had sex with twenty differ-
ent women. Sex is all that she knows. She is a street person, she
likes to pick up on shit, or, if it isn't shit, she will turn it into shit; as
a matter of fact, she attracts shit everywhere she goes. She is another one who will continue to have her mind in between her legs for
the rest of her life. She can never be no more than what she is
now—below the political spectrum of white trash.*

*Still, another one of your friends have had sex with 20 to 30
women. She likes social unity. She has shown signs of mental
problems in recent years.*

*Given what has been said of late by you, you think what's in
between your legs is special. There is no gold in between your
legs. Your focus, not like others, isn't between your own legs but
in between men's legs. It appears that you have socially elevated
yourself on the erection of a penis. You are on a very low level.*

*More can be said on the things I have heard of late. There is
no need for me to say anymore. It isn't worth the time, for too
much time has already been given. I will let you and your friends
to continue to talk about the dirty shit of race and sex.*

Jerri copied this document and called us all, and we met in the living
room of my house and read it together. Later we sent copies to all the people
who were still in. After the shock to my stomach had worn off, I thought to
myself, "Thank you, Theo. This is what everyone needed. Now we know
you are a crazy psychopath. You have lifted our guilt, you have given us our
villain, here in such extraordinary prose."

We were even able to laugh about it. The "twenty or thirty women" I'd
slept with—me, heterosexual to a fault! And Betty's so-called adventures with
the six men at once! Even Zack was a running dog! But after the laughter,
God, such hate, such filth, such anger. Here was the face of the psychopath
with none of the charm, the cleverness, the manipulation that he'd used all
those years. This was raw hate, lashing out, sickness.

We all of us got thrown back into our fear. But we were also stronger
in some way, knowing we had escaped, perhaps late and damaged, but at
least, finally, escaped.

The next afternoon we went as a group to a demonstration on the
North Side. The men who'd been captured on videotape beating Rodney
King had just been acquitted, and the United States was erupting in one of its

irregular spasms, trying to shake off the extremities of injustice. While South Central Los Angeles burned, hundreds of black North Siders and a handful of white supporters marched down Plymouth Avenue towards downtown. We marched with the now teenaged Beth and with Julie and Bill's black neighbors. Ted stayed home with all the other children; he was not ready for this, which was quite understandable to me. Beth had not wanted us to come, afraid of the black community's response to white faces in the march, but we felt little hostility, mostly a strange joy that penetrated the anger—the joy of people who've said "Enough!" and found themselves in good company in the saying of it.

Feeling the immediacy of the soon-to-be-victorious struggle in South Africa, this mixed crowd of Midwesterners bravely attempted a bouncing but clumsy rendition of the *toyi-toyi* as we headed past the concrete ugliness of the City Center, a place hated for its targeting and harassment of black youth by police and store owners. I felt embarrassed and saddened that I could teach them little of this political dance that my father and sister, I knew, had stepped out to do in London celebrations of the ANC. But our small group comically *toyi-toyi'ed*, too, in our own celebration, dancing for a personal liberation.

After the demonstration, we moved Jerri and Anthony out of 801 with Theo's last document fouling the atmosphere. That year we had moved people every month, it seemed, from one place to another, trying to help each other resettle, remove ourselves from the properties tied to Theo. Bill, Zack, Julie, Betty, and I were there to help. At the last minute, Debbie and Dave refused to let Bill come into the house. We didn't know why they picked on him, but the Enemy of the Week seemed to always change at random. We backed off from the fight, and Bill stayed by the moving truck to load instead of coming into the house. Debbie brought out a video camera and aimed it at us as if it were a machine gun. We burst out laughing. This was the 1990's version of what the O. used to do back during the expulsions in 1976, when the paramilitary units went around to the resisters wearing dark glasses and carrying cameras.

I felt an unfamiliar rush of sympathy for Debbie. She had the video camera up to her eye, and I approached her, stood talking to her through the lens, my body blocking the moving of boxes and furniture going on behind me. I spread my hands out, appealing to her, "Debbie, I know you are in there somewhere. I know there is a person under all of this. Just try to think. Try to use your mind. You're a good person, too."

The lens stared at me unblinkingly. I backed away and turned into the house to help the others. Later I laughed to think of them reviewing their carefully planned documentation of this event. They would have me up in their face, pleading for Debbie's humanity in a kindly sort of way, and then two hours of intensely boring footage of people sweating as they carried Jerri and Anthony's boxes of household living into the beat-up rental truck.

Another O. member, Sara, and her ten-year-old son, Frederick, lived in the top floor of Betty's duplex, 905, three doors up from 801. When Betty left the O., she too had to go through a complex negotiation to determine the ownership of 905. Unfortunately for Betty, she got saddled with the title to that pathetic piece of property, even though it had greatly improved since my days of caretaking it as an unwilling slum landlord. Sara and she had put a lot of money into it, also, and remodeled it (of course, hiring Theo to do the work) and it was brighter and cleaner than before. But still, the place was structurally unsound, bizarrely architected, unmarketable and, worst of all, too close to 801, carrying the heavy memories that most of the O. properties bore.

But Betty didn't have much money, and she needed a place for her daughter and her to live. Finally, Sara sold her share to Betty and moved out. Betty returned from work that day and checked the upstairs duplex. She found the following:

The carpets were all ripped from the floor.

The light fixtures were gone.

The white plastic plates that covered the light switches had been not-so-carefully unscrewed.

The sink in the bathroom was ripped off the wall.

No, I couldn't believe it—the toilet had gone again! When Betty called me to witness the damage, I found myself staring down that bottomless pit again. What was it about that toilet?

Wood molding from around the bottom of the walls had been pried off.

Doors were gone from their hinges.

The kitchen cabinets had been torn off the walls.

In short, they trashed the place. Betty, would spend the next year trying to make it livable again. We all came and trooped through the ruins. We hugged Betty. She became scared again. She bought a dog. She loved her dog.

CHAPTER 38

Television

1992. We have elected a president. Clinton waves through the television to us, his generation. We have all voted earlier in the evening, and now we're gathered in Jerri's living room in her new house. It is furnished with pretty, floral-patterned furniture—no longer the Sears-drab of our O. years. Anthony pops the cork off a bottle of champagne. We celebrate the coming of age of our peer group; the demonstrators of the sixties have entered the White House, the old men of World War II are moving on. Our war was Vietnam; we are veterans of this war of jungles and booby-traps that divided the nation, exaggerating still further the great divides of, first, the McCarthy fifties, and then the internal war of the Civil Rights Movement. Ours was not the Good War, the one that united the nation briefly in the top-heavy romanticism of the heroes of D-Day.

The sweet bubbles of the champagne give us a heady feeling and we celebrate, too, our own delayed participation in this flawed democracy. We don't expect too much from this fluent president who has ambled across the floors of television studios with such familiarity and skill. But he talks about feelings, and he parlays empathy into the currency of votes counted. Though he is obliged to hide it, we who remember know that he too remembers the sharp thrill of power when thousands of voices bellowed against Our War. Perhaps he was in London with me, scared of the horses as they backed up against the crowd, driving us away from the U.S. embassy. After all, in the 1960s he was a Fulbright Scholar in Oxford and organized there against the war.

We who are gathered in this comfortable living room have come out of the cave. Perhaps not entered the mainstream—some of us will never do that. But we recognize our place in the world now. We watch television, read the newspaper, feel powerless to change the slaughters that are sprinkled so liberally around this planet. We are as powerless as our neighbor, no longer an imagined elite.

We discuss these questions:

"We have a black woman as the mayor of Minneapolis. This is good," says one.

"Yes, I called up her campaign office and they brought a sign, and I put it up on my lawn. I could do that," says another.

"I give money now. To CARE. To Amnesty International. To the World Wildlife Fund. I'm on all their mailing lists—I must get five requests a day. I don't know how to say no."

"We must be a good market," I say. "Ex-political cult members. I give them money too. A small market, but lucrative!"

"Each One, Teach One. That's what I can manage now. No more changing the world. No more big answers. If I can help one person—that's one more than I did for all those wasted years."

"Achievable goals!" says another.

"Yes, but I still believe in Marxism. We still have to organize."

Some of us sigh.

"I don't think I'd call myself a Marxist anymore. I'm not sure I would call myself anything. Perhaps I will just try and *do* instead."

It is the conversation of tired people, of people who are struggling to stand up again after a long fall.

"I try to volunteer—our neighborhood has a revitalization committee—but I can't deal with the commitment. I get too scared. I have to leave. Perhaps I'll never be political again."

We are quiet for a moment, contemplating this reality.

"Small steps. One day at a time."

"It's got to feel all right. It's like we used to say, before the O.: the process is as important as the goal."

"The personal *is* political."

We shift positions. Tune back in to the TV.

"It's incredible, they're the same age as *us*."

Hillary is in trouble because she doesn't bake cookies. Neither do we.

Leaving a cult, the imprisonment of mind control, is a long, slow fall off the edge of a very small world. Only a primitive, instinctive faith in life is what keeps us from blackout. We're all hanging on, hoping to God that someday there'll be a piece of ground beneath our feet again.

It's a violent mix that brought us here. Our generation has sucked this up like milk, and the violence has spewn forth all over the country in a bloody clash of economics and culture. We are the ones who understand this. Some day we'll be able to bring our heads out from under the blankets and, one by one, with no grand schemes, we'll reach out to a friend or a neighbor, a school or a community center. Perhaps we'll be able to add a touch of wisdom here and there; every once in a while nudge one another out of the path of danger; be alert to the tricks of history as it swells up beneath us. Beyond that we do not know.

The relationships begin to crumble. We are out—those of us who will come out in this round are out. Still left are Suzanne, Debbie, and Dave, Nancy's parents and a handful of others. We have tried with them, but they are stuck, absolute and unrelenting.

The rest of us are in flux. I look it up in my dictionary.

FLUX: [From the Latin, fluere, to flow] 1. a flowing. 2. a continual change. 3. a substance used to help metals fuse together, as in soldering.

My eye moves to the next entry:

FLY: flew, flown, flying [OE fleogan] 1. To move through the air in an aircraft or by using wings, as a bird. 2. to wave or float in the air. 3. to move or pass swiftly. 4. to flee.

We are in flux. We are re-evaluating everything. Our jobs—the jobs that Theo instructed us to do. Our politics—the same politics that people the world over are re-evaluating. Our marriages—arranged or approved by Theo.

We, none of us, re-evaluate our children: they are as much a part of us as blood or bone, whether biological or adopted; this clearly does not lessen the intensity of our love and identification. Their world has become richer for our escape: we have a loving community now, aunts and uncles for the children, people who will come in an emergency, who will answer a midnight call for help. We solidify our support for each other in this way.

But the marriages crumble like the desiccated pages of a book left too long unread. The safe worlds of the children collapse about their heads as the families that contained them disintegrate. We cannot stop the erosion. We just ache and ache.

Bill is leaving Julie. Slowly. He wants to write, to find his passion. He and Julie have learned to love each other over the years, but it is a relationship grown in a soil of powerlessness, a relationship that neither chose, after Bill's forced divorce from Jerri—something which he did not choose either. Bill wants the opportunity to choose.

Suzanne is still in the O., so it goes without saying that Zack and she will divorce. He is clear about it; they never loved each other—he regrets marrying her. Their battles over custody are intensifying. It is their children who will be hurt.

Surprisingly, Jerri and Anthony, childless, are able to keep their relationship going. Anthony has dispassionately sat in on our Wednesday evenings of recovery, listening without comment to the stories as they rolled out of us, one by one. He and Jerri stick together through the turbulence.

I have loved Ted. Perhaps I have tried too hard to get him out. The exit-counselor warned me about this. Ted is out now, and I want my reward. But there is none forthcoming. I have imagined that Ted would jump into freedom feet first with the rollicking glory the others of us felt in those first few months.

But things seem to slide over him. I want to meet his eyes, but he keeps them from me. I want to kiss him, touch tongues in wetness, but he does not. I want to share stories and tears with him, tell him the hurts, accuse him, forgive him—but he does not. I want so much from him. He cannot talk about the O. with me. Perhaps I am overbearing, perhaps I can't give him room to find his own way. Perhaps I am too far out and cannot reach back any longer to where he is. We talk about the children and the business. We talk about the business and the children.

I love the children, am always happy to talk about them. But I hate the business. I don't want it to be my life. I am trying to find my life. The business came out of our endless contortions to fit ourselves into the narrow funnels that Theo had defined for us. I am trying to fly—I am in flux—I need continual change, to flow, to fly, using my wings, as a bird, to wave or float in the air.

There is something unbearable about this quiet conflict between us. Perhaps there is *flux* lacking between us. I remember when I welded metal to metal. I took two pieces of iron—thick black quarter-inch sheetmetal—placed them next to each other and put the heat-proof cylindrical mask over my head. A nod of my head shook the grimy visor down over my eyes and then my thumb turned the knurled knob of the oxy-acetylene torch to a flameless hiss while the other hand squeezed the double handle of the striker until the blue flint spark jumped into the invisible noise to kindle a pointed blue-and-white fire that, always remarkably to me, could melt this toughened metal. I applied the flame spear to the proximate metals, caressing the edges up and down until the relaxing occurred: the hard-edged shoulders softened, gave of themselves and became red—this was the time for the solder, the *flux*, and into the little spear, held close to the separate entities, keeping them warm and affectionate like the beginnings of love, into it I held the innocuous-looking solder stick and pulled it down the seam in the heart of the cool-blue burning spear's path, and the whole of this magical chemistry collapsed in a meltdown to produce a weld that, if I held steady, was straight and strong. A weld done right makes the joint stronger than each of its pieces. The metals fuse together, and at that point in the weld they become something other than themselves.

This was the bond that formed among some of us who left together that year. The crisis gave us to each other. We had no room or time or courage left over to appear other than we were. But Ted drifted from me like a person lost at sea. I could not reach for him anymore.

Huey P. Newton had died in 1989. Now that he was gone, the memoirs were coming out. Elaine Brown's *A Taste of Power* described that piece of history she had witnessed from the inside. Rising out of the Civil Rights Movement, the fires of the Watts riots, and smashing into the Vietnam War, Huey arrived in this slice of time, a brilliant megalomaniac who seduced and threatened and caught the light of people's imagination. Elaine Brown described his penthouse apartment, the place in which I had met Slim Coleman of the InterCommunal Survival Committee so many years before: "A visit to the penthouse had become an awesome experience. It was where truth was both explored and extracted, the house of redemption, or damnation."

Elaine described how Huey habitually kept the windows wide open and sat bare-chested while Elaine shivered with the cold and the fear of the twenty-five-story drop beneath her. Here she'd seen Bobby Seale lashed twenty times with a bullwhip on Huey's orders. Seale was expelled, and two days later Elaine became the reluctant chairman of the Black Panther Party. She too suffered both physical and psychological violence at Huey's hands.

Finally she'd fled with her daughter.

And David Hilliard, the first chairman of the Panthers. His book spoke of his identity—shattered after the hot years when he was a national hero, but living under the shadow of Huey, who returned in a state of paranoia after his exile in Cuba. While Hilliard was in jail, he too was expelled. A year later, back on the outside, he stumbled in drink and crack cocaine into craziness. He hit bottom, then stripped himself down to his humanity, understood his commonness with the common man, and became to himself, at least, a person, not a hero.

I began to discover the other Left-wing political cults of my time. Sally was a white working-class feminist from Oakland and an old friend of mine. She'd joined the African People's Solidarity Committee, led by their own black Chairman Yeshitela. Over a Japanese dinner one night, she described to me their armed patrols, shotguns hidden in the car as they guarded the party's headquarters in San Francisco. She described the procurement of women for the chairman, the break-up of her marriage to the love of her life when she finally left: he remained in the group and remarried another loyal member. Their group remained small—perhaps the organizing call of "Join the movement for white people's reparations to the African community!" was not a compelling enough come-on for the average activist.

I remembered sweet Chuck Wheeler. A thin, music-loving man from Philadelphia with whom I'd worked for years in the San Francisco food system; I'd met him first in the Peace and Freedom Party, and he'd been in several of my study groups. Chuck had left us to return to his working-class roots in Philly, and the last I'd heard of him he was married and working for the National Labor Federation—now known to me as a political cult run by Gino Parente and including the Eastern Farmworkers and California Homemakers. That was another group in which I'd been interested for a while before I joined the O. They did grassroots organizing, were dedicated and disciplined, organized whites. Now I had heard stories of teenagers separated from their families, living in Parente's armed compound, working those endless days I remembered so well, and all this, once again, for the world revolution.

There was Janet Tijerina, my solidly middle-class white friend from LA who'd married a tiny Chicano man, Carlos, who used to teach me Spanish. She'd divorced him, joined California Homemakers, one of Parente's groups. Janet had a creative spark; together we'd organized back in 1973 to keep the women's clinic attached to the Free Clinic in Berkeley. We were against the separatists, wanted to keep the women's clinic accessible to working-class women and women of color—and we fought what we felt was the middle-class separation. I thought of Janet. I didn't know how to find her. I wondered where she was now, twenty years later. Had she found her way out?

Another old friend, Helen, had been in the New Alliance Party—this was still going strong. They used the particularly ugly technique of recruiting poor women through psychotherapy groups. This was close to the work I had wanted to do in organizing women: to find ways to provide support for them, but it, too, had become a baited trap. Once in, power was wielded by a white man, Fred Newman, with Lenore Fulani, a black woman being his front person. They had been taking over and destroying AIDS support groups and other activist organizations in New York and California and were universally disliked throughout the Left. Recently they had formed an alliance with Scientology and the Sun Myung Moon organization to fight anti-cult organizers.

I read more memoirs. This time from China, from the years of the Cultural Revolution. *Wild Swans*, by Jung Chang, *Red Azalea* by Anchee Min, *Life and Death in Shanghai* by Nien Cheng. I saw the new movies coming out of China, among them *Farewell My Concubine*. The image that remained with me was that of the flower beds being dug up. In the Cultural Revolution it had been decided that flowers were not proletarian. Well, I had to admit, this was true. All over the country, to prove their loyalty, to deflect accusations from themselves and their families, ordinary people took shovels to flower beds, ripped out the beauty, built destruction as an icon to Mao. They denounced each other, read no books but Mao's, dared not speak to each other, stuffed their thoughts into a slim volume of quotations, buried their selves in the fuzzy layers of thought-stopping.

As I stepped through this world of memory, South Africa shimmered with a new kind of freedom. The elections in which the ANC was surely going to win were around the corner. My hope. Now South Africa would be in the forefront of the bitter struggle of democracy. A struggle I knew to be impossible without culture and love and beauty and complaints. A struggle impossible without thought and dissension, joy and disunity, compromise and negotiation. The South African darkness of some of the most intense repression on the planet was coming to an end. A multi-racial government would emerge, tens of thousands of people would return to their country, perhaps an extraordinary culture of vast differences welded with the heat of the South African sun would flower in between the battles for territory and power. Here a people in common cause had found the current of history and pushed it on with the weight of their bodies.

I began to imagine returning—remembering the smells of my childhood: the salty *biltong* jerky, vivid purple bougainvillea, the giraffe-necked lavender jacaranda trees. There was an opening there. A place to return to. A looking forward.

Meanwhile, in the former Soviet Union, mind-control groups were swarming, eager with the scent of fresh blood and, like the mafia gangs, opportunistically seeking to turn a profit from these new countries' chaos. The Reverend Moon had quickly found his way there, as had Transcendental Meditation's Maharishi (also well-ensconced in Mozambique), along with the Hare Krishnas and Scientology. Perhaps I would make this my task—perhaps this was where my history had placed me: to hammer out a warning. It is an old story: the abuse of power in the name of Freedom or Truth. We must learn the methods and the mechanics. Diagnose the condition. Practice preventive medicine. For it is a killer. But if we can learn what it looks like and teach our children well, we can move on to the next stanza of the song, the one I always wanted to sing:

> *I'll sing about the love between*
> *my brothers and my sisters,*
> *all over this world . . .*

I sat and set pen to paper. I was a product of my history and history is what I would describe. I always knew where my story would begin . . .

I was fourteen in 1968. Martin was dead, Malcolm had just been killed, and George Jackson would die soon after . . .

EPILOGUE

Over ten years have passed since the events that end this book. Ted and I eventually divorced. Our ability to work together still serves us well as we co-parent our children together in a caring and cooperative way. The others who left the O. in the early 1990s have all moved on and rebuilt lives that are perhaps more ordinary but certainly happier. Many, including myself, went back to school to follow long-deferred goals. As far as we know a few souls remain in the O., although it has probably changed its name yet again.

SUGGESTED READING

Arendt, Hannah. *The Origins of Totalitarianism.* Orlando: Harcourt Brace. 1948/1979.

Brown, Elaine. *A Taste of Power: A Black Woman's Story.* New York: Pantheon Books. 1992.

Chang, Jung. *Wild Swans: Three Daughters of China.* New York: Simon & Schuster. 1991.

Cheng, Nien. *Life and Death in Shanghai.* London: Grafton Books. 1986.

Cialdini, R. *The Psychology of Influence.* New York: William Morrow. 1984.

Crossman, Richard H.S., and Arthur Koestler. *The God That Failed.* London: Hamish Hamilton. 1950.

Hearst, Patricia Campbell, and Alvin Moscow. *Patty Hearst: Her Own Story.* New York: Avon Books. 1982.

King, Dennis. *Lyndon LaRouche and the New American Fascism.* New York: Doubleday. 1989.

Koestler, Arthur. *Darkness at Noon.* London: Longmans. 1968.

Lalich, Janja. "The Cadre Ideal: Origins and Development of a Political Cult." *Cultic Studies Journal.* 1992. 9:1-77.

Lalich, Janja. Forthcoming. *Bounded Choice: The Dilemma of True Believers and Charismatic Commitment.* Berkeley: University of California Press.

Layton, Deborah. *Seductive Poison: A Jonestown Survivor's Story of Life and Death in the Peoples Temple.* New York: Anchor Books. 1998.

Lessing, Doris. *Prisons We Choose to Live Inside.* New York: Harper & Row. 1987.

Levi, Primo. *The Drowned and the Saved.* New York: Vintage Books. 1986.

Lifton, Robert Jay. *Thought Reform and the Psychology of Totalism*. New York: The Norton Library. 1961.

Lifton, Robert Jay. *The Nazi Doctors: Medical Killing and the Psychology of Genocide*. New York: Basic Books. 1986.

Lifton, Robert Jay. *Destroying the World to Save It: Aum Shinrikyo, Apocalyptic Violence, and the New Global Terrorism*. New York: Henry Holt. 1999.

Min, Anchee. *Red Azalea*. New York: Pantheon Books. 1994.

Muller, Robert. *It Happened One Summer*. Great Britain: Sceptre. 1941.

Orwell, George. *Animal Farm*. New York: Signet Classic. 1946.

Orwell, George. *1984*. New York: New American Library. 1949.

Orwell, George. *Homage to Catalonia*. New York: Harcourt Brace. 1952.

Tobias, Madeleine and Janja Lalich. *Captive Hearts, Captive Minds*. Alameda: Hunter House. 1994.

Tourish, Dennis and Tim Wohlforth. *On the Edge: Political Cults Right and Left*. Armonk: M.E. Sharpe. 2000.

About the Author

Alexandra Stein was born in Johannesburg, South Africa, and has also lived in England, France, and the United States. She writes creative non-fiction and is currently studying for a doctorate in sociology at the University of Minnesota. She lives in Minneapolis with her two children.